Spartan Supremacy

Spartan Supremacy

Mike Roberts and Bob Bennett

Pen & Sword
MILITARY

First published in Great Britain in 2014 by
Pen & Sword Military
an imprint of
Pen & Sword Books Ltd
47 Church Street
Barnsley
South Yorkshire
S70 2AS

ISBN 978-1-84884-614-2

Typeset in 11pt Ehrhardt by
Mac Style, Beverley, E. Yorkshire

Printed and bound in the UK by
CPI Group (UK) Ltd, Croydon, CRO 4YY

Pen & Sword Books Ltd incorporates the imprints of Pen & Sword Archaeology,
Atlas, Aviation, Battleground, Discovery, Family History, History, Maritime,
Military, Naval, Politics, Railways, Select, Transport, True Crime, and Fiction,
Frontline Books, Leo Cooper, Praetorian Press, Seaforth Publishing and
Wharncliffe.

For a complete list of Pen & Sword titles please contact
PEN & SWORD BOOKS LIMITED
47 Church Street, Barnsley, South Yorkshire, S70 2AS, England
E-mail: enquiries@pen-and-sword.co.uk
Website: www.pen-and-sword.co.uk

Contents

Maps and Plans

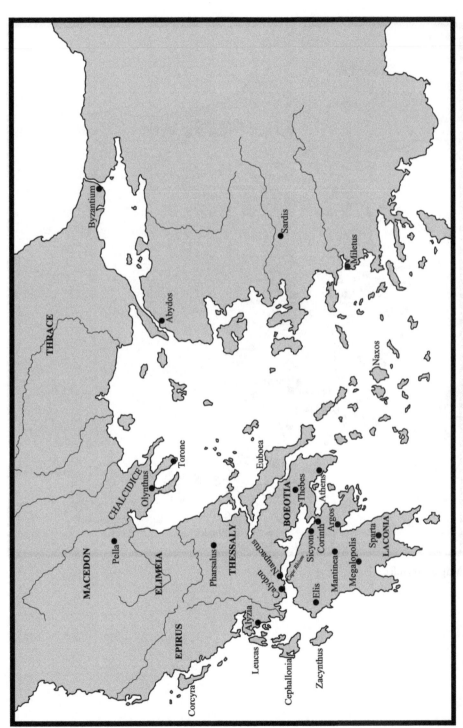

Map of the Aegean

Map of Anatolia.

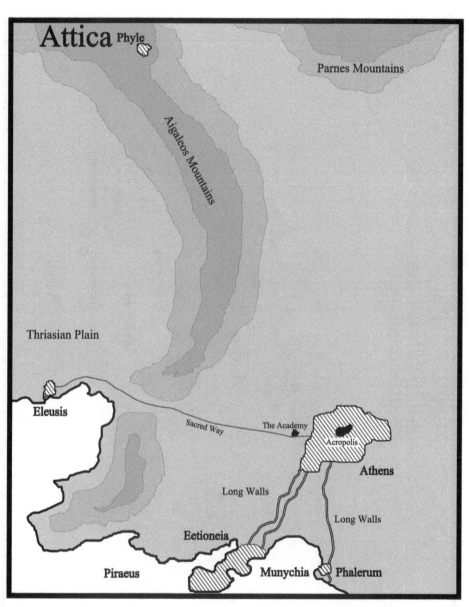

Map of Attica.

Map of Boeotia.

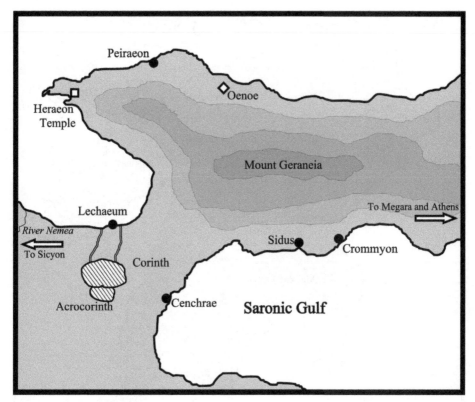

Map of Isthmus of Corinth.

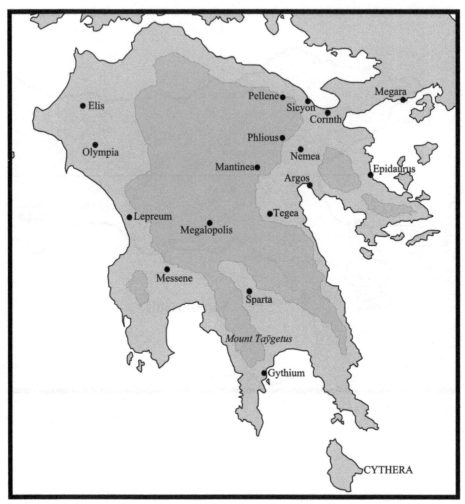

Map of the Peloponnese.

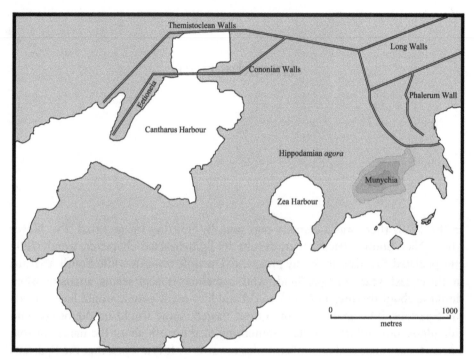

Themistoclean Walls

Long Walls

Cononian Walls

Eetioneia

Phalerum Wall

Cantharus Harbour

Hippodamian *agora*

Munychia

Zea Harbour

0   1000
                    metres

Map of the Piraeus.

Introduction

In the 1980s there was a comedy pop song by Spitting Image titled 'I've Never Met a Nice South African' that, despite its light-hearted character, wonderfully encapsulated the distaste felt by progressive people towards white South Africans in those last years of apartheid. And somehow it also seems apposite when thinking about the ancient Greek world and how many people would have viewed the Spartans. The analogy is, of course, flawed, some would no doubt contend ridiculous, but still does contain something of the truth about the nature of that extraordinary state and others' attitudes towards it. It is not just that the Spartans practised a sort of apartheid against the helots both in Laconia and most particularly in Messenia, enslaving other Greek peoples to do the work that allowed them to dedicate their lives to the practice of arms, they also exhibited a xenophobic arrogance and philistinism typical of many apartheid era white South Africans, and, like them, they inevitably took a polarised attitude to the world outside their own bizarre and twisted polity. Most were extreme chauvinists who had little but contempt for what they saw as essentially weak and feeble people who they always beat on the battlefield and whose behaviour did not match what they considered to be the exemplar they themselves demonstrated.

Many might contend the comparisons between the two places falls down because while apartheid South Africa was a pariah state in most of the world, to many Hellenes Sparta was held up as a model; a place to be admired; in fact a polity that could often call on the loyalty of people outside her borders, some of whom were even prepared to betray their own communities to further Spartan interests. Particularly this was the case with the well born and wealthy, who felt acutely the threat to their hereditary power from the rise of democracy in their own countries, people who loved the *eunomia* or good order that the Spartan system seemed to guarantee.

But we should remember that it was not so very different in the Britain of the 1970s and 80s. There were still plenty of individuals who hankered back to imperial days and covertly admired the South Africans' intransigent treatment of the black population, wishing perhaps they had behaved in that way in their days of power.

And these were not just some absurd 'Colonel Blimps'; it is no coincidence that a man like Thatcher's son should become involved in the world of African politics in tandem with characters with connections with South Africa. He and his like retained an attitude of entitlement to exploit black Africans that made them very much in tune with the ethos of Botha and de Clerk. Very far from all sportsmen and entertainers at the time boycotted the place and the most bizarre excuses were trotted out to justify the unjustifiable. Certainly to most of the civilised world white South Africa was outcast but this should not make us blind to the fact they had many friends in high and low places in Britain, the USA, Europe and elsewhere; partly because the regime was seen as a bastion against communism in Africa, but also because from some there was a covert sympathy with the very racism that was the reason for most people's opprobrium.

Yet this analogy should not be pushed too far; there is no likelihood that apartheid South Africa will be remembered in the way Sparta is, as a place where everybody finds something to regard and the very words Spartan and laconic have entered everyday language. The Nazis were well known for their love of 'The Spartan Way' but this attitude had deep antecedents. The Prussian cadet corps' education was modelled on Spartan lines in the nineteenth century and so to a lesser extent were English Public Schools. But it is not only the privileged and the right-wing who can find something to admire. Liberals and nationalists have embraced some of Sparta's ideals and even leftish intellectuals. Indeed feminists have expressed their admiration and approval for the Greek city's treatment of women. They were relatively free in comparison to their other Greek brethren and were allowed to own property – not a concept their neighbours and feted radical democrats in Athens would have indulged or even understood.

Everybody can find something to hang a story around in the social and political arrangements of this polity that seemed so often to punch above its weight and never stopped punching until the advent of Rome made Greek intercity politics an irrelevance. Whether it was under traditional kings against Persians, Athenians and Macedonians, under apparently radical reformers like Agis and Cleomenes, or under tyrants like Nabis, they never allowed the peoples of the Peloponnese, and often the whole of Greece, a moment's peace. Yet few, if asked to name a time and place they would have liked to live, would say ancient Sparta: food that made death a sweet release, an upbringing of institutionalised abuse and barbarity, an economy that revelled in its own backwardness, and all this with no sign of the kind of political and intellectual ferment that at least would have made life at Athens and other places interesting. But the heady aroma of heroism is strong; self-sacrifice can pull at the heart strings. Leonidas and his 300 are icons of western consciousness in a way that it is difficult to exaggerate and, whatever the peculiarities of the state that produced these men, their heroism can be compelling.

Yet these grim warriors who killed and died with such facility at the 'Hot Gates', only on one occasion in their long history, around the end of the fifth century BC, seemed about to entrench themselves as ascendant in the Greek world. This time under study is the only occasion that these belligerent philistines actually became the dominant power in the whole of Greece and around much of the Aegean. In this generation of hegemony, as opposed to the regional Peloponnesian dominance that was almost a default situation, they made themselves hated in a way that no other past and future imperialists did whether they were Athenian, Theban or indeed even Macedonian. They were uniquely bad as international players showing the kind of qualities that make any ascendancy, however well founded, likely to crumble in a short enough time. Their state had eschewed the use of money, to the extent that it could, but once the treasuries of its tributaries were prised open Spartan imperialists showed themselves rapacious and grasping to an extraordinary degree. They had a knack of exhibiting arrogance and brutality that went well beyond that which even their natural friends around the Greek world expected. They did have instinctive adherents; peoples deeply afraid of the Persians and more generally oligarchs who were perennially frightened of the indebted and dispossessed in their own backyard. To cultivate these groups would not have been difficult, and indeed to completely alienate most of them *was* difficult, but the Spartans achieved it. To dig a bit more into the South African analogy these factions were not unlike the western powers of the 70s and 80s who were desperate to bolster the apartheid regime, because it offered crucial strategic support in Africa and the southern hemisphere against Soviet influence yet the unpleasantness of the people in charge and their refusal to try and look even a bit more acceptable made it just too embarrassing to cosy up to them as they would have liked to.

It is the intention of this book to try to understand the interstate relations, the military developments and the cultural and social dynamics in the Greek world in the period 410–370 BC to the extent that our sources allow. In so doing we will range from the great Greek cities of Western Asia, to Athens and the Peloponnese, to Byzantium and the Hellespont. This was a wide world, but the centre of much interest has always been the city of Athens at a time of great political change and social trauma when larger than life characters, particularly from drama and philosophy as well as politics strutted the avenues and alleyways of a place that in the Parthenon still boasts the presence of an edifice that almost defines the Classical Greek world. But to get out from under the omnipresence of the Attic capital is important; there were other places, Corinth, Thebes and Argos that played major roles. And of course it is worth trying to understand how Sparta itself worked. Other ancient polities we can grasp pretty much how they functioned; whether it be the kingdom of Macedonia, the mixed oligarchy of Rome, or a Greek League where the final say in key matters like war and peace might be given to the mass of the people in assembly while the everyday power was wielded by city delegates and elected war leaders. An almost Homeric set up so different from Athens and her equivalents where real assembly based democracy held sway, with all these there is at least an idea of how the elixir of power was dripped out but Sparta is something different. The constituents are familiar, the kings, the *Gerousia*, the ephors and the assembly; but how they really functioned is not so easy to know.

In the period under scrutiny there are times when the Spartan state was really only of regional significance, and others when it is a truly great power. This is relevant not just for itself but also to try to redress a balance that concentrates much more on the Athenian dimension in a time when the Peloponnesian power was the one in the driving seat. History is of course all about the sources fragmented and biased as they are but historians should never be prisoners of the evidence they work with; imagination and perspective adjustment is an imperative to draw a picture that expands understanding and does not merely regurgitate what has been left from ancient writers.

In the effort to see Sparta operate we may learn something from an interesting glitch; that some of the great Spartan movers and shakers in these years seem to deviate from the ideal civic norm. Lysander, it was claimed, was born of a non-Spartan mother, something that theoretically should have debarred him from being a full citizen. King Agesilaus, arguably one of the greatest soldiers of all the Spartan kings, had a deformed leg. It is a wonder, if the state rules were so rigid, that he was not tossed as a baby into the death chasm. Clearly in Sparta, it was one rule for the royal family, and another for everybody else. No absolutely defined image will emerge: power and politics are always opaque. Class, faction, family, financial interest, personal ambition: all impinge and are as important as statute, title and the constitutional glove that fits over the iron hand of power. But the real extent of ephor influence, how independent was a king or navarch on campaign, these are things that can be discovered to a considerable degree in this period when we have good details of imperial Sparta in action.

This is a world with an overpowering presence, as Greek rivals bustle the Great King is always over the horizon. History is always about money and the gold darics available in the treasuries at Susa and Babylon were the almighty dollar of the time. The ability of 10,000 Greek infantry to win a battle in the Euphrates valley and then defy the Persian Empire on their return home described in Xenophon's *Anabasis* was an event of real note but still should not be made too much of. One hundred and fifty years of experience had already shown that the Persians were no race of supermen. The Greek colours were emblazoned with victories at Salamis, at Plataea, at Mycale and at Eurymedon but this had been foozling at the edges; in no sense could any of it be seen as precursor to the Alexandrine conquests threatening the very heart of the realm of the king of kings. Persia was not invulnerable on the battlefield but she was a juggernaut, particularly in the purse, and a divided Greek world was bound to be vulnerable to pressure exerted from the empire in the East. But of course the Iranian superpower was no monolith. There were divisions between great satraps, squabbling factions at court and revolts by fiercely independent subjects that all meant the Greeks always had wriggle room to exploit and effective military forces were important in exploiting whatever advantage came their way. Yet still in the end there was a big man with lots of money at the end of the room who always had to be taken notice of.

Most commentators manage to push the Xerxes invasion of 480 BC into a box described as 'west versus east' and 'freedom versus tyranny' with the battles at Thermopylae and Salamis as the great tipping point that allowed the freedoms developed in the west to survive and flourish until the present day. Whilst this Eurocentric stuff, admittedly first peddled by the wonderful Herodotus, is becoming a tad less fashionable it is still well entrenched despite the fact that in terms of slave states the one that was the most extreme was the one that provided the heroic 300 defenders, not the attacking hordes of Asia. Certainly other Greeks like the Athenians were at the forefront of democratic civic developments; developments usually opposed by Sparta and the many oligarchs from other cities that loved the radical reactionaries from Laconia. And even had Greece been conquered by Xerxes' great invasion force it is probable a fairly light Persian hand would not have stopped and perhaps hardly set back what was developing in some of the mainland Greek cities. Indeed Thebes, a community that famously medised, would develop into a yeoman democratic exemplar that would forge the tool to remove a Spartan hegemony that was looking to be far more ugly and oppressive than anything a distant Persian monarch might have imposed on his westernmost province. It is a moot point whether the soil would have been more fertile for the advancement of progressive freedoms under Spartan or Persian supremacy had either been sustained in mainland Greece. Sparta had an ideological bent towards the suppression of democracy on behalf of its aristocratic pals whilst on the other hand Persia's only real dogma was getting the money in. If a democratic assembly organised efficient tribute the satrap in charge, as often as not, had few qualms, as illustrated on more than one occasion in Western Anatolia. And, anyway, it should not be forgotten that hegemony was never that thorough or monolithic in pre-modern times. With either the Spartans or Persians in charge the probability is their regional administrations would have left the elbow room needed for peoples under their sway to develop those aspects of government and culture for which we have such regard and consider the gene pool of our own modern souls.

The years in question are not well covered by modern writers, understandably enough as these last lees of the Peloponnesian War and the short generation of Spartan hegemony come just after the end of the output of the extraordinarily influential Thucydides. The ancient writers that cover this time stand in his rain shadow and their reputations suffer for it. Our main source, Xenophon, lived through the events he was describing and was witness to some of them. Although his pro-Spartan and anti-Theban bias and his omissions were noted, until the turn of the twentieth century he was regarded as a fairly accurate and reliable historian. But the discovery of the Oxyrynchus papyrus in 1906 changed all that and the following years have seen a catastrophic decline in his academic standing, for the papyrus, while confirming some of Xenophon, was at variance with much else and seemed to bear out a lot of the much derided Diodorus Siculus, the other main source for the period. Though there has subsequently been some rehabilitation of Xenophon it remains the case that he must be treated with extreme caution. Yet we should not despair; it is not a thin period for sources. Many epochs are much more opaque than this one with more light shed by Plutarch, Pausanias, Polyaenus, Cornelius Nepos and others. There are also of course Aristotle and Plato, to give another dimension to a period that contains its fair share of political and cultural titans. But clearly historians used to the lucidity of Thucydides (though one wonders what would happen to his reputation if an alternative source for the Peloponnesian War was ever found) have tired quickly of trying to make sense of what is certainly a mishmash and with its main plank heavily derided as parochial and biased.

Balance demands a move in the angle of the spotlight. The concentration of interest on the fifth century, with the Persian wars of Darius and Xerxes at the beginning, great cultural outpourings and architectural achievements soon after, and finally a war defined by its sole historian, is unreasonable. This is not all of Classical Greece: Socrates, Plato and Aristophanes were all alive and well when Thucydides dries up. In the story of the Thirty and their overthrow in Athens, and the revival of a second naval empire almost the equal of the first, there is much extraordinary material. The idea of a golden age coming suddenly to a close must not be accepted unquestioned, people are too easily hoodwinked by the paraphernalia of time; the end of the century signifies nothing in itself being merely a later imposed chronological construct not a change of culture. The decline of Classical Greece certainly might be picked out with the death of great artists, great thinkers even great politicians whose footprints are not perhaps filled by quite such seminal figures. But great comic plays were still being produced well into the fourth century, Praxiteles was still creating great sculpture, Plato the most influential philosopher of all time was fashioning his works, and architecture of great merit was still being built. The backdrop to much of this was the emergence of resistance to the dominance of Spartan imperialists. The campaigns around the Gulf of Corinth and in Boeotia are as interesting as the wars of Brasidas in the Chalcidice or Demosthenes in Sphacteria. None of the events we will cover perhaps has the extraordinary drama of the Syracusan war that has attracted the pen of so many wonderful writers, but there is plenty of rich material almost as good and with as much dramatic colour that has received little attention in recent years.

Many of the names in these pages were once very well known but in recent times it has been rare for these characters to get star billing. Lysander for one, a man who in his day was given demigod status a century before Alexander, strained to win the same standing, and apart from him the times were littered with other great figures. Thrasybulus, as towering a presence as is possible to imagine, yet not now well known at all; Iphicrates, a military reformer who influenced the way of waging war as far down as Philip of Macedon; Conon, a sailor who almost singlehandedly reinvigorated the naval might of Athens; Epaminondas and Pelopidas, the Thebans, who dominated the middle years of the fourth century in a way that would have been difficult to imagine to any stranger who viewed their homeland in the early 380s when the Spartans held them in thrall through a garrison-backed oligarchy. To revivify these reputations is surely timely and productive as a contribution to the continuing rebalancing of the story of the Ancient World.

The period is also well worthy of attention due to the availability of detail on major campaigns fought on sea and land; enough to make attempts at reconstructing important military events eminently possible. And the actions considered comprise some of the greatest contests ever engaged in between Greek peoples that in magnitude at least approach the dimensions of the battles of the Persian Wars. Arginusae, Coronea and Leuctra are great affairs; the first being probably the largest sea battle ever fought between Greek states and the others as considerable in terms of numbers as any ancient combat in the Greek peninsula without the involvement of outsiders like Persians, Macedonians or Romans.

Chapter One

Alcibiades' Return

In 407 BC a strikingly good looking man of middle age strolled with friends through the streets of Athens on his way to the assembly. He paced the half mile west of the acropolis with the citizens joining him from their houses along the road. There the flag had been raised that called the enfranchised to attend, slaves hurried them along with a dyed rope corralling them onto the Pnyx Hill, the gathering place that looked proprietarily out over the flat roofs of the city houses. Once there he mounted the platform with its rock cut steps where he had triumphed so often in the past, as the congregation stood, apart from the council of Five Hundred who were provided with wooden seats. A few years before, this same man, now making ready to address the people, had been arraigned and threatened with death for sacrilege after it was discovered that the *hermai*, the guardian statues of Athenian houses, had wholesale had their phalluses knocked off in one night of outrage. When charged he had not stayed to face the music but fled into exile. The complication was that at the time of his arrest he was jointly leading one of the greatest armaments Athens had ever fielded against the city of Syracuse in Sicily – a project that he had himself been at the forefront of bringing into being. Without him to lead, it had gone down in disaster. Many hundreds of ships and many tens of thousands of combatants, Athenians, allies and hired men were lost and the pathetic remnant, as an awful reminder, were worked to death in quarries on the outskirts of Syracuse. And, more than this, the man had played his part as adviser in exile to the Spartan enemy in bringing about the collapse of both that botched enterprise and in more general guidance on how to drive the war against his own homeland. It is claimed he not only persuaded the Spartans to resurrect a waning Peloponnesian War in support of Syracuse and to send a Spartan general to guide them, but that he recommended to the Spartans they set up a permanent year-round fort at Decelea just twelve miles to the north of Athens city to heap up even more agony than that inflicted by the annual raids that had been their previous strategy in the conflict, denying any dependable access to most of their fertile acres and to the silver from the Laurium mines. After the dreadful disaster at Syracuse he had led the Spartan offensive that encouraged and exploited the insurrections amongst the islands and West Anatolian subjects of Athens. The breaking away of places like Chios, Athens' most powerful subject, and Miletus could be laid at his door, as could the delivering of the first Spartan/Persian treaty that crucially loosened the purse strings of the eastern power to the advantage of the Peloponnesian axis.

This was no Lord Haw-Haw, an irrelevance made sacrifice to a population embittered by years of privation, or a Bernadotte, who in regal guise had been a small part of the coalition that brought his own country and emperor down in defeat. He had been the head and brains in the process of the crumbling of Athenian power that came after the disastrous enterprise that he himself had midwifed. But now circumstances had allowed all this if not to be forgotten, at least to be forgiven in the hope that the same man now might make the difference on behalf of hearth and home against an enemy who had had the upper hand since the Sicilian calamity brought grief and despair to the ebullient inhabitants of the Attic city. The man's name was Alcibiades, a cousin of the great Pericles, a playboy politician who now seemed to be the only hope for a community on the ropes. The government that called him back felt his talents; his proven military qualities might just enable them to claw themselves up out of the pit into which events of the last years had hurled them. He himself had some time since left the bosom of his Spartan hosts when the reprobate, never able to resist salting the tail of his host, had seduced the wife of Agis II, one of their kings. He had been buttering up the satrap of Lydia, Tissaphernes, with the aim of inducing the Persians into an alliance with the Athenians, so that with money and ships he would have the leverage to earn reinstatement at the heart of his home city's government. This was always going to be difficult while the radical democracy remained in power at Athens both because of their suspicion of Alcibiades as an aristocrat long tainted with oligarchic inclinations, and also because of Persian misgivings over those Jacobin elements in the city that were currently ascendant. Much would have to happen to allow Alcibiades' reappearance at the core of the city regime. Rehabilitation he knew would take some time, but he had not just waited in the hope that domestic developments might mature in his favour. Instead he had insinuated himself with the Athenian forces on the island of Samos. Embedded there he hoped for the opportunity to show off what use he could be to his fellow citizens on the front line.

In this war at sea, access to the money to hire the best oarsmen was going to be of massive importance, and it was by dangling access to the Persian purse that Alcibiades had made it possible for people to consider his recall. A swift built trust with the satrap Tissaphernes, constructed while he was still acting for Sparta, allowed him to do just this, and Thucydides claims there had always been a long term aim to worm his way back into the Athenians' good books. To commence his restoration he sent spokesmen to Samos to flush out the Athenian officers there who might not be completely committed to the democracy, 'the best people', to make it plain to them that if the authorities in control at Athens could be subverted the result might be that the Persian moneybags would come over to the anti-Spartan cause. The agenda his people outlined was clear, that while the Great King or his officers would never sully their hands by dealing with the kind of democrats who had been running Athens for decades, they might if Alcibiades and his kind were calling the shots. This prospect did not just appeal to the friends of the plutocrats back in Athens who were whingeing in their political clubs about the cost of the war. This refrain was far from new but it was Persian money, the famed 'daric archers' that could sustain an effort towards victory. This was bound to be attractive to the Athenian military men on Samos, even those who never had any commitment to an oligarchic agenda; Eastern largesse that had always seemed to be at the beck and call of the Spartans now hovered like a mirage on the horizon. Its appeal was across the political board to men who had been fighting for years and were almost prepared to countenance any policy change if it brought victory.

The island of Samos was a dynamic centre whose loyalty to the Athenian cause was well tested; most members of the Athenian League had fallen off years before but Samos would continue to hold out even after the battle of Aegospotami. Sailors and soldiers from Athens had been based there for sometime, a military home from home where many would have relatives in the cleruchs – communities that had been there since the middle of the century and where officers no doubt found comfortable billets between campaigns with guest friends from the local aristocracy. This strategic island had grown as a kind of military Athens overseas, particularly after an army sent to suppress the Milesians had in good part remained there after the end of the campaign. These hoplites mixed with the sailors and marines from the navies that the Athenians now based at a place so useful for fighting an Ionian war. It was handy to strike at Miletus and Ephesus, not far from the important islands of Chios and Lesbos, the scenes of bloodshed since the Peloponnesian War moved east after the epic of Sicily.

Here one man would do much that made possible the rehabilitation of Alcibiades, a key figure, who achieved enough for his city that he could legitimately be inducted into an Athenian pantheon of greats that included the likes of Miltiades, Themistocles and Pericles. Much will be heard later of this Thrasybulus, but on this occasion his role was to kick off the process of reintroducing into civic favour the one man who might make the difference in pulling off an Athenian victory. He led a group of officers who were prepared to swear a binding oath to replace the current Athenian administration with one that would allow Alcibiades' return to the fold. These men who ranged from hard line oligarchs to moderate democrats were a good start, but knowing they had to get as wide support as possible they looked for approval from the Samos Assembly where the main body of sailors and soldiers left the austerity of leather or canvas tents, near the beached triremes, to listen to what was being proposed. With both pay and victory at stake, the majority there saw the advantage of the Alcibiades idea and envoys were appointed to test the waters in the home metropolis. A man called Peisander was chosen to head them up. He had history as a demagogue, leading a witch hunt in 415 in the wake of the *hermai* incident and even proposing lifting the ban preventing the torture of Athenian citizens. This schemer, who was in fact determined on an oligarchic solution, arrived in Piraeus in late December 412. The men from Samos peddling Alcibiades and moderate reform to make the Persians happy, at first met strong resistance as the assembled Athenians listened, but the need was great and anyway they could sweeten the pill by emphasising that the changes they were proposing might be reversed if they were not liked, after victory. So reluctantly the citizens acquiesced and dispatched Peisander and his people back to thrash out details with the exile and his Achaemenid backers. But, if this was the official face Peisander was showing, by February or March 411 he had revealed his real hand at the political clubs in the city where the old elite gathered, that he was preparing a takeover by a hard line oligarchy. The deep dyed intriguer then departed a fermenting political scene at Athens to lead the deputation to Tissaphernes.

In three long negotiating sessions they bargained. The Persians wanted the Athenians to give up Ionia and the off-shore islands, but if this had been acceptable they still baulked at the Great King's fleets being empowered to enter the Aegean. With nothing finalised Peisander retired first to Samos then to Athens on a journey where he made every effort to secretly mobilise support for an oligarch takeover not just in Athens but in key subject cities too. Once back in Athens, Peisander in cahoots particularly with Antiphon, widely regarded as the silver tongued brains behind the business, decided to act. Calling an assembly that he claimed was to consider constitutional reform, what he was really brewing was the coup for which his confederates in the city had been preparing the ground. On the Pnyx Hill the audience was persuaded that ten trusted leaders should be chosen with full interim powers to put formal constitutional changes before the people. But those selected, in fact, had very different ideas and were working towards a very different outcome.

While much of the citizenry were occupied defending the walls, keeping a wary eye out for the Spartan enemy at Decelea fort, the new ten leaders called the next assembly outside the city in a narrow precinct dedicated to Poseidon. There they pushed through legislation they intended would end the democracy for good. Paid office holding by lot that allowed the poor to participate in government was abolished and five men were elected as presidents who then selected a hundred of their supporters who then sponsored three hundred more. These Four Hundred were given executive powers, only needing to consult a restricted assembly of Five Thousand men of the hoplite class when they felt the need to. The putschists, backed by rich young bravos, foreigners and colonists from Aegina, all hoped to benefit from the change in the government. Not only had they set these Four Hundred oligarchs in power, they also swiftly evicted the incumbent council of officers selected in the previous regime. The Four Hundred new rulers and their enforcers, sporting long hair and red cloaks in homage to the enemy city whose politics they so admired, wanted peace with Sparta at almost any price and sent envoys to King Agis encamped outside the walls to offer very advantageous terms. But the Spartans were more interested in winning unconditional victory than hobnobbing with kindred Athenian spirits. Hoping the political turmoil had made the city vulnerable, they spurned the peace offer and deployed to assault the walls, while sending home for reinforcements. But despite change at the top they found the Athenian military as alert as ever and the defenders briskly pounced on the attackers with cavalry, hoplites, archers and javelin men, forcing them to fall back to Decelea in disarray.

As the oligarch express had trundled into Athens station in 411 so similar things were being tried at Samos. Three hundred Samian bluebloods attempted a takeover but the likes of Thrasybulus and Thrasyllus with the local democrats, and particularly the crew of the *Paralus*, Athens' sacred trireme used on state business, managed to foil the insurgency. So now there existed two divided and antagonistic centres of power. But it was really this island that was the muscle. Here lay the fleet and much of the army who were never going to be happy while their rivals lorded it in the streets of Athens. Thrasybulus and Thrasyllus and other trusted officers were elected as generals and undependable oligarch-tainted ships' captains dismissed. In this new environment the soldiers and sailors with no hope of pay or support from a hostile mother city were bound to look even harder for an alternative.

Though Alcibiades had initially dallied with the oligarchs, they had soon fallen out in the negotiations with the Persians and he was still felt vital to the cause by moderates on Samos. His claims of easy access to Persian money and their Phoenician fleet still seemed plausible enough and Thrasybulus found him with Tissaphernes and whisked him off to rejoin his compatriots on the island. There he was quickly acclaimed by the island assembly and elected a general.

They were a mixed bag those who had supported the takeover of the Four Hundred. Some may well have originally had motives shot through with patriotism, but now the project had been usurped by those with overtly sectional interests. Still even they could not discount the element of Athenian military might residing on Samos and overtures were made hoping there would be enough natural allies in the officers of the fleet and the army to ensure a favourable reception. But it was never going to happen: there might be hoplites and officers with whom their ideas resonated but not the hard core democrats who manned the navy. The Four Hundred's ten envoys received a rough passage at the Samos Assembly and indeed some of the wilder heads would have attacked them there and then except that Alcibiades got them safely off. As duplicitous as ever, as they were spirited away he emphasised that he could work with the government at Athens if the moderates of the Five Thousand franchise both ditched the Four Hundred and could find money to pay the fleet and army.

When these ruffled envoys reported back Alcibiades, with Persian money, certainly looked good to lots of unhappy moderates and even oligarchs at Athens who saw in his attitude an opportunity to reconcile the factions. People who had initially been overawed by the Four Hundred's bald power grab began to think of a push to overthrow them, and even some of their leading men felt sufficiently insecure to contemplate compromise, if only to protect their own hides under future governmental arrangements. Despite this groundswell there were still plenty of intransigents like Peisander who loathed Alcibiades and Aristarchus, who hated all democrats with a vengeance, but with the ground slipping away they could only see hope in an accommodation with Sparta. These men were prepared to offer almost anything that might save them from their domestic rivals' vengeance and had sent agents to the government at Sparta to try for peace again. But these traitorous oligarchs were not just depending on being rescued by their foreign connections, they took practical measures as well and prepared a stronghold in Piraeus where they might bolt to in *extremis*. We hear of continued building of a defensive wall at Eetioneia, the mole at the Piraeus by the entrance to the harbour where there was already a land wall. Now another one was being thrown up on the sea side fit to command the whole place, including two towers that secured the harbour mouth. From there the Four Hundred had agents who made sure all the corn entering the port went through their hands and the money so earned into their coffers. But if the leaders of the Four Hundred saw this as simply preparing a fallback position it was openly spoken in the streets of Athens that their real motivation was to control the port so they could let the Spartan fleet in if it suited them.

Then a new dimension intruded into the divided city when a Peloponnesian fleet was reported to be on its way and the threat of a Spartan takeover looked like becoming a reality. Much was gossip but people still believed that these reactionaries would rather a Spartan tyranny than be the victims of a restored popular rule. To many anarchy appeared around the corner, particularly when Phrynichus, one of the Four Hundred's envoys who had just returned from Sparta, was assassinated in the marketplace. The government's failure to react to this open murder could only embolden the opposition. Then extraordinary developments rolled out down on the Piraeus mole, by the walls that Themistocles had long ago conjured up to secure Athenian power. The soldiers and workmen building the wall at Eetioneia fort were divided and fractious, and Aristocrates, a senior officer backed by soldiers from his own tribe, arrested the oligarch in charge of construction, an action that seemed to receive general support. The Four Hundred in Athens had to act against this plain subversion, but they themselves were panicked and divided. Finally they sent Theramenes who, though not completely trustworthy, persuaded them he could rescue the jailed man. With this trimmer they dispatched a trusted general and some horsemen, patrician cavaliers dreaming of the days when blood was almost all that counted. Unity, loyalty and cohesion were a dead duck now at Piraeus and when Theramenes and his party arrived, a pantomime of abuse began. But still, citizens, hoplites or blue blooded bullyboys, they were all Athenians and squaring off the groups began to debate, arguing whether they should pull down the wall or that it should be kept as a real prop to the port defences. The upshot was that most turned; first to demolish the stonework, and then geared up to proceed against the Four Hundred in Athens itself. The next day, after assembling at the theatre of Dionysius, near the Munychia, they took the short road up to the city where at the sanctuary of the Dioscuri they were met by spokesmen of the authorities. Negotiations began but were soon halted as news arrived that the Peloponnesian fleet was now approaching the port. The hoplites and men from the oarsmen class rushed back down and manned what ships there were, or got in place behind the port ramparts to face the threat. But once arrived they found the Spartan admiral had sailed on past them around Cape Sunium and was heading for Euboea.

The men who had come to defend Piraeus now launched the home fleet triremes in pursuit and joining an Athenian squadron already near the island of Euboea went into battle. But they only found defeat. Their 36 ships led by overconfident and lax officers got themselves comprehensively outmanoeuvred. Even though the Spartans did nothing decisive to exploit their victory, still the Euboea effect had done for the last shreds of credibility of the incumbent administration at Athens. This setback impacted badly on morale. Some even compared it to events after Syracuse when the city had been left without a fleet and a generation of warriors had perished. The Pnyx was packed again as the people assembled to throw out the Four Hundred. Not full democracy yet; that was still anathema to too many, and the key provision, payment for office holders selected by lot, was still completely debarred. The Four Hundred had lasted barely four months and now these quisling oligarchs either kept their heads down or hightailed it to their Spartan friends at Decelea fort. And while Agis was still encamped nearby and a victorious Spartan fleet remained, the new administration was bound to try to do something about these present dangers. To achieve this they needed help, so the rift with the forces on Samos needed healing, even if part of this, the recall of Alcibiades, had to be swallowed.

The context of all this civic commotion was the closing stages of the Peloponnesian War sometimes called the Decelean or Ionian War, a conflict fought largely at sea by fleets of triremes that manoeuvred close to the shore and could only function with safety in those months when the weather was clement. We know a great deal about these vessels, the same sort of ships that had won the battle of Salamis under Themistocles in 480. A leader who had persuaded his fellow citizens to forgo some immediate spending money from a recent silver strike in order to invest in warships to go head to head with the intimidating merchant princes of Aegina, local rivals they could see as a threat in a way they could not the distant Persia, though Themistocles knew it was this eastern power they were really required to combat. Mainly through the efforts of wonderful obsessives in the 1980s most arguments about the construction of these ships have been resolved to the extent that a full scale rowing replica could be constructed[1]. These mortise and tenon built rockets of oak, fir, pine and beech were light as a feather, held together by wooden pins and linen string, and only given strength by two great hawsers pulled tight around the whole length of the vessel's frame. We know the dimensions of these ships, which were the backbone of all the contending navies, pretty near exactly: they were about 121 feet long by 20 feet broad, with 170 oarsmen and sixteen officers and sailing crew. These triremes were not given lead encased bottoms like many merchant ships, and if not very regularly beached (a process eased by waxing the hull) to dry out, despite liberal pitching they would soon become waterlogged and suffer the ravages of worms and barnacles.

The bronze beak was the real weapon in the sea fights between the contending fleets, driven forward by men clutching oars made of young firs, divided into three different levels. The beaks were the cutting edge, though of course the men on board also fought, throwing missiles or boarding and fighting hand to hand. Apart from the oarsmen there would have been a helmsman (often the captain), boatswain, lookout, quartermaster, shipwright and a flautist to give the rowers rhythm. In addition there were two officers in charge of the rowers on each side of the ship. They usually carried between ten and twenty hoplites and up to five archers. The hoplites, apart from fighting the enemy, also had a disciplinary role: next in social status to the captain they helped keep the rabble of oarsmen in line. Under oar they could travel 130 miles a day, rowing for sixteen hours. The likelihood is most triremes were fully decked over, certainly those that doubled as troop transports, and some indeed given further protection by leather curtains hung along the side to ward off missiles aimed at the oarsmen and a rail around the deck. Some however were probably specifically kept undecked, losing protection in order to gain speed.

In the Peloponnesian War the Corinthians had recently introduced the practice of reinforcing the bows and in particular the catheads with thick stay beams in order to give them an advantage in frontal ramming. This innovation had been used to good effect in the battle of Syracuse harbour in 413. With Syracusan ships coming east to continue the war against Athens they would surely have spread this successful advance, though perhaps these changes that made the difference in the confines of Syracuse harbour would have made them unseaworthy outside.

The arena these racehorses of the sea battled in was one where there were three great islands dominating the coast of the West Asian mainland: Lesbos in the north, then fifty-odd miles south of that was Chios, half a day's easy rowing, then a little further again was Samos. These were the battlegrounds, because who controlled them controlled the coast. Certainly the mainland cities Ephesus, Miletus and the rest were rich and important, but they were less secure places to base a martial force, situated where it was necessary either to fight or come to an arrangement with the great inland Persian power. Cos and Rhodes further south, where Anatolia bends round east, were fought over too. They were affluent and significant but not quite as key as the big three that controlled the region opposite mainland Greece along the eastern flank of the routes the grain convoys to Athens had to take.

411 saw the sails of a well drilled Peloponnesian squadron appear beneath the walls of Abydos town intending to boost troubles for Athens along the grain routes that brought the food to sustain the population. Corn convoys concentrated in the Bosporus around early autumn: over fifty years later Philip II of Macedon would show how vulnerable they could be on an occasion when he had fallen out with the Athenians. Whether these men arriving in the north knew that Alcibiades had now joined their enemies on Samos or not, it had certainly not slowed them down. They were anyway probably relieved to be up and doing under a new commander. The man in charge before had not endeared himself to many. This was Astyochus, the Spartan commander of the fleet based at Miletus who had not done well in getting the Persian government man, Tissaphernes, to come up with the promised pay on a regular basis.[2]

There was fudge at the heart of the Peloponnesian/Persian axis against Athens: cooperation between a Sparta who claimed to be heading a drive to free the Asiatic Greeks and island cities from Athenian oppression, and their partner who demanded they receive back all the places that had ever been under their rule, was bound to be difficult. But if this was the big picture, it was the trifling over their money that concerned the men in the fleet. They and their allies from Italy and Sicily demanded they be given their wages, or if not to be led out to fight to win for themselves the fruits of victory. They had even in frustration attacked a Persian fort near Miletus and this was the atmosphere of deep distrust that the new Spartan commander Mindarus found when he arrived. For him there would be no meeting of minds with his sponsor at the satrapal court either; he was deeply unhappy with a 'barbarian' backer who was not only slow in disgorging funds but showed no signs of bringing up the Phoenician fleet whose help had been promised. These skilled veterans at Aspendus seemed very disinclined to move, either because their chiefs saw no reason to bring a conclusion to Greek bloodletting, or that troubles brewing in Egypt and Arabia required them to be kept uncommitted.

By summer Mindarus and his men had become more and more suspicious of the Lydian governor. But while Tissaphernes was revealing himself as a broken reed, Pharnabazus, the northern satrap, had been sending to Mindarus to come and join him in the Hellespont to oust the Athenians and their allies currently dug in there. With no sign of money or supporting squadrons he now seemed the only game in town. Ten ships had anyway already been sent off north by Astyochus from his 112 based at Mycale over the gulf from Miletus and soon enough another sixteen were ordered after as well. When it was reported these 26 had made progress in gaining a foothold around the Chersonese, Mindarus decided on action to reinforce this success. The passage to the north for the Peloponnesian fleet was not going to be easy especially as another thirteen ships, under Dorieus, had had to be dispatched to suppress a rebellion at Rhodes where they had been tailed by Alcibiades with thirteen Athenian ships. So it was a depleted force of only 73 that would need to pass by Samos where the Athenians were thought to be sitting with 108 triremes, that still ship for ship were of better quality than their Peloponnesian counterparts.[3]

If it came to fighting against these odds, to get north near the Hellespontine shore would definitely be an advantage for Mindarus as Pharnabazus' army would be around to support him. But how to get there safely was the quandary. In fact, though Mindarus did not know it, the Athenians had themselves been weakened by dispatching twenty triremes to the north, quite apart from Alcibiades down around Rhodes with his thirteen ships, so in reality only seventy-five Athenian vessels were beached at Samos when Mindarus made his attempt to slip past his watching enemy. In the event foul weather, though buffeting his fleet, gave him a real advantage. The Peloponnesians were forced to put in for five or six days at Icarus Island, a place not much smaller than Samos itself and something over ten miles to the west, but crucially the weather conditions kept the enemy landlocked and allowed the battered squadron past to Chios without being intercepted. As soon as the weather eased the Athenians launched and chased after Mindarus, but when their scout boats saw the prey safe in Chios harbour the main force sailed on to Lesbos intending to concentrate there and block the Peloponnesians' further passage north. But again the nimble Mindarus was up to the challenge. First he sailed to the harbour of Carteria on the mainland near Phocaea, a distance of 45 miles and after a midday meal continued for thirty more to the Arginusae islands at the southern end of the channel between Lesbos and the mainland. After an evening meal and night's rest they prepared for the last leg where they would again have to pass the enemy fleet. They sneaked between Lesbos Island and the mainland before the sun was up and by midday had passed safely through the channel. Revitalised with a meal taken at Harmatus on the mainland opposite Methymna, the fleet managed in a day of hard sailing to reach the town of Sigeum at the Asian mouth of the Hellespont, a total of nearly 145 miles in one day. This breakneck second passage had been aided by the Athenians on Lesbos being distracted by a local conflict. There at the city of Methymna the oligarchs had been making trouble. Though unable to suborn the loyalty of their less well-heeled compatriots, they managed to establish themselves with some mercenaries at Eresos, a fortified place in the west of the island. This peripheral stuff seemed to have particularly distracted Thrasybulus when he should have been keeping Mindarus in his sights. When the Spartans' ruse was reported, the Athenians pulled out of the siege of Eresos and chased after, determined not to be outsmarted again, though in the rush only three allied ships managed to join them as reinforcements.

The upshot was that on the second day after sailing the bleary signallers on the heights above Elaeus saw Mindarus' fleet and managed to alert the eighteen Athenian vessels based at Sestos. These guard boats, now horribly outnumbered, tried to sneak away, and hugging the shore dropped down the channel hoping to exit the straits and sail into open water. Though avoiding the sixteen strong enemy force based at Abydos, in the following dawn, almost in open sea, they bumped straight into Mindarus' armada who chased and captured four triremes that failed to scatter for shelter on Lemnos or Imbros. The Spartans, though failing to take the enemy base at Elaeus, moved on to Abydos, a strong city further up the channel on the Asian side, the best harbour on that bank and the shortest crossing point of the Dardanelles. Only a mile broad, Hero and Leander had done their stuff there and this Milesian colony had been where Xerxes started his bridge of boats into Europe and where both Agesilaus and Alexander would cross the other way too. Revolting from Athenian control in 411 it had since shown firm adherence to its new Spartan friends.

The Athenian fleet from Samos chasing after were close behind and even picked up three of Mindarus' most laggard ships before they concentrated at Elaeus to prepare for battle. This town, on the European side of the absolute western lip of the Hellespont, now became the base for a great Athenian fleet, just as Abydos was for the Spartans. Thrasybulus was in charge now in what would become an epic of multiple combats. He was a thorough officer and prepared for five days, training and equipping the 76 strong war-fleet that had been pulled together. On the sixth day, in column ahead close to the Gallipoli shore, the Athenians moved out, eager to fight in this narrow place close to the friendly European coastline. They needed to dispose of the Spartans to ensure the freedom of those trade lines through which the lifeblood of Athens flowed.

When the fleets met they numbered 76 Athenians against Mindarus' 86.[4] The Spartans had had more success in concentrating their forces than their opponents, nor were they lacking in battle preparation: they had also dedicated five days to sharpening up their fighting skills. The combat would start with two lines of battle each with its back to a friendly shore, from Abydos south to Dardanus, a distance of over seven miles. Mindarus deployed with the Syracusan triremes on the right while he personally commanded on the left. On the Athenian side Thrasybulus himself led on the right while Thrasyllus took the other end of the line opposite the Sicilians. The Spartans, knowing their superiority in numbers, were confident and determined to try to turn the enemy right in a manoeuvre that might cut off their line of retreat, and then to overwhelm the centre which would have little room for manoeuvre with their wings on either side and the shore close behind. In the rear of the Athenian line there was also a headland that ensured that after the Athenian left had rowed past they would not be able to see what was happening to the rest of the fleet following them. Both sides extended their flanks from the beginning of the fight which meant that the Athenians, by stretching out dangerously, thinned their centre. So when the Spartans made their move and drove in at the middle of their line, Thrasyllus who was past the headland could not see what was happening and saw no cause to return (even if he could have done so with a battle of his own on his hands). All the while Thrasybulus on the far right was extending his wing to stop it being flanked and cut off from the escape route back down the channel to Elaeus, so equally was in no position to help.

In the middle of the line the Peloponnesians forced their enemies back onto the beach. All was seemingly going to plan for Mindarus. But naval warfare at this time was a chancy business both at the tactical and the strategic level, and this day would be no exception. The tables turned in a manner most dramatic and not easy to completely credit. The centre of the Athenian line had backed onto the shore and the noise of keels grinding on stone and sand was accompanied by cries that Spartan marines were disembarking to capture the immobile ships. Soon armoured men from both sides were fighting in the shallows. There the Athenians were disordered and vulnerable and it is asserted that the Peloponnesians, believing victory won, scattered to secure these prizes. An indiscipline that meant a considerable part of the Spartans fell into disarray and may even have affected what happened on their own left wing.

The contest on the side where Thrasybulus faced Mindarus had begun with considerable manoeuvring to gain the benefit of the current. 'At the outset both sides strove stubbornly for position in order that they might not have the current against them.'[5] This was to the advantage of the Athenians whose crews were better at handling their vessels, suggesting that any Persian money coming through had not yet begun to seriously impact in the market for oarsmen. In this melee the Athenians were very successful in ensuring their ships were not exposed but kept ram to ram when the Peloponnesians attacked guaranteeing they did not find it easy to board. A key factor as though their sailors were inferior the Peloponnesian marines were of better quality. Indeed when craft became disordered in the current, Spartan numbers were cancelled out by the Athenians' seafaring skills as they were able to outflank Mindarus' ships and to hit and hole some of them in the flank. This is detail from the sources that makes it believable that the two Athenian wings were able to overcome their opponents.[6] With Mindarus' wing beaten and indiscipline rife, the Peloponnesian centre was soon in trouble as the hoplites who had thought they would shortly be owners of tens of Athenian beached triremes were called back to their own ships. The Spartan commanders who had taken their eye off the ball to go for individual prizes also began to understand how matters had changed as they saw the whole of the Peloponnesian left and many of their comrades from the centre fleeing up the strait.

On the right the hard fighting Syracusans were equally being pressed back by the squadron under Thrasyllus and when they perceived their confederates beating a retreat, it was the end. The Peloponnesians only just managed to get away, firstly to the River Midius then back to their base at Abydos which fortunately was not too much of an oar pull away up the channel, though on getting there it became clear that the Athenians had achieved a winning score, if only a marginal one. They had bagged eighteen ships: eight from Chios, five from Corinth, two from Ambracia and one apiece from Syracuse, Pellene and Leucadia, for a loss of fifteen themselves.

'Thrasybulus set up a trophy on the cape where stands the memorial of Hecabe (Hecuba)'[7] and then proceeded to exploit his just-won local ascendancy. Like ripe fruit eight Byzantine ships, discovered at anchor at Harpagium and Priapus, were captured while the Athenians went east into the Sea of Marmara to retake Cyzicus, an unfortified place that had recently cried defiance. Then after extorting money with menaces from the locals the Athenians shipped out for Sestos which they took over as more convenient to control the eastern mouth of the Hellespont and to defend the grain fleets sailing out from the Bosporus and the Sea of Marmara.

Yet while this was happening Mindarus was far from down and out. He crept down to Elaeus without being noticed and retook some of the prizes lost after the battle – the rest had been burned by locals, while Hippocrates and Epicles were sent to fetch reinforcements from Euboea. This did not go as smoothly as he could have wished: one squadron of fifty triremes was shattered and every man drowned, except for twelve wretched survivors, when a gale blew up round Mount Athos in the Chalcidice.

The Battle of Cynossema was fought in the previous year in the summer of 411 but the roughed up remnant from Euboea did not get through until well on into autumn, and the same was true of the squadron under Dorieus who had been left in the south when the main force sailed. This Rhodian who had command of the Italian ships and apparently had 'quelled the tumult in Rhodes' before turning north with the intention of joining Mindarus recouping at Abydos from the rigours of the previous battle. Everybody was congregating now; even Tissaphernes was wending his way up north following the war he was patchily financing. When Dorieus with his thirteen ships sailed north Alcibiades knew he must move where the action was and no doubt Thrasybulus had been calling him back anyway. The man he was supposed to be chasing reached the mouth of the Hellespont without encountering hostile ships, but then all changed. The October tides would have worried his pilots, with strong currents powering down from the Sea of Marmara to the Aegean, and a robust north easterly wind blowing. Also the Rhodian knew he was nearing Athenian ports that probably held many more ships than he could deploy. The sun would just have been coming up when they rowed hard into the Hellespont channel. The first to respond to the desperate warnings of the Athenian signallers on the heights were twenty ships, most likely from Elaeus, who launched and fell on the enemy with a will. Dorieus could not fight it out at sea but retreated to the southern shore near Rhoeteum just over the lip of the channel and north of the site of old Troy. The twenty Athenians could make no headway against the ship-defended perimeter on the beach and pulled off to find the rest of the fleet at Madytus just opposite Abydos keeping an eye on the Spartan base. Scouts had anyway been alert and had sent the news to where the 74 Athenian triremes were anchored; they were quickly got underway and began to run down the straits to finish off the newcomers. Mindarus meanwhile learned of all this while making a sacrifice at a temple in Ilium (Troy) and he covered the ground back to Abydos in double quick time to get the main fleet out to rescue Dorieus. Eighty-four vessels pulled out of Abydos harbour barrelling down to enter the fray. Mindarus, pulling out all the stops, also sent to Pharnabazus to come with his army to rally round in the anticipated confrontation. Out in the channel they found Dorieus who, once the twenty-strong Athenian fleet had withdrawn, had progressed up as far as Dardanus, a promontory some ten miles inside the Hellespont on the southern shore. Urgent action had allowed their combination but once joined, now numbering 97, they found themselves confronted by the entire Athenian fleet that had come sailing south out of Madytus, and a set piece encounter developed. Both sides deployed as best they could; the Peloponnesians took station with the Syracusans on the left and Mindarus on the right, while the Athenians led with Thrasybulus on their right and Thrasyllus on the left. Flags and trumpets conveyed the orders and the two great fleets, bronze beaks and garish painted figureheads showing, moved forward to attack.

Seamanship on both sides is praised, with pilots highlighted who would turn their ships at the last minute to avoid a ram or make sure when they struck it was prow to prow. 'For whenever the triremes would drive forward to ram, at that moment the pilots, at just the critical instant, would turn their ships so effectively that the blows were made ram on. As for the marines, whenever they would see their own ships borne along with their sides to the triremes of the enemy, they would be terror-stricken, despairing of their lives; but whenever the pilots, employing the skill of practice, would frustrate the attack, they would in turn be overjoyed and elated in their hopes.'[8] So it is reported to the huge relief of the marines, seen in this cameo of terror as an enemy bears down, beak forward, against their ships' flank. The air was full of javelins and arrows and slingshot as the boats came together, until the moment of contact when it came to hand to hand, spear, sword and shield, with men leaping onto the enemy deck to attempt a decisive boarding action. The clashing of metal the shouting and screaming of men is transmitted over the millennia in a way that allows an authentic imagining of what occurred in the battle.

The battle of Abydos was an even combat that was turned in the most dramatic manner, by the arrival of Alcibiades with twenty fresh ships. It is reported he had appeared in the Hellespont by chance from Samos, but the evidence is against this as it is probable he had been following Dorieus' squadron up from Rhodes. Alcibiades had been active in the south Aegean since his appointment as general on Samos and this sojourn had included forcing money out of the administration at Halicarnassus before heading for Cos where he built a fort, left a governor in place and then went back to Samos. There in September he boosted his popularity by doling out some much needed money for the troops. These activities do not reek of great purpose, perhaps he was just revelling in the experience of untrammelled command but as hot war flared in the Hellespont the likelihood is his core brief was to shadow the Peloponnesian squadron under Dorieus and keep it shackled while the main task force was off up north. He had followed him when he left the region and on the track of his prey Alcibiades now arrived at the crucial moment. When these onrushing entrants were spotted, water creaming under the thrust of their oars, both sides thought the reinforcements were for them, so when realisation finally dawned on the Spartans the shock was devastating. Alcibiades had let his comrades know that he was on their side by raising a purple flag.[9] With hopes dashed morale was broken and the Peloponnesians gave ground. Slowly at first but then more and more ships turned to disentangle themselves from their enemy and fled. Ten could not get away and were caught and captured while the rest had at least some good fortune. Violent winds blew up and the seas they raised made life very difficult for the Athenian triremes as they pressed the pursuit; 'for because of the high waves the boats would not respond to the tillers, and the attempts at ramming proved fruitless, since the ships were receding when struck.'[10] The Peloponnesians turned to flee but the only possibility of haven for most was the shore. There they beached their ships and, as bottoms scraped the beach, soldiers leapt down to form what defence they could against an Athenian armada that was bearing down on them at speed. The weather had allowed some wriggle room for Mindarus, but now his only hope was to get everybody onto dry land and fight it out from there.

To form a defensive perimeter with the ships and make a stand was the only hope and this tactic of transferring a sea battle to land was made the more attractive by the fact that Mindarus knew there was support to be had nearby. They could even see friendly troops from the town on the shore all set to help them when they landed. Dragging up the boats onto the beach and setting their prows facing out they placed the marines from the fleet and the soldiers from the town with all the missiles they could lay their hands on to defend their ships. The Athenians, like wolves round a sheep pen, crowded in and tried to drag the enemy boats off with grappling hooks, so once back in the water they could surround and capture them. But the defenders were well organised and brave – though time was bound to be against them because of the number of their foes. This was not Phormio manoeuvring at Patrae or Naupactus, but more like Ajax in the Trojan War on the stern of his black ship fighting with a long boat spear a land battle aboard or amongst the stranded, immobile triremes. Fighting from deck or sand with archers picking off where they could and hoplites pressing and stabbing in the centre of the battle line was only a place for the brave. But Spartan captains and other officers were losing control and formations were falling apart as the Athenians pressed the attack.

What saved the Peloponnesian forces from utter disaster was the arrival of the Persians. Pharnabazus and his army had been marching to the noise of battle, and the Athenians as they tried to drag off and capture more ships found, with the numbers of Persians growing by the moment, that they began to be thrown back. Here the Persian bowmen and other missile troops had the advantage over the hoplites on board ship who found it difficult to get at them on the shore.

Pharnabazus, in heroic mould, even rode his horse up to its chest into the water leading, with his companion guard behind him, to aid his allies in fighting off the Athenians. Another deciding factor was the light; it was night by the time the Athenians got back to Sestos after the battle so it may well have been dusk as this last stage of the combat flared, which effectively brought an end to the encounter. Frustrated but happy with a second considerable victory in these waters, the Athenian vessels backed oars into the main channel before returning upstream to their base. They had not overwhelmed the last ditch defence, but they had captured thirty enemy hulls and also recaptured many of their own ships previously lost to the enemy.

The fight had been turned by the great exile and only the Persians' intervention stopped the victory from being decisive. This was Alcibiades really establishing himself. Thrasybulus was a key sponsor, gifts of money to soldiers in Samos helped, and it was always the anticipation of Persian gold that he might win for them that gave the man his worth. His position was still tricky, the breach in trust had been deep and before the battle of Abydos his achievements had been useful but hardly crucial. But now arriving at the darkest hour to win the day he began a rise in the eyes of the Athenians that, if it continued, bid fair for him to re-establish himself in the home city. The exact hierarchical relationship in the Athenian command structure at the time is difficult to ascertain, and where in it Alcibiades fitted is even more so. To many in Samos, particularly amongst the radical democrats, acceptance of him had been grudging and he had had to plough a lone furrow for a time. But now with the triumph at the battle of Abydos there was a sea change and this would become even more apparent with events in the following year.

After the victors had withdrawn, Mindarus returned once again to Abydos with a defeated fleet. But the man was resilient, he hardly took breath before sending messengers off to Sparta for reinforcements while he contacted his Persian allies to encourage their resolve and settled down to draw up plans for further attacks on Athenian collaborators in the region. Still in terms of real action he kept quiet over the winter of 411/410 looking to salve his bruises and recoup his strength. But as for the Athenian camp, another Alcibiades escapade is detailed. Tissaphernes had moved up towards the Hellespont in the off season for reasons unknown, but to bring him thus to his rival satrap's heartland they must have been important. Surely it was to do with a concern he was losing his grip on the war? Down in Ionia and Caria he was able to play both sides against the middle, confident that whatever the Spartans or the Athenians could achieve he could constrain or encourage them depending on his own interest. But now it seemed the situation was out of control; could he continue to apparently support the Spartans while double dealing with Alcibiades when the Athenians were on the up threatening to gain complete sway over the Hellespont and Sea of Marmara? This was a development that might not be to the liking of the Great King at Susa, and Tissaphernes was bound to worry that when he heard, it would be he who would be blamed. When he learned of the satrap's arrival, Alcibiades immediately set out to visit him despite the fact that Tissaphernes was formally a Spartan ally and Alcibiades was now a bespoke Athenian general again. Clearly the need to show he still had a relationship with the Persians made the risk of this venture into the enemy camp worthwhile. But it backfired: Tissaphernes was having none of this shifty man who had no herald status and directly had him arrested on the grounds that he was under orders from the Great King to make war on all Athenians. He was sent in chains to Sardis, a dire outcome that is described with little drama, yet for a time it must have seemed the end of everything for an individual whose star had been on the ascendant, certainly in Athenian affairs. But Alcibiades was not a man to be kept down by mere prison walls. After thirty days his captors became lax and, with another prisoner, he slipped out of jail one night, found some horses in the sleeping town and rode like the wind to Clazomenae on the coast. The fugitive then contrived to pick up five triremes and a rowing boat, getting help from local officials probably by putting it about that Tissaphernes let him go, before getting to Lesbos on the way to joining the rest of the Athenian navy now at Cardia.

While Alcibiades was away the Athenian command had found it a very up and down war. Though seemingly getting the better of two encounters, they found the new year of 410 opening in a most threatening manner. Frequently in wars that go on for a long time the story becomes the same: the strategic function of the armed force develops into essentially one of trying to feed itself. The aim of the campaign became about squeezing enough supplies and money out of the locals for the commander to keep his forces in being. It had already become a pattern in this war between Athens and Sparta that had been going on for over two decades: virtually every campaigning season included a cruise of extortion as the old mechanisms of support from the home government and the resources to sustain them became eroded over time. The corollary of this was that the victims who were on the receiving end either became deep died enemies, or if allies tried to make their complaints heard at the home city which might well impact on the reputation, career and even life of the commander in charge. On this occasion after the battle at Abydos all except forty ships of the Athenian fleet went on such an extortion cruise while Thrasyllus went back to Athens to bask in the congratulations of the home folk and to try to persuade them to follow up their success.

While the Athenians had been scrabbling round for cash, Mindarus had been active conjuring up triremes 'from the Peloponnesus as well as from the other allies' and suddenly the Athenian captains in Sestos felt themselves extremely vulnerable if the reinforced Peloponnesians decided to pounce. Their fright was such that they upped sticks and skedaddled out of the Hellespont altogether only pausing to set up a new base once they reached the protection of Cardia on the other side of the Chersonese. But once there, they got to work recovering the squadrons under Thrasybulus and Theramenes who had been showing the flag in Thrace, and when Alcibiades arrived from Lesbos with his triremes the mood of terror rapidly transmogrified into one of confident ambition. Maybe it was his arrival or just the consciousness of their numbers but the Athenian high command now seemed to put aside any personal differences and got down to encompassing the downfall of Mindarus and his Persian cohort Pharnabazus. Cyzicus was the chosen arena, an Athenian ally that had fallen to her enemies again despite having been re-secured after Athenian success at Cynossema. East of the Hellespont channel this town was at the base of a large and rugged peninsula that almost crossed right over the Sea of Marmara, and any force located there was well placed to interdict the corn routes that much of this fighting was all about. The Athenians moved from their base at Cardia and relocated all the ships they could gather to Elaeus, eighty-six in total, enough to make a good fist of it against a Spartan fleet that on their latest reports only comprised eighty triremes.[11] From that base at the mouth of the channel they slipped up past Abydos at night so the enemy scouts on duty should not discover their strength and with Lampsacus on the right entered into the Sea of Marmara. A good long pull brought them first to Parium, on the north Asian shore, then on to the large island of Proconnesus (modern Marmara) north west of the Cyzicus peninsula, and there they anchored.

The Athenians took enormous pains to keep their arrival a secret, even impounding the local fishermen and their boats. The intention was to surprise the enemy fleet and army that they had discovered was concentrated at Cyzicus, and the Athenian commanders were aided in this by the weather. In driving rain and heavy mist the Athenian triremes were launched and ploughed through the water towards their unsuspecting prey. The initial scheme had been to assault Cyzicus town and a general called Chaereas was delegated to land with most of the hoplites for that purpose. As for the fleet, after they had dropped the assault force off, with Alcibiades in the van, they cruised past the Artace headland and came into sight of the Spartan fleet that was exercising in the bay of Cyzicus. 'As for the generals themselves, they divided the naval force into three squadrons, Alcibiades commanding one, Theramenes another, and Thrasybulus the third. Now Alcibiades, with his own squadron, advanced far ahead of the others wishing to draw the Lacedaemonians out to a battle, whereas Theramenes and Thrasybulus planned the manoeuvre of encircling the enemy and, if they sailed out, of blocking their retreat to the city.'[12] There is a feeling here that Alcibiades was designated to act as a bait, and that the enemy were already out of port was something of a bonus.

The twenty ships of the Athenian van was what Mindarus saw when they loomed out of the rain and, assuming it was the whole force, he gave orders for his entire fleet of eighty ships to chase and engage. But as the Spartans and their allies pursued Alcibiades west past the Artace promontory, they saw his flagship raise a signal to his colleagues and soon became aware that away on their right were a large number of other enemy vessels. There the squadrons of Thrasybulus and Theramenes with the remaining 66 ships were drawn up in battle order menacing the Peloponnesians' exposed right side. And at the same moment Alcibiades ordered his captains to about ship and the erstwhile quarry became something very different with their bronze prows turned to face them. Mindarus' ships responded well enough, they had plenty of expert crews paid with good Persian gold, but by now they could not get back to Cyzicus harbour as the Athenian main force had cut off their escape.

The ambushed fleet was not heavily outnumbered but the initial manoeuvres had left them disorganised, exposed and almost surrounded: they knew they were not well placed for a fight in open water. Mindarus decided his best chance was again to make for land and the protection Pharnabazus' forces might afford him. He ordered his commanders to head for a place south of Cyzicus called Cleri but while they tried to escape, Alcibiades, the nearest enemy, chased them hard towards the beach, getting in amongst them, ramming some and sweeping the oars of others. Even so most of the Peloponnesian vessels did manage to land, though some were seized at sea, but the Athenians, far from stopping when the enemy were beached, endeavoured to drag them off wherever they could.

Here the archers, javelineers and peltasts came into their own, where there was no room on the triremes' decks to form a phalanx. Certainly when it came to hand to hand fighting the hoplite with shield, and stabbing spear or sword would carry the day. But in these circumstances reaching hand to hand was not easy. In fact the struggle was as often as not conducted with grappling hooks as with swords, the Athenians hurling them to catch the beached enemy and then their oarsmen straining to drag their ships into the water. If successful the ships were surrounded

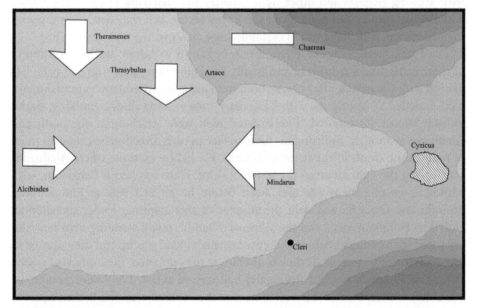

The Battle of Cyzicus 410 BC.

and captured with all the crew who had not been able to jump into the shallows and escape.

Not all of Alcibiades' men were thus engaged, a good number had disembarked to form up in line and make an attack along the shoreline. On the beach, Pharnabazus' mercenary infantry once more supported the Spartans as best they could though we do not know what sort of soldiers they were. They were numerous but not able to turn the table against the Athenians, so perhaps they were light troops and not up to a shield to shield battle on the sands. Into this balanced picture Thrasybulus now intruded and, seeing the key fight was on the beach, disembarked his marines to form up alongside those of Alcibiades. He also sent urgent orders to Theramenes to bring in his soldiers and the hoplites under Chaereas who had been left to attack Cyzicus town. These men must have been ferried across from near the Artace promontory as it would have been tricky if not impossible for them to march past the town that blocked off the narrow neck of the peninsula. While they were on their way Mindarus was still with his ships fighting off Alcibiades' men who were striving might and main to drag them off with their own craft. But he did not disregard the shore fight, ordering his general Clearchus with some of the Peloponnesian troops and units of the Persian mercenaries to boost that front. These men initially all but overwhelmed the Athenians Alcibiades had landed, but just in the nick of time Theramenes' and Chaereas' troops arrived to save the day. Thrasybulus' marines, lined up backs to the wall alongside Alcibiades' men, were also in desperate straits when the rescue party arrived. Now with numbers not hugely unbalanced it came to a real push of battle: each side settled into a phalanx with archers, peltasts and other light infantry manoeuvring to cover the flanks. The Persian cavalry had not arrived yet: a vital factor, as if they had, their capacity to outflank the Athenians would certainly have changed the face of the affray.

Then 'the mercenaries of Pharnabazus began to withdraw and the continuity of their battle line was broken; and finally the Peloponnesians, who had been left behind with Clearchus, after having both inflicted and suffered much punishment, were expelled.'[13] Mindarus, with Clearchus' men and his allies crumbling, found himself almost surrounded; Theramenes' men were attacking at one point and Alcibiades at another. Splitting his force to face in each direction he called on them to fight to the death in the name of Sparta. He led by example where Alcibiades was forcing the fight amongst the beached ships. Here was heroic behaviour, with Mindarus cutting many enemies down before he himself was surrounded and brought low. Once he was slain the absence of this inspiring leader signalled an end. The Peloponnesians and the allies who had been still standing firm now slid away and soon enough broke into flight. Athenian blood was up and they wanted to finish these deadly foes while they could but, as they pursued, their officers became aware that Pharnabazus with his cavalry had arrived at last. They were going to be extremely vulnerable to these newcomers as they chased after the broken Spartan army, so they settled for what they had already gained and orders were given to return to the beach. There it began to dawn on them that this fight they had just won had virtually bagged them the whole enemy fleet.

The Peloponnesians who were left in the city looking for protection from the Persians saw none coming and took to their heels, so the cherry on the cake, the city of Cyzicus, came effortlessly into the victorious Athenians' hands. 'They set up two trophies for the two victories, one for the sea-battle at the island of Polydorus, as it is called, and one for the land-battle where they forced the first flight of the enemy.'[14] This seemed enormous: the Spartan power at sea subsidised by Persian darics had been undone and done for. When news arrived at Athens they sacrificed in thanks to the gods and also sent out 1,000 hoplites, 100 horsemen and 30 triremes to reinforce success. And it was to Alcibiades they directed both their thanks and these very practical resources. It was apparently Hippocrates, Mindarus' vice admiral, who famously composed the laconic but clearly despairing report back to Sparta: 'The ships are gone. Mindarus is dead. The men are starving. We know not what to do.'[15] The Spartans had lost their whole fleet, captured and dragged off to Proconnesus Island, except for the Syracusans who had burnt their ships refusing to contemplate letting their hardware fall into the hands of the people who had almost destroyed their home city a few years before.

The Spartan response to the catastrophe of Cyzicus was to sue for peace.[16] The head of the negotiating team they sent to Athens was shrewdly chosen. It was Endius, a guest friend of Alcibiades (a relationship between their respective families which dated back to the 550s) and experienced ex-ephor who they no doubt hoped would still have sufficient influence on their erstwhile ally. His speech was typically laconic seeking to point out the advantages the Spartans possessed in their paymaster the Persians. 'While to the Laconians the war has brought many allies, from the Athenians it has taken away as many as it has given to their enemies. For us the richest king to be found in the inhabited world defrays the cost of the war, for you the most poverty-stricken folk of the inhabited world. Consequently our troops, in view of their generous pay, make war with spirit, while your soldiers, because they pay the war-taxes out of their own pockets, shrink from both the hardships and the costs of war. In the second place, when we make war at sea, we risk losing only hulls among resources of the state, while you have on board crews most of whom are citizens. And, what is the most important, even if we meet defeat in our actions at sea, we still maintain without dispute the mastery on land – for a Spartan foot-soldier does not even know what flight means – but you, if you are driven from the sea, contend, not for the supremacy on land, but for survival.'[17]

The Athenians just recovering from the final throes of the Four Hundred chose to reject the offer of the status quo, mainly under the influence of Cleophon, a leading radical democrat, though Alcibiades' influence cannot be discounted even if he was away in the Hellespont at the time – it would certainly not have been in his interests for a peace to be concluded. Certainly there were some who favoured accepting the offer, but in the new found ebullience after Cyzicus it was felt total victory was in sight. The battle had been fought either in April or May 410 and the peace negotiations followed on shortly afterwards, but though most of a full campaigning season lay before them the Athenians did not do much to exploit their success. Apart from the forces sent in the first flush of victory to Alcibiades, when another effort was made under Thrasyllus, it headed not to the Hellespont but to Samos. The cities of Miletus, Cnidus and Antandrus in the south Troad had all thrown out Tissaphernes' garrisons and this was seen as too good an opportunity to sniff at. In fact Thrasyllus landed and campaigned around Ephesus with mixed fortunes, and only after this messing about on the periphery did they head north, reaching the Hellespont just before winter set in. So the Athenians did not at all make decisive hay in the aftermath of Cyzicus. What they achieved was not derisory but it did not seem commensurate with the dimensions of the triumph. Once again the chronology is confused but the reasons for the lack of activity are obscure. The restoration of democracy was occurring around this time and may well have played its part in diverting people's attention. It should also not be forgotten that Athens was suffering severe economic hardship, being reduced to melting down silver and gold from the temples in order to issue emergency coinage. Presumably they did not have the wherewithal to finance major military projects.

The most immediate and important benefit of the battle was that it gave Athens control of the customs house at Chrysopolis north of Chalcedon and across the water from Byzantium, though this domination of the Bosporus and the corn trade was not to remain uncontested for long. But apart from this, for well over a year the Spartan maritime vacuum was hardly built upon at all. For the vanquished this respite was a godsend they could not have expected and it allowed them from disaster to begin to pick up the pieces. Blows had landed hard and repeatedly like a trip hammer against the Spartan cause, but various factors meant they were not decisive. Mercifully Pharnabazus had stayed onside and he had money and timber to get a comeback started. Shipyards at Antandrus, presumably either never lost or retaken, were soon busy building new triremes, and Spartan allies were pressed to send whatever they had left in their arsenals to get them back in the ring in this crucial Propontic war. Also the Spartan Clearchus had connections at Byzantium, and took charge there and at Chalcedon, beefing up these allies' efforts with a contingent of troops from Megara that were shipped over in 15 allied ships. Though this was still dangerous territory they traversed and 3 transports were afterwards sunk by Athenian patrols active in the area.

At the end of 409 the Athenian forces took up the cudgel again. Thrasyllus' reinforcements had not gelled with Alcibiades' soldiers on the spot, but simmering rivalry did not prevent them cooperating to the extent of decamping together to Lampsacus on the Asian shore of the Hellespont, a place ideally situated to loot both Pharnabazus' satrapy and threaten the Spartans in Abydos. Good use was made of the winter season as both Thrasyllus and Alcibiades' men sweated to comprehensively entrench their encampment at Lampsacus. But when the fighting season began it became clear they were not staying put and that Abydos was their objective. The city port dominated one of the narrowest points along the Hellespont shore and was the last Spartan stronghold on the waterway. To take it would enshrine full Athenian control so Thrasyllus took thirty ships south to attack the place. But he found when he landed the Persians were soon on the scene with a good number of horse and foot and attacked him. While this Athenian force had gone by sea, Alcibiades led the Athenian cavalry and 120 hoplites overland down the coast road. Good fortune was his partner: finding Pharnabazus engaged with Thrasyllus' men he ordered his men to charge and they put the startled enemy to rout pursuing them until darkness called a halt. With the region now clear of the enemy the invaders were able to plunder at will and accrue a good quantity of booty, but for the larger picture Persian resistance had at least distracted the Athenians and prevented a surprise attack on the city. In fact they never managed to take the place and Abydos remained a Spartan stronghold, as the Athenian forces were called back to shore up the grip of their comrades on the Bosporus.

There the Spartans at Byzantium and Chalcedon under the harmost Hippocrates had recently become more active and the Athenian man on the spot, Theramenes, was feeling the pressure at Chrysopolis. He had off his own bat been wasting Chalcedonian territory on his side of the channel but this had stirred a hornets' nest, so he was anxiously waiting for succour from the main Athenian forces to the south to ensure he did not get back too much of his own medicine. When they arrived, the Athenians had accumulated 190 ships: an altogether overpowering force. The people in Chalcedon, seeing the size of the enemy, did not even bother to try to defend themselves but, handing over their valuables to some friendly Thracians in Bithynia, fled their homes. Unfortunately for them Alcibiades, hearing of their plan, intercepted the convoy carrying their property and confiscated almost all the goods. Well provided with this Chalcedonian booty to remunerate the troops, the intruders now settled down to the serious business of besieging the town from which it had come. It was first cut off by a ditch and palisade, built from the Bosporus to the Sea of Marmara, to defend against any attempted relief by the Persians. Hippocrates, knowing the Persians to be near at hand with a large army and hoping they would march to his aid, led out his men to drive off the besiegers. They encountered the Athenians under Thrasyllus in a bloody affray. Alcibiades with the cavalry and a small number of hoplites did not join the fight till near the end, perhaps being needed to defend the palisade against Pharnabazus' men. Eventually when he did intervene Hippocrates was killed and the Spartans routed. But again victory in the open was not decisive, as sufficient defenders got back to hold the walls of the city.

The Athenians stuck at it, but the need for money was forever a distraction and Alcibiades went on tour to press the Hellespontine cities to drum up financial contributions. There now transpired some shenanigans involving the Athenians, Persians, Chalcedonians and eventually even the Spartans that are difficult to credit and to comprehend, and reflect the complex political and diplomatic situation at the time. The presence of the Persian army was once more proving decisive in keeping the Athenians from achieving complete victory. It had been the case down by the Hellespont and was equally so up by the Bosporus. The Athenians' own in-house tensions did not help either, Alcibiades was a talisman, but a tainted one, and his brother officers often seemed more comfortable when he was away doing his own thing rather than in camp with them. On this occasion the Athenian commanders at Chalcedon, frustrated by their lack of progress, came to an accord with Pharnabazus that a truce should stand while an embassy was fitted out to visit Susa to propose peace between Athens and Persia. In addition the satrap would pay them twenty talents and the Chalcedonians would stump up their usual tribute pending the result of the talks. The Athenians anxious to defeat the Spartans after Cyzicus desperately needed to try to neutralise the Persians. When Alcibiades returned and heard the news of this he became a worried man. His unique selling point was his claim to a special relationship with the local Persians, and to retain his reputation he could not just be seen as having the equivalent relationship with Pharnabazus as the other generals. So he persuaded the satrap to go through a special form of agreement just including those two. But this jaw jaw had not been the end of war war, now Byzantium across the water came into the cross-hairs of these Athenian generals and their assorted hosts.

Theramenes and Thrasyllus shipped their soldiers across the Bosporus while Alcibiades who had taken over at Selymbria just west along the coast also piled in. Again they got down to digging, throwing up a wall to cut off the city of Byzantium by land as the fleet did by sea. But big well defended cities like this were never a pushover at this time particularly before torsion throwing machines had come into use. Clearchus was there on the walls directing the defenders including some troops from Laconia, a few Megarians, Boeotians and mercenaries as well. Only when he left to try to recruit men at Chalcedon and to distract the Athenians by attacking their friends in the Hellespont did things begin to move for the besiegers. The Spartan was, it unsurprisingly turned out, not loved in the city he defended; his arrogance and barely disguised disdain for his allies, so typical of these harmosts, raised hackles across the classes. So this time it was not the usual suspects who inclined to sell the pass to Athens, it was upper crusters who contacted Alcibiades; they no doubt considered this Athenian of the highest pedigree more naturally on their wavelength. On a promise of good treatment they contracted to let him in after the Athenians and their allies had drawn their fleet and army out of sight of the walls to ensure the Spartan loyalists would stand down from high alert. With nightfall the Athenians returned in earnest and the guards who had stayed on duty were drawn down to the harbour, when the Athenian fleet attacked the vessels anchored there. The defenders showed very well down at the port and if the assailants were not to be denied a lodgement, there was going to be more bloody fighting. By announcing through Byzantine friends that nobody would be harmed Alcibiades took some of the steam out of the defence, but still he and Theramenes commanding on either wing had to fight it out in formal order until only the garrison struggled on. Five hundred men, Peloponnesians and their most stalwart allies, were eventually left with no option but to flee for sanctuary in a temple. But at least the victors were as good as their word restoring autonomy to the citizens albeit with tribute paid as usual. Winning hearts and minds seemed well worth attempting now Spartan influence around the waterway to the Euxine seemed to have been crucially undermined.

While these developments were underway Alcibiades himself made the move he must have been contemplating since he had travelled to the great military camp at Samos in 411. Since then he had made himself the heart and head of a resurgent Athenian war effort that saw the Spartans virtually swept from the Aegean, and had re-imposed Athenian authority over the choke points on the Black Sea corn routes. Others had shared the glory but he had been consistently there, mobilising, paying and inspiring the Athenians and their allies, and seeming to accomplish feats of military and diplomatic prowess that others could not. He was dusted with glory and glamour in the way no other was, just as he had been fifteen years before when he was seen as the young heir of Pericles. Thrasybulus had been his sponsor but he had grown greater than him now and despite Alcibiades' appointment having been made at Samos not Athens. It was well known in the military now that with the Four Hundred overthrown the people had voted to bring him back from exile. But these were volatile times and though there was no doubt of the *demos*' inclination now, not long before these same citizens had wanted to tear him apart.

Cyzicus had been the decisive rubber, and the man who had made the difference was Alcibiades. The whole of the Peloponnesian fleet had been captured apart from the Syracusan bottoms whose crews had burned them; Mindarus had been killed, many men captured and Cyzicus town had been taken. The other generals had been on top form during these north Anatolian campaigns but Alcibiades got the headlines, riding to the rescue at Abydos and fighting like an ancient hero against the odds on the beach at Cleri. The battle of Cyzicus had taken place in the spring, March or April 410 and when word of the victory arrived at Athens a stressed people for the first time for a while could breathe easily. They thanked the gods that their bellies would stay full with Pontic corn and that once again the sea, the element so close to their hearts, was again largely in their control. Now with two or more years' achievement, when Alcibiades sniffed the air he perceived a genuine welcome on the wind. He had done a great deal to revive Athens' situation in the years since he arrived, a prodigal son back at Samos, but attitudes amongst the people could still be ambivalent. The *hermai* were not forgotten, his switch to the Lacedaemonian side that might have been crucial to the defeat at Syracuse certainly not forgiven, but if he brought victories – well then? None denied his talent but his real bedrock support was small. The rest would accept back with signs of enthusiasm the glamorous victory machine, but what would happen if it broke down and no longer delivered?

Perhaps this was why Alcibiades tiptoed back into town, examining the Spartan shipbuilding at Gythium from out at sea on the way. His confidence was based on what he could bring to the table, but the actual timing of his return was probably to do with the election of that year's generals. Only when he heard he had personally been elected and that no obvious enemies were amongst their ranks did he decide to turn the prows of his ships towards Piraeus.

While one source has Alcibiades playing the triumphant hero with his triremes decked out with 200 captured enemy figureheads and sundry spoils of war to the accompaniment of celebrated flute blowers and the cadences of purple clad actors, most have the exile stealing back into town not completely sure of his reception. However most of the population of Athens crowded the road down to Piraeus between the long walls, and each perhaps had a different Alcibiades in their head. The lordly types wanted a leader to put the *hoi polloi* in their place, while the poor saw an imperialist whose plans would give them employment and bring back the great days of imperial tribute. But all bought into the idea that this man trailed victory and triumph wherever he went. When his trireme slipped into the port every eye was on him. He worried all the way, even hesitating to disembark, and only stepped onto dry land when he saw some of his relatives and realised the crowds he saw pouring out from the city had come to acclaim him, not to task him for past treachery and sacrilege. He apparently 'called a meeting of the assembly, and offering a long defence of his conduct he brought the masses into such a state of goodwill that all agreed that the city had been to blame for the decrees issued against him ... but went further and cast into the sea the stelae on which were written his sentence and all the other acts passed against him; and they also voted that the Eumolpidae should revoke the curse they had pronounced against him at the time when men believed he had profaned the Mysteries.... They also chose as generals others whom he wished, namely, Adeimantus and Thrasybulus.'[18] So in 407 the pariah of the past was made commander in chief of all Athens' forces. The people gave him back his property, which mattered; he had been a very rich man, voted him gold crowns, and made him *strategos autokrator* over land and sea, while the priestly cooperatives that had cursed him to hell and back rescinded their invocations. A limelight hogger all the way, in late summer of the same year he led the procession by land to Eleusis, a place of key spiritual pilgrimage that had been blocked for years by the Spartan forces at Decelea, which had meant the people who had gone there in the past few years had had to go by sea. It was the greatest showman the city had known for years putting on a show that harked back to their days of glory, Alcibiades was back with a whoosh but the question was: could he keep it up?

In fact a stuttering in the Alcibidian juggernaut was not long in showing itself. After about four months since coming home, as commander in chief he led out a considerable task force of 100 ships, 1,500 hoplites and 150 cavalry, indicating an intention to wage an aggressive campaign on land perhaps to retake some of the

Ionian cities. In fact first he sailed to Andros, an island south of Euboea that was a key staging post on the grain route to Athens particularly since Euboea itself had been lost to the city. To get it back he was intending to attack Gaurium, north up the west coast from Andros city, and then strengthen it with a strong defensive wall to act as a base for future operations. Initially when the locals from Andros and their Peloponnesian allies deployed to take on the intruders Alcibiades led his own hoplites and other men in a devastating attack, routing them back behind the city walls. But though he had defeated them in the field, behind their walls the defenders fought on doggedly and looked like bogging him down in a protracted siege. He had no desire to linger there long and led his infantry in several assaults to try to decide the matter. But none of these came off and the fretful Athenian supremo determined he had to leave, so detached an officer called Conon, who we will hear much of later, to hold the fort and maintain the siege. Alcibiades himself launched the ships again, this time to descend on Cos and then Rhodes, hoping he might find sufficient booty on these prosperous islands with which to remunerate his soldiers and sailors.

As Alcibiades was the new principal at Athens another had also come to the fore in Sparta. This was Lysander who was appointed the new navarch or admiral of the fleet. Arriving in Ionia he mobilised what ships were left in fighting condition and sailed to Rhodes picking up vessels from Ephesus, Miletus and other allies along the way. Chios chipped in too with possibly as many as 25 warships and soon there were 70 triremes concentrated at Ephesus. This place, which Lysander had determined would become his base, was north of the old centre of operations at Miletus and had the great advantage of being strategically placed between the enemy on Samos and the Hellespont, and politically it was more accessible for the Persian court at Sardis. Lysander made considerable efforts to refurbish the dockyard facilities and defences that would make the city a real strategic competitor for Samos in the region. Then he put in hand the plan on which all depended, visiting in the summer of 407 the Persian prince Cyrus, just arrived in Sardis.

There had been a context to this which had been part of the wheeling and dealing that had gone on at the siege of Chalcedon. Then it had been agreed that an embassy, made up of Athenians and Argives, should be taken to Susa by Pharnabazus to see the Great King, but the satraps had made no great rush to pack them off. It soon became clear that this was in order to give a free run to a Spartan group who were already at Darius' court. These envoys, led by a smooth talker called Boeotius, had looked to resolve the matter of who got Persian support in favour of the Peloponnesian suppliants. In fact this man and his fellows were already on the road back and bumped into the Athenians coming the other way at Gordium in Phrygia. The Spartans had in fact not only got the promise of support but were accompanied by the Great King's son Cyrus, with a remit of overarching governance of West Asia Minor and a real commitment to aid the Spartan war effort.

So now Lysander in a manner that is detailed as sycophantic and deeply un-Spartan successfully negotiated a deal, in which he apparently came away with

10,000 darics and promises of more. These funds now allowed the payment of an extra obol a day on top of the usual Athenian stipend. He now began the process whereby he would both end the never-ending war and for a time stamp his own authority over almost the whole Greek and Aegean world. Initially he set about cementing a local power base that he knew he would need to effect a long-term impact. He called the aristocrats from the Asian cities to organise themselves into cabals ready to take over when he had constructed an environment in which they could prosper. Promises of power loosened their purses too: 'and that Lysander was quickly supplied in startling fashion with all the equipment that is useful in war.'[19]

While Lysander grew his power bloc and skewed the market for oarsman, Alcibiades, after his money gathering excursions to Cos and Rhodes, took off back again to the great base at Samos. The new Athenian commander in chief had kept himself well informed of his rival's busy programme. When his agents reported the fiscal arrangements with Cyrus that allowed such a fleet to be readied at Ephesus, he decided to act. First he himself made overtures to Cyrus, through Tissaphernes, to make a peace that might take the Persians out of the equation, then when this failed he prepared for battle with the force of 80 triremes at his disposal, he had left 20 with Conon at Andros. Offering battle to Lysander's squadron he was refused, despite the Peloponnesians now deploying 90 triremes in good condition, Lysander had just had them beached to dry and be repaired. So Alcibiades dropped anchor at Notium, a harbour of the nearby cities of Colophon and Claros and by what is the modern holiday mecca of Kusadasi. With his enemy apparently bottled up and time passing with no great achievements to his name in that campaigning season Alcibiades felt the need to make an impact elsewhere. He left the fleet under the command of his pilot Antiochus with all the triremes but with orders not to get involved in battle while he was away. It is something of a mystery why he laid such responsibility on this junior man – perhaps it was because he thought him less likely to bring on a fight than the other senior captains or commanders, but if so his plan backfired.

In very early 406 Alcibiades took a large force on board troopships and sailed north from Notium to what is now the bay of Smyrna. Winter warfare was not normal but Alcibiades was under great pressure to achieve and to achieve soon. If Lysander would not come out and fight him Alcibiades could not afford to just hang about and to take some cities in Ionia might anyway put pressure on the Spartans to emerge. We are offered two options as to what he did next: the first that he went to Clazomenae on the south side of the gulf to help this allied city that was suffering from exiles attacking its property; and the second that he went to assist Thrasybulus in the siege of Phocaea town on the north of the bay.[20] Whichever is correct, while he was away Antiochus the pilot fatally overstepped his remit. The man was eager to make a name – perhaps he was a little miffed by the officers who looked down their nose at a mere professional being given command – and set out to do another Cyzicus if he could. Keeping most of the ships out of sight he sent bait of ten vessels to challenge the enemy entering the harbour of Ephesus, 'past the very prows of the ships of Lysander'.

Lysander was not one to be caught on the hop. He understood from informers that Alcibiades was absent and meant to take advantage even if it entailed risking a battle. Launching his triremes either in sections or as a whole (depending on who is followed) the intruders found they had bitten off more than they could chew. 'He encountered the leading one of the ten ships, the one on which Antiochus had taken his place for the attack, and sank it, and then, putting the rest to flight, he chased them until the Athenian captains manned the rest of their vessels and came to the rescue, but in no battle order at all. In the sea-battle which followed between the two entire fleets not far from the land the Athenians, because of their disorder, were defeated and lost twenty-two ships, but of their crews only a few were taken captive and the rest swam to safety ashore.'[21] Antiochus, the careless pilot, managed to get himself killed, but the result was important and when Alcibiades heard of it he returned to Samos eager to patch things up. He again took the whole fleet, the bruised remnants of Notium and Thrasybulus' thirty he had brought back with him, and deployed outside Ephesus harbour offering combat, but Lysander once again refused. The man who had moved from exile to supremo had been significantly undermined as he again fell back to the main naval base at Samos.

Initially it seemed the reverse was not that crucial and that elsewhere the Alcibidian project was holding up well. Thrasybulus, who had moved on to Thasos, even without most of his ships was very successfully holding his own. 'Thrasybulus, the Athenian general, sailing to Thasos with fifteen ships defeated in battle the troops who came out from the city and slew about two hundred of them; then, having bottled them up in a siege of the city, he forced them to receive back their exiles, that is the men who favoured the Athenians, to accept a garrison.'[22] With this place brought back into the fold, and then Abdera, an important town opposite Thasos in Thrace, there were plusses for the Alcibiades team, but it was not to be enough. In the end the need for ready money was the catalyst for Alcibiades' fall. With his men demanding pay (his expedition was costing fifty talents a month) he now tried to squeeze Cyme, Athens' ally, the largest and most important of the twelve cities in Aeolis on the Asian mainland, laying 'false charges' to cover a blatant looting expedition. But while he was collecting plunder and rounding up prisoners the incensed citizens got into armour and attacked in numbers. Alcibiades' troops were disorganised and though the looters put up a fight as more locals joined in, they were forced to leg it for their ships. Alcibiades was enraged and determined on revenge. He had a hoplite garrison at Mytilene on Lesbos Island across the strait and, calling these up, he drew up in battle order outside the Cymaeans' walls. Facing the whole might of the army the citizens would not come out, allowing Alcibiades now to systematically pillage the countryside around. But it was not only Cymaean fighters that troubled Alcibiades, much worse was to follow when the city dispatched ambassadors to complain at Athens that they, a loyal ally, were being attacked by this sacrilegious mad dog. The envoys' arrivals were timely, as already Alcibiades' enemies from Samos had been at the city badmouthing him as a traitor in cahoots with Sparta, and worse, intent on using Pharnabazus' support to impose himself as tyrant at Athens. A different man also called Thrasybulus had come from Samos complaining that Alcibiades caused the Notium debacle when he left the fleet in charge of a drunkard just because the man was a boon companion and entertaining raconteur. Despite his having been recently hurled into a dungeon in Sardis by the Persians, the idea that he was really in their pocket was soon circulating again. All the old worries surfaced now without the man himself being in the city to blind them with his charm and charisma.

The problem was Alcibiades made the Athenians fearful as well as giving them hope, a heady and unpredictable brew. The questions kept being asked in the *agora* and political clubs, what was he cooking up with the Persians? Did he harbour ambitions of tyranny? What was his relationship to the Spartans? This was of particular moment, as King Agis had just made a night attack on the city walls with a strong force. 'He had twenty-eight thousand infantry, one-half of whom were picked hoplites and the other half light-armed troops; there were also attached to his army some twelve hundred cavalry, of whom the Boeotians furnished nine hundred and the rest had been sent with him by Peloponnesians.'[23]

In fact after a cavalry battle under the ramparts and some posturing the coup was abortive, but still it was worrying. The year's deep fears of this talented but dangerous man festered, and many in that litigious city who laid charges against him before began to brush off their old paperwork. He was a moving target that, if it faltered, would become a sitting duck. A bit like Caesar after he came back to Rome after the Gallic campaigns – if he did not dominate and disarm his enemies they would eat him alive. Alcibiades could not shackle his many detractors and was not present to dominate them, so with failure at Notium, complaints from Cyme, and with the Ionian campaign faltering, Alcibiades was coming into the sights of many who hated him still.

Regular elections were held in early March but probably even before that the assembly had passed a proposal to remove Alcibiades from office. Of all his many enemies it was Cleophon who proposed stripping him of his office as general: a man of impeccable patriotic credentials even if he was something of a figure of fun to many. The assembly selected ten generals, many not Alcibiades' friends. It had not taken that much, a setback in battle, complaints from Cyme, and already law suits were simmering and people were even bringing up old charges about dodgy horse race practice in years before involving the dubious outlay of eight talents.[24] Alcibiades had no reservoir of goodwill to fall back on; once the momentum slowed it was over. He was left with little option but to hand over the reins of command to Conon – a poignant cameo of the waning star handing over to the rising one – and return to familiar exile on his estates in the Chersonese.

Chapter Two

Lysander Triumphant

As one big time player quit the stage – barring a small cameo role in the future – another very different leading man came forward. But before Lysander emerged as the fulcrum of the future one of the grandest and most dramatic naval encounters in Greek maritime history occurred. Traumatic in terms of both scale and public consequence for the Athenians, as a generation of war moved to a close. After Alcibiades had slipped again into exile, Conon had taken command of the Samos fleet. By February 406 this latest commander had sufficient men available to man seventy of his one hundred ships but morale was apparently low; perhaps the disappearance of Alcibiades had hit spirits amongst the men who had certainly won victories with him. And without doubt the inducement of Persian gold meant oarsmen were slipping off to the Spartan fleet at a rate that made clear a real change in the balance of power at sea was under way. But Conon was an active officer and decided he would at least carry out a swoop on the enemy coast and get some looting in, in an effort, if nothing else, to pay his men while he waited for reinforcements from home.

Pitted against him in the coming campaign Conon would find the navarch Callicratidas. Like Lysander he was apparently a *mothax* and associate of King Pausanias.[1] He took over command of the fleet at Ephesus in about April 406, three or four months after Notium. From the start he was determined to be his own man and considered his predecessor's methods had strayed a long way too far from the proper Laconian path. He was 'a very young man, without guile and straight-forward in character, since he had had as yet no experience of the ways of foreign peoples, and was the most just man among the Spartans; and it is agreed by all that also during his period of command he committed no wrong against either a city or a private citizen but dealt summarily with those who tried to corrupt him with money and had them punished.'[2]

This exemplar tyro, one of the few Spartan imperialists without sticky fingers, inherited 140 ships, a force that should have been able to crush the Athenians had they been prepared to come and face him. But they were not, so his first move was to transfer his base from Ephesus to Miletus, as much as anything to get away from a place riddled with Lysander-philes or Great King's placemen. This was independent stuff but without Persian gold it meant achieving early success was even more imperative, before his men began carping about lack of wages. Nor was it just money worries, as of his 140 triremes 90 were crewed by Lysander's old sweats who had little faith in the new man, and their old chief may have briefed his friends in the Greek cities to undermine the upstart in any way they could in an effort to force his return. The divisions eventually reached such a peak that Callicratidas called the Spartan officers together to try to impose his authority. But petulant prosing by the newcomer was not best designed to win over these veterans and now, beyond alienating half his own side, the commander decided he could spurn those resources that had been Lysander's secret weapon – Persian money. He was determined to take exactly the opposite tack to that of his predecessor and was adamant he would never end up in the Medes' pockets. The young admiral had already visited the Persian prince Cyrus but this had only stoked tensions. He was forced to cool his heels in the potentate's glitzy antechamber (the prince probably still saw the decision to remove Lysander as perverse) and an already self important personality was soured by the experience. He let everybody who would listen know that he thought any kind of peace with Athens preferable to dependence on a degenerate 'barbarian' despot he left without even getting an audience and crucially without any money.

Only by sending to Sparta and approaching the Milesians did he achieve even some financial liquidity. The local elites knew they needed him on side and they and their Chian compatriots fed him enough gold to keep the navy functioning. With at least some money in their wallets, the fleet set sail and descended on a fort on Chios that Alcibiades had built called the Delphinium, defended by 500 Athenians. It was quickly picked off, with the defenders happy to get away under a truce while Callicratidas dismantled the place; the removal of an irritant that was an immediate pay-off for the Chians who had stumped up hard cash. Then they cruised to Teos on the mainland which also quickly succumbed as his men 'stole inside the walls of the city by night and plundered it.'[3] Success ensured loot for the soldiers and any Athenians discovered were sold into slavery; all grist to the mill for a commander who had purposely closed up the money pot that had been available to his predecessor. Methymna on the north of the large island of Lesbos, governed by friends of the Athenians and held by a garrison of 500, was his next target. This was the largest and most northerly of the great offshore islands so crucial for controlling the seaways along the Anatolian coast and to gain control of it would be a huge advantage in further campaigns aimed at closing the Hellespontine grain routes to Athens. Callicratidas assailed the place with little success in the beginning, but where Athenian friends governed, traitors always existed, primed to sell the pass. This fifth column managed to let the attackers inside the walls and once in they plundered what they could, though the inhabitants were themselves spared. Callicratidas even 'returned the city to the Methymnaeans.'[4] Clearly something of a man for the grand gesture, 'all the captives Callicratidas assembled in the market-place; and when his allies urged him to sell into slavery the Methymnaeans as well as the Athenians, he said that while he was commander no Greek should be enslaved if he could help it.'[5] This, though, did not stop him from selling the Athenian garrison; what he objected to was the enslaving of the inhabitants of captured towns in the possession of the Athenians. Next he indulged in some bizarre verbal gage throwing down with his opponent Conon, declaring that he should stop fornicating with the sea as it belonged to him, before he got matters in hand to get the better of the man he had insulted. Much had been accomplished even without Persian gold but it had only been a step towards the major prize on the island, Mytilene. To accomplish its capture he disembarked all the heavy infantry he had on board and sent them south overland under the general Thorax while the fleet sailed around the coast under his own command.

These strongpoints the Spartans had been picking off were all well north of Samos. It showed, based as they were at Miletus, that they were unafraid of any sortie by the Athenians – indeed they would have welcomed a fight with Conon who remained holed up in port. But if previous knocks had not forced him to react, a threat to Lesbos was a very different matter. Lesbos was a plum strategic station so Conon, who had been training up his navy of seventy ships and confident in their expertise, prepared to risk them in defence of this crucial island. When dispatches reached him that Methymna was being besieged he sailed, but on arrival at the Hundred Isles (the Hekatonnesi islands in the channel between Lesbos and the mainland north of Mytilene) he learned from his scouts not only that the place had already fallen but of far greater concern, that the whole Spartan fleet, informed of his coming, was deploying out of the dawn in a bid to envelop him. Outnumbered, he ordered his captains to manoeuvre their vessels back down the channel to get as near as possible to the friendly city of Mytilene, so if they had to fight and it went against them they would at least have a bolthole at hand.

When this comfort zone was almost reached, with plenty of marines on board and full crews, Conon decided he was at last prepared to engage. Callicratidas' fleet was disorganised in pursuit and well spread out. They 'pushed the pursuit hotly, and they wore out the rowers by their continued exertion at the oars and were themselves separated a long distance from the others.'[6] It was almost as if Conon had been trailing his coat all along to accomplish just what had happened. Something certainly suggested by the report that: 'having put his soldiers on board ship, he set out with the oars at a leisurely stroke in order that the ships of the Peloponnesians might draw near him. And the Lacedaemonians, as they approached, kept driving their ships faster and faster in the hope of seizing the hindmost ships of the enemy.'[7] Whatever the truth, whether by strategy or chance they were now vulnerable and the Athenian supremo hoisted his red banner as a signal to his captains to turn and fight. They raised a paean, trumpeters blew for all they were worth and the attack was commenced.

For the Spartans it was a shock. They thought they were chasing down a defeated foe but now it had turned on them snarling. They tried to form a line but it was not easy with the rest of the fleet far astern. Conon's triremes, fully crewed with well trained oarsmen, picked them off, ramming many and shearing the oars of others. The Spartans tried to backwater hoping their comrades would come up in time. For a period those facing the right of the line under Conon held their own but the Athenian left wing particularly was making hay against the disordered foe. They dispersed all the vessels in front of them and then made hot pursuit, turning the tables on those who had recently been on their tail. But Conon was cognisant this was only a small part of the enemy fleet that had been routed and that when the rest arrived he would again be badly outnumbered. With desperate cries and orders shouted across the water he called together the 40 ships in his own squadron but the men on the left wing ships' blood was up and determined to catch the fleeing foe in front of them. They either did not hear or ignored their admiral's orders and paid the price. It was not long before they found themselves faced by the rest of Callicratidas' fleet bearing down in overwhelming numbers. For them it was soon all over and all they could do was beach their craft, jump ship and flee down the coast to Mytilene leaving their vessels to the enemy.

There is another tradition describing this encounter, with Conon surprised at dawn and fleeing for his life, and losing the thirty ships in the narrows of Mytilene when the Peloponnesian fleet overtook them.[8] But whatever the exact particulars, the ships captured and the remainder trapped at Mytilene is common to both accounts, so either after an early setback or smooth as silk from the start, the upshot was that all was going very well for the young Spartan admiral. Conon on the other hand was in deep trouble as Callicratidas, thirty triremes to the good to cover any losses, arrived to bottle him up in the place he had been intending to besiege from the start. But outside the city harbour in the larger outer port the Athenian admiral prepared his defence. He sank small boats full of rocks to block or at least narrow the port entrances and in deeper water anchored merchantmen full of men armed with large stones to throw down from their yardarms onto the enemy decks. In addition, soldiers were massed on the breakwaters to fend off any enemy vessels attempting to land their men, and any locals who could be trusted with arms were called in from the countryside and deployed, geared up to repel what was expected to be an assault by both land and sea.

These *ad hoc* fortifications were timely as the enemy army, assembled from the troops that had taken Methymna and others from Chios, disembarked on a beach not far away, was soon detected swinging up the road and laying out an assault camp on the land side of the city, while ships were also approaching in battle order towards the harbour defences. There had been a little respite, as Callicratidas' men had set up a victory trophy to commemorate the previous fighting but that was the only breather allowed as the next day revealed the Spartan admiral's best ships bristling with fighting men advancing menacingly towards the harbour of Mytilene.

The Athenians' defensive show was brave with their triremes' beaks facing out and full of marines packing the mouth of the harbour, while their comrades from the fleet and city manned the breakwaters and larger ships: all to offer a resolute face to the adversary bearing down on them.

The previous victory had boosted the Spartans' morale. 'Advancing with their ships in mass formation and with their best soldiers lined up on the decks they made the sea-battle also a fight between infantry; for as they pressed upon their opponents' ships they boldly boarded their prows, in the belief that men who had once been defeated would not stand up to the terror of battle.'[9] But equally the defending Athenians were determined, seeing their only hope as living or dying where they stood. Hoplite marines tussled, archers and javelineers sped darts in thousands but the Athenians were better positioned and the stones dropped from yardarms and men fighting and throwing from firm ground or steady grounded ships found it easier to find a mark. The first assault was bloody but achieved little and Callicratidas was forced to order his men to withdraw for breath. But the Spartan was resolute and tried again and this time superior numbers started to tell. The barriers were broken down and the attacking vessels gained the outer port, anchoring there and forcing Conon, with those ships he could rally, to pull back to the inner harbour. Athenians 'fled for refuge to the harbour within the city'. Now the Spartans could disembark their troops to occupy the outer harbour defences and the siege of Mytilene got properly underway. 'It may be explained that the entrance for whose control they had fought had a good harbour, which, however, lies outside the city. For the ancient city is a small island, and the later city, which was founded near it, is opposite it on the island of Lesbos; and between the two cities is a narrow strait which also adds strength to the city. Callicratidas now, disembarking his troops, invested the city and launched assaults upon it from every side.'[10]

Nor was this all. Callicratidas heard from messengers that his friends in Methymna and Chios were sending troops to help attack the city from the landward side and that prince Cyrus, perhaps realising the new man was not such a dud after all, had finally remitted money to pay the crews. Conon was in great danger and knew he needed help if he was to have any chance of survival. He outfitted two of his fastest ships which managed to trick their way through the blockade. One was chased after and caught, but the other reached Athens with desperate pleas for aid. The besieged forces though were not completely without succour on the spot. Diomedon, an Athenian general, hoping to aid Conon had crept with twelve ships into the straits of Mytilene. But the besiegers were alert: they pounced and captured ten of these potential rescuers. The reality was that the only hope would come from Athens, if it came from anywhere.[11]

The mother city did not disappoint, coming up trumps with an expedition that was extraordinarily formidable considering the attrition of the recent past. Athens had been scraping the bottom of the barrel for some time, but now they had made the supreme effort to get together 150 triremes at their base at Samos. It had taken under a month; some were from a newly built home fleet. As the summer had drawn on, the buzzing of insects had been matched with the buzzing of saws and the noise of axes and adzes. Soldiers and civilians were mobilised for all the daylight hours to throw up the yards and to provide the materials required to build some sixty new triremes. The big ship timber trees had long gone from Attica's hills, cut down to create the fleets that built her empire. It was materials from estates in Thrace and friends in Macedonia that ensured the Piraeus shipyards were kept busy in this last great throw of Athenian ship building in the war. There were also other triremes mobilised from their allies, and any ships in any area they could press into service. To crew the new fleet 22,000 more men were required so they enrolled both below and above the norm. Hoplites and cavalrymen found themselves forced to adjust their arses to the rough feel of an oarsman's bench and *metics*, aliens and slaves were enfranchised and liberated to eke out the numbers.

The differences between the crews of ancient oared warships and those of their early modern counterparts that contested for the control of the Mediterranean in fights like Lepanto in AD 1571 and Preveza in AD 1538 are in general clear. The latter were manned by chain linked slaves, usually criminals or prisoners of war, while in the Greek and Roman worlds the motor power of maritime warfare was provided by free, waged men. But this is not the whole story; we know apart from this special case at Athens that it was not that unusual for slaves to man the oars at this time. Thucydides, describing the results of an early battle of the Peloponnesian War against a fleet from Corcyra, states that of 1,000 men captured 800 were un-free. And he also specifies that Syracusan and Italian crews who on one occasion defied the navarch Astyochus were freemen, an indication that a good many others must have been servile or the point would not be worth making. Probably the mix of slave and free was infinitely variable and even in the least servile of ships there would have been bondsmen, body servants present to service the hoplites and officers, who would have acted as oarsmen when required. We also on occasions hear of rich individuals providing slave labour to fill the benches as part of their financial responsibilities to the state. In the ancient world the continuum along which stood the slave and paid man was perhaps less clear cut than in more modern times. What is probable is that most ships had some slaves at the oars but not that many, it was the free oarsmen who might be attracted by Persian gold that were the majority. Indeed their mass use on this occasion of Athens' peril, that extraordinarily even offered them their freedom if they served, was clearly exceptional. So desperate was the manpower demand that the city itself, it was declared, was left defended only by boys and old men, who luckily were not tested, as King Agis failed to press an attack from his base at Decelea, an example of inaction that is not a little difficult to understand.

The mint new fleet sailed in the middle of July to rendezvous at Samos where 10 Samian ships and 35 from other nearby allies brought the total to around 150, the command of which was divided equally between eight generals. This product of an enormous outlay and effort, by a people on the ropes, put out into the seaways and, sailing between Chios Island and the mainland, approached the Arginusae Islands where they intended to base themselves in preparation for the attempted rescue of Conon and his beleaguered men who had been sustaining themselves obstinately in the intervening weeks. Callicratidas decided to bring on a fight when news leaked of the Athenian relief armada being on the way. Leaving 50 ships under Eteonicus to keep the enemy holed up he sailed with 120 to intercept the Athenians he knew were bound to come up from Samos to the south.[12] Cruising south east along the shore of Lesbos Island he allowed his men to stop at midday for a meal at Cape Malea and, by accident or design, he found himself almost directly opposite the enemy he had come to find, who themselves had stopped to eat on the island of Arginusae that rose about six miles in the distance over the channel.

When evening fell the sight of the fires in the darkness over the water suggested a night attack to the Spartan high command but a thunderstorm prevented it getting underway. When dawn broke, with the waters quieted, the Athenian fleet stowed sails and rigging ashore, set nets to protect against boarding and sallied out, led by Thrasyllus, in command that day, to meet the old enemy.[13] The Greeks had fought many bloody encounters with each other at sea over the years but this was to be the largest until that time in terms of numbers of ships involved, so perhaps it is only appropriate that it turned out such a dramatic affair, not just in itself but in its aftermath as well. The Attic generals deployed gallantly as was their wont, but now it was they who had to try to compensate for the fact that they had largely new and untrained crews, and so decided to try to turn the combat into, as near

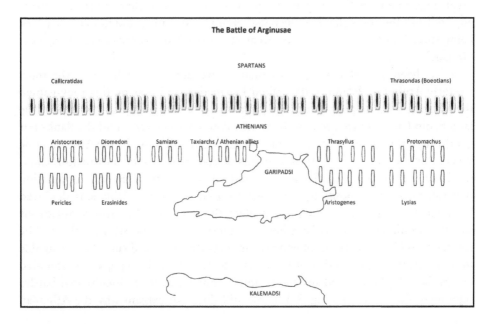

The Battle of Arginusae

as was possible, a land battle on the water, so their foes might not confound them with skilful manoeuvre. This was a far cry from earlier in the war and indicated the impact of Persian money which had clearly been spent well. The Athenian high command comprised eight generals each leading fifteen ships. On the far left of their line out to sea was Aristocrates in overall charge of that wing. On his right came Diomedon leading his fifteen, bearing plenty of grudges from the encounter of a few weeks before. We know the ships on the left were deployed in a double line, Pericles with his fifteen was behind Aristocrates and Erasinides tucked in behind Diomedon. In the centre were ten Samian ships, commanded by a local man called Hippeus, which are specifically described as having been in one line as were the next ten Athenian vessels under the commanders of tribal contingents called taxiarchs; then came three more Athenian triremes and some others from her allies.

As for the right wing, also deployed in a double line, the squadron under Protomachus was nearest the mainland coast and Lysias' triremes were lined up behind him; then on his left came Thrasyllus, the commander in chief, with his fifteen backed by Aristogenes. Where the islands fitted in respect of this deployment is not exactly clear. Certainly they were an integral part: the Athenians included the Arginusae Islands in their battle-order, but exactly how? Two things give us a clue, firstly that the Athenian line was mainly arrayed two deep, apart from the centre, yet it was still longer than their enemies' line which while fewer in terms of numbers was laid out in just one line. It is also settled that the fleets were observed to be divided into virtually four different divisions that ended fighting each other almost in separate battles. 'Consequently he (Callicratidas) aroused great amazement in the spectators on many sides, since there were four fleets engaged and the ships that had been gathered into one place did not lack many of being three hundred. For this is the greatest sea-battle on record of Greeks against Greeks.'[14]

It has been argued that the Athenian centre deployed in front of the most westerly Arginusae Island, today called Garipadasi and that by this they gained the advantage that so positioned they did not need a back up squadron because the land behind acted to ensure that the enemy could neither get round the flanks nor get through their line.[15] But this is problematic as it still suggests the Athenian line was continuous and that as most of it was double banked such a formation could not have been longer than the singly deployed enemy line. The only explanation that satisfactorily accounts for what we are told is that the Athenians deployed between the islands using them to protect the flanks of the various squadrons and this would certainly make it look like there were several separate fleets. The reference to Callicratidas' deployment supports this too. 'And since he was unable to make his line equal to that of the enemy by reason of the large space occupied by the islands, he divided his force, and forming two fleets fought two battles separately, one on each wing.'[16] Yet this still does not explain why the Athenian centre was left only one line deep unless this was done to extend the line in a place where it was safe from a flanking attack even if it did still risk being broken through with no defence behind.

So the Athenian ships were double banked on the wings but only singly in the centre when they came out to face a Peloponnesian fleet that now packed up camp and pulled out into the broad straits between Lesbos and the islands. This outfit was now comprised of mostly seasoned self-assured seamen, eager to take the initiative and who expected to use superior skills to carry out the devastating tactics of the *diekplous* and *periplous*. The Spartans high command may have been pretty confident in their men's superior seamanship but not so much that worries aren't mentioned. Apparently a nervy Megarian named Hermon warned about the disparity in numbers – which seems strange as the Spartans had at least 120 and maybe more well-crewed triremes underhand. Perhaps the Athenians' reputation continued to hold sway over men still young in maritime bellicosity. The Peloponnesian fleet spread out about 2,400 yards from wing tip to wing tip in a single line.

With Callicratidas commanding on their right, the place of honour, the instruction was given. Trumpets ordered forward the triremes at speed to try to get between the enemy vessels confronting them and then to turn and ram their victims' exposed flanks. The Spartans 'enthusiastically struck the waves, vied with one another, every man being anxious to be the first to begin the battle.'[17] But in attempting the *diekplous* manoeuvre many warships exposed themselves to the Athenian second line. The Spartan admiral himself spotted the ship carrying an Athenian general and drove for it, undaunted by seers who predicted his death, or perhaps intent on going down in a blaze of glory. The first blow of the flagship's ram apparently holed the vessel so successfully that it sank immediately while the other ships of his squadron plunged into the enemy opposite, ramming, sinking and smashing off the oars of many of the triremes they encountered. This was heroic between ships and men who were eager to end a war that had gone on so long. The Spartan admiral himself, having penetrated the first line, ordered his ship against the vessel of Pericles (the bastard son by Aspasia of the greatest Athenian of the last fifty years).

His beak stuck in the planks of Pericles' craft. The Spartan oarsmen pulled like madmen to back off and disengage but the two ships were completely stuck together. The Athenian sailors threw grappling irons over to ensure they were held tight together, just as other Athenian ships from the second line converged on the exposed flagship. The Athenian marines jumped over the deck rails and the Spartan admiral, like a Homeric hero of old, fought with spear, shield and sword against a mounting tide of men, but it could not last. Callicratidas was either cut down or fell overboard and his armour dragged him straight down to the seabed. With his demise the morale of the men around him was badly dented: his flagship was taken and the others in the squadron seeing it were shocked and dejected. Yet while the men in this section of the line began to waver and then turn and flee, those in the other parts of the battle line were made of sterner stuff.

On the left of the Spartan line a Boeotian squadron under Thrasondas the Theban was the core, supported by some Euboeans and others who had been Athenian subjects in the past and who could expect little mercy if they succumbed. In fighting for their lives they equally were fighting for their cities which if they lost could expect to fall once more under a vengeful Athenian yoke. Thrasyllus, Protomachus and Aristogenes on the Athenian right contested all the way against these bitter foes but it was not until the battle elsewhere was decided that a winner also appeared here. Seeing the chaos to their right with their allies either in flight, sunk, or captured the Boeotians and other allies were bound to be affected. They had fought like lions but now with their comrades gone and their enemies concentrating on them, resistance could not last. Soon the whole fleet was turning to flee, and from then on it was each ship for itself: 'then began a flight of the Peloponnesians to Chios, though very many went to Phocaea.'[18]

The Athenian generals, either drawing together to talk from their ships or convening on the nearest strand, debated about priorities, whether to pick up the dead and shipwrecked or raise the siege of Mytilene and bag the enemy vessels still left afloat. But the delay meant there could be little interface between intent and achievement as a storm blew in that made sailing anywhere an impossible task. The wounded found no succour as the elements scattered them to the four winds and no ships could launch to go to the aid of survivors and soon the 'coastline of the territory of the Cymaeans and Phocaeans was strewn with corpses and wreckage.'[19] The Athenians had lost 25 ships and perhaps 5,000 men while the Peloponnesian butcher's bill was huge: 77 vessels and 15,000 men. News of this great victory was not long in reaching Eteonicus outside Mytilene. He at once understood his position was untenable and the 50 ships he had been left with were immediately got ready and piled up with what could be moved easily before the enemy got news and sortied out from the city or the triumphant Athenian fleet arrived. The vessels were ordered underway to hopefully find safety with allies at Chios while the general himself marched his land forces to Pyrrhaea town, a partner they hoped would cleave to their Spartan allies even in adversity.

So another Spartan supremo died in battle within a few years. This was beginning to look careless, if heroic, and in this last case completely unnecessary. Callicratidas had attacked the Athenian fleet in its secure position when he had no need to. The Athenian strategic aim was to relieve Conon in Mytilene, and to get to that town they would have had to move away from the Arginusae Islands and into the open channel where the Peloponnesians with their superior oarsmen could have outmanoeuvred and chopped them up, just as Athenian fleets had done in the past under the likes of the great admiral Phormio earlier in the Peloponnesian War. As for the victors they did not dally to deal with these Spartan detachments but moved to Samos to pick up reinforcements before descending on the main enemy bases in the region which must have seemed ripe for the picking after the virtual complete destruction of the Peloponnesian navy.

But the aftermath that would be remembered was not one of victory trophies raised, or of cities falling to the victor and celebrations by a community proud of its winning warriors. Instead, famously, the Athenians poisoned what should have been the hour of their triumph by trying to execute most of the generals who had been in charge during the battle. Theramenes and Thrasybulus, who had fought not as generals but as ship commanders, had been deputed to carry out the rescue after the battle, but they failed to do so and had hurried back home to Athens. The joy that the citizens felt at the victory at Arginusae was tempered by the huge casualty list and the feeling that more could have been done. The two commanders not unnaturally felt themselves in a vulnerable position especially when the generals – still away – tried to dump on them. Accusation and counter accusation were the order of the day and trial before the assembly followed. The details of the trials and convictions are complex and unclear, but the core was that it was alleged the generals did not make a sufficiently vigorous effort to rescue the lives and bodies of those Athenians lost in the combat. They argued convincingly that they could have not done much more than they did because of the weather; there was a cameo appearance by Socrates himself; but in the end six of the victorious generals of Arginusae (two others, Aristogenes and Protomachus, had fled before they could be arraigned) were forced to drink lethal doses of hemlock by their own people. Leaders on both sides are recorded dreaming before this encounter, for some predictions of death had come true and even for the survivors it turned out a nightmare whether on the day they had been victor or vanquished.

The whole stew can only be understood in the context of the trauma of the recent imposition on the city of the oligarchic government of the Four Hundred. Unlike Rome of the proscriptions or the Civil Wars we seldom imagine the gutters that led down the hill from the Pnyx running with blood, but on that occasion it was certainly stained by the gore of many Athenians. The capacity for vicious violence of any propertied class in defending what they owned is almost unlimited and the trauma of the Four Hundred's activities should never be underestimated. The confusion over motives in the trial, the apparent unreasonableness of the decision all makes it a compelling drama. The city had given of its all, the youngest and oldest of all the classes; it had enfranchised *metics* and even slaves to fill the oar benches and so broken every tradition and taboo to get the fleet together. And it seemed to many that a great victory had been won by the efforts of the people but their leaders had made little attempt to save these very brave men when they were being swept by storm, hanging onto flour barrels and spas and desperate for rescue that never came. The fear of the rich that pervades the motivation of the assembly was not unreasonable; generals by their nature were moneyed aristocrats, tainted anti democrats who could not be trusted. The natural condition of the Greeks was conflict between oligarchs and democrats and though this had been to some extent subsumed in the Athenian system nothing could hide how near the surface the blood disputes were. And after ordeals like the Four Hundred and later the Thirty tyrants the *demos* could become very irrational whether in response to the foibles of a crusty philosopher or aristocrats who seemed to have been more content to bask in the glory of victory rather than saving the citizens who had earned the triumph for them.[20]

There had been extraordinary ups and downs over the years, since the disaster at Syracuse had seemed to offer a decisive end to the war between the alliances headed by Athens and by Sparta. Even after the Athenian victory at Arginusae, there was still to be another decisive turnabout. These bloody encounters at sea had for the most part gone the way of the Athenian alliance yet this was far from the full story. The achievements of putting out these huge armaments had taxed the city to the limit in an age when its empire was shrinking and the tribute coming in dwindling. Achievements had been won by the people of the city themselves and their closest allies like the Samians. Perhaps well over 5,000 Athenians had been lost in battle over these years, many drowned at Arginusae. They had been spending the principal in the years after Syracuse not the interest. For the enemy it had been different: for six years Persian money had allowed them to face disaster and bounce back. But the Spartans' benefactors were unpredictable and had their own ideas as to the people they were prepared to deal with. This was the context in which the return of Lysander, the victor of Notium, was demanded by both Cyrus and the Aegean allies, who sent messages to Sparta leaving no doubt that without him they could not guarantee their continued support of the cause.

The government at Sparta was prepared to respond to this request favourably as in the immediate aftermath of the disaster of Arginusae they had offered terms to Athens, terms that included evacuating Decelea and then peace on the basis of the *status quo*. But Athens refused demanding that Sparta vacate all the cities they had taken from them including amongst others Abydos, Chios, Cyme and Ephesus. In this determination the Athenians were apparently 'completely deceived by Cleophon, who prevented the conclusion of peace by coming into the assembly, drunk and wearing a corslet, and protesting that he would not allow it unless the Lacedaemonians surrendered all the cities.'[21] It was a decision they would come to regret. And that the project of coming to terms with Athens, had been the programme of Lysander's domestic opponents did not hurt his case. Even a hard ruling that no navarch should serve more than one term of office was not allowed to impede the promptings of necessity and in the circumstances this was just another problem that must be overcome. Lysander was designated as the aide or secretary to the new commander in chief, Aracus, but in reality with full authority over the Spartans and all their allies' armed forces in the Aegean.

Lysander whether the upfront name or *eminence grise* had no intention of keeping his head down. Sailing with 35 triremes collected from what are described as 'neighbouring allies' in the Peloponnese he put in at Ephesus. That he established himself there and not at Callicratidas' old stronghold of Miletus suggests he could not depend on the leadership at the more southerly port. Though it is unlikely he would have accepted this situation indefinitely and this may well be context of Diodorus' aside about the oligarchs in Miletus butchering their democratic rivals with Spartan help. Very probably the result of underhand chicanery orchestrated by Lysander to establish a government at Miletus more to his liking. The fleet from Chios under Eteonicus now came in too. His men had been forced to keep body and soul together by working as day labourers on farms in Chios and when winter closed off this avenue of income, these rough necks tried an abortive coup against Chios town which even if it had failed gave some leverage for Eteonicus to persuade the city fathers on the advisability of coughing up rather than being left to the mercy of these beached sailors. So it was this undisciplined gang that had taken the remnants of their navy over to meet their new commander. The whole gathered at Ephesus and from this great Ionian port city Lysander sent messages to the local oligarchs, his political friends, who had come up with funds before. But the trump card he played was the resuscitation of his relationship with the man with the real money. Cyrus, the Great King's son, was who mattered and though he had in fact just been called to the interior Diodorus tells us: 'and Cyrus, since his father was summoning him to Persia, turned over to Lysander the authority over the cities under his command and ordered them to pay the tribute to him.'[22] The suggestion of Lysander as virtual satrap in his absence is not very believable and almost certainly we are hearing of an arrangement where he was given the authority to ensure money designated by Cyrus to help the Spartan cause would be handed over to him.

With pockets full and more to come, Lysander none the less still felt the need to put some clear blue water between himself and the considerably larger fleet from Samos that was raiding the coast between Chios and Ephesus. He moved south with most of his ships, taking the Athenian allied city of Iasus in Caria not too far from Halicarnassus. There he put the defenders to the sword and razed the buildings. But this was all surely something of a feint, as soon after it was the communities of Aegina and Salamis the other side of the Aegean that to their surprise found the man and his followers raiding their shores. Lysander even landed in Attica to meet with King Agis at Decelea; he did not intend to be forgotten by the other key movers in Spartan policy. From this strategic summit Lysander led the Peloponnesian fleet, manned by happy sailors flush with plunder from the Attic countryside, off to the Hellespont where matters would finally be resolved. It has been suggested he was forced in that direction by an Athenian fleet that had come up in pursuit from Samos, but while this may have been a factor it was surely strategy that directed Lysander's steersmen, not panicked retreat.[23]

Once on the spot 'he himself attacked Lampsacus from the sea with his ships, while Thorax, cooperating with the land forces, assaulted the walls. He took the city by storm, and gave it up to his soldiers to plunder.'[24] This port on the Asian side of the Hellespont at its egress into the Sea of Marmara was now refurbished as the main base in this new theatre of war. The Athenian generals from Samos were apparently soon on his tail. They had been little concerned while Lysander and the Peloponnesian navy had been scrabbling around Caria, particularly after what they had done to them at Arginusae, but with this most recent threat they had acted. Triremes were called in from all stations and 180 were manned and launched to chase after an enemy who seemed once more intent on interdicting the all important grain convoys. Philocles had brought the navy down from Athens after the trials of the admirals, to join Conon at Samos; Tydeus, Adeimantus, Cesphisodotus and Menander were the other commanders mentioned as appointed to lead the 180 ships and 36,000 men that comprised an intimidating pursuit. These generals it seems amicably rotated overall command amongst themselves. Whether some of these were tyros whose incompetence would soon hurt the cause is not clear, but it has been suggested the Athenians found it difficult to get good men to stand as generals after the executions of the previous year; this despite the fact that Conon was still there, and others who we have no reason to think were of particularly poor calibre. The *kudos* that went with the top jobs makes it likely that ambition would trump pusillanimity as often as not. But leadership failings could have been an increasing factor when the post Arginusae culling of admirals came on top of the fact that competent officers like Thrasybulus and Theramenes, trierarchs at Arginusae, were also out of the loop of high command because of being tainted with association with Alcibiades.

Certainly it is clear despite a team command structure that there was little indecision; the Athenians wanted a fight despite the great losses they had suffered in battle and to the storm in the last encounter. The quality of each side's personnel at this time is not known with any certainty. We hear of an order by an Athenian general to cut off the fingers of any enemy oarsmen captured; a desperate design suggestive of a command who knew their best oarsmen were haemorrhaging away for better wages. But against this is the specific testimony of Cornelius Nepos, a first century BC Roman biographer, who claims the Athenians were still the superior sailors even at this time.

On their arrival the Athenians, after pausing at their old base of Elaeus, heard that Lampsacus had fallen and that the Spartans were still there. They victualled at Sestos but did not stay. Another beaching place was required and they found it at Aegospotami or Goat River. The exact site is still argued over but was probably either opposite Lampsacus by modern Gallipoli or somewhere further round to the north at beaches where the Hellespont begins to open out into the Sea of Marmara itself. Any further west is not likely as it would have meant a long pull against the current to get the ships up to attack the enemy at Lampsacus. The place chosen by the Athenian generals was an open spot where two small streams met and there was plenty of water to drink, room for their encampments and crucially the position was tight on the neck of the enemy so they might not slip away and attack the grain convoys soon due to arrive. The stretch of water between the Spartan and Athenian bases was not great and observation not that difficult. It was probably around four miles between the two contestants and though distance and promontories meant they could not exactly peer into each other's faces, with the aid of spy boats and watchers on the heights it was reasonably easy for each side to make out what the other was up to. Thus the sailors, soldiers and captains at Goat River would surely have been kept appraised of any activity leading to the launching of Lysander's navy, and that in the event they were taken unawares does not speak well of their vigilance.

So, almost cheek by jowl, Lysander needed all his cunning to encompass his enemies' downfall. This man was in many ways, by traditional laconic norms, a very un-Spartan commander indeed. As comfy on the cushions of a satrap's headquarters as any sycophant, he handled money with real aplomb, acting as the conduit whereby Persian darics brought over the very best crews to man the Peloponnesian fleet. He was a wily politician as well, constructing an active faction of oligarchs in the Ionian cities attached to himself as much as to Sparta and the Peloponnesian League. These were all activities that made him a figure of suspicion to Spartan conservatives yet one whose success could not be denied and gave him an almost uniquely unassailable position in the state. Stories went round that he was not fully Spartan having a non Spartan mother but surely this is really just the usual *topos* to stress how far he had climbed by emphasising how lowly his origins were. Clearly Lysander was from the highest echelon of Spartan society whatever his mother's origins. His father had the wherewithal to ensure a true Spartan upbringing, and that it is claimed he was the lover of the later King Agesilaus makes obvious what is already probable. These youthful relationships were important political matters and near status parity would have been crucial in the choices made as much as any matter of personal attraction. Equally if a story is to be believed that Lysander intrigued to make the kingship open to any true Spartan so he might aspire to it, this shows too what a blue blood he was. It is inconceivable that such a plan might be mooted as possible except by someone with an impeccable pedigree.

This was the man who faced a larger enemy fleet that had been almost unfailingly victorious over some years now. All sources agree that after establishing their base the Athenian fleet for several days sailed out from Goat River to offer battle and that on each occasion Lysander refused. This was not the script and it left the Athenians in difficulties situated as they were away from a proper port on an open beach. As supplies ran short, the longer they stayed, the further men had to travel to forage or buy food at local markets. Indeed it seems that this, for many officers, had become the priority rather than keeping alert in the face of an enemy who seemed completely quiescent. It was at this time that a familiar face was espied approaching the gate of the Goat River site. Alcibiades himself was noticed riding down from the hills above the Athenian camp. When he spoke with the officers of the day it turned out he had come from a fortified residence on his estates at Pactye about twenty miles away on the Chersonese. This region had long been a place where Athenian aristocrats purchased estates and on occasions they found them useful as hideaways when their fellow citizens became tired of them. Miltiades, the hero of Marathon, had done the same well over a century before and the historian Thucydides had retired to family gold mines in the region when his career collapsed to a premature end after a setback at Amphipolis. Now this latest golden boy to have lost his lustre had apparently not lost his patriotism and wanted to point out the dangers that the fleet's current camping ground placed them in. He felt his local clout might be useful as he had the ear of two Thracian kings who could provide their armies as auxiliaries if he asked them. He proposed that if he was given a share in command he would unleash them against the Spartans on land if they continued to refuse to fight at sea. Indeed this proposal might support the contention that the Athenian fleet was still better crewed as it seems Alcibiades' suggestion was that his Thracians should defeat the enemy on land so then they would have no option but to fight at sea or surrender. But he found his intervention not at all appreciated and the men in charge, Tydeus and Menander, sent him away with short shrift, no doubt realising hitching their star to this man would not be in their interest. If things worked out well undoubtedly Alcibiades would garner all the credit but if it went wrong he would slip from under leaving them to shoulder the blame. As a parting shot the exile suggested the fleet should move twelve miles down the coast to Sestos where they would be less exposed, but this was not taken up as they had from the beginning rejected that place as too far away to keep a tight lock on the enemy fleet. A great story, and if it were not for the wholesale accreditation it would be tempting to put it down as an invention to show up the hubristic stupidity of these officers who refused good advice and suffered for it.

All we hear records the Athenians for four days launching their whole navy to offer battle to the Spartans at Lampsacus, and that on each occasion an 'Odyssean' Lysander refuses combat and pulls his beard reflectively as things fall out in the shape of his master plan. Lysander ordered the oarsmen, sailors and pilots to take up their stations at sunrise but not to make any stir that might be noticed by the enemy. So when the Athenians drew up before them challenging them to battle, they were all well deployed, but held back, prepared to defend but refusing to be lured out to accept the gauntlet laid down by the enemy. Officers in small boats were warned particularly to keep an eye on the foremost ships that might be tempted to engage the vessels out in the channel in front of them. By evening the Athenians had had enough and sailed back across the water to Goat River. But Lysander was not making rash assumptions and kept his men in fighting trim, not allowing them to stand down until his spies had actually seen the enemy disembark from their ships. Each day, after battle was declined, the Athenians returned to their beach encampment and the crews disembarked so the men could find supplies and cook and eat their meals. This routine apparently made the Athenians complacent so that after a time they dropped their guard against an enemy so close and so dangerous.

This was the pattern for four days but on the fifth everything changed. As usual the Athenians launched their ships and deployed across the strait offering battle to the men at Lampsacus. All seemed the same with the Spartans refusing combat so the Athenians, after another day of frustration, returned to their beach camp. But this day Lysander was not inclined to follow the programme of the days before. He had prepared some boats with keen eyed crews to follow the enemy and when they saw the Athenians had beached their craft, disembarked and complacently let their guard down, they rowed back and halfway over alerted Lysander by signal from a flashing shield. The Peloponnesian crews had kept to their craft and were ready and encouraged by Lysander sailing around in a small boat demanding they strike quickly and boldly when the trumpeter on the admiral's vessel sounded the attack. The warships exited Lampsacus port and began the crossing, dropping off their sails, masts and rigging at a convenient promontory to be in top fighting shape. The distance between the two bases was crossed with some strong pulling on the oars of the Spartan ships that put them well placed to take advantage of their enemies' confusion. Soon more and more of Lysander's triremes appeared in the channel off Goat River, while some swept in to try to pull the unmanned enemy craft off into the sea. A land force was put ashore under Eteonicus, whose job was to attack the Athenian camp in double quick time from the landward side. There were men at the bows of all Lysander's triremes as they approached the Athenian beached boats and each carried a grappling iron. These were hurled as the Peloponnesian vessels rowed along the shore, and with the empty warships caught, the assailants pulled hard to drag them off and capture them. Lysander encouraged as more and more of his men got in close enough to throw grappling hooks over the rails of the beached Athenian ships. Behind the palisade the Athenian camp was in uproar. The soldiers and sailors surprised, there seems to have been little success in either getting aboard to launch their ships or to set up a perimeter on the shore to defend them from the land. Panic was in the air and in causing it the simultaneous landward attack was undoubtedly critical. The sight of Spartan and allied hoplites charging down the beach against the walls of the camp was too much. Taken on two fronts, some manned the defences for a while, throwing javelins and fighting behind their hoplite shields but there was no organisation and if one section held out the enemy poured in elsewhere where the resistance had been more brittle. Eventually the palisade defenders and the men who had reached the boats were overwhelmed and all they could do was flee for their lives. That with cooler heads much more could have been done was shown by Conon who after only a short moment of paralysis managed to round up sufficient sailors to man nine triremes and got them to sea and away.

As to the beached triremes, while some made efforts to fight off the attackers from the decks of their ships, with great tugs of war the Peloponnesians pulled on their oars to take off the grappled craft while the Athenians tried to hold them back and cut the hawsers that clasped them tight. Empty trireme hulls were pulled off and others were captured when the few men who had got on board failed in their defence against overwhelming numbers. The rest of the Peloponnesians then disembarked to slaughter the unarmed Athenians and their allies in their tents; or if they had reached their weapons they were too disorganised to resist a prepared and rampant enemy with spears and shields deployed in professional fashion. Thousands were killed, all the ships apart from Conon's captured, and three thousand men and the rest of the generals taken prisoner. Even so, many got away, having probably never been involved in the battle. They managed to get to Sestos while the Peloponnesians settled down to plundering the camp, procuring their spoil and taking virtually the whole of the Athenian fleet back to Lampsacus. It had taken not much over an hour to win a battle that would finally end a war that had seemed never ending.

The picture peddled by Xenophon of, apart from Conon, a collection of foolish Athenian generals bamboozled by the cunning Lysander and too arrogant to listen to Alcibiades when he offered a way out seems almost too pat. The very symmetry inclines us to listen to alternative accounts and certainly Diodorus does have a different slant, though the outcome was the same, and indeed he also gives little credit to the Athenian high command. He suggests there was desperation in the Athenian camp before the battle – 'famine gripped the army' – and it was from this, not from overconfident complacency, that disaster followed.

With it now transparently clear that they needed to move base Philocles, the Athenian general commanding that day, set out with thirty triremes and ordered the rest of the ships to follow him. Whether this was just relocation or whether there was another plan and they were a bait to bring out the enemy so the rest of the Athenian fleet could engage them, is unclear but in a way neither make a lot of sense. If a relocation, why travel in vulnerable smaller squadrons, and if a bait why was the rest of the Athenian fleet so woefully unready for battle when the lure was taken? Whatever the project was it went awry. Lysander had certainly not been surprised. Deserters crossing the short spread of water between had let him know what Philocles intended. He was prepared and his men ready to go; oarsmen were on their benches, steersmen at their oars, and marines armed and eager for the fight. Philocles' ships rowing down the channel were overwhelmed by an all-out attack that he clearly had not expected to be so devastating. After the Athenian vanguard was disposed of the whole Spartan fleet was now in a position to fall on the rest of an Athenian fleet that was in a state of total unpreparedness at least as great as that suggested by Xenophon.[25]

Whether the story was one of Lysander being able to pounce on Philocles' detachment or to carry out a surprise attack on the Athenian camp, the outcome was the same. And one thing is clear: though everybody in the Athenian disturbed ants' nest was doing something only one officer was doing anything to a purpose.

The only Athenian leader at the Battle of Aegospotami with his wits about him was Conon; the rest of the officers had allowed their men to go off to market, to cook their dinner or to go to sleep in their tents. He had bullied sufficient oarsmen sailors and marines to man nine ships, including the sacred ship, the *Paralus*, and just managed to launch and get them downstream before the enemy, shouting and singing their war paean, descended on them just as they had the rest of the unprepared camp. These few alert characters were lucky too: finding where Lysander's ships had dropped their sailing gear on the way to the battle, these fleeing Athenians picked up the masts and rigging they needed from the pile left behind; so once underway with the purloined equipment they were likely to have the legs in this race for safety. Soon Conon's little squadron was boiling along down to the Hellespont away from the danger. But once free of pursuit the canny admiral decided against risking being held as scapegoat by his compatriots and, while the *Paralus* was sent back to Athens to inform the government of the disaster, the rest sailed south on a voyage that would end at Cyprus. Apart from these escapees, the rest of the generals had been abysmal and suffered for it. Philocles who, if we credit Diodorus, at least was not caught on the beach with his pants down, was still taken with his ships, and was swiftly executed when brought back to the Spartan base. The rest of the over 3,000 Athenian captives had their throats cut at the insistence of enemies with plenty of hurts to repay, though Adeimantus, a friend of Alcibiades, was spared, either due to having opposed the move to mutilate captives, or as is even claimed, because he had helped the Peloponnesians during the course of the battle.

After the satisfaction of all this bloodletting the first stop for the Lysander victory train was no surprise, he went north and accepted the submission of Byzantium and Chalcedon, the double lock on the Bosporus channel where the commercial fleets carrying Pontic grain must exit from the Euxine. There he left a Spartan called Sthenelaus in charge as he returned to the Hellespont and his old base of Lampsacus. The imposition of harmosts and ten-strong oligarchic committees was becoming the norm now – Spartans he could trust in charge, and local oligarchs completely dependent on his sponsorship to support them. This was hard hand occupation that would soon make many remember with something close to fondness Athens' much lighter touch imperialism. Lysander commanded 200 ships by now and feared no one, as the main force sailed down to Lesbos. This much fought over place was quickly brought into line while Eteonicus took ten ships to Thrace and pacified that region with little trouble. Samos held out for the old alliance and some troublesome blue bloods who might have thought of handing the place over to Lysander were swiftly butchered. The island was clearly still going to be a considerable nut to crack even for the triumphant commander so he decided not to delay there but instead to aim at cutting off the head of the beast. Forty ships were left to keep Samos under siege as Lysander sailed for Athens itself. Before this move he had prepared King Agis, based at his fort of Decelea, for his coming. In fact there would be two Spartan kings on campaign in Attica when he arrived, the first time this had occurred since the sixth century. Pausanias was on his way with the main Spartan and Peloponnesian army – all the levy called up this time, not just the normal two thirds. But Lysander had no intention for it to be forgotten who provided the real muscle that had just won the war. After all, Spartan kings had wasted Attica for years without any decisive result. What had made the difference this time was the awesome panoply of maritime might following at his back, a navy he had almost singlehandedly created by his ability to tap into the moneybags of Persia and by mobilising the opponents of Athens in the islands and along the Anatolian coast. Even before his arrival he was not reticent in advertising his power: on the route over at Aegina and Melos and other places not named he reinstated exiles who had been expelled by the Athenians, he ruined Salamis just off the coast of Attica, and when he arrived at Piraeus around October, instigated a complete blockade.[26]

Finally the pendulum had stopped swinging. Aegospotami would be decisive in the way the other naval battles of the last few years had not. Of course in these circumstances divine intervention is unsurprisingly attested: aid from Castor and Pollux and the effects of a giant falling stone. But celestial marvels could not hide what had really occurred, who had really had the impact in this epic contest. Lysander had proceeded brilliantly against an Athenian high command that without Alcibiades, Thrasybulus and Theramenes had been divided and incompetent and who paid the price. It was the final crumbling: Aegospotami as it turned out was the last straw for a city and empire that had exhausted all it had to offer. Athenians had come back from disaster before, but not this time. The grim arithmetic of their losses was decisive; she could produce no more fleets, and without these her overseas position was untenable. When Lysander sent out his victorious squadrons to exploit the victory history would have suggested his enemies might hunker down behind their walls; that strategic strongpoints would have to be brought to heel through long sieges as in the past. That Athenian colonists placed to sustain friendly regimes would likewise take a real struggle to winkle out whether they were in Thrace, the islands, Anatolia or the Propontis. But it did not happen, partly because Lysander offered seemingly generous terms allowing Athenians and their allies to retain their lives, arms and goods and enabling them to return to the home city. It was a thought through strategy not some altruistic turnaround by the bloody and hardhearted veteran: he knew the final round would be fought outside the walls of Athens itself and when the siege began he wanted the place rammed with hungry mouths that would need feeding. He wanted swollen bread queues whose requirements would become more and more difficult to satisfy as the Peloponnesians gained control of those places from where they could completely interdict the grain routes. And soon he would threaten the death penalty to anybody found trying to smuggle grain into the city.

Lysander had begun the cruise to Athens as September moved into October and now he had put an iron grip around the throat of the Athenian mother city. Since the *Paralus* had slid into night time Piraeus bringing news of Aegospotami, the people and their leaders knew it could not be long before they were besieged. Fear was a spur; memories of rough treatment dished out in their days of power was an inspiration, as they got the walls in as much order as they could and barricaded the port entrances, except for one left open in the hope of future succour. The preparations it soon was shown would be very much required as word came of the vast Peloponnesian panoply arriving to camp in the academy so near the city walls; apparently every folk from the Peloponnesian peninsula had joined this army except the Argives. But it was when Lysander and his mighty fleet anchored in the roads outside Piraeus the population really began to hear, the crack of doom rolling down around them. Yet people were by all accounts dying of malnutrition before anybody was even prepared to consider suing for terms.

How long it was before they caved in is uncertain but almost certainly in the time it took, the siege had changed into a blockade with Pausanias' main army demobilised. King Agis and the Decelea troops and their Athenian oligarchic exile auxiliaries remained, but Lysander took what ships he could spare from closing Piraeus to have another crack at Samos. Without quite so many Peloponnesian spear points glistening outside the city walls we can perhaps believe the citizens could remain intransigent for some time, despite the hammer blows they had sustained. But the Athenians were bound to have to treat eventually and when they did it would be with a very poor hand indeed. The first bluff was opened with Agis and entailed offering submission but with the proviso they could keep the fortifications at Piraeus and the long walls leading up to the city that had always been the root of their capacity to resist invasion. The men who came to offer this were sent on by the king to Sparta but turned back at the border town of Sellasia, not even being allowed to enter Sparta proper, by a government totally unwilling to consider what they proffered. Back at the beleaguered city there was still plenty of spirit. One weak link was imprisoned for even suggesting the walls could be touched at all. Indeed the redoubtable demagogue Cleophon – who like other democrats, had little to expect for themselves after surrender – had even managed to get a law passed forbidding discussion of such a thing again. With people dying in the streets and no capacity to put significant forces in the field this lusty patriotism began to look like empty posturing. Strain and starvation soon stitched the faces of the assemblymen who began to consider the inconceivable. Theramenes, a real snake oil salesman – if we are to believe Lysias, a contemporary orator and speech writer – with a history of facing both ways in the days of the Four Hundred, now made a play to be the man to win decent terms for his fellow citizens.

There are some extant details of convoluted negotiations over many months involving Theramenes apparently hobnobbing with Lysander on Samos then with the ephors back in Sparta. But eventually the nakedness of the city's condition forced reality, and other envoys were sent bustling behind him determined to accept virtually any terms their persecutors would offer. It was finally fact-facing-time on Pnyx Hill. The assembly heard the sentence laid on them and though some spoke in opposition, the argument of empty store houses and dead in the streets could not be gainsaid. There is evidence that groundwork had already been done to ensure compliance, with Cleophon eliminated and a number of democratic generals put under arrest, even before the peace was agreed.[27] Any lingering reluctance to knuckle under would have been swept away when word was heard of how close a run thing their very existence had been in the conference of the Peloponnesians and their allies at Sparta. There the likes of Corinth and Thebes had demanded the complete abolition of the city and the turning of Attica into pasturage but this had not been agreed, conceivably for the love of Athenian drama as some claim but far more likely by Sparta's concern that an empty Attica would allow the very places that demanded it to fill the vacuum in a way detrimental to the postwar balance she intended. But the child that was surrender had no parents easily prepared to own it. No one wanted to be associated with responsibility for the most awful day in Athens city's life – even worse than when Xerxes burned it down. However, finally the destruction of the long walls, the return of the exiles and the acceptance that Athens must follow Spartan foreign policy was swallowed. And with these expected terms came a condition less easy to understand: a demand that the Athenians must organise the government in line with their ancestral construction. This was a condition likely to favour Lysander who wanted an open brief to ensure he could mould the city government in his and his oligarchic friends' favour.

Chapter Three

Liberation and Tyranny

In October 403, not much more than a year since the flute girls had accompanied the first shifts put in to pull down the long walls, a fascinating scene was played out outside Piraeus that tells us much about the Greek world after the Peloponnesian War. The participants included Lysander, the architect of Spartan victory, at the head of a group of mercenaries, his half brother Libys with forty warships, one of the Spartan kings, Pausanias, with the main Peloponnesian levy and any number of Athenian contenders who had been taking part in an extraordinary drama over the last long months. As the various members of the army present – hoplites, peltasts and cavalrymen – milled around and placemen rushed in and out of the public tent it became clear the foreign policy of the Spartans was by no means a monolithic thing; there were real tensions between the agents of that state gathered there.

The process that highlighted all this had begun when the Athenians, in spring 404, though the chronology is uncertain, broken by the Spartan siege, accepted terms that included the destruction of the walls from Athens to Piraeus and Phalerum bay, the reduction of their maritime arm to a derisory twelve warships, and the return of the anti-democrats in exile, many of whom had only recently been ravaging the Attic countryside as part of Agis' army at Decelea.[1] There existed now an Athenian political class finding it hugely difficult to come to terms with defeat and added to them came the exiles from 411 many of whom wanted to replay those years of oligarchic power. The surrender terms did not solve anything and the declaration that an 'ancestral constitution' should be returned to was a stipulation that ensured debilitating divisions, which no doubt were the intentions of those who imposed it. What the high sounding intent would mean in practice, the extent of the franchise and the mechanisms of authority, was soon up for argument from all sides. So in the shadow of the long walls being prepared for destruction, in the crushed *polis* enfeebled but still contentious, the old factions, hard core democrats, oligarchs and those in-between, took up familiar positions.

Of these blocs, known democrats were naturally a little reticent: it was after all they who had lost the war. But there were still moderates, frightened by intransigent oligarchs in hock to national enemies, who would be prepared to argue their corner for some form of limited franchise. There was not much room for compromise, in a political atmosphere, poisoned by the events of 411, as the citizen body, much changed during years of war, prepared to haggle over the disposal of power. What with plague, near thirty years of bloodletting, and the Spartans sitting on their neck at Decelea for almost the last ten years, the people that started the war had been dramatically affected. Many of the middling landowners had gone from the land for good, not returning to their old fields at all or, if they did, failing to prosper in a country of destroyed vines and burnt olive trees. A return to normality would occur though and soon enough; the hoplite franchise based on land, the ubiquitous currency of the ancient world remained, and would continue strong as the bedrock of moderate democratic suffrage right down to the end of the fourth century in the days of the Macedonian rulers Antipater and Cassander. For the moment sectional groupings assumed accustomed attitudes but as they wavered in carrying out what they had agreed as the price of survival some of the oligarchs, who had shown in 411 how little they put the demands of patriotism above their own interests, prepared to play the Lacedaemonian card. To facilitate this they crucially managed to persuade enough of the people who mattered to have five of their faction declared in charge, tasked with moving the constitutional debate along. These office holders were named ephors though such a designation was certainly not traditional at Athens and already suggests an inclination to model the city's future along Spartan lines.

While these new principals arranged the detention of many of the most prominent democratic leaders, the most important decision they made was to call for intervention from Lysander. He had just wrapped things up and put his exiled friends back in place in Samos. The defenders, finally despairing, had agreed to leave with their lives and a cloak each to their name. Returning now, backed by a hundred ships, Lysander was in no mood to accept anything but the same for Athens as he had just realised at Samos; the most direct imposition of his policy. He justified his intervention by claiming the Athenians had been slow in tearing down the long walls and now on arrival he not only enforced those harsh clauses that had given the Athenians so much trouble to accept but also ensured his own people, client oligarchs who admired everything Spartan, got into the power seat. A disposal that, to the backing track of the sound of the rest of the long walls tumbling into the defensive ditches in front of them, would begin a massive crisis in Athenian life.

The men Lysander imposed became known as the Thirty Tyrants but the constitutional adjustment that brought them in was not made without considerable debate. Theramenes, who we know from the time of the Four Hundred as a trimming oligarch but one who had retained sufficient patriotic credibility to avoid exile, was part of it. He initially supported proposals that would put in place thirty men to act as a constitutional convention rather than as an executive, but when Lysander flexed his muscles he and his ilk could not resist, though the Spartan tried to keep him on board by allowing him to nominate a third of those chosen, with another ten being picked by the ephors and the remainder by the currently constituted assembly. Just to make sure it was clear who really called the shots, Lysander had already appointed ten governors to be in charge at Piraeus.[2] But whatever influence Theramenes retained he was unable to restrain the Thirty, who ditched any inclination towards constitution construction and wasted no time in setting themselves up in complete control of all the levers of power. With their feet under the table, friends and supporters were swiftly sited in the key jobs for the coming year, particularly the law courts, and these thirty prepared for a purge that eventually turned into something Sulla would have been proud of.

The new government though did not start with a bloodbath; it was some months before they really showed their hand. The process began with the proscriptions of informers from the old regime. This culling was not that unpopular, but the career of the Thirty was from the beginning not all smooth and easy. They never had much real legitimacy and managed to force their will only by the threatened muscle of rich young bravos and foreign bully boys, a Spartan garrison of 750 men under a harmost called Callibius had arrived at some stage.[3] The man who emerged as the leader of the Thirty was Critias; the scion of an old aristocratic family that also produced the philosopher Plato. A sophist, he wrote several works including tragedies and some that evinced his great admiration for Spartan ways. Unfortunately these now only exist in fragments. As a young yahoo he was implicated in the *hermai* incident that put paid to Alcibiades' plans to triumph in Sicily and, like him, was a pupil of Socrates. Though he had followed a teacher who prided himself on claiming he knew nothing, Critias and his followers were going to show they certainly did know one thing, and that was how to bring down their rivals in rivers of blood. Claims are made that they wanted to bed into Athens the discipline of *eunomia* ('good order') they knew from Sparta; that the new Athenian institutions were built in parallel with that place, with the Thirty matching the *Gerousia*, the Three Thousand the peers, the rest of the citizens downgraded to *perioeci*, and with foreigners periodically kicked out just like their exemplars did. This is arguable but whatever their philosophy the Thirty's intention to rule with a rod of iron was unquestioned. With cold determination they began to eliminate those who they considered in any sense a threat to them. Apart from known democrats, anybody who had a good name amongst the citizen body soon became fair game, many of whom had never been part of an anti-oligarchic faction at all. This was the stage when the likes of Thrasybulus realised Athens was no longer a place for them and looking to their survival took the hard road to exile.

With Spartan swords on hand as back up, Critias and his crowd let rip the bile of decades when under the Democracy they had been forced to accept their social inferiors as equals. Now it was death to any they perceived as enemies and as time went on also to men of wealth whose confiscated money they needed to fill their coffers. They sold off the ship sheds at Piraeus for a pittance of three talents though they had cost a thousand to build. This was part ideology as well. Rejecting their nautical past, they even turned the speaker's platform on the Pnyx away from the sea and pointed it inland. They knew the city's maritime orientation had always run hand in glove with democratic power. They were acting like tyrants of old with their mercenary guards but now these armed men were provided by Sparta, the very city that had years before made a name as the nemesis of tyranny in the Peloponnese.

But this government was not without its own problems. Soon a fault line became clear between the two greatest of their number. Critias not only wanted revenge for the pains and indignities of his own exile but was prepared to go to any lengths to get the money needed to pay for his Spartan friends; while Theramenes saw the rich and well born as a natural bulwark of support, not a cash cow to be milked. For Theramenes, men of property with popular support were the key to long term power not the road to short term riches. Critias, elitist to the core, was only inclined to allow 3,000 citizens approved by himself to have any sort of political say in the city and now he moved to enshrine his inclination. A list was drawn up of these safe men, while everybody who was not on it was disarmed and their weapons taken to the acropolis. These neutralised and disenfranchised were clearly in no sense the poor; they were not the foot soldiers of radical democracy, they were of the hoplite franchise, at least of middle income, with the funds to own their own arms. Theramenes wanted no part of this social engineering that he realised would serve only to strengthen Critias' position.

It was not the 3,000 list that actually brought the break; that occurred when Critias' gory fundraising took off in a really organised way. Now it was not to be just democrats and enemies that would be taken down dark alleys; the need for gold made them mark out any men who had it. Rich men, mostly resident foreigners ('*metics*'), were targeted in a systematic way, with members of the junta being delegated one of these moneybags to eliminate and despoil. It was now we learn of Theramenes determined to say so far and no farther, despite the fact that this resistance was going to be very risky indeed in the dangerous city that the Thirty were now running. In the council chamber matters came to a head. Critias had isolated his rival but he was a belt and braces man and had some of his blue blooded bravos on hand, men always brave with a knife pressed against the backs of the defenceless. He singled Theramenes out as one who, though useful in the past as part of bringing in the Spartans, was now lacking in what it took to go the final mile; of not being prepared to raise the war cry against a *demos* that in democratic guise had made war on him and them in the past. He berated him as a trimmer who had first stood at the head of the Four Hundred in 411 but later turned and led the democratic backlash and whose survival would now encourage enemies of the Thirty.

Theramenes, in response, finally declared his manifesto that put faith in horsemen and hoplites – that they should rely on not disarm these sturdy well heeled folk without whom they would be completely at the mercy of the Spartans. None of this was helping him, and the thugs brought in by Critias were signalled the order to take their man. But 'when Theramenes heard this, he sprang to the altar and said: "And I, sirs," said he, "beg only bare justice... . I know, I swear by the gods, only too well, that this altar will avail me nothing, but I wish to show that these Thirty are not only most unjust toward men, but also most impious toward the gods."'[4]

However the 'eleven' officers charged with responsibility for prisoners and executions dragged him off and any in the council inclined to protest were intimidated by not only the oligarchs' bully boys but Spartans from the garrison who were also present in the council house. There is a generally derided suggestion that Socrates unsuccessfully tried to save him but failed to influence any of the junta, despite many of them being his old pupils. Others propose that the author of the last ditch plea for clemency was in fact Isocrates, none of which stopped the hemlock being got out and the most significant adversary of Critias dealt with. The regime now had the shackles off and if our sources are to be believed nobody was safe. They went for the men of the highest reputation and pedigree if they could be identified as not being behind the Thirty. Well off patriots who had in the past funded two triremes for the city were executed. In fact now the policies of the Thirty became quite extraordinary, driving out of Athens all the citizens who were not part of the Three Thousand and confiscating their property, and evicting people from houses and land their families had lived on for generations. It is claimed 1,500 all told were killed by the Thirty so it is hardly a surprise that hordes of men and their families now filled the roads to Piraeus, Megara and even as far as Thebes to escape the men of blood who had taken over town.

Thrasybulus had always been too big a man for the Thirty to have around and had suffered exile early along with many others. Athens' Thirty Tyrants hated with a vengeance and years of democracy that they considered had taken away their birthright of power and pre-eminence had embittered them into virtually any foolhardiness. The Thebans were happy to give refuge to Athenians looking for sanctuary. The Spartans, eager to boost their friends' chances of survival, had commanded the rest of the Greeks to refuse refuge to Athenian exiles but this not only left a sour taste but was completely ignored by Argos and Thebes. Indeed the rulers in the latter place even proscribed penalties against those who did not give succour to the troop of democrats limping down the road that ran from the Attic border. Thrasybulus, already waiting at Thebes, must have not been able to believe his luck. His enemies were cutting their own throats, turning everybody outside the Three Thousand into his natural allies. Never likely to be content with some government in exile sinecure, living on the charity of these central Greek friends, he did not delay long. Acting with Anytus (best known for later prosecuting Socrates) and 70 other supporters he slipped out of Thebes and marched down the road over the frontier and up into the Parnes Mountains where the fort of Phyle was sited. His commandos seized the place; we are not told how, presumably it was not garrisoned but they had won themselves 'a commanding position.'

This was probably in January 403 and they were playing out a kind of internal version of the strategy utilised in the Peloponnesian War when a strongpoint would be set up in enemy territory to encourage helots and other subjects to rebel and come over. But now it was Athenian citizens they were wanting to attract. Word of the descent from Boeotia came quickly to Athens and Critias did not let the grass grow. He intended to snuff out these upstarts before they could become a serious alternative centre of loyalty. He knew how many people might be drawn to the new player and wanted him eliminated. The Three Thousand got down their shields and spears or accoutred their horses and marched out in bright fine weather not expecting the newcomers to put up much of a fight. The under twenty miles was covered well before the first day of marching was over and when they came in sight of the walls of the fort some of the eager bloods began to dismount and deploy to make an attempt on the defences. But the defenders were ready and not a few of the scaling party got hurt by missiles as they tried an escalade. Put off by this unexpectedly stout resistance, once the commanders arrived they decided on a siege and set about walling the place in to deny the defenders supplies. But now the weather changed dramatically with snow falling heavily in the night, a meteorological excess that continued into the next day, making it impossible for the besiegers to dig up the wood and stone needed to construct a wall, and causing extreme discomfort for the attackers exposed in the open as they were. Neither leaders nor men were up for this kind of hard campaigning and soon began to trickle back to the city, even leaving or losing some baggage to the defenders as they decamped.

Without men willing to bear spears for the cause in the face of disagreeable conditions Critias had to call on the Spartan garrison. These 750 tough combatants backed up by two divisions of Athenian cavalry set up a camp a mile and a half away from Phyle to try to contain Thrasybulus and his followers, but they turned out not to be sufficient to suppress the burgeoning numbers of their enemy. Soon enough, in April or May, the democrats had organised and armed themselves to the number of 700 and, eager to have a go, crept out of their fort and up to the besiegers' camp just before dawn. As the sun was rising they stood up and ran hell for leather to get at the enemy while they were still unprepared. The work put into the defences must have been slipshod as sentries were easily cut down at their posts while the rest just gave up and ran. The besiegers lost 120 hoplites and 3 horsemen before Thrasybulus and his men, after a mile, gave up the pursuit; then the rebels put up a trophy and withdrew back to the fort. When later more cavalry came up in support they found only the bodies of their own dead comrades and, accepting they could not keep up their position in front of Phyle, they picked up the bodies of the slain and took the downhill road back to Athens.

With their Spartan friends defeated and their antagonists on the increase Critias and the Thirty began to get cold feet. They had successfully managed to alienate virtually every Athenian outside the Three Thousand and were getting desperate as it became clear how isolated they were. Their policy of removing most of the disenfranchised citizens beyond the town walls (5,000 troublemakers were even relocated to Piraeus despite this being already a hotbed of democratic support) had clearly acted as the most effective recruiting tool for Thrasybulus' party. When realisation dawned, Critias and co were completely unnerved and took another of those decisions that would be difficult to credit if it was not so generally attested. The Thirty decided they would now decamp. They began to prepare a more defensible base at Eleusis, a town about eleven miles north west of Athens and famous for its sacred mysteries for over a thousand years, while leaving mercenaries in the city to keep a lid on things. And having made their name mud inside Athens itself they now acted to ensure the same result in places roundabout. Local folk from Eleusis were arraigned for helping the exiles and numbers condemned to death at an assembly where any opposition was quietened by the presence of Spartan troops. Similar treatment was apparently meted out to the inhabitants of Salamis as well.

Thrasybulus had made himself a player and even the Thirty could not deny it. Sending envoys about prisoner exchange they tested the water to see if he might throw his lot in with them. They suggested he take the erstwhile place of Theramenes at the top of government and as a further sop conceded he could bring his ten most important supporters with him. But they did not know their man, who rejected their offer out of hand, and they were left with no option but to look to defending what they still had. The Thirty girded for battle, getting all their men concentrated outside Athens at a place called Acharnae, and also sent to Sparta for more help. The man who had put such a scare in them was well up for a fight and was getting good support from important people. The orator and metic Lysias, whose brother had been a victim of the Thirty, was one who stumped up funds, not just to arm the rebels but apparently to recruit mercenaries too. There were 1,200 fighters with Thrasybulus now and with these he marched at night down the Piraeus road, attacked the defenders' camp in the dark, killed a number and bundled the rest back to Athens. After that it was on to Piraeus, where the people had long been deeply hostile to the Thirty. Here they took over the Munychia hill as the civil war came to the boil in real earnest. This was stasis red in tooth and claw on the streets of the great port.

But it was not just gardeners, hairdressers and waiters versus high-born bravos, not just poor folk with stones slings and javelins stirring up frisky horsemen. The middling people crouched down behind their *Aspis* shields were the core and they, as so often with these sort, were split. Some followed Critias under a banner of snobbery while others were only too aware how far the Thirty had strayed from honest virtuous Aristotelian aristocracy. The Thirty were oligarchs to a fault only interested in protecting their own, not caring to govern in the interest of all.

Not long after, down the wagon road from Athens to the port, an armoured column moved with the Spartan garrison at its head and Athenian cavalry and hoplites crowding after. Thrasybulus first attempted to stop them in their tracks but when it became obvious he was seriously outnumbered he pulled his men back up the steep streets to the top of the hill of Munychia to make a stand. This prominence, rising above the two smaller harbours and the Dionysian theatre, is still impressively contoured today and must have looked daunting to the troops from Athens as they deployed in the Hippodamian *agora*. The houses along the side of the road did not allow the attacking phalanx to deploy with much width. It is recorded as having been fifty deep, a depth that presages the Theban tactics at Leuctra, but in this case forced by necessity rather than by choice. The defenders, outnumbered five to one in hoplites, only stood ten deep but they were determined, and behind them they had numerous peltasts and light infantry, well positioned on higher ground to make a terrific impact with their missiles. The numbers of these warriors fighting with javelins, rocks and slings had been augmented by the local populace, many of them seamen, always the heart and soul of the democracy since Athens' imperial heyday.

In the hiatus before it came to blows we hear of Thrasybulus geeing up his men by reminding them of the outrages of the Thirty, their own past victory in the snow, and the advantage they had firing downhill into a packed street where they could not miss. The spirit of his party was only increased by the seer who, after determining from the entrails of his sacrificed beast that someone must be killed or wounded before the main body could attack with any chance of success, himself ran forward onto the spears of the enemy to allow the rest to advance. This was just what was needed and with a shower of rocks, javelins and anything that could be thrown raining down on the oligarch troops the 'Phylites' charged. Many of the Thirty were in the front rank and Critias and at least one other of the tyrants fell at the beginning. Whether it was this or that many did not have their heart in it, the deeper phalanx was pushed back down the hill to the point where they had started. Surely indicating a lack of steel as in this street fighting a deep column with flanks all covered by the buildings on either side ought to have had the edge in a confined push, even going uphill. Over 70 of the men from Athens were killed but more importantly they markedly failed to dislodge the rebels even with Spartans fighting on their side. It was a tipping point and, with a truce to bury the dead agreed, intercourse began between the two sides that had just been at each other's throats. It was stalemate but a stalemate with benefits for the men from Phyle. For many in the oligarch ranks were unhappy with the way things were going and a number of these started to slip out of their lines and join Thrasybulus' side while others affected by the rebel chief's assurance of brotherhood to all but the Thirty themselves returned to Athens intent on reforming their leadership. With numbers and confidence boosted the rebels launched a surprise attack and drove the Thirty's army right out of Piraeus town.

Piraeus had been drawing any Athenians alienated from the city government like bees to a honey pot. It was the crisis as it became clear the revolutionaries now could count on far more armed support than their adversaries. Holding the initiative, Thrasybulus and his followers put in place plans to besiege the mother city itself, the combat at the port had changed the game in Athens completely. The people left there despite being part of the junta's chosen Three Thousand started to divide over how to deal with the threat from the powerful party down the road. It is known that those of the Thirty left met the next day in the council chamber but far from taking control they lost their nerve completely when they heard of proposals mooted in the city to ditch them and vote in a government who would be dedicated to ending the civil war. This new administration was to consist of ten men, one from each tribe, only two of whom were to be from the Thirty. But it turned out this lot when appointed had no other policy than the men they replaced and set themselves up as tyrants, sending to Sparta for another army to save them from the ravening democrats outside the city gates. While this was going on those of the Thirty not part of the new setup scuttled for it to Eleusis taking their Spartan bodyguards with them. It was like the Four Hundred over again building a fort down in Piraeus harbour in 411, when threatened these oligarchs were programmed to find a fortress to defend themselves and from there look for help from Sparta.

Under the new Ten the administration was coming apart; the men who were still on board were jumpy as hell, sleeping in the *Odeon* with their horses and weapons, and patrolling in the day so as to be prepared if the men from Piraeus advanced. Down at the port increasing numbers were arming themselves into a numerous strike force; some even prepared to fight with improvised wicker shields, and were looking after themselves by foraging wood and summer fruits. All this lasted for ten days, with military preparation and mutual encouragement the order of the day. It was one for all and all for one now, even the *metics* who had joined up were assured in the new Athens they were about to create they would only have to pay the lower citizen tax rate rather than what they had before. It was a cross class coalition; the behaviour of the Thirty had driven all sorts into the opposing camp. Thrasybulus could even count on seventy cavalrymen, showing some of the toffs had changed their colours in the light of events as well as plenty from the hoplite franchise as well. It was a triangle of dispute now: the remnants of the Thirty were at Eleusis with their diehard supporters; Thrasybulus, the man with the momentum in Piraeus, where the people were solid in the democratic cause, and his armed forces swelling by the day; and at Athens in the middle were the ten oligarchs and those not completely tainted with subservience to the Thirty, hoping to keep a hold of something in incredibly uncertain times. In Piraeus they were confident and prepared to take the struggle against Athens itself, while the defenders in the city were preparing for a siege, blocking off the road by the Lyceum racetrack to the east of the city along which they expected the insurrectionists to bring their siege engines. But before matters were resolved there was a response to the desperate pleas for help sent to Sparta. Lysander, when the oligarchs called responded, in

June or July 403, got himself made governor and his brother Libys navarch for the year 403–2, and went up to Eleusis with 40 ships and 1,000 men where his old friends were based. Once there he sent out the word to mercenaries around that he was paying good wages, while his brother set out to harass the democrats at Piraeus.

This was the situation when Pausanias entered the picture. He was the grandson of the Pausanias who had achieved wonders at the Battle of Plataea in 479, but had subsequently become caught up in several intrigues involving the Persians and died in disgrace. Despite this, and the fact that he was only ever regent, his son Pleistoanax ascended to the throne and was there a good long time from 458–409. He was very much seen as of the peace party who were reluctant to go full throttle in the war with Athens, and indeed he was exiled for allegedly taking a bribe from Pericles. Recalled and restored to the throne by 428 he continued to press for reconciliation, a position that resonated with many after disasters like that on the island of Sphacteria. Now Pleistoanax's son Pausanias II had inherited the mantle and the family commitment to a less belligerent policy. The more subtle approach also resonated well with conservative tendencies in the *polis* who worried that campaigns outside the Peloponnese would expose true Spartan heroes to the enervating impact of foreign ways and temptations. And of course they were right – though to oppose these influences in defence of Lycurgan propriety was never going to be easy in the long run, if even possible.

On this occasion Pausanias had persuaded three out of five ephors back home that to let Lysander have his way in Athens would be dangerous and that the whole of Sparta's armed might was required to intervene. They put him at the head of the full levy and Peloponnesian allies and as the autumn came on he marched them over the isthmus into Attica to pick the bones out of what had occurred in the heartland of their old rival. The force he disposed of was likely to be decisive, though ominously the Corinthians and Thebans had both refused to send their contingents. So now a tableau is shown of two Spartan forces vying for control that tells us much about policy making in the post Peloponnesian War world. Pausanias represented a considerable faction who feared and distrusted Lysander and when they rendezvoused we can imagine a very fraught council indeed. Yet whatever the rifts between the two leaders, the Spartan army was there in force and something had to be done to solve the festering problems of Athens' future. The troops of King Pausanias and Lysander combined, and marched east along the coast to camp on the edge of a marsh sited just north of Piraeus.

The democrats there were called on to withdraw from the town but they had not come so far to give up now. They threw up defences, wooden palisades, ditches, anything to slow the enemy down. It was more than the Spartans had expected and though they approached with the king holding the right wing and Lysander and his mercenaries on the left their effort seems to have been feeble, hardly threatening the ramparts at all. But Pausanias could not hold fire forever:

whatever his real feelings towards his colleague, he had to show some intent. With a strong force of two regiments and some Athenian cavalry still loyal to the Thirty, he made a reconnaissance in force near where the Eetioneia fort stood. This had been the epicentre in 411, and from that breakwater, with the great harbour to the east, he seemed to be contemplating setting up an assault wall to cut off the defenders. But when the Spartans turned and were marching back to camp, the democrats holding the walls began to pester them. Eventually the attackers were seen off by the cavalry and younger hoplites and, after killing thirty, the remainder were chased back towards the theatre of Piraeus. At this point it looked like the battle was over – but far from it. When the pursued and pursuers arrived, they found a goodly number more of Thrasybulus' supporters. Hoplites and peltasts were exercising there and when they saw the enemy they began to hurl everything they had at them. The Spartans now found themselves badly outnumbered and in danger, so began to withdraw. At this point fighting became vicious and several Spartan officers were killed (including two polemarchs whose skeletons were famously unearthed at the Kerameikos ancient cemetery in Athens in 1930 where a communal tomb featured an inscription in Laconian with the names of the very polemarchs mentioned by Xenophon).

It was beginning to look like a general bloodletting when Thrasybulus brought up his main hoplite force and deployed them 8 deep outside the port almost to the edge of the marsh where the Spartans were camped. Pausanias now called out everybody he could from their posts and drew them up in serried ranks. This straight phalanx fighting was meat and drink to the Spartan warriors who seemed to have been drawn up deeper than usual and soon got the upper hand in the struggle. It was shield against shield and spear against spear though in places soldiers on both sides lost their footing on the marshy ground. It seems 150 Athenians were killed in the encounter, well sufficient for Pausanias to claim victory and put up a trophy. But Thrasybulus' men were not routed and fell back to their defences while the Spartans withdrew again to their own camp. With this hiatus it began to become clear what the agenda of Pausanias and the two ephors who marched with him was. It was not unusual when practical for these executives to be present when kings went on campaign and on this occasion these men accompanying the army like Pausanias were very suspicious of the power of Lysander.

They were far from natural allies of the democrats but they at least had the merit that unlike the Athenian oligarchs they were not Lysander's stooges. With no love for either party the feeling is they wanted a compromise with no one getting the upper hand. To this end they secretly sent to the Piraeus party and those in Athens and asked them to dispatch envoys to them to discuss reconciliation. When the democrats and some in Athens responded positively the king and ephors proposed sending them to Sparta to make their case. But this turn of events deeply worried other of the oligarchs who tried to get the Spartans back on side by offering both to give up hostages and hand over the walls of the city to Spartan troops. And to up the *ante* further they suggested the democrats should show good faith by agreeing to these terms as well. All this backstairs lobbying and dirty work in the late summer could not get a decision out of the men on the spot and soon envoys from all sides were directed to take the road to Sparta and argue their corner there.

Eventually the upshot of all this squabbling at Sparta was the sending out of 15 worthies to act as intermediaries, though this of course did not curtail jockeying at Athens. Thrasybulus and his men had moved up from Piraeus to Athens city itself taking over the acropolis and calling an assembly of all of the citizens remaining in the disordered town. Now it was clear the balance of power had changed; the insurgents were now in control. Only the Spartans could have done something about it but that would have meant war and that was not about to happen. The arrangements made in Autumn 403 by the winners were tender enough, even property confiscated by the Thirty in their days of power was not demanded back and the bloodlust of the returning democrats was kept well in hand as they allowed even their most virulent opponents to slip off to Eleusis with their hides intact. Perhaps the anticipated joy of celebrating in procession to the acropolis to sacrifice to Athena made them misty eyed and forgiving because only the Thirty themselves, the Piraeus Ten and the eleven commissioners of police were proscribed and even some of those were allowed the chance to win forgiveness if they could satisfactorily account for what they had done in the time just gone.[5]

Though in the end understandably Thrasybulus could not resist dressing down those of the Thirty who remained in the city and attended the assembly, but that all they got was harsh words was in itself pretty extraordinary. Not that the next few years were without rancour, famously Socrates suffered fatally from the handiwork of his pupils, who included the likes of Alcibiades and Critias. There was much squabbling over the years about who should be awarded the benefits of citizenship, or to what extent *metics* and even slaves who had helped with the liberation should be enfranchised. But, however heated the wrangling, the democracy did not totter; there was not for a long time a return to the kind of infighting between the haves and have-nots that landowners and mariners had engaged in so many times before. The trauma of the Thirty had just been too much and the bitter moneybags and their friends had been too awful; there was no constituency that wanted to go into bat for a return of the likes of Critias. The butt end of the civil strife itself occurred sometime later when the remnant of the Thirty at Eleusis made themselves a sufficient nuisance, by 'trying to hire foreign soldiers', that the authorities at Athens determined to suppress them. They mobilised to attack with the citizen levy, but in the end it did not come to a fight, as the oligarch leaders were tricked into dropping their guard at a conference and murdered. Their followers, left leaderless, agreed to reintegration into the Athenian community on the promise that they would not be prosecuted for past deeds.

Like Athens, the country that had sent one of its kings to sort out the folk from Attica, had undoubtedly changed from a couple of generations before; wars always change things and none more so than the Peloponnesian War. Sparta had long been a conservative landlocked power inclined to isolationism whose people did not like or trust outsiders and eschewed many of the sorts of interaction others thought to be the cornerstones of civilisation. It is only necessary to visit the site of Sparta to see the difference. Here there is no ostentation; it was a city of mainly xenophobic people who felt no need to try to impress others. Indeed, feeling little respect for outsiders, they were happy to dupe and oppress as the occasion dictated. In this, of course, they were not alone but in Sparta such behaviour was honed and perfected. How they would respond to victory on a world stage was always going to be one of the key questions of the age. The organs of state were still there, the Kings, the *Gerousia*, the five ephors, all remained intact as did the assembly of Spartiates, but the stresses of war and victory were likely to have impacted to the core. On a larger stage, with a bigger pie to be divided, the rivalries that already existed, and new ones yet to be played out, could not but be more intense.

The intensity and complexity of the situation is nowhere better exemplified than what happened to King Pausanias when he and his army left Attica after the settlement and returned to Sparta. It was not only Lysander who disapproved of his Athenian policy, and he was brought to trial over it – a reminder that for all its peculiarity Spartan government had some remarkable democratic aspects to it. There are unfortunately no details – only the bare bones of what happened.[6] The king was arraigned before the five ephors, the *Gerousia* who comprised 28 elders, and the other king, Agis. The *Gerousia* split down the middle and Agis also voted against him, but the ephors (who Pausanias had no doubt assiduously cultivated during his sojourn in Attica) all voted for his acquittal and so he walked free. However, suspicion of his motivation would always remain.

The concerns of many power players at this time were similar to those felt by King Pausanias, that Lysander's growing clout was making him the kind of figure Sparta just had not seen before outside the royal lines; indeed few kings had ever reached the apex of influence in the world that the victor of Aegospotami had. The structures Lysander had put in place in the new empire did not sit well with many, and the removal of his placemen from Athens turned out to be only the beginning of an expression of these concerns. Lysander had, since Goat River and even before, been setting up an imperial edifice centred more on loyalty to himself than to Sparta. It had become only too clear what kind of status he had achieved when, with his ships garlanded with enemy prows, he returned to his home city. His moneybags were full with almost 500 talents and he led in triumph all the triremes from Piraeus except the derisory twelve left to the Athenians. But, amidst all the celebration of Lysander's achievements, the very magnitude of what he had accomplished meant the whole epoch had become the age of Lysander. The regimes he had established at Samos and Ephesus had even had statues put up to him at Olympia and Delphi, and word got about that in those places he was worshipped as something like a god.

The competitive elites of the ancient world frequently could not function when one person became so much more important than his peers. The Athenians instituted ostracism just to get round such a problem, other places failed to face it head on. The Roman republic was buffeted and eventually sunk when the likes of Sulla, Pompey and Caesar made their own the power, that the system demanded should be shared amongst the ruling class. This skewing of things could be sustained when the individual was kept abroad for the most part, but once at home it became thorny. The kind of personality that had achieved so much and become used to a subservience he would never receive at home, was unlikely to enjoy being pulled about by the strings and levers of domestic politics, particularly as most of the others pulling would have had uppermost in their mind the desire to drag him down a peg or two. Lysander, knowing this, had from the start made a priority of storing up political credit outside Sparta.

Nor was it just the power that Lysander had accrued; it was his interaction with the wider world that upset so many, antagonising a group of naysayers who wanted Sparta to remain in a bubble uncontaminated by the outside world and saw the influx of imperial money and foreign influence as completely destructive. This tension had been at the heart of much of Spartan politics for generations but now in the age of Lysander the dangers of contamination by the outside world had reached new dimensions. So opposition to Lysander's design was peopled by those who resented the man's achievements and status, his ubiquity, and also in part by a strong faction of 'little Peloponnesers' who saw it as tainting almost any dealings with peoples outside the peninsula. Some, like Pausanias, were all for peaceful co-operation with Athens and the rest, whilst others did not care a damn what happened to folk they wanted nothing to do with and longed for a return to the time when the writ of Lycurgus was the gold standard of political business.

To chip at the edges of Lysander's influence was not going to be easy, but ammunition was soon to be had as news came in on how things were progressing in the world he and his people had built. Neither a king nor an ephor, he was entrenching himself in overarching power in the places that had been won after the fall of the Athenian empire. Brutal arrangements had been put in place at Chalcedon, Byzantium, Mytilene and Thasos where Lysander had personally superintended the massacre of a number of dissenters. Thorax, a hard navy man, who would later suffer for his sticky fingers and for his adherence to Lysander, was put in charge at Samos, and Sthenelaus was initially left as harmost of Byzantium. On the mainland there had been Callibius at Athens; there still was Aristodemus at Oreus; and Herippidas at Heraclea. But the harmosts, garrisons and quisling tens were just not going to be enough to make a credible Spartan hegemony last. It looked as if abuses perpetrated by these regimes were getting the Spartans a reputation that even many of these hard faced people would not relish. The Spartans might show themselves incredibly insensitive when in positions of power, but still most remained concerned about the city's reputation.

The example of Clearchus in Byzantium in 403 showed the problems these violent men with power but no real responsibility or control from home could cause. The Byzantines, after Sthenelaus left, had been in difficulties with faction fighting and raiding by their Thracian neighbours and asked Sparta for help. Clearchus was dispatched and granted complete authority to resolve matters, but he abused the trust he had been given and set up as a tyrant, funding his mercenary bodyguard by what he squeezed from the citizens. He started his reign with a bloodbath by inviting the chief magistrates to a party and assassinating them, before having thirty more of the most prominent citizens strangled to death to get his hands on their money. When news of his rogue activity got back, orders were sent to stop him in his tracks. But the new tyrant of Byzantium was not backing down for anyone and even when the Spartan authorities sent an armed force to arrest him he prepared to resist. Clearchus took up station, with army and treasure chest at Selymbria, just west of Byzantium; he was worried about being stabbed in the back by the Byzantines if he stayed there. An unpleasant man he may have been, but a brave one, and he took on the men sent against him. Fighting for his life, and with his mercenaries loyal to their salt, after an impressive stand he was overrun and the Lacedaemonians forced the renegade back into Selymbria town, besieging him there. But far from done for, he slipped out over the walls at night and, easy come easy go, left his realm so recently won, and crossed over to Asia to find service in the expanding army of Prince Cyrus of Persia that would soon be on the road to Cunaxa.

This kind of incident was not untypical of the world order that the end of Athens had allowed, but for Sparta it had not just meant troublesome proconsuls, it meant new wealth too. Tribute from the cities Sparta controlled raised more than 1,000 talents a year. Yet both the behaviour of her enforcers and the monies that poured in caused problems that were both personal and ideological for the elite of the Eurotas valley. The extent to which the new Spartan place in the world would undermine the Lycurgan way was something many people were not prepared to countenance. The issue of specie was always difficult for a state sustained on tribute from its new empire but that still technically banned the private ownership of money. This attempt to achieve parity between the peers as the basis of community life might never have been fully applied but still the idea had a strong pull. Strong enough to get Thorax condemned and executed for the possession of a silver hoard though for his prosecutors this had as much to do with the fact that as a friend of Lysander getting at him was a way of hitting at the great man.

Lysander's personal stature and the reputation his arrangements had brought down on the head of Sparta: all was tinder for the fire that might burn him up. The existence of this big beast was causing problems. But what remained to be seen was if it was huff and puff or whether a comprehensive effort could be made to put some restraints on this Spartan titan. By about 403 or 402 it was clear that much had been accomplished in this direction. It was not just that those who resented his ubiquity were made into bitter opponents, but also natural rivals came together to bring him down off his high horse. The kings Pausanias and Agis put away differences to join forces against him; an unusual cooperation between the two that allowed a real strike at the roots of Lysander's power, and its effectiveness was soon made apparent. The Spartan State declared that all the Greek cities where harmosts, and 'tens' that had been put in place were to be allowed to once again choose their own governments. The grounds given for the dismissal of the harmosts and the dissolution of the tens were that these proxies of Lysander were endangering relations with the Persians, who the Spartan administration were still at this stage keen to keep onside; but the reality was an intention to crumble Lysander's power base outside Sparta.

The stresses in the Spartan body politic may have been the backdrop for events in Attica and for the partial eclipse of their greatest military leader but this was not all. Back in Sparta itself events unravelled that indicated much deeper problems at the heart of the imperial polity, events that resolved around a man called Cinadon whose social designation was an inferior (*hypomeion*), a Spartiate who had lost his citizen rights through poverty and the inability to pay his mess bill. Such men clearly could have a role in Spartan society – he himself seems to have carried out police duties for the ephors on occasions – but was at a grave disadvantage compared with full Spartiates. One of his accomplices was a seer named Tisamenus, descended from an Elean who had earned full Spartan citizen rights for services in the Persian wars, but due to poverty he had also now found himself disenfranchised. Both of these were figures on the margins, but in the Sparta at the turn of the century they were far from alone.

The Athenian war was a strain the Spartan state could not take and remain the same. The number of true Spartiates was decreasing and these people who had become disenfranchised were the inevitable detritus of the development. Without land redistribution, over time agricultural plots had to be split between children until some became so small they could not support the required mess fees. Despite claims of equality between peers some fell into debt and plots had to be mortgaged. Rules that women could inherit meant that land would end up not even supporting a warrior at all if there was no son or husband involved. More crucially – though money in theory was supposed to play no part – as is always the case the rich accrued more and more land both by buying up what became available and by ensuring that land married land. The old order was crumbling and failing to provide the military manpower sufficient to fight the wars Sparta needed to fight. It had not become absolutely critical yet but it soon would be. There was no sign of any will in the ruling elite to use the windfall of victory money to fund an expansion of citizen manpower by funding plots to allow those who had lost their status to again afford their mess bills and be fully reintegrated back into the community.

So an underclass had swelled, composed of those who could not afford the cost of full citizenship, those whose parents were not of the required social standing, or of those who through misbehaviour had fallen out of the group of peers who filled the ranks of the citizen levy and attended the assembly. Apart from these fallen from grace there were plenty of other bitter folk about too. The *perioeci* had been around for centuries. Free but not enfranchised they provided the craftsmen, the metal workers and shipwrights without whom imperial Sparta could not have functioned. They lived round about, in towns such as Gythium, the port of Sparta. They were already fighting as hoplites at the battle of Plataea in 479 – indeed half the warriors captured at Sphacteria during the Peloponnesian War were *perioeci*, and more and more they served to bulk up the haemorrhaging Spartan war machine. Nor was it just as rank and file hoplites that they served, but as officers too. We hear of admirals and diplomatic envoys who came from this group. It is likely the sons of very well heeled *perioeci* and even privileged foreigners (e.g. Xenophon's sons) experienced a Spartan education. But again this did not guarantee citizen rights. Even lower down the class hierarchy a blood tithe was expected too, there were the *neodamodeis* who we first hear of as soldiers under Brasidas fighting in Thrace in 428. Helots recruited to fight as hoplites in a war where Sparta was feeling a manpower strain and emancipated but not enfranchised when the campaign was over. Few of these people had been kept sweet; the Spartans were not great sharers, this would be a problem with her allies soon enough and internally all these groups had a major gripe in common, not being full Spartiates they received little in the way of spoils in a war they had done much to win.

This was the powder keg that ignited the stuff of most Spartiates' nightmares. Strange outcomes at rites performed by the new king Agesilaus were the first signs of trouble afoot, before a snitch alerted the ephors to the details of what was happening. The informer named Cinadon was the instigator of a plot to mobilise a coalition of non-Spartiates to rise up and murder the citizens, kings and officials. The stool pigeon, who Cinadon had tried to recruit, described this brave and charismatic young man gathering potential recruits in the market place. Cinadon had taken him to the edge of the market-place and directed him to count how many Spartiates there were in the market-place. 'And I,' he said, 'after counting king and ephors and senators and about forty others,' asked 'Why, Cinadon, did you bid me count these men?' And he replied: 'Believe,' said he, 'that these men are your enemies, and that all the others who are in the market-place, more than four thousand in number, are your allies.'[7]

In fact the plot had not spread very widely as yet but everybody knew that the potential constituency for such talk was huge. Beyond the *perioeci*, the freed men and downgraded Spartiates any such call was bound to resonate with the helots; public slaves who could only be manumitted by an act of the government, so largely lacked even that desperate hope of most down trodden ancient un-free, that a beneficent master might liberate them.

The knowledge of being outnumbered by those they exploited and who hated them was the whole *raison d'être* for the Spartan security state so the terrified ephors did not hesitate to act. They called out an action committee, described as the 'little assembly', selected from the *Gerousia*, and they put a plan in train to get the troublemaker out of town and separate him from his followers. Cinadon was sent on a mission to Aulon in Messenia on the Elean frontier. It would not have seemed strange; he had done such work for the ephors before. His instructions were to arrest some locals, but unknown to him the six or seven young soldiers made available by the guard commander to go with him were specially picked, and knew it was their leader who had to be apprehended. To make quite sure, the ephors also sent a cavalry detachment to follow and ensure the ploy was not botched. These swift riders arrested Cinadon when they overtook him and, after they wrung the names of his fellow conspirators out of him, hurried back to the ephors with their information. They arrested all those named, including a prophet called Tisamenus, and he and Cinadon and most probably others named under torture were tried, condemned and brutally scourged round the streets of town until they expired. No effort was left undone to ensure the servile population saw what happened to those who might have contemplated revolution.

This was far from the first example of Spartiates not singing from the same hymn sheet, it had happened before. Those who had experienced the humiliation of capture by the Athenians at Sphacteria in 425 became a significant dissenting group when the peace of Nicias allowed their release. They pushed for an immediate war of revenge hoping to regain their lost honour on a new battlefield and by doing so clashed with compatriots who had not experienced the same disgrace and, at least for a time, were tired of conflict. But these had been differences between peers, now what threatened was altogether different, essentially domestic contention based around class lines that had been heightened during the stresses of the Athenian war. The state was endangered by men who had known better times but dropped down the social scale, people dangerous in every age. And the cry of the chief agitator when asked why he aimed at revolution 'to be equal to the best in Sparta' is again so typical of people recently excluded. These men actually wanted in, not to destroy the state but as so often, short term thinking on the part of the haves turned these have nots into enemies of the state rather than soldiers for the cause.

This was Imperial Sparta, ever fearful of her helots and unprepared to share much outside her home-grown elite. This miserly state, divided and beginning to suffer from serious structural degeneration, was finding itself with few friends and too many enemies, and faced with real crisis in a world where she had just attained top slot. With her pool of warrior citizens declining and no leadership able to take on a solution to this dilemma she was going to depend more and more on friends that she had failed to value and done little to reward. Circumstances that would mean a future with a weakened Sparta had their attractions for many, not just her perennial rivals. Even some of those who stayed true often did not fight well beside their Spartan comrades and there is a feeling that amongst allies, old and new, there would be those who would see the upside of a Sparta brought low on the battlefield.

Chapter Four

The Hobbling Prince

As for his deformity, the beauty of his person in its youthful prime covered this from sight, while the ease and gaiety with which he bore such a misfortune, being first to jest and joke about himself, went far towards rectifying it. Indeed, his lameness brought his ambition into clearer light, since it led him to decline no hardship and no enterprise whatever[1].

The other king apart from Pausanias who had ganged up on Lysander had been around a long time. Ruling for over twenty years he had been the victor of Mantinea in 418 and it was he who since 413 had hunkered down at the fort of Decelea in the Attic hills and stayed there through the remainder of the war to ensure the Athenians could never enjoy a moment's peace. Agis II, though he had joined his fellow monarch to clip the wings of a high flying commoner, was not a natural partner of Pausanias. His vision of Sparta's role had more of the Greek policeman about it rather than the more cerebral and conventional inclinations of his fellow monarch. The law he wanted to impose was Spartan law and soon after the fall of Athens he was swinging the truncheon again. Though some Spartans might be reticent about getting too involved in the wider world, it was very different when it came to what they considered their own bailiwick. So when Agis took up an old quarrel with Elis, a peninsular neighbour, it was pretty much without dissention from his compatriots.

The slow burning fuse in this conflagration was the little town of Lepreum that had brought out the bile between the people of Elis and Sparta on not a few occasions in the last century. Elis itself had only gained its importance following a synoecism (amalgamation) in the 470s but since that time she had determined on becoming the main dog in this particular backyard. Lepreum, down south towards the border of Messenia, had had trouble with a neighbour and called on Elis for aid. After the intervention had worked out successfully, the Lepreans had agreed to pay tribute to their benefactors. When the Peloponnesian War had begun the Lepreans had appealed to Sparta and they, always concerned about activity near the borders of Messenia, and in order to curtail Elean influence, sent some of the enfranchised helots who had fought so well for Brasidas in the early part of the War to set themselves up as colonists in the area. A move that did not ease relations with the Eleans who if previously members of the Peloponnesian League were not always happy ones. They had even joined up with the Argives in the anti-Spartan alliance that had led to the battle of Mantinea in 418, though her men did not actually fight in the battle, returning home in disgust as they had been refused the chance to attack Lepreum.

There were other wrangles between Elis and Sparta, as often as not around issues at the Olympic Games, held every four years under the aegis of the Eleans. Thucydides tells a story of dirty deeds on the race track from years before, and in the 420 Games, because they had attacked a fort during the Olympic truce, the Spartans were refused permission to compete; and to make it personal, on a later occasion Agis II was denied authorisation to sacrifice at the Great Temple of Zeus, a proscription that he undoubtedly saw as spite rather than procedure. After that, the Eleans showed no sign of paying up the contributions they owed as part of their effort in the war just gone. Why the Spartans took such a hard line on this occasion is difficult to exactly know. Wherever the organs of resentful memory resided, in the headquarters of the kings, the offices of the ephors or the *Gerousia*, payback was always their credo. So after the way Elis had occasionally backslid in the Great War, once she had the chance Sparta was always going to punish this uppity place over the mountains. And apart from past misdemeanours the basic Spartan concern was that Elis and the local league she was constructing in the north west of the peninsula might turn into a threat to her dominance. Also there was an ideological dimension, over the century the political complexion of the ruling elite in Elis had changed; staunch oligarchs at the beginning of the fifth century had gradually morphed into something like democrats. They had even given money to Thrasybulus and his rebels to take on the Thirty. None of this sat happily with the men of power in the Eurotas valley, the Elean League was getting too big and independent. The Spartans undoubtedly felt they had to make an example of somebody to emphasise their imperium, and with the onset of local troubles they took advantage.

Even before this the Spartans had done some local power housekeeping. In 400 they drove out and dispersed to Sicily and Africa a rump of free Messenians who had been resettled for generations in Naupactus on the north shore of the Gulf of Corinth. But they began the main fixture by dispatching an ultimatum that required Elis to give up hegemony over some outlying communities and when this was refused they mobilised an army under King Agis. The Spartans took a northern route marching by way of Achaea and then down the Larisus River into Elis itself. But once over the border and putting a real effort into plundering the fertile countryside, the invaders were brought up short. The earth started moving under their feet as the country was shaken by a major tremor. The Peloponnese is earthquake country. Indeed a concentration of these seismic events had almost certainly contributed decisively to the downfall of the Mycenaeans and the ushering in of a so called 'Dark Age' over half a millennium before. This was a shock significant enough to give pause to seers, kings and commoners alike in this superstitious age and the Spartan leaders, completely unnerved, hurried their army back home. It was the end of the war for that year and the men disbanded. Whether Agis' response was really over angering the gods by attacking the guardians of Olympia, or because from the beginning the intent was just to put a scare into their neighbours is not at all clear. Certainly on this first assay Agis had not gone in full panoply; the Peloponnesian League allies had not been called to the colours, which suggests the intent was limited.

Whatever the king's intentions had been with this reprieve, the Eleans looked to take advantage to try to build a coalition with anybody who they thought ill-disposed to the Spartans. Though it is difficult to believe there were not a few such states around, none were prepared to put their heads above the parapet against the recent victors in the Great War. So it was Elis on its own that faced the next round as Agis had another go. This venture was begun at the close of the year, so a winter campaign, and this time they intended to march with the whole League levy, though, significantly for the future, the Corinthians and Boeotians refused to send their contingents. All the rest acquiesced including the Athenians so it was still a heavyweight force that travelled up by Aulon on the Elean frontier with Messenia. This time they were marching up through the country where the contested towns were situated, and this turned out to be a real advantage. They soon found they had friends in these satellites of Elis. The Lepreans, the Macistians and the Letrinians all revolted and as the Spartans closed in the people from Amphidolia and Margania did the same, places both north and south of the River Alpheus that ran past Olympia. At that place Agis made a point of stopping to finally make the sacrifice to Zeus, before marching on Elis itself.

This was famously rich country and the plunder they were garnering tickled the cupidity of neighbouring Arcadians and Achaeans who joined the party as volunteers to swell the invaders' ranks. 'In fact this campaign proved to be a harvest, as it were, for Peloponnesus.'[2] The suburbs were stripped but Agis did not attack Elis itself, aware as he was that recent developments in the town might drop the place into his lap with no effort at all. There was an oligarchic plutocrat in the place called Xenias who hoped for much from a Spartan takeover and he tried the crudest of coups. With swords unsheathed he and his confederates hunted out the democratic leadership intending to cut them down. But an adrenalin overload warped their judgment and almost unbelievably they killed a man who looked a bit like their main opponent Thrasydaeus, and having done this got down to celebrating. In fact the man himself had been sleeping off a hangover, and when he found out what was happening he led his followers, who had gathered at his house to find out if he was dead or not, to drive out the oligarchs who in double quick time found their fortunes changed from putative rulers to exiles begging succour at the camp of the Spartans outside. With this incompetent revolutionary now a busted flush, Agis decided against an all out attack but still his reaction was determined and uncompromising. While he slipped back over Alpheus River he left a good number of men under an officer called Lysippus backed up by the local exiles at Epitalium, to keep the Eleans in check. They kept the country in uproar for the rest of the summer and winter to such an extent that the government of Thrasydaeus were persuaded they had to treat. Envoys trudged to Sparta offering much of what had been asked before. Elean forts at Phea and Cyllene would be broken down, and they offered to release their hold on the Triphylian cities of Phrixa and Epitalium, as well as on the Letrinians, the Amphidolians and the Marganians. They let go Acroria, Lasion (the Arcadians claimed this place) and Epeum.

This story of peninsular bullying would seem clear enough except that once again there is real confusion between the sources. Diodorus has the whole campaign conducted by King Pausanias, and while the siege is also indecisive it is not because of the failure of a coup but that the Spartans are driven back by the Eleans with the aid of, amongst others, 1,000 Aetolians. In both cases a frustrated king takes out his bile by ravaging the country around. This is all too similar to be describing two separate events: much more probable is confusion about which king took the lead in the punitive expedition. Whether our informants push Pausanias or Agis as the most likely participant they are pretty much agreed on the shape of the campaign and when everything is considered the upshot is not in dispute: the Eleans just could not face their powerful tormentors and had to accept the same curtailment of their local power as had been demanded in the first place. Most likely they also gave up the majority of their small navy and had to allow Sparta access to important ports on their west coast that had been the scene of some fighting. The Eleans kept their overall supervision of the Olympics but the sight of Spartans swaggering in to sacrifice at the Temple of Zeus left no doubt as to where the real power lay. The chronology of all this is rather fuliginous, though it is probable the campaigning began sometime in 402 and was certainly over by the time of the Olympic Games in the year 400. But whatever the timeframe what is not in doubt is the impact it had amongst the rest of the Greeks. If the Spartans could treat a people who had been a long-time, if occasionally wayward ally in such a manner, perhaps the rest of them ought to start looking to how to safeguard their interests in a world where a rampant Sparta occupied 'The Chair' at the power table.[3]

Accepting that Agis is the right king, this campaign in fact would be virtually the last act of this old warrior. He had reigned almost thirty years. A trip to Delphi to dedicate a tithe of campaign spoils to the gods may have improved his spiritual condition but it did nothing for his physical. He arrived back at Sparta in an ambulance and was soon a candidate for the undertakers who apparently did him proud. Every citizen household was forced to provide the traditional two mourners, and thousands of others were drafted in from the country to accompany the cortege to the Eurypontid burial ground outside town.[4] Though if his departure was spectacular it left those behind with a succession crisis of some complexity. There are no completely satisfactory narratives of how the Spartan state functioned in matters of disputed kingship, and though when Agis II died we know the who and the why of the participants, the exact mechanism of decision is opaque. There was a son and heir called Leotychidas but the ongoing speculation over his actual progenitor meant his accession was not likely to be unchallenged. And once it became clear that it would be a contest, not a coronation, Agis II's half brother Agesilaus, the obvious alternative, did not wait placidly while matters were decided. He mobilised to push his case as hard as possible and Lysander we learn was behind his candidature and badmouthing his rival. Though it is not necessary to believe his spreading of the rumour of illegitimacy, it was hardly required: the prince's mother was unashamed about the father being Alcibiades. The affair had been the talk of every gossip shop for years despite Agis II signing up on Leotychidas' legitimacy at the very end of his life.

Amongst the ephors and the *Gerousia*, Lysander and his protégé had the pull, an influence they had long played for, a credibility that must have made a difference to Agesilaus' eventual success. Clientism was always a factor, not perhaps the institutional kind familiar from ancient Rome, but still it would have mattered in Sparta too. People are mentioned swarming around Agesilaus in Sparta when he leaves his house to go for a swim, in a manner not so different from the crowds attending on the doors of consuls and senators in the city on the Tiber. The network began with the family, and we see it when Agesilaus raised his half brother Teleutias and his brother in law Peisander to high command, but it went well beyond it. Rich men might sponsor another's mess bills or arrange advantageous marriages and in return expect a shout for his friends at the assembly, in *Gerousia* elections, and support in other policy decisions that might come before them.

Most members of the *Gerousia* probably had some sort of client base. Most were well off: human social arrangements are seldom absolute and though equality was a key part of Lycurgus' ideals, Spartiates were far from being equals. There was a minimum property qualification, but it is certain from the start that there were richer and poorer amongst them. Even at the original, quasi legendary, division of the land into lots, the rich and powerful probably got the biggest share, and as time went on wealth went to wealth and land to land. And the *Gerousia*, filled as it was by acclamation, apart from those with exceptional reputation, it is likely it was men with wealth who could pull strings and financially sponsor less well off compatriots that were favoured. These 28 old men, sitting with the kings, could set the pattern of state activity and it was probably here as much as anywhere that politics played out, factions developed and kings tried to find firm support. It was its permanence that was the key, and that it controlled the agenda of an assembly that had only the power to approve or disapprove the proposals put before it.

The five ephors were critical too. They called the assembly and one of them chaired it. They had access to patronage overseeing the *agoge*, and choosing candidates for the elite guard unit called the *Hippeis*. In charge of the treasury, taxes and tribute crucially they were in a position to restrain the most powerful of monarchs. They supervised a once in eight years bout of star gazing that might get rid of a king for no reason, and were empowered to take royalty to the bar on capital charges if they did anything they did not like. They not infrequently accompanied the monarchs on campaign acting as a major curb on the commander in chief's independence. But their Achilles heel was their tenure: it only lasted one year and in general ephors were allowed to hold office only once. There was no wealth qualification to be one of the five ephors, except the wherewithal to pay your way in the mess, though, as with the *Gerousia*, being elected by the assembly meant no doubt money talked much of the time. Even so it is attested that the very poorest of full Spartiates might get the nod and Aristotle makes a point of grumbling that this often made them eminently bribeable.

It was imperative for a candidate for the throne to win support amongst all these key players, and Agesilaus, prior to his accession, had always shown himself eager to get on the good side of the establishment giving ephors and elders presents and going out of his way to be courteous and amenable when they visited him. But in the end it seems probable it was the clout of Lysander that made the difference that swung the votes and swayed those who might have vetoed the decision in favour of Agesilaus. It might have seemed from his 'king-of-the-world' moment after Aegospotami and the fall of Athens that things had gone sour for Lysander – not long before first Athens was liberated and the system of tens and harmosts he had implanted elsewhere were to a large decree broken up by his own compatriots, and he had suffered when he found both kings Agis and Pausanias in cahoots against him. But this monarchical teamwork was always going to be unsound, the kings tended to be rivals, heading opposing groupings, far more than cooperating with each other. So it is little surprise that very soon normal service was resumed and Agis was found voting in court to condemn Pausanias for having not suppressed the democrats at Athens. And though it was probably soon after the court case that Lysander found Sparta too hot and took himself off on a diplomatic mission to Syracuse, consensus between the kings was shattered which would be bound to allow Lysander's re-emergence as a major player.

His prestige as the man who had won the war against Athens and the power of patronage gained in those successful years of campaigning meant that to oppose his protégé would have been difficult. Indeed as 'the state chose Agesilaus king' Lysander's intervention is the last event described. But still the constitutional clues are exiguous and we do not hear if a full assembly or the *Gerousia* met to ratify the choice or if the ephors had the final say. However at this key moment Lysander had the clout pushing a contender who had long been an associate, even a lover in the days of their youth, and whose thinking on much of state policy was compatible. How important each ones contribution was in relation to the other is not knowable but what is not in dispute is that this heavyweight pairing had been hand in glove in taking the lead to ensure the candidature of the hobbling prince. Interestingly after gaining the throne and getting control of the estates of Agis, now Leotychidas was disinherited, he gave half the land to his mother's family, who, though of the best lineage, had fallen on hard times. A popular move, emphasising that already there were many poor Spartiates who might like to see such largesse go to people in their own condition. And it might suggest Agesilaus had received backing from the increasing number of those Spartans who hovered on the brink of failing to fund their attendance at a military mess, a step absolutely necessary to gain the privileges of full citizenship.

What is sure in these years between emerging from his teens and when he came to the throne is that he would have aimed at amassing a personal following. It was a time when any high status Spartans began to gather round themselves friends and supporters who might have started as boyhood friends or lovers but in later life could be of crucial political significance. And this was even more the case when there was an heir apparent tainted by illegitimacy, making it likely many ambitious young Spartans would be inclined to pin their colours to Agesilaus' mast, hoping their stars might rise with his. Indeed the standing and support this prince managed to achieve was sufficiently noteworthy for us to hear of the ephors trying to bring him down a peg or two just because of the popularity he was gaining in so many quarters.

This meant that in 400 BC at over the age of forty a Spartan king began a reign that would last a very long time. If Lysander had loomed large over the years around the turn of the fifth to fourth centuries, when he came to the throne this new man was to be part of the power furniture for almost the next forty more. There is little good evidence to reconstruct Agesilaus' youth yet something can be essayed. As the younger son of king Archidamus II he was not slated to ascend the throne so, unlike such a designated heir, he went through the traditional Spartan military education, the *agoge*. Indeed it is suggested this gave him a real pull with his contemporaries who had also experienced that gruelling preparation; a shared experience he could not have claimed if he had been raised as a king in waiting. The *agoge* was the distinctive schooling endured by all Spartiates only after which could they become full citizens of the state with all the rights and responsibilities entailed. During the years of this training Agesilaus and his class mates, between the ages of seven and nineteen, left their families to live in barracks and experienced a regime of instruction meant to turn them into hardened, skilled, fearless and disciplined warriors. Grouped into herds (*agelai*) they were ruled and guided by a boy hardly older than themselves and underwent a kind of specifically designed '*Lord of the Flies*' experience. They would have wandered the wooded hills north towards Sellasia, where Pausanias, centuries later, describes the continuous darkness under the canopy of oaks at nearby Skotitas, or west to penetrate the extraordinary wall of the Taÿgetus Mountains that rose so stark in the west of the Eurotas River valley or over the Parnon range to the east or south towards Gythium. In just the barest covering, even in winter, after the age of twelve all they were given for protection was a threadbare red cloak. The youngsters had to steal to survive, perpetuating a code of behaviour that continued into manhood when few of them seemed to be able to keep their fingers off the precious goods of those who came into their charge. Either with his cohorts or alone Agesilaus learned to scavenge to supplement a meagre diet and to rough up the local helots in the kind of routine terrorism that the Spartan state saw as vital to keeping its subjects cowed.

Living together engendered extraordinary loyalty to mess mates and sleeping in the open with river reeds for their beds. Always hungry, they learned the skills of foraging, fishing and hunting small wild animals like deer and hares, so qualities of resourcefulness, perseverance and endurance were built. A bare knuckle boy scoutism of tramping hills and drinking the cool water of mountain streams was vigorous outdoor stuff and it lasted without cessation for years and, while Laconia could be beautiful and fertile in spring and summer, in winter it was cold and hard. This training camp for young Spartan manhood might even involve encounters with wild boars and wolves but it had to be endured despite the hardship and dangers. Loitering around the stalls in the market place looking to steal a sweetmeat or even taking the remains of sacrifices from temples may have honed useful skills and made life a bit more worthwhile but if they were caught the punishments were savage. Perhaps there was a little compensation in that the whippings they received were for getting caught; there is no suggestion of any guilt needing to be felt for either the ethics or the victim of this culturally sponsored criminality. The unpleasantness of some of what these children and young men went through must be contextualised by the knowledge that a child's life in most other parts of Greece was not so wonderful either. Child mortality in all pre modern societies was high, making great investment in an individual child neither emotionally or financially profitable. Childcare was pretty slapdash even in better off households and survival very much a matter of luck, though no doubt the lack of adult supervision was not unappreciated by many of the more adventurous and independent souls. A few toys, companionship of their peers was probably a good enough start for many and for males the big change at about seven was when they were taken out of the world of women and the home. But if this severance occurred in most Greek societies it was particularly stark in the upbringing of a Spartan male.

Apart from becoming inured to the sort of hardship that their future life of constant warfare would entail, weapon training and other martial arts was their life; their shields, spears and short swords all adored objects. Not just weapons but symbols of their warrior status and from their earliest years they learned their lifework was to kill. Mock battles with savagery imbued were part of the training that nicely compare to the ancient, kicking, gouging and biting ball games of the early English Public Schools. Though there was a limit; we are told a boy called Drakontios was exiled for killing a playmate during his *agoge* years. Of their intellectual development little is known; certainly most learned reading and writing as part of barracks life. But what else was inculcated about their lands and culture we just don't know. History must have been taught, and no doubt family lore and the triumphs of the state in arms, to inculcate patriotism. Apart from Homer, it is improbable that they were exposed extensively to the drama, the poetry or the philosophy we think of when considering ancient Greek culture. However there was masked ritual and comic drama of sorts, and songs were learned, but mainly as military anthems and marching aids, for, as they were fond of pointing out to the Athenians, they 'were making a great mistake in wasting their energies on amusements, that is to say, in lavishing on the theatre what would pay for great fleets and would support armies in the field.'[5] Not that of course this would have been everything. Spartans were after all Greeks, and when older the more privileged would have been aware of the theatre. Indeed it is claimed that this is what saved Athens from obliteration after its surrender in 404.

When they reached eighteen the very best of the graduates took a stint in the gruesome *Crypteia*. These young men formed death squads who slipped out in the hours of darkness and circled the rural villages looking to cut the throats of any helots they found wandering out alone: homicides authorised by the ephors who annually declared war on these subject peoples. Plato claims the *Crypteia* as a kind of endurance test with no murder attendant but this brutal class bullying to keep their serfs in their place is otherwise very well attested though whether Agesilaus had any part in it is inconclusive.

Agesilaus before all this had survived a difficult inspection as a baby. Despite being lame in one foot he was not exposed as was generally demanded. One suspects this was a very minor disability well compensated for by the fact of his royal birth; or perhaps his survival shows that already Sparta was suffering a severe manpower shortage, so a disability if not debilitative could be overlooked; or even that it was just humanity, and a family with royal prerogative might ensure that the rules would not be perhaps as rigorously adhered to for their own offspring. In the *agoge* he dissipated any disadvantage this might have brought by being the first to laugh at himself and his disability made him only more eager to excel. He was otherwise reported as a beautiful child, though of quite small stature. His father was fined by the ephors for marrying a small woman – they took breeding seriously in old Sparta. Like most of his ilk he was hugely competitive, but he reportedly combined this with charm and an easy going manner. He was loyal to his friends whatever the circumstances even 'sharing in their misdeeds'. The contests, running, wrestling, javelin throwing and other games that were meant to prepare them for the hardships of war were eagerly participated in by the young Agesilaus. A distinctive feature of all of these activities was they took place on foot. There were few horses for these young aristocrats and princelings, such as would have been the case in Athens and most other Hellene communities. For Spartans it was the length of a man's stride by which they judged distance not the rate horseflesh could travel at. Agesilaus and his peers were being trained as heavy phalanx infantry not cavalry, though the *Hippeis*, the name of the elite unit that would guard the king in battle, certainly harks back to some ancient pre-Lycurgan tradition when an old riding aristocracy ruled the roost.

The kind of childhood Agesilaus experienced in the *agoge*, like the English Public Schools that so admired them, tends to produce conformists rather than experimental thinkers but on occasion the stresses of that kind of environment could create eccentrics of altogether more interesting kinds. Agesilaus was comparatively unusual in his ambition and energy and retained it into very old age; yet the experience undoubtedly made him as deeply conservative as most of his peers. At twenty, like his age group, Agesilaus joined the main body of the Spartan army and gained acceptance at a public mess of about fifteen men, though it is possible a royal mess existed that the young Agesilaus would have joined, sitting with the likes of his half brother Agis II. On reaching thirty Agesilaus would have begun to attend the assembly, not to speak, as to do so would have been very un-laconic, but he would have heard orators, the ephors or ambassadors from other states, and have voted at the end of the debate. Full Spartiates had a voice but only one that could say yes or no; the agenda was the province of others, members of the *Gerousia*, ephors and kings.

Though we do not hear of the king-to-be's army experience, he must have had a considerable amount as when he steps out onto the pages of history it is clearly as a veteran. Those handbooks for generals from the ancient world are full of examples of his military exploits. He never seems to have been much of a naval man though, and always delegated command at sea to others, so it is reasonable to assume he did not take part in the great maritime operations in the latter years of the Peloponnesian War. He surely marched with King Agis on his invasions of Attica and did a stint on duty at the fort of Decelea. His formative years saw the early campaigns of the Peloponnesian War and it might have been expected he would have developed a malevolence towards the people who had humiliated his people at Sphacteria and tried to raise the helots and other subject peoples against their Spartan masters. Whatever his personal feelings, Agesilaus actually spent most of his life fighting not Athenians but Persians and Thebans, both of whom had been largely his country's friends in the great internecine Greek war.

In the greater Greek and Aegean world Agesilaus was about to enter as king, there had been two men left holding the prizes after the dust of the great Greek war had settled, and both of them had major ambitions beyond just seeing off the power of Athens. Lysander wanted to set in stone his power and influence, to exploit the new Empire he had won with the network of powerful locals he had already built up around the Aegean. The other man was Cyrus: his father, King Darius II of Persia, was on the way out and though his elder brother Arsaces was the heir, Cyrus had other ideas. Ambition gnawed at the young man's bosom as was only going to be likely in this product of a pushy parent; his mother had sweated, wormed and done anything to ensure her Cyrus got pushed to the front of the dynastic queue, despite the fact that the heir was her son too.

When Cyrus first came west to Anatolia in 407 at only sixteen years old he had been given authority over the whole region, Cappadocia as well as Phrygia and Lydia, with instructions that after crushing the hill folk of Pisidia and the Mysians he was to reassert dominance over the Asian Greek cities that the Athenians then controlled. Any dallying with a divide and rule policy between Athens and Sparta was to be ditched and the whole might of Persian influence brought to bear against the occupiers. There is little doubt the young prince saw benefit for himself in this arrangement. Cyrus, from the beginning, wanted Sparta as a committed friend for when he might make his play for the imperial throne and this almost certainly explains his supporting the Spartans so unequivocally from the first. He was aware that a Sparta wanting a piece of Greek Anatolia might be a Sparta that was prepared to pay for it by supporting him against the Great King.

The Asian Greek cities had, for the most part, long been components of the Athenian empire, but in the years running up to and after the defeat of that city they had fallen under Spartan sway. Lysander had foisted on them the councils of Ten, local oligarchs and Spartan harmosts, but when these disagreeable tyrants were got rid of it was only to become once again tribute payers in the Persian state, though with the compensation that they could generally chose their own leadership as long as this did not actually affront their Persian masters. Arsaces, once he had established himself on the throne as Artaxerxes II, sent Cyrus, who had returned for the enthronement process, back west. It was not with complete comfort he let his little brother out of his sight and he put a hold on a good part of his funds by entrusting control of the revenues of the Greek cities to the local satrap and setting up an officer called Orontes as independent commander at the citadel of Sardis. Cyrus' nose was not unsurprisingly put out of joint when he realised much of his potential income was to be withheld. Without it he was bound to find it difficult to do all a mighty Achaemenid prince should. Palaces, bureaucracy, retainers, mercenary forces, courts at Sardis and Celaenae, all would be hard to fund without the gold of the Asian Greeks. But fortunately for the young Prince, governmental *diktat* could be shaky so far from the Imperial centre, and the reality was that he was actually able to access most of the key economic resources in his bailiwick.

With these means Cyrus pressed his plans to replace his older brother, gathering an army with a hard core of Greek heavy infantry. He contacted Clearchus, the veteran Spartan ex-governor of Byzantium, who led a mercenary band in the Chersonese, engaging him ostensibly to fight the Thracians but really to be on the books when the prince made his move. In Thessaly and mainland Greece his recruiting sergeants were active too, claiming it was all in the cause of harrying the turbulent Pisidians. When the royal rebel finally threw off the mask and made his move he was lucky in his timing if in nothing else, as an Egyptian revolt had flared up to entangle the Great King's resources, a liberation movement that in fact would not be fully suppressed for sixty years. So in good heart Cyrus and his army, including 13,000-odd Greek mercenaries, marched east in a bid to take his brother's throne from him. But despite a kind of victory at Cunaxa in Babylonia in 401, the death of the insurgent prince in the battle called a halt to the endeavour, a throw of the dice that not only removed a considerable player from the table, but also kicked off the great trek of the 10,000 made famous by Xenophon's firsthand account in the *Anabasis*.

But while Lysander and Cyrus had been the big picture, two Persians, Tissaphernes and Pharnabazus, had provided a deeper regional context in Asia Minor and would continue to do so for some time to come. Tissaphernes had been a power there since at least 415 when he won a great name for the suppression of one Pissuthnes, the ruler of Lydia who had hired some Greeks under an Athenian general called Lycon to set up against the Great King as his own man. Tissaphernes acted quickly, subverted these mercenaries at the price of a few towns for Lycon and his men to retire to, arrested the rebel and took him back to face death at the hands of his king. Though an illegitimate son of Pissuthnes called Amorges did maintain himself in Iasus for some time in face of the satrap's power. Indeed it was probably dalliance with this man by Athens that was one of the factors that persuaded the Persians initially that it might be in their interest to support the Spartan side in the Peloponnesian War.

Tissaphernes had acted as Cyrus' adviser when he had first come to Anatolia. It was not perhaps an easy cooperation though the relationship was still sufficiently tight for him to accompany the party, probably in 405, when Cyrus was called back to court. Back at the centre, where they stayed until the old king died, they were both embroiled in a bitter rivalry between two great queens. One was Darius II's wife, Parysatis, the mother of both the heir to the throne Arsaces and Cyrus. Parysatis hated the wife of Arsaces, called Stateira, leading her to favour the younger son who also had the extra *kudos* of having been born when his father was actually on the throne. The poison between the two women had been put down when members of Stateira's family revolted against the throne. The rebel was her kin, Terituchmes, who was a scion of one of the finest aristocratic houses – an ancestor was one of the famed seven who had killed Darius I's rival and so established that Great King on the throne in 522. But blue blood has never been a bar to degeneracy; Terituchmes was married to Darius II's daughter Amestris but lusted after his own half sister Roxana and to further the affair had his wife murdered and led 300 followers in a rebellion, each of whom committed themselves irreparably to the cause by stabbing her while she was restrained in a sack. The putsch came to nothing and the queen Parysatis took vengeance for her daughter by wiping out the whole family apart from the wife of her son, the heir Arsaces, and also Tissaphernes, another relative whose previous services to the throne in Anatolia saved him.

These two queens were still in play when early in 404 Darius II died and Arsaces came into the kingdom with the throne name of Artaxerxes II and with him his queen who had escaped Parysatis' wrath. Poisonous dealings between queen mother and queen incumbent in the seraglio are the meat and drink of politics in such places but this was something different. In the years to come Parysatis would both engineer the poisoning of Stateira herself and though suffering temporary banishment for it, by 395 would make a comeback that would allow her to eventually put an end to Tissaphernes as well. But that was later, and now Cyrus and Tissaphernes, still in tandem, went west once more. If there had been any chance of smooth cooperation between the two men designated to administer the area it was lost when Cyrus found in his orders that his brother had determined that the tribute from the cities should be given not to him but to Tissaphernes instead. Actually when it came to it most of the Greek oligarchs still widely in control preferred Cyrus, Lysander's old friend, to Tissaphernes who they thought would favour their democratic rivals. So they revolted and placed themselves under the protection of the prince. Only the city of Miletus stayed loyal to the satrap because he had arranged the elimination of the leading oligarchs there, though expelled exiles who survived the cull found Cyrus a willing sponsor who armed them up and sent them back to retake it. So the Asian Greeks soon enough found themselves something of a battlefield between Cyrus and Tissaphernes, warfare by proxy between satrap and prince. Between these two it was conflict from then on and it is no surprise when Cyrus pulled the veil from his intention to dispute the throne with his brother. Tissaphernes fled east down the royal road to warn the Great King and assist in the preparations for resistance to the rebels' advance.

Tissaphernes has had rather a bad press as the man who dallied in a two faced manner with both Alcibiades and various Spartans. Though this was a consistent policy – that the Persians should let neither of the sides win completely but continue to weaken each other in everlasting warfare – he found it overturned with the advent of Cyrus. More opprobrium is heaped after he commanded the left division of Artaxerxes' royal army at Cunaxa where his men suffered first hand from the charge of the Greek brazen hoplites. It was he who tricked these Greeks when they floundered in the heart of Babylonia, manufacturing divisions between their generals and leading them by the nose north before killing their leaders at a conference he had invited them to under a truce. After this he chased the 10,000 out of the lowlands and into the mountains and if they eventually survived it was against all his endeavours. He was well rewarded for seeing off the troublemakers: the government of Western Asia Minor was returned to him and a wife provided from the royal family itself.

Persia had been a major gainer by the ruin of Athenian power. The rich Anatolian provinces with their great Greek cities, as well as local tribes and landowning barons, were now expected to produce the tribute to keep the court accountants at Susa happy. But along the coast the population and landholding context was complex. The Greeks who had dominated for centuries had been punished after the Ionian revolt at the end of the sixth century; Miletus, for instance, lost lots of land (*chora*) to both Carian and Persian colonists in that vengeful time. Administratively the area was complicated as well; three chancery languages Lycian, Greek and Aramaic were used at the city of Xanthus in the south. We know local leagues existed, from Ionian Greeks to native peoples like the Carians, but if once centres of resistance, they were now kept for the administrative convenience of their Iranian rulers. It was Tissaphernes who stood once again at the apex of local power in this western march of the Great Empire of Persia.

Pharnabazus was the other key local power player. A descendant of one of Darius I's highest officials, he had taken up the reins of power in 413 or 414 in Hellespontine Phrygia, a fiefdom his family had run for ninety-odd years. If he was perhaps not such an important man as Tissaphernes he would remain significant both in Asia Minor and in other parts of the Persian Empire for a longer time. Like Tissaphernes he had played a considerable part in the concluding years of the great Greek War and in 404 had also brought to an end the life of the extraordinary man Alcibiades. The Athenian was on his way to the Persian court to warn Artaxerxes of the revolutionary intrigues of his brother that were common knowledge even as far as the Chersonese where he was holed up. Pharnabazus, hearing of his intention, arranged his murder on the road, aiming to get the credit for bringing the timely warning to the king. In the Cyrus war itself nothing is heard of Pharnabazus but when the remnant of the 10,000 entered his province he was still very much the man in charge around the Hellespont and remained so even when Tissaphernes returned to Asia Minor. Their exact relationship is unclear but it looks like Tissaphernes had some sort of supervisory standing, so the man who had so recently fled the region with his tail between his legs now claimed a form of authority which could not have pleased the man whose family had been boss hog in the Hellespontine region for almost a century. Rivalry between local bigwigs was far from unusual in the story of the Persian empire, indeed in a sense it was a method of government, ensuring no provincial governor got too big for his boots however glorious their lineage. Cyrus was the exemplar of this over mighty subject and his was a warning that was heeded, it is no coincidence that in a few years the Persians set up a local dynasty, the Hecatomnids, whose most famous member was Mausolus, in power in Caria, however ambitious such foreign folk were they could never actually hope to make a bid for the Persian throne itself. These regional entities with their satraps with almost vice regal powers were far from being necessarily hereditary but it was not unusual for great families to become settled and attached to a particular region. Though in some senses the Persians were aliens in Asia Minor they had been there for a very long time and freely intermarried with their subjects and Tissaphernes and Pharnabazus in cooperation or contention would be the context in which a new war was about to be detonated.

With the imminent return of Tissaphernes in 400 few of the Greek cities of the Eastern Aegean had any illusions about what was coming to them. These communities by the sea knew they could expect summary punishment for their involvement in what the dead Cyrus had done. They had backed the prince against Tissaphernes even before he had openly rebelled. This would have been enough to poison the satrap's attitude, but now he was returning charged with the Great King's remit to punish those who had supported his brother. Their tribute had gone towards paying for the army he led into Babylonia and their citizens had provided at least some of the soldiers that gave Artaxerxes such a scare at Cunaxa. So if for the Persian Empire the death of Cyrus was central, for the Greeks it mattered too. Tissaphernes, who took 'over all the satrapies which bordered on the sea,' would no doubt consider them a mob of rebels, and the men who had placed faith in the young prince Cyrus could not have looked forward to anything except pain and plenty of it. Whether they were Greek cities or local Persian officials, they approached the returning governor in trepidation and waited with sweating brows to learn what his verdict would be. Not all just sat and waited for his judgment; some of the Greeks, hoping to avoid having to make a grovelling arrangement with the returning power, defended their walls. But to do so they needed friends, so playing the helpless card they sent to Sparta with pleas to save them from being 'laid waste by the barbarians'. The Spartans feeling themselves a power in the region took it upon themselves to warn the representatives of the Great King, the very people who had paid to put them in the power seat, not to give their fellow Hellenes a bad time. But this posturing had no impact and hardly had Tissaphernes arrived when he led an assault on the city of the Cyme. Only the onset of winter stopped him from taking it, and even despite the weather he ravaged the open country and captured plenty of locals who he ransomed back at very high prices.

The return of Tissaphernes ignited a tinder box in Anatolia. It turned out that with Athens gone, Sparta was about to be sucked in to replace her as defender of Greek Asia. Fear by the Asian Greeks of receiving their just deserts for involvement in Cyrus' treasonous adventure sparked off what was to be the middle of the three Greco-Persian wars of ancient times. The first was the one recorded by Herodotus that included the battles of Marathon, Artemisium, Salamis and Plataea and the last was when Alexander the Great of Macedon ended the diarchy of Hellene and Achaemenid by the demolition of the Persian Empire. But the one in the middle, if it lacked perhaps the drama and glamour of the other two, did see the emergence of a man who would be a virtual ever-present in the years we are considering.

The start of the conflict had roughly coincided with Agesilaus' accession but his direct involvement only commenced after some years when news arrived that the Great King Artaxerxes was preparing to attack on land and sea, racheting up a rumbling war that had been going for some time. The involvement of a Spartan king in this enterprise was warranted by a threat gestated when Pharnabazus had convinced his ruler that a major naval campaign in the Aegean would be in the empire's interest. And he had a man in mind to lead the effort to counter Spartan sea power, uncontested since the fall of Athens: Conon, the refugee from Goat River, who had been enjoying for some years the hospitality of Evagoras, the king of Salamis in Cyprus. The news of this menace filtered through to the men in charge at Sparta in 397 by the agency of Herodas, the Syracusan, a merchant trading in the ports of Phoenicia who had heard talk of the Persian plans. A major response was deemed appropriate and Peloponnesian League delegates were convened to ensure everybody was behind the strategy. Lysander, for his part, supported the initiative and orchestrated appeals to Sparta from his friends in Asia, and when the expedition was decided upon, involved himself from the start. It is even suggested that Agesilaus was pushed in the direction of a campaign in Asia as a *quid pro quo* for Lysander putting the crown on his head.[6] But if that man was pressing, it was on an open door: Agesilaus' career shows from the beginning he was not just of a martial bent but enthusiastically bellicose. On this occasion he only demanded thirty Spartiates go with him as an officer council, plus 2,000 enfranchised helot hoplites and 6,000 allies as his expeditionary force.

The invasion force was gathered at Gerastus at the southern tip of Euboea in spring 396 where we hear Agesilaus dreamed of Agamemnon at Aulis sacrificing his daughter to gain fair winds for the journey to Troy. But when he tried to ape the ceremony, with a deer not a daughter, taking the paraphernalia on only one trireme to the mainland while his seers were setting up, all were interrupted by magistrates from Boeotia. Backed by armed men they upset the plans of a superstitious monarch who never really forgave them ever after for this slap in the face in what he saw then as the defining enterprise of his life. Not absolutely believable stuff and possibly contrived to give a context to the king's future antipathy towards the Thebans, though it is certainly mentioned by all the sources. Whether in his rage he pondered more rational worries that in leaving a bristling and contentious Boeotia in his rear there might be real danger for his country, is not clear. Anyway this crossing of the Aegean was not kicking anything off, the Asian War had been a well trodden path for some years; Agesilaus was only the latest on a list of those who had been meddling in Persian Anatolia.

Back in the winter of 400/399 a Spartan commander named Thibron had been sent with an expeditionary force to defend the Greek cities against Tissaphernes. Spartan hopes had been enhanced by a swiftly concocted alliance with Egypt, a province that had recently thrown out the Persians and declared independence under the pharaoh Amyrtaeus. The new Spartan supremo in Asia Minor had been dispatched with an army of 1,000 emancipated helots armed as hoplites and 4,000 Peloponnesian troops. It is noted that he travelled to Corinth to summon his allies to join him. 300 Athenian cavalry amongst others responded with the blessing of the reconstituted democratic home government who were only too keen to be rid of these potentially subversive blue bloods. This taskforce had shipped over to Ephesus on an uncontested Spartan sea and while based there 2,000 soldiers raised from local Greek Asian municipalities joined them. Thibron, though he now headed a strong force of over 7,000, still had a very puny mounted arm and was so anxious about the Persian cavalry that he initially remained inactive, encamped up in the hills, unprepared to drop down into flatter country where the enemy horsemen were at their most effective.

What got the Spartans going seems to have been the arrival in camp of some veterans whose career over the last few years had been a great story for contemporaries and has continued to be so down through the centuries. They were the remnant of the 10,000 who had enlisted under the banner of Cyrus, the Persian pretender, professional fighters who had cut a swath of destruction through the heart of the Persian Empire before turning back through Anatolia on their extraordinary journey back home. Their military achievement against all the greatest empire in the world could throw at them already had a considerable impact on the minds of contemporary Hellenes and the impression would be even greater for generations to come. Now these fearsome warriors would merge into the story of this war that soon involved a king whose campaigns in Anatolia in the 390s reinforced the impression that good Greek infantry could see off effete Persian hoards and their degenerate leaders almost at will, a pleasing truism fostered by the likes of Isocrates that would eventually help to gestate the great Macedonian project of Philip II and Alexander the Great. These would echo too Agesilaus' claim that his was an Asian Crusade to revenge the Persian invasion of Greece in 480. The actual *Anabasis* reported by Xenophon though is no part of our account. Not until the time the rump of Cyrus' mercenaries come out of the mist of 'Amazonia, out of the lands of tower dwellers and head-hunters' do they take on significance here. Halfway between Heraclea and Byzantium at Calpe Harbour however they begin to impinge on characters who had played a bustling part on the Aegean stage for some time. At this moment, in a place that Xenophon lords as perfect to found a city to settle his caravan of freebooters, Pharnabazus takes notice of them to the extent of joining with local Bithynians to attempt to harass them out of the country. They only had sufficient forces to snipe at the edges of the 10,000, despite these veterans being clearly reduced by what they had been through. They were still a potent force, and when they materialised near the grain routes around the Bosporus, out of control with unknown intentions, both local potentates and more distant powers could not help but sit up and take notice.

Their arrival certainly stirred things up in Byzantium, upsetting the local Spartan agent, who not only worried about them kicking up trouble in his bailiwick but might have been getting instructions from home to suppress these intruders whose presence could enflame an already difficult situation with the Great King's people in Asia Minor where the Spartans had not yet finally decided to go to war.

Unfortunately for the peripatetic army's long term future they had begun showing divisions and men were dribbling away. There were only about 6,000 of them left when they got temporary employment with Seuthes, an Odrysian Thracian king, who wanted them to harass one of his rivals. And once back in the Greek world their options were bound to be found within the parameters of what the Spartans allowed so it was no surprise when they became a crucial auxiliary in the plans for Thibron's Asian war. When they were called upon to join up they had just had a thrash at some Thracians living on the south west coast of the Black Sea. The people there were wreckers from way back. 'Accordingly the Thracians made it their practice to lie in wait in those parts and seize the merchants who were cast ashore as prisoners.'[7] The mercenaries invaded, defeated them in battle and burned their habitations before, with Xenophon probably still at their head and eager to have a chance to have a go at their old bugbear Tissaphernes, they marched across Lydia to join Thibron's army – only pausing on the way to do some vigorous looting near Pergamum in the lands of a Persian official called Asidates.

Marching north and joining with these belligerent remnants near Pergamum, Thibron gained confidence and decided to move into the open and face the Persians despite their effective and numerous horsemen. The newly adventurous general immediately reaped the benefits. Pergamum, Teuthrania and Halisarna, important inland towns in Aeolis, all opened their gates, these last being the hereditary holdings of descendants of Demaratus, an exiled Spartan king, who had served the Persians in the great Greco-Persian War. Indeed there were echoes of this epic conflict at every turn, as now two brothers, descendants of an Eritrean who had medised in the same war, brought over the communities of Gambrium, Palaegambrium, Myrina and Gryneum that gave the invaders control down to the sea. These new friends had just previously been cooperating with the Cyrian remnants in pillaging the estates of their Persian neighbours. The first real military act of this cakewalk was the assault on a place called Egyptian Larissa that controlled the valley of the lower Hermus that led upriver to Sardis. Siege lines were drawn and Thibron's men dug a tunnel to cut off the water to the place, but the defenders were clued in and constantly sallied out to fill in the shaft the enemy were digging with wood and stone. The attackers then covered the duct with a shed but the town's folk came out again at night and set fire to it. This was a frustrating business and worse was to come as messengers arrived from the ephors back home telling Thibron to leave the Larissians alone, pack up and take the war into Caria far to the south.

While all this sounds quite convincing another very different itinerary for the Spartans has been suggested where it is claimed that after arriving at Ephesus with 5,000 men Thibron marched south, not north, to Magnesia on the Maeander River, one of Tissaphernes' cities, and after he had taken it continued on up the river valley to Tralles. This he found too tough a nut to crack and withdrew back to Magnesia. A un-walled city and thus indefensible, Thibron decided to transfer the people lock stock and barrel to a hill nearby called Thorax and having prepared some defences against the return of the Persians, after 'invading the territory of the enemy, glutted his soldiers with booty of every kind'[8] he returned to the main base at Ephesus with its strong defences and port. In this account, this is the moment when the remnant of the 10,000 arrives in camp. It is not easy to choose between the two versions and one option is to crowbar both campaigns, with a winter season between, into Thibron's time in charge.[9] But our second source makes us question his accuracy when he claims Thibron's army included 'a thousand soldiers from their own citizens.'[10] This number of Spartiates just were not being sent overseas by this time, unless he is using citizen in the loosest sense, meaning any person, Spartan, *perioeci* or helot from Laconia. But whatever the sequence of events what is not in doubt is that when Thibron settled himself at Ephesus he received a nasty jolt. His progress had been sound enough but too leisurely by half and he now learned he was to be replaced by an officer named Dercylidas, ex-harmost of Abydos, who arrived in time to scoop up the glory while Thibron returned home to condemnation, trial and exile as Spartan allies heaped blame on him for letting his men riot and pillage their property. A harsh judgement perhaps as he had a difficult bunch to control, but still the first general in Sparta's Asian war had not really impressed at any level and first impressions would be confirmed when after rehabilitation his services were called on again.

Dercylidas was a famously subtle leader who had studied his satraps and was prepared to play off one against the other and also particularly hated Pharnabazus because of a previous encounter. When he was serving as harmost under Lysander at Abydos he was given the humiliating punishment of standing on guard while carrying his shield due to some tale telling by the satrap. With this personal agenda and an inclination to profit from the divisions between these Persian officials he approached Tissaphernes and negotiated an arrangement by which they would each leave the other alone so he might turn his attention against Pharnabazus. To put the boot into the hated satrap of Hellespontine Phrygia he marched his column of veteran mercenaries, citizen hoplites, enfranchised helots and local Greek warriors up from Ephesus through 'friendly country' to Aeolis. Dercylidas was clearly a man of real authority, as he managed to keep them from pillaging until they reached Pharnabazus' lands in a manner Thibron had just not been able to do. The local Persian ruler of northern Aeolis had been Mania, the wife of the previous governor. She had proved an effective and loyal successor to her husband even bringing Larissa, Hamaxitus and Colonae on the coast of southern Troad back into the Persian fold with a force of Greek mercenaries she had hired, also joining Pharnabazus in police actions against Mysian and Pisidian peoples who had been giving his administration trouble. This formidable widow had, herself, recently been murdered by her son in law, Meidias, propelled into action by people saying 'it was a disgraceful thing for a woman to be the ruler while he was in private station.'[11] So when the Spartans arrived they found this usurper preparing to defend himself against Pharnabazus, who was bent on extracting revenge for the slaying of his loyal executive.

Dercylidas reaped the benefits of this internal dissention. 'In one day' the towns of Larissa, Hamaxitus and Colonae, situated around the flanks of Mount Ida, sent to the Spartan to offer submission. Other Greek places were also encouraged by the newcomer to revolt and Neandria, Illium and Cocylium, further up towards the Hellespont, agreed to let Dercylidas put his men in to garrison their defences. Yet not everybody was happy: the Greek mercenaries billeted in some of these places under the old order were unhappy about their treatment since the woman who recruited them had been killed. Presumably they had not been paid and certainly at Cebrene, up the Scamander valley, the officer in charge thought he had a better chance of back pay from Pharnabazus than either Meidias or the newcomers; so staying loyal to his salt, he closed the gate on the Spartans. Dercylidas was profoundly irritated by this stand and not at all inclined to let them remain in peace behind the town walls. Though reputedly something of an intellectual the Spartan general had the deep superstition of his race and allowed four days to elapse without action because of bad omens; and this despite being in a lather of worry that Pharnabazus himself and the whole satrapal army might arrive at any moment. But not everybody had his patience. Amongst the officer corps a man called Athenadas from Sicyon who, less god-bothered than his leader, took matters into his own hands and with his own soldiers blocked off the town spring to pressure the defenders to give up the ghost. But without support he and his men were driven off by the inhabitants, who wounded the Sicyonian in the process. Yet this display of fortitude, though impressive, only hid deep division in both the garrison and the citizens, as many locals thought they should be facilitating the Greek army and not helping the Persians. So when Dercylidas finally got going he found the gates were opened to him and secured the place without a fight. Leaving men to hold the town the army was ordered onwards to Scepsis and Gergis, a short march to the east.[12]

Meidias, the mother in law killer, was now in despair both at the prospect of Pharnabazus' appearance and at the apparent hatred he had managed to inspire in the local people. So with the Spartans' arrival his only hope, he threw himself on their mercy and at Gergis town showed his value when he ordered the garrison there to open the gates to his new sponsors. The experience of Spartan hospitality and his realisation that it was them using him rather than the other way round quickly began to worry Meidias. While at Gergis he wriggled to try to improve his chances in a world where he was between the rock of Pharnabazus and the hard place of his Spartan hosts. But his attempts at repositioning himself only made things worse and soon Dercylidas had had enough of this slippery collaborator and, claiming the residents had told him everything in the whole region, particularly that the treasure Meidias had taken from his mother in law belonged to Pharnabazus, he claimed it to be his own as spear won goods, and that all he would leave Meidias was the house in Scepsis he had inherited from his father. Another source corroborates the fall of the places in the Troad to Dercylidas and indeed claims all the rest of the places in the area came over either as a result of persuasion or by assault. Clearly Dercylidas had taken note of what had happened to his predecessor due to his inaction; he had taken nine cities in eight days in this campaign and the plunder taken amounted to a nice nest egg to keep the troops happy.

But the year 398 was drawing to a close with winter just around the corner and billeting the army had been a real problem before. With the men spread out in winter quarters, the towns they now controlled were more vulnerable to Persian forays and the presence of thousands of idle warriors would cause tension with the locals – the very thing that had done for Thibron. To try to ensure the places he had won over would not suffer enemy depredations he asked for and got a truce of several months from Pharnabazus. The satrap apparently was as worried about the Greeks attacking his own lands in Phrygia as they were worried about him. With this problem sorted Dercylidas, to avoid burdening his allies, decided to winter his army in Bithynian Thrace, up around the Bosporus, where they could live off the land and plunder non-Hellenes, a solution not without its attractions for Pharnabazus as the 'Bithynians were often at war with him.' Over the straits from Dercylidas lay Odrysian Thrace, the fiefdom of King Seuthes. Whether as a plan to keep the intruders at a distance or of their own accord a force of 200 cavalry and 300 peltasts appeared at the Spartan camp offering themselves as allies. They had soon established themselves at a stockaded camp just over a couple of miles from the headquarters and asked and got a hoplite guard from their new found friends. Soon the combined raids of Greeks and Odrysians had obtained great quantities of booty.

Hard pressed they may have been, but these Bithynians were made of stern stuff. Keeping these two bands of brigands under observation they picked a time when only 200 Greek hoplites had been left on guard while the rest were off on the loot. They then attacked at dawn and skirting the stockade they hurled in their javelins very effectively, killing and wounding many, forcing the Greeks inside to desperately throw down their own wooden posts to get at the attackers outside. It was no good; the Bithynian peltasts kept out of reach of the heavy infantry weapons and struck from afar. Eventually only fifteen hoplites escaped back to the main Greek camp and these only because they had hidden themselves at the height of the fighting. Meanwhile the Bithynians pressed on and slaughtered the remaining Odrysians who had been guarding the tents of their camp while all this was going on, and the attackers had the great satisfaction of recovering their plundered property. When the main force of Greeks and Odrysians got back from their looting spree, the Bithynians, who knew they could never face the whole force in the open, had gone. Seuthes and Dercylidas' men contented themselves by continuing the winter harrying of Bithynia, vandal conduct apparently fuelled by copious amounts of wine.

In spring 397 the Greeks force marched out of winter camp, bid goodbye to a devastated Bithynia and took the direction of Lampsacus on the Hellespont. Thereafter on his foray to the east Dercylidas found himself once again within the remit of the home government. Shortly after he got to Lampsacus three commissioners from Sparta arrived to review the situation. They confirmed him in command but, under instructions from the ephors, addressed the soldiers. They told them that while they commended their current behaviour they would not tolerate any ill-treatment of their allies as there had been in the recent past. At this point the leader of Cyrus' former troops replied: 'But, men of Lacedaemon, we are the same men now as we were last year; but our commander now is one man, and in the past was another. Therefore you are at once able to judge for yourselves the reason why we are not at fault now, although we were then.'[13] The speaker was almost certainly Xenophon himself trying to divert blame for any misdeeds onto the conveniently departed Thibron.

Having completed their lecture they further suggested a good use of the army's time would be to go over to the Chersonese where the men could build a defensive wall to keep out those Thracians who were brutalising settlers who had gone into that region encouraged by the Spartans and now expected protection from them. The commissioners now carried on to Ephesus on their fact finding tour, while Dercylidas completed another truce with Pharnabazus and crossed the Hellespont into Europe. Here he hobnobbed with Seuthes (some of his men had done mercenary service for the king in the past) and from there he headed for the eleven communities in the Chersonese that were suffering the attention of these particular Thracian raiders. It was under five miles across the isthmus where the barrier was meant to cross, possibly following the line of a wall built by the Athenian dynast Miltiades in the later sixth century, and the soldiers got down to work in a manner that would have done Hadrian's legionaries proud. Competing to throw up their particular section of wall, each unit, with a prize for the quickest in mind, worked so hard and effectively that the whole project was completed between spring and harvest. All this was good work done in double quick time but now on his return to Aeolis the Spartan general found himself bogged down in the siege of Atarneus – just opposite Mytilene – where some 600 exiles from Chios, thrown out in 410 and still bearing grudges, had holed up and were harassing Sparta's friends in the area.

They were a tenacious lot these Chians and to capture the town took about eight months over the winter. In the meantime back at Sparta ambassadors from Ionia had arrived complaining that Tissaphernes had not allowed the Greek cities he controlled there more independence. To put pressure on him Dercylidas and his army were ordered by the ephors (the commissioners presumably having gone home) to decamp there. Dercylidas heeded the call cutting short any inclination to celebrate the successful conclusion of the long siege and now with the fleet, under Pharax, nearby it looked like they might make that impact in the decisive arena of Caria that had been intended for some time. Caria was always important. Dominating the Maeander valley meant controlling the main highway from Ionia to the interior and the heartland of the empire. As for their opponents Tissaphernes, as chief officer in Persian Anatolia, called Pharnabazus, buried their differences and agreed to coordinate their response to the threat. The plan the two decided upon was to garrison the strong places in Caria while they themselves with their main army of 20,000 infantry and 10,000 horse crossed back over the river to defend the road into Ionia. The Spartan army made no apparent attempt to work in tandem with the navy, a strategy that might have borne fruit in terms of gaining complete control of the coast, and instead followed the Persians inland out of Caria across the Maeander River and were hard on the heels of the satraps and their forces when the road they were taking approached a large burial mound.

At this landmark Dercylidas, with his own men in some disarray, found the enemy drawn up in battle formation across the road. Tissaphernes held the right of the line with his Persians, local Carian troops, his Greek mercenaries and large numbers of cavalry, while Pharnabazus with his Greeks and cavalry was on the left. The Spartan commander clearly had been let down by his scouts – it had been thought the Persians were further on down the road towards Ephesus – but fortunately for him the enemy did not take advantage. In fact the two armies squared up without making contact and Dercylidas had time to form up his 7,000 men. This heavy phalanx was eight deep, with its wings protected by peltasts and the few horse he had. The army's spirits were not uniform as they took position in the high standing corn of the Maeander plain. The local recruits from Ionia and the islands were shaky and some dropped their weapons and fled. But the Peloponnesians were solid as a rock, and though on the Persian side Pharnabazus wanted to attack, Tissaphernes was worried about what he had seen these soldiers had been capable of doing at the battle of Cunaxa when they had carved through that part of the Royal Achaemenid army that stood in their path. He persuaded his colleague of the reasonableness of a more cautious approach and, finally deciding talking might be the better option than battle, dispatched an envoy to the army opposite to ask for a conference. A truce was arranged and the Persians withdrew to Tralles where they could control most of the roads going up the Maeander valley and down into Caria, while the Greeks moved to a place called Leucophrys where there was a lake and good drinking water for the men. Again things settled down to one of those diplomatic exchanges that were so typical of these years. Dercylidas, feeling that the Persians were on the back foot, demanded independence for the Greek cities, but in response the satraps delivered their bottom line that the Greek army should leave the country and the Spartan officers get on the first boat back home. There was predictably little meeting of minds here yet neither wanted to risk the lottery of a battle, so an extension of the truce was agreed while the terms were sent back for perusal at Sparta and by the Great King at Susa.

This was the situation Agesilaus found himself in when he arrived, with a war that was not quite on fire and himself sent to counter what was seen as a dangerously aggressive Persia intent on contesting Spartan hegemony both in the Aegean and mainland Greece itself. So in a complex situation where his predecessors had frequently got bogged down it was no surprise that when he arrived in Asia, diplomacy was the order of the day. Another truce of three months was arranged between the forces, passed on by Dercylidas (who had remained to work for the man who displaced him and indeed was one of the ambassadors who orchestrated the armistice) and Agesilaus' own men on one side, and the satrapal forces on the other, so the issue of how the Asian Greek cities should be governed could be argued further before the Great King at the Achaemenid court. This, plus the fact that the king was only given supplies sufficient for six months, perhaps suggests that the goals of the expedition were not that ambitious and the government of Sparta intended only a limited intervention. While a response was awaited, mostly what we are given are tales of Persian deceit and Spartan forbearance. Tissaphernes supposedly sent to Susa for more troops against the agreement while Agesilaus, though well aware, did nothing to break the concord, nor even matched the duplicity by raising reinforcement himself. All this fits badly with other reports that laud the Persians for their honesty, except for the usual rationale that the current generation of Achaemenid lordlings had fallen into degeneracy since the time of Cyrus the Great over a century before. But the gist is confirmed by Plutarch who has Tissaphernes indulging in 'jaw jaw' rather than 'war war' while he bulked up his forces.

Whatever the reality, Agesilaus had remained in Ephesus while these intrigues were reportedly underway, getting more and more irritated as the local bigwigs paid court to Lysander rather than him. This is, of course, far from surprising when Lysander, though officially only part of the royal entourage, so recently had been the great power in the region. When he had arrived at the commencement of his triumphant campaign against the Athenians in 405 it had been as the power behind another official figurehead, so it was unexceptional that local people saw in Agesilaus a parallel with admiral Aracus, who had been the official man in charge on that occasion. But the thirty Spartan peers at headquarters did not see it that way and vocalised their dislike of Lysander putting on airs that 'would have been excessive even in royalty.' The king tried to dissemble the personal pique he felt but could not hide his feelings altogether and we are told he vented his emotions by ensuring anyone coming for favours sponsored by Lysander got very short shrift. Inevitably with two such non-self-effacing personalities tension could not fail to surface and Lysander suggested as a way out that he be detached for service elsewhere. As the only way out of these egos clashing the commoner packed his bags, mobilised his associates and shifted up to the Hellespont, putting a few hundred miles between himself and his monarch. Agesilaus was glad to be rid of him, but he must equally have known it was unlikely a man of Lysander's stamp would keep his head down for long and that he was far from being without friends in the quarters that mattered. In any case his feelings were complex: he knew how much he owed to Lysander for putting him on the throne but also could not allow himself to be put in the shade by anybody, even him. In fact, Lysander hardly stayed quiet at all but unearthed a worthy named Spithridates in Hellespontine Phrygia, 'with much money and two hundred horsemen' who was angry with Pharnabazus. He encouraged him to revolt and, while leaving his own people in charge at Cyzicus, Lysander took ship with the rebel and his son down the coast back to Ephesus. Agesilaus was apparently happy enough with their arrival. If Lysander like a bad penny kept on turning up, Spithridates had potential as a very useful card in the game he eventually intended to play against Pharnabazus in the north.

But before he could have any impact in that region things hotted up locally as Tissaphernes, reinforced by troops from the king, voided the truce and demanded the Spartans get out of Asia without further ado. The locals, with all to lose, were worried when the Persian's declaration of war was circulated but the Spartan king himself was all insouciance. He had done some good intelligence work already and decided to take the offensive and give the impression of attacking Caria, sending envoys to get the cities along his route to prepare markets and ordering allies from Aeolis, the Hellespont and Ionia to direct their troops to the military camp at Ephesus. Caria was logical as the Spartan's choice of target because it was broken, indented country that did not suit the Persian mounted arm at all, and also Tissaphernes' personal land holdings were concentrated there. But in fact it was a ploy, and when the Persians got their infantry over and dug in behind the Maeander River, and the cavalry were in the valley where they could manoeuvre, Agesilaus turned about and took the high road north in the direction of Phrygia. The benefit for him in this was not only that he avoided the prepared Persian positions but also he was able to pick up troops from allies, most of whom were in that direction rather than south towards Caria. As advantageous was that the local people allied to the Persians were caught napping and had not brought their goods into protected places, so they were picked clean with ease when the Greeks arrived.

It had been a long old hike past Ionia, Aeolis and the Troad, and it was improbable that everything went without a hitch. Though our sources never mention much about straggling it must have occurred over these hard miles, particularly as at times soldiers passed places where they knew people and might expect shelter if they deserted. Apart from problems within their own ranks, when the Spartans and their allies made it as far as Dascylium, Pharnabazus' headquarters, they encountered serious resistance for the first time. In the field opposed to them there were a number of mounted units under the officers Rhathines and Bagaeus, the latter a bastard brother of Pharnabazus. Both were veterans who had tangled with the remnants of the 10,000 when they emerged from the interior a few years before.

The vanguard of Agesilaus' army comprised an equivalent number of horsemen, and both groups coming up from either side of a hill only saw each other when hardly more than a hundred yards apart. Both sides were in deep formation, for the line of march rather than combat, the Greeks four deep on their small unshod mounts, while the Persians were massed twelve broad and many more deep. The Persians started first and the attack was devastating with their cornel wood javelins being very effective. Reeling back, twelve Greeks were killed and the rest fled, only to be rescued when Agesilaus and the main body of infantry came up and the hoplites showed a serried row of spear points to the pursuing horse. Either because of this show of resistance, or as we are told a dodgy liver lobe, the Greeks feeling themselves exposed headed back to the coast. The next move certainly suggests it was policy not divination that was directing the Spartan king's policy. Once securely settled he set about recruiting some cavalry as his recent experience showed he just could not do without some more horsemen to protect his flanks and line of march. The allied Greek cavalry class in the area were pressured to help, though most were allowed to provide a well horsed and armed substitute rather than needing to parade themselves. Agesilaus just wanted good cavalry, the social standing was of no interest to him; indeed he no doubt thought these hired men might be more pliable than self important locals with interests to protect.

These troopers rode good horses raised on better fodder and with superior blood than the typical animals the Spartans had known in Greece. Without saddle or stirrups the riders made do very well with the pressure of their knees and primitive bits and probably wore body armour not so different from their hoplite compatriots but without a shield. The Persian cavaliers they would have been familiar with even had part-armoured mounts and scale aprons that went down to their boots. So these troops of horsemen meant it was with a better balanced force and a well trained one (the gymnasium and hippodromes around Ephesus where he had returned to had been well utilised over the winter) that Agesilaus set out the next spring to do some hurt to Tissaphernes who had been so bad to his word the previous year. The much reduced remnant of Cyrus' 10,000 were now led by general Herippidas, while Xenocles and an unnamed officer were deputed to lead the cavalry; Scythes headed the helot hoplites and Mygdon was in charge of the allies. All these were members of a group of thirty Spartiates who had come out to replace the original thirty who accompanied the king but had been called back home with Lysander having done their year of service. Tissaphernes we learn, reinforced by troops from the Great King, had kept his men in position to cover Caria despite Agesilaus letting it be known he would be advancing on the shortest route against the heart of Persian power in Lydia. The satrap it seemed anticipated a double bluff, but again he was shown to be wrong headed as the invaders took the high road for Sardis just as had been promised (though a comment by Polyaenus suggests a campaign of misinformation may have been at the back of the Persians' flawed defensive).[14]

Xenophon, who was almost certainly present, tells us that a three day hard march was accomplished without incident but in that time the Persian horse had been alerted and marched out hard on the heels of the army. Lydia was much more cavalry country than Ionia or Caria so in some confidence their squadrons of horsemen made camp on the River Pactolus near its junction with the Hermus, just north of Sardis, and prepared to get down to harassing the Greeks who had sent out servants and light armed men to plunder the countryside. Now Agesilaus' new model horse would be tested as he ordered their officers to deal with these enemy gadflies who were disturbing what so far had been an untroubled progress. He ensured these green troopers should not be without back up: the phalanx was deployed in support, particularly the younger men who with the peltasts could keep pace with the cavalry. It worked, the Persians, who drew themselves up in deep lines, first held their own against the Greek horse but when the young hoplites and peltasts piled in, without infantry support of their own the Persians were pushed back, some driven into the water, then overwhelmed and hurled in flight back across the river. Agesilaus ordered his men on. Dripping wet but eager, they followed over the watercourse to capture the enemy camp. The plunder taken there was rich indeed, amounting to more than seventy talents worth and included camels that we are told ended piquing the curious in Sparta when Agesilaus returned in triumph back to Greece.

There are other versions which give us more detail on the intruders' movements. They claim Agesilaus marched his men to the plain of the little Maeander just north of modern Seljuk and from there went west around the mountains to the north and nearby where modern Izmir stands, then on into the Hermus valley that led east towards the city of Sardis itself. This was enemy territory and Agesilaus made the people feel the pain of war, which had the required effect as Tissaphernes came out to fight the men who were tormenting his subjects in the country around. But the strength the satrap arrived with must have come as something of a surprise if we are to believe claims that 10,000 cavalry and 50,000 infantry were gathered. This is not very credible: we never hear of any such numbers in the armies raised by these satraps before and even with reinforcements from the Great King this sounds excessive. Whatever their exact numbers they acted quickly and the invaders had not penetrated deep into the valley on the road to Sardis when they appeared. The Spartans had Mount Sipylus on their left (on its north side the great battle of Magnesia was fought centuries later) when the Persians hove into view and Agesilaus, seeing the threat of the enemy cavalry, sensibly put his men in a square and made sure he kept to the foothills where rough terrain would make it difficult for the Persians to get a good run on his men and their wagon loads of plunder. But despite this defensive posture he intended to retain the initiative here, and was only waiting for an opportunity to go for the enemy in an advantageous circumstance. That again militates against the credibility of their very high numbers which would surely have made such a policy too daunting.

The invaders got as far as Sardis, roughing up the suburbs and creating havoc in the 'pleasure paradises' and orchards along the way that belonged to Tissaphernes, and as this took them out into open country the square formation must have worked effectively or the Persians were inept and failed to pounce in force when the enemy were on level ground. These places were the satrap's pride and joy and what happened next suggests Agesilaus was trying to provoke his enemy to make a move that would allow him to get at them. Retreating halfway to a place called Thybarnae, on the road away from Sardis, they passed a thickly wooded area and the king dropped off 1,400 men under the cavalry commander Xenocles to lie in wait for the Persians following on. Camping there, with the next dawn the rest of the army swung out on the road. As usual the Persians began to harass their rear but 'without battle order'; it was easy pickings they were after, not an all out fight. Now the king turned, formed up his men with spears levelled, and faced the forces harrying them. This done, he signalled to the hidden men and they, chanting their battle hymn, came out of hiding at the charge. With Agesilaus' spears in their front and the 1,400 others coming in behind it is no surprise the Persians hardly put up any fight but just looked to personal survival. In pursuit it is claimed 6,000 fell but this is probably an exaggeration equivalent to that of their original numbers; and the great multitude of prisoners claimed is also not that credible. The Oxyrynchus historian mentions only 600 casualties – a much more convincing figure and also suggests that only a few prisoners were bagged in the camp itself. Hoplites were not great pursuers at the best of times and if the peltasts and the Greek horse could move pretty quickly their numbers would not have been sufficient to scoop up many more than a few score of what were mainly horsemen with all their advantages of speed and mobility. But it is probable that their camp, where the spoils were rich, was pillaged and great stores found; and also that Tissaphernes, thunderstruck at the daring of the Lacedaemonians, fell right back to Sardis while Agesilaus pushed over the mountains out of Lydia and on into greater Phrygia with some remnant of the Persian horse still following but at a respectful distance. Before turning in this direction though, it is suggested that the king had contemplated exploiting his showy victory by pressing further down the royal road against Celaenae in the interior, only to be dissuaded from this course by more bad omens.[15]

The battle of Sardis had badly shaken Tissaphernes. The arm he had most confidence in had been bested. Word began to spread that the satrap was being deserted by his own men and, worse than this, reports of his poor performance had over time been reaching the ears of those in power at Susa. There the failure to deal with the Greek invaders and restore the Asian Greek cities to tribute status had been causing more and more irritation. Tissaphernes, who with the queen mother still baying for his blood, was likely to carry the can and the Great King decided on the most radical action to register his displeasure. An official called Tithraustes was dispatched west on the royal road with orders to purge the failing servant of an unforgiving throne. The actual deed was done by Ariaeus, a man with a history. He had fought as Cyrus' lieutenant at Cunaxa, probably commanding the left wing of the army; though some claim he fought alongside the prince and inflicted a wound on Artaxerxes himself. After refusing the Greek mercenaries' offer to make him their claimant for the Persian throne he rehabilitated himself with the Great King by betraying those Greek generals, who had been his comrades, by persuading them to join under truce a conference that ended with their detention and death. So by the hands of this deep dyed double dealer, the man who had done so much to secure Artaxerxes on the throne was decapitated in his bath. With this accomplished, Tithraustes took up the other part of his remit. He essayed talks with the tormentors from over the Aegean and suggested that with Tissaphernes gone and a new administration taken over at Sardis a peaceful way forward might be found. In fact after some usual horse trading it began to look as though an Artaxerxes-approved formula, whereby the Asian Greeks would be autonomous but still pay tribute to the Achaemenid, could be acceptable to both sides. This laid the groundwork for purposeful talking, but to get the intruders out from the region Tithraustes was also prepared to hand over hard cash. It cost him thirty talents to get Agesilaus to bid adieu and turn off north in the direction of Pharnabazus country, but no doubt after what had happened to his predecessor it probably seemed money well spent.

By the time Agesilaus' army, counting their Persian gold on the road north, reached Cyme on the coast in southern Aeolis, the king met envoys from home bringing good news. A fleet was being constructed that was to be put under his command and in brisk order 120 triremes came in from the building and repair yards of allied cities on the Asian coast and the islands. It had been a long time since anybody had been entrusted with such forces on land and sea. 'This was an honour which no one ever received but Agesilaus. And he was confessedly the greatest and most illustrious man of his time.'[16] Agesilaus' receipt of command of both army and navy in his Asian campaign showed just how dominant a figure he had become. But never a saltwater man, he installed his brother in law Peisander as the admiral, and from this managerial business soon returned to concentrate on military matters. Now it was to be Pharnabazus whose toes he would tread on. The leaves were turning when he packed up the army, and the tramping Greek footsloggers headed for the Hellespont hoping to get the Mysians on his side. This turned out to be a complicated matter as the locals resented the pressure put on those who would not join him. It all backfired for them as he passed 'Mysian Olympus' finding that as he moved through some defiles, the locals took advantage by attacking the rear of his column. He lost fifty men in the first attack but made up for it the next day by leaving Dercylidas and some of his veterans in ambush along his route. This worked perfectly; they pinned down the Mysians while Agesilaus and the main body rushing back completed the rout that cost the enemy 130 dead. After this bloodletting the locals turned co-operative, and guided by those they had recently been fighting, the invaders pushed on into Pharnabazus' satrapy.

The evidence is that Agesilaus even got as far as Gordium, the old capital of Phrygia, but was held off by a garrison commanded by Rhathines who we have come across before in the first attack on Pharnabazus.[17] Frustrated, Agesilaus turned to Spithridates, Lysander's turncoat, who had been functioning as guide at least since the troubled crossing of Mysia. He urged them to aim for Paphlagonia where he assured them the king there would give them a rapturous welcome, join the cause and stump up plenty of warriors to beef out their strike force. This policy of subverting local rulers was what Agesilaus was planning from the start; indeed it was the only realistic way he might get the resources he needed to strike any kind of significant blow against Persian power in Anatolia. The king they encountered was called Otys who had already burned his boats with the Persian authorities by refusing a summons to the court at Susa. Well pleased to find a powerful friend coming to back him up he was persuaded by Spithridates to contribute 1,000 cavalry and 2,000 targeteers; very welcome reinforcements – the kind of numbers that the invaders must have thought boded well for a great invasion campaign in the future.

After a balmy domestic interlude of matchmaking between the children of Otys and Spithridates, Agesilaus determined to put the squeeze on Pharnabazus and marched against Dascylium, the satrapal capital, situated in rich country near a lake on the banks of a river, where generations of Persian aristocrats had beautified the country. Here the Greeks settled down to enjoy the winter perhaps with ambitions to invade Cappadocia the next year. The army was able to supply itself pretty well until after the passage of time the foragers got slack and left themselves open to attack by a vigilant enemy. Pharnabazus had found a couple of old scythed war chariots and with these he also got together 400 cavalry. With this mobile corps he rode into the region where the Greeks were encamped and swept down on about 700 scattered soldiers foraging in the country. The antique war vehicles were in front and the horsemen just behind when they charged, and though the Greeks had got into some sort of formation when they struck it was not solid enough. The chariots broke them completely, chopping up any unfortunates found in range of the wicked axle mounted blades, and the cavalry mowed down the disordered men to the number of 100. The rest escaped to Agesilaus, who was not too far off with the hoplites, and they reached their protection before the Persians could do any more damage. There these Greek infantry, who had not turned their back on Persians in arms for many years, cowered behind the friendly phalanx having dropped spears and shields in their eagerness to get away. It had been a rare example of the successful use of war chariots as a contact arm and there is no doubt the key was that the target was ill prepared, neither able to show a unbroken hedge of spears that would have put the charging horses off, nor able to open lanes for them to harmlessly career down.

The Spartan king was determined to retaliate. He was fortunate that Spithridates was well cognisant of what was happening in the neighbourhood. Pharnabazus had kept moving, keeping his treasure with him, and after four or five days it was discovered that he had based himself at a large village called Caue. Spithridates decided not to inform the commander straight away but talked to Herippidas, leader of the Cyrian remnants, who he knew was aching to get more achievements to his name. These two then approached the king and persuaded him to let Herippidas lead 2,000 hoplites, an equal number of peltasts, all Spithridates' cavalry, the Paphlagonians, and any Greeks who volunteered, to make a surprise attack on the enemy camp. This large force was ordered to gather at the camp gate and though for an undisclosed reason only half those expected turned up, Herippidas did not let this obstruct him in his hour of glory. He marched the men he had out into the night and at dawn was overlooking the objective where the largely Mysian soldiers employed by the satrap on outpost duty must have been very lax. These shoddy sentinels barely gave any warning to their comrades before the attackers descended, swords and spears bared on the camp. The main force fled with hardly a fight, and the whole business was so unnerving for Pharnabazus that from then on he kept moving never staying in one place, if he was going to be target at least it would be a moving one. But these Spartans, even in corporate triumph, could upset anybody when it came to a contest in cupidity. Both Spithridates and the Paphlagonians were incensed when Herippidas confiscated all the loot for himself allegedly in order to distribute it properly though this is hardly convincing given the usual work of so many Spartan officials when it came to other people's money. But the victims this time were not some down trodden citizens in an oligarch ridden Greek city; they would not endure it and Spithridates and the Paphlagonians, their friends and followers downed tools and marched off to look for sanctuary with Ariaeus the local commander at Sardis.

But if Agesilaus was worried by the desertion of these crucial local collaborators and not just for their own sake but also apparently because Spithridates' son had caught his predatory eye, his spirits must have lifted when Pharnabazus decided he needed to deal and sent Apollophanes of Cyzicus 'a guest-friend of both' to open up negotiations. The king and his thirty Spartiates guarding him agreed to meet the satrap in an open field, allowing a smug tale of the contrast between the hardy and excellent Spartans lying on the bare grass while the satrap sat in luxury with his Persian followers on beautiful carpets surrounded by gorgeous trappings. Apparently Pharnabazus soon saw the error of his ways and stepped away from his carpets and cushions to join the Spartans lying on the ground. Whatever the real interaction between these two potentates from different worlds, Pharnabazus immediately took the opportunity to point out some obvious truths. It had been he who funded the fleet with which the Spartans had defeated the Athenians in the late war, and at the battle of Abydos in 411 he had ridden his horse into the sea to fight beside the very men who were now prowling his country, destroying his houses, cutting down his trees and stealing his animals. He contrasted his own good conduct with the treachery of Tissaphernes. This all apparently brought a blush to the cheeks of the thirty Spartiates but not to the king's. He blasély contended that Spartans fight the enemies of their fatherland even if they are personal friends, and that as the war with the Great King was ongoing, Pharnabazus as one of his officers was a legitimate target. From these preliminaries Agesilaus cut to the chase, declaring that Pharnabazus' best interests demanded he declare his independence from Artaxerxes' empire and set up as his own man who would then get powerful support from a Sparta that commanded thousands of devastating battle-winning heavy infantry. It was the Cyrus ploy all over again and clearly the divisions Agesilaus was looking to exploit were real enough as the satrap did not refuse outright. Instead Pharnabazus asked: 'Shall I, then, tell you frankly just what I shall do?' 'It surely becomes you to do so.' 'Well, then,' said he, 'if the King sends another as general and makes me his subordinate, I shall choose to be your friend and ally; but if he assigns the command to me – so strong, it seems, is the power of ambition – you may be well assured that I shall make war upon you to the best of my ability.'[18]

With Agesilaus congratulating him on what a good man he was it was agreed that the Spartan king would remove his men until it became clear what the outcome of the court intrigues over the satrap's position would be. It was coming on spring now and the Greeks agreed to leave Pharnabazus' territory and move to the plain of Thebe at the base of Mount Placus in the Troad. So after some gift exchange and flirty fraternisation with one of the satrap's sons (an interlude that had an epilogue when the Spartan king helped the young man as an exile in the Peloponnese and had fallen in love with an Athenian athlete) the king left the satrapal lands but with intentions far from peaceable all round.

For Agesilaus the truce was just a breather to bulk up his army and press on into the interior to raise as many peoples as he could against the Persian king. Plutarch certainly claims he was intending to head for Ecbatana and Susa if not further still and that the mission was only aborted when Epicydidas arrived from Sparta and recalled him to Greece on orders of the ephors. He had been away nearly two years and had made an impact not just as general but as a man whose simplicity and life of moderation contrasted for the Greek locals with the Persian *apparatchiks* who had oppressed them so frequently in the past.

Whatever Agesilaus' personal standing – and the evidence was he had showed tactical flair and panache – these had not seemed decisive years, and the key strategy of stopping Persian advances in the Aegean had not been achieved. As we shall see, Conon had been allowed to erupt into a Spartan world in a massive way. What had this Spartan king, who would do much in the next few decades, and die with his boots on at over eighty years old, really been up to in this Anatolian war? His ambitions had been partly shaped by the achievements of the 10,000, and like many he had begun to perceive the Persian Empire as a hollow thing, but how high his ambition vaulted is far from clear. We should not forget it was on an Egyptian shore his life ended, and who is to say that in earlier years he did not see himself riding roughshod over feeble Persian defences at least as far as the Levant. Was it some kind of proto-Alexander campaign with Agesilaus supremely confident in the fighting prowess of his compatriots and prepared to go for the Persian jugular? Hardly: the numbers don't add up. The amount of cavalry mentioned are in the hundreds, not even a twentieth of the mass that the Macedonians brought across the Hellespont in sixty years time. Certainly he had good infantry hoplites and peltasts but not enough and anyway he knew cavalry was the key. The Spartan king's tramping never took him very far from where plenty of Greeks had gone previously. He may have attacked Sardis but other Hellenes had trod that high road centuries before in an adventure that triggered the whole Greco-Persian conflict and was the first stage on the road to Marathon, Thermopylae, Artemisium, Salamis, Plataea and Mycale. Agesilaus' strategy was essentially pragmatic and exploratory. He was the ambitious king of a victorious state with a blooded veteran army to hand, and that he used it in the direction of the largest most prosperous political entity is hardly surprising.

Certainly he would have chased the Persian beast to its lair if he could have, but that was not within his power and the only way his efforts could have been anything more than pinpricks would have been if he could have raised in rebellion warlike tribes and powerful peoples within Artaxerxes' empire which might have created an independent buffer zone between the Asian Greeks and the Persian power. He knew this and hoped victories over the Anatolian satraps might encourage the grievances of such peoples in the region, but this never happened to the extent that would have made a difference. The perennial rebels in the Achaemenid state were the Egyptians and the wild men of the upper satrapies. Anatolia by and large was a peaceful place for the Great Kings residing at Babylon, Susa and Persepolis. All in all if the aim had been to march deep into the east to advance along the royal road through Anatolia into Cilicia and beyond, it had not happened. The great fortress towns along the route did not fall to Spartan arms – he could not even take Gordium. He does not seem to have taken a great siege train with him nor could his forces field the torsion engines that were in use when the Macedonians tore across the world. Indeed in the end the impact for the Spartan war in Asia was not even sufficient to build a threat that might have sucked back the Persian men and resources that were being mobilised to take the sea war into their own backyard.

Chapter Five

A Year of Battles

In 395 a familiar figure was again the key man in the Lacedaemon power landscape. Lysander had been instrumental in the years before in getting Agesilaus onto the throne and into his Asian war, showing he could still mobilise his supporters when needed. And though it had not gone smoothly when they were tied in tandem, soon after, back home, it is clear he was still very much on the bridge of the Spartan ship of state. Trouble with ephors, the *Gerousia* and monarchs: Lysander had had them all over the years since his triumph in the Great War. Even his reported dabbling in the canons of kingship could not take away from how great his contribution had been and how important his power base still was. Lots of people, Spartan and others, had benefited from his success, and they had not forgotten. But it was in fact something else, not rivals at home, that would finally bring an end to an extraordinary career, and its gestation occurred in country he had not been much involved with before, central Greece.

A quarrel had been brewing between the Phocians and the Locrians over a piece of land, and such was the bellicosity on both sides that it became a sufficient spark to light a fuse. The disputed territory that started the war is differently identified by our sources as to who exactly was involved. Certainly the Phocians were one of the disputants, and some place in Locris that was under contention, though some of the border incidents cited sound more like big time sheep rustling than anything else. The Thebans had plenty of history against the Phocians and when the Locrians asked for aid they joined in with alacrity, mobilised an army, marched west and invaded up the Cephisus valley from a base at Orchomenus.

What happened once there is not detailed but the Phocians were tricky men, known for on one occasion booby trapping the ground enemy Thessalian cavalry would charge over and for back to the wall desperation, so perhaps this time they also put up a sufficient defence. In any case the strike took place at harvest time so the whole thing was perhaps anyway more a raid than an invasion. The Thebans returned via the town of Hyampolis where they unsuccessfully tried a surprise escalade before presumably disbanding and heading home. The most significant result of all this was that Phocian envoys were soon heading over the

Gulf of Corinth and down through the Peloponnese to put their case before the Spartans.

In both our main sources it is specifically stated the Thebans had induced the Phocians to invade Locris as an excuse to provoke the Spartans into war as 'they could never persuade the Boeotians or the rest of the Thebans to make war against the Spartans.'[1] Whatever the cause, once the ephors had vetted them, the envoys found once more that Lysander was the flavour of the month and that he and his compatriots were still angry with the Thebans since they had complained about the distribution of spoils after the conclusion of the Peloponnesian War. This was getting on for ten years ago, but when they had claimed a tithe of the booty from Decelea, just by asking they had deeply offended King Agis, and many Spartans were still angry at their allies' presumption. Recently they had failed to back up the Spartans in their other enterprises, whether in the conflict between the Thirty tyrants and their democrat rivals in Athens, or in the demolition of Elis' power.

Though bitterness and distrust were certainly not one sided; equally important from the Thebans' point of view was a northern dimension that had poisoned relations between two states who had stood shoulder to shoulder against Athens for a generation. The issue was the growth of Spartan influence in Thessaly and around the Malian Gulf. Strategic Heraclea in Trachis, just four miles west of Thermopylae, had been founded by the Spartans as a colony in 427/6 and initially they had done this with the support of Boeotia who saw the place as a buffer against the Thessalians. Fear of Thessaly had been a major motive behind the Boeotian League getting together in first place at the end of the sixth century. But it was not long before Spartan presence in the region came to be resented. Their garrison at Heraclea had been kicked out in 419, but in 399/8 the Spartans took back control from the Thebans when Herippidas marched an occupation force there slaughtering 500 locals in the process. Perhaps this was why Lysander asked the Boeotians whether the Spartans should travel through their country with spears upright or levelled, in peace or with warlike intent. The story may be fanciful but the intrusion had become a real stress point, particularly when many locals who would not play ball with the Spartans were exiled to Thessaly and a garrison was put in Pharsalus too. Thebes saw this region as very much her own backyard and the permanent intrusion of another major power there was not to be contemplated.

It may well have been these events at the turn of the century that caused a moving of the tectonic plates of faction power in Boeotia, and were going to revolutionise the whole Greek world in a generation's time. The pro-Spartan faction led by Leontiades had been dominant for years; his grandfather had even been in charge at the time of the Persian Wars. But there was always opposition in Boeotia: the Delian campaign in 424 illustrates the existence of dissident democrats in Orchomenus calling on the Athenians to help overthrow the regime in Thebes. The people at Thespiae also frequently acted as a fifth column and the stresses of both regional and class divides affected the Boeotian League as elsewhere. Even so mutual hatred of Athens kept the Boeotian ruling classes onboard, and anyway they had done well out of the recent war with much profitable raiding of Attica as well as the acquisition of the key port of Oropus and the border town of Eleutherae after the crushing of Athenian power. However if they enjoyed the spoils of war, the end of Athens as a great power meant there was no longer this threat to make a Spartan alliance so attractive. A new faction is discernible as becoming important around 400 led by Ismenias who had started to make a splash after being the beneficiary of a large inheritance. He and his people may have been calling some of the shots even earlier when a base was offered for the Athenian democrats to arm themselves in a process that eventually ended with the overthrow of the Thirty. This Sparta-phobic group were definitely in the driving seat by 397 when the Boeotian Leaguers refused to send troops with Agesilaus for the Asian war. All in all the Thebans were looking for an excuse to start hostilities and the Phocian Locrian dispute provided a perfect pretext. So when the Spartans sent heralds demanding the Thebans halt their military preparations against Phocis and submit to mediation it is no surprise they received an absolute rebuttal.

When the Phocian envoys had put their case at Sparta, Lysander pushed for a war of conquest against Thebes and persuaded the ephors to this point of view rather than just offering limited aid to the petitioner. Once this was decided, he also secured high command and was dispatched in person to organise the Malian Gulf front in this new confrontation. He clearly moved quickly with only a small number of troops, probably no more than a few hundred Spartans who Agesilaus would find in garrison at Orchomenus the next year, hoping an immediate impact would be more efficacious than a time consuming and steady build up. So within a very short time he is discovered in Phocis most likely having crossed from Sicyon over the Corinthian Gulf and then on. He rounded up an army from allies from the regions of Ainis, Malis and Mount Oeta. This character who found himself once again at the head of Sparta's military affairs had such a name that it must have seemed the war would be over before it even started, despite the limited army he had been vouchsafed to carry out the campaign. The Spartans had many friends amongst the locals. An eager, armed and vengeful army of Phocians assembled at their federal capital of Elatea, and it was with the support of these and others that Lysander hoped to sustain himself while the Agiad king Pausanias collected the full Peloponnesian levy and came to join him.

He was in decent strength now. Apart from the men who had come with him, the allies must have provided a couple of thousand warriors at least, and the Phocians mobilised 3,000 hoplites a hundred years later to fight invading Galatians so now very close to home turf they surely put up almost that number as well. So Lysander crossed the border from Phocis into Boeotia probably commanding 5,000 plus men as he looked to undermine the Thebans by exploiting those local rivalries that were the meat and drink of Greek political life. He targeted Orchomenus first, this city had always stood in the shadow of its grander sister Thebes and succumbing to local spite, not for the last time, fell in with a people who wanted to injure the seven gated city on the *Cadmeia*. She would suffer for it too when Thebes, elephantine in memory, in 349 razed the place at a time she herself had become the master in most of Greece. With these friends mobilising, Orchomenus, together with Hysiai could provide 2,000 hoplites and 200 horsemen so presumably added something under half of that number to their new saviour, the bolstered Spartan task force moved a little down the main road, plundering the town of Lebadeia as they went.

At about that stage Lysander, feeling a little exposed in the heart of enemy country, decided to make contact with the other arm of the invading pincer. He sent messengers with written orders off towards Plataea where he thought Pausanias with his 6,000 men would be, to meet him at Haliartus the next day. The

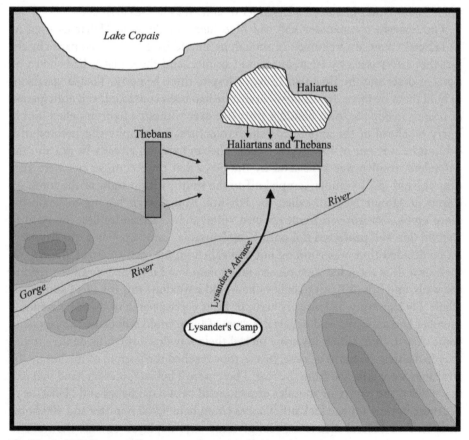

The Battle of Haliartus 395 BC.

king was not far from there, having raised men from Sparta itself: *perioeci* levies and allies like Tegea and the Arcadians, though interestingly not from Corinth, who had refused. He had had an easy passage over the Gulf of Corinth and crossed the Cithaeron Mountains, south of Plataea, on the borders of Megara and Boeotia. The plan was that the prongs of the pincer should combine under the walls of Haliartus at dawn the following day, a place twelve-odd miles along the main road west out of Thebes city and right by Lake Copais (this great body of water is drained now but the marks showing its old extent are still clear in the level basin stretching between Orchomenus and Haliartus). But one of Lysander's couriers was caught by scouts from Thebes who were out roaming the country trying to make sense of the various sets of intruders appearing on their frontiers. So, armed with the Spartans' plans in their hands and boosted by Athenian allies who had just arrived, the Thebans prepared to mass against the northern arms of the enemy pincer. It was classic use of interior lines, but success would depend on many factors. The whole Theban levy marched as evening was coming down, giving their Athenian comrades sufficient strength to defend Thebes town itself and get to Haliartus either just before Lysander or at least as he was arriving.

The Spartan commander had had high hopes of doing at Haliartus what he had already done at Orchomenus, though he should have been given pause by the fact they had passed by Chaeronea and Coronea, and these places had shown no signs of deserting the Boeotian League, despite there being no Theban garrisons to hold them by force. It was possible that he had been contacted, and anticipation of friends inside the town handing the place over without a fight impelled him to hurry on ahead of the appointed rendezvous time. Yet despite this mooted fifth column he was out of luck: there was a Theban garrison already in *situ* and the defenders' resolve was kept solid by the news that their compatriots were very near at hand. So Lysander camped off to the south, within sight of the town, on a spur of Mount Helicon called the Fox-hill. And though hoping to scoop the place up he also worried about his own vulnerability. Lysander first intended to wait on this well protected hill until King Pausanias came up, but as the day went on he decided time was running out and called on his men to attack the city on their own. It is recorded they turned into column and marched down the road to the walls, and it is difficult to believe he would have done this if he had known the whole Theban army had already arrived. So it is reasonable to think he assumed no relief had appeared and believed a show of force could still cause the people to come over to him. When his army picked their way down the hillside they found they had entered a hornets' nest. Just as they reached the bottom of the hill by the river they were attacked from the rear. There were Theban forces on hand that had flown down the twelve or so miles of main road between Thebes and Haliartus to get there in time for the kick off. Thebes could field 4,000 hoplites and 400 horse from its four federal districts. Most of these were deployed outside the walls to the right of the town and were well positioned to manoeuvre against Lysander's columns as they moved along a road by a fountain locally known as Cissusa. But it was not just the Thebans outside. Others inside the walls with their Haliartan allies were formed up and ready and, seeing their confederates' actions, opened the gates, rushed outside, charged down the road and fell on the head of the enemy formation. Lysander was killed immediately in the first contact. He had been out at the front with his soothsayer, somewhat ahead of the rest of the soldiers. The rest of the front men buckled and fled back the way they had come.

The rest of the Spartan force already under attack, seeing the men who had been up ahead with Lysander in flight, were deeply alarmed. The sight of the troops from the city coming rushing after them was too much. These soldiers were a mixed bag with not that many veterans or Spartans present. They quickly became disordered and were forced to withdraw back up the road they had come down, looking for the protection of Mount Helicon. The Thebans were determined not to let them get off scot-free and the hoplites, reordering quickly, doubled off in pursuit, intent on scouring the hills to annihilate the invaders. It was a massacre along the road. One thousand were killed and the rest were only saved by getting onto rough ground. Once in this terrain with rocks to hide behind and few paths for the enemy to climb after them the Spartans and their allies showed their teeth. Soon rallied, hoplites with spears in sweating hands were jabbing back, men were beating the enemy down with rocks to great effect, and the peltasts were discharging their javelins. This took a toll of the Theban front rank and when they began to roll great stones downhill and followed up with a counterattack with spear and sword, the pursuers began to think better of what up to that time had seemed like a walk in the park. The Boeotians lost 200–300 men before the end of this tangled combat, enough to put a damper on what should have been a great victory. In fact accusations had been flying around that some of the locals in Haliartus had indeed wanted to sell out to the Spartans, just as Lysander had hoped when he arrived so precipitately under the walls of the town. So it is feasible that these men, tainted by the suspicion of siding with the invader, were overeager to show their patriotic credentials and came to grief by pressing too hard in the pursuit of a still dangerous enemy.

All this seems somewhat out of character for foxy Lysander, to rush headlong into battle without knowing the strength or even position of his enemy. Was he quite astonishingly negligent or did he have good reasons for celerity? Had he hoped to bring the place over before more Thebans arrived to stiffen the resolve of the inhabitants? Maybe it has always been too easy to paint him as the great calculator above all else. As much as any Greek he craved personal glory and to get success here without having to share it with Pausanias, a bitter rival for years, was perhaps enough to make him chance a gambler's throw.

Anyway perhaps the most important Spartan in their whole history was dead. Not the most orthodox or the most famous maybe, but the one whose talents made the greatest difference. King Leonidas of the 300 is the most celebrated but in a sense all he did was what any Spartan king would have done, the number of Spartan leaders who died in the front of their battle line is ten a penny. Others like the later Agis IV and Cleomenes III pushed for the social change required to buttress Lacedaemonian power that would have enshrined their reputations, but their efforts ultimately ended in failure. Lysander by his own efforts and talents ended the Peloponnesian War in such a decisive fashion that it gave his people for a brief time a position of predominance in the Greek world. A hegemony that was flawed but no imperium can be without flaws and the ones exhibited by the Spartans, extreme cupidity, arrogance and stupidity can be paralleled in every empire from the Assyrian to the American.

As for Lysander himself he remains an ambiguous figure. He is very much out of academic favour now but in centuries gone by he was the staple of a ruling class education (he is after all name-checked in the seventeenth century marching song 'The British Grenadiers'). A man whose policy was 'to cheat boys with knuckle-bones, but men with oaths.'[2] He has been painted by most of our sources as a vicious and ambitious character even for a Spartan. Frustrated by the fact that he was not king, he is supposed to have considered pushing a radical reform of the monarchy, opening it up so that rulers could be chosen from outside the two royal lines (the Eurypontid and Agiad). To this end he massaged various oracles and portents, slipping coins into the hands of oracle attendants. The chronology and context of this is all very opaque however – it can be placed after the fall of the Thirty in Athens and in the context of the two kings Pausanias and Agis ganging up against him or in events after his death – but the papers alleging this conveniently were not found by Agesilaus till after his death, and it should also be noted that Xenophon who knew Lysander personally mentions nothing of it. As for any trial it 'was proposed, but he presented a persuasive defence of his conduct.'[3] He was never brought to book in any meaningful way by the notoriously litigious Spartans. It is remarkable that the most powerful figure in the Greek world after the Peloponnesian War never tried to impose his dominance on his homeland. Indeed all the evidence seems to indicate that he remained to his death a loyal servant of the Spartan state.[4]

One of the Spartan virtues embodied by Lysander was a lack of interest in material wealth. 'The poverty of Lysander, which was discovered at his death, made his excellence more apparent to all, since from the vast wealth and power in his hands, and from the great homage paid him by cities and the Great King, he had not, even in the slightest degree, sought to amass money for the aggrandisement of his family.'[5] Thus amongst the first who felt the impact of Lysander's death were a number of bachelors back home. They had been engaged to the dead man's daughters but when it came out that he had virtually no money or property to leave his children they broke off their engagements only to be taken to court and fined for such tawdry behaviour.

But they were not the most prominent to feel the fallout of this huge character's demise; another to do so was his co commander in the war. News of what had transpired at Haliartus became known to Pausanias as he led his army from Plataea to Thespiae, west of Thebes, and only a few miles from the battlefield. He kept on the road reaching the town and once near there was reinforced by some of Lysander's remnants. The Phocians and other local troops had made use of the night to head home but the Spartans and others with nowhere else handy to retire to would have found their way to his camp. But despite having a sizable army he was disinclined to look for revenge in another battle or to make an attack on the town now that Thrasybulus had arrived from Thebes with the main Athenian contingent of the confederate army. A strong reinforcement that included cavalry under Orthobulus, Lysias mentions the campaign to illustrate how the life of a cavalryman was easier than that of a hoplite. So when a more stock Spartan response would be baying for revenge Pausanias proposed a peace conference.

While it had looked to many as if a major encounter might be in the wind, both sides may have concentrated forces of over 10,000 strong by this stage, it was not to be. The whole Spartan campaign had been planned as a short term venture with easy conquests but it had not turned out that way so now heralds escorting Pausanias' truce envoys approached the enemy camp. The Thebans would only agree to what was asked if the invaders would consent to leave their territory on the direct route out by Phocis. This indignity was agreed but for Spartan hard liners even worse was to follow; enemy soldiers abused the evacuees along the way and manhandled any of them who strayed from the confines of the road. A real humiliation and reports by angry returnees certainly explains the attitude of the *Gerousia* when the homecoming king gave his version of events. Pausanias had consulted his officer council on the decision to avoid immediate battle and these men largely plumped for caution too on the grounds the enemy were at an advantage both in morale and number of cavalry. And because it would be bound to be problematic getting the bodies of Lysander and the other fallen away from under the walls in the face of armed opposition. A truce was the only sure way and the importance of getting back the corpses was not just an Athenian thing; any leader might fear an 'Arginusae effect' anywhere in the Greek world. But, if the decision was corporate and the sources are at some variance about how unanimous it was, Pausanias knew as king that he would carry the can.[6] With the truce pledged the invaders carrying their comrades' corpses marched out of Boeotia halting in Panopea, just over the border into Phocis on the road from Delphi to Chaeronea, to bury the body of Lysander, though there is a dispute and Pausanias claims he visited the man's tomb at Haliartus itself. Only Spartan kings were brought home for burial, others' bones remained near where they fell. Not that the Spartan axis was giving up the ghost in this region altogether, when the retreating army withdrew a garrison of Spartans was left at Orchomenus to hold up their end for the next round of fighting.

For Pausanias it was nothing but trouble back at Sparta. A mood of sullenness had set in with his men after he failed to get straight back in the ring. The *Gerousia*, incensed at what they saw as pusillanimous behaviour both in failing to support Lysander and in retrieving the bodies of the fallen by combat, immediately put him on trial. This was capital stuff particularly if it is to be believed that he was at the same time re-arraigned for the old charge about his failure to succour the Thirty outside Piraeus in 403, an accusation of which he had already been acquitted once. He had been around and knew a stacked deck when he saw one and expecting the worst jumped bail and fled up the road to Tegea seeking sanctuary at the temple to Athena. Here he saw out the rest of his days, though he continued to intervene in Spartan affairs and is known to have written a pamphlet accusing his enemies of violating the laws of Lycurgus.

So Lysander, the man who had done the most to found Spartan hegemony, departed as the first great test of his creation got underway. The exact causes of what became known as the Corinthian War are, like so much else at this time, open to argument with a whole host of contributing factors. Matters at Rhodes were certainly a catalyst; those islanders threw off the Spartan imperial yoke in 396 and this despite the city's merchants having been firm friends of Sparta in the last years of the Athenian war. But they had not just fought to exchange one imperium for another and when the presence of Sparta's enemies with ships aplenty announced a change in the power balance at sea, they took their chance. The defection of Rhodes cut Egyptian aid to Sparta and militated against any opportunity of co-operation between their navy and army and concerted actions in Caria. But it was more than just the appearance of this first crack in the Spartan edifice; another player had also taken a crucial hand in affairs. Lacedaemonian support for Cyrus had stirred up a tide of resentment at Susa and the advent of Agesilaus digging even deeper into Persian Anatolia only made things worse. So it is hardly surprising Persia had laid long and well made plans to make trouble for these new imperialists and the torch they used to light the hoped for conflagration sparkled with the radiance of Persian darics. The man on the spot, Tithraustes, in charge in the west after disposing of his predecessor Tissaphernes, had already spent thirty talents to get a temporary respite from the Spartan king's depredations and now was prepared to outlay fifty more – little enough cash to permanently rid the Persian empire of Agesilaus, so he now utilised some Rhodians to enter into negotiations and foment dissent against Sparta with the other Greek powers. His first emissary, Dorieus, had been caught and executed by the Spartans, but undeterred by this setback he soon waved off another Rhodian agent called Timocrates with his bags of money en route to mainland Greece.

Whether Athens was visited is unclear, war wounds were perhaps too raw and recent, but Argos, Corinth and Thebes were, and at each Tithraustes' man found he was pushing at an open door. It was not just money, it was also opportunity. All knew of the absence of significant Spartan forces in Asia and this undoubtedly warmed up antipathy to Spartan hegemony; a two year absence by Agesilaus and his army counted in the minds of those in Argos, Corinth, Thebes or anywhere else that the experience of Spartan pre-eminence had soured. As this included to some degree most of those in south and central Greece, when payback came it was inclusive and considerable. Resentment at the treatment of Elis and anger at demands for troops to fuel Sparta's Asian wars were crucial but though some people claim this turning on Sparta was a reaction to the great sea battle at Cnidus the evidence does not fit. Everything points to combat having occurred some time after the Corinthian War began. This disaster would be crucial in ungluing Spartan thalassocracy, but the possibility rather than its accomplishment had been the key. Whatever the chronology there is no denying that after an extremely short period the supremacy of the taciturn men from Laconia was definitely under serious threat.

The motives of Thebes in being not just unprepared to support the state that had led them in years of war against Athens, but actually to contemplate fighting against it were complex. It was not just turpitude; some old allies had been deeply disappointed over the share they received when peace was made following the fall of Athens. Thebes had been hugely resentful – feelings her leaders could not disguise when Agesilaus tried to make an event out of leaving Aulis for Asia. Androclidas, Ismenias and Galaxidorus are mentioned as the recipients of money at Thebes. These men coming to the fore represented the triumph of a new faction in the Boeotian League at about the turn of the century. An essentially pro-Spartan group including Leontiades and Erianthus (who had fought with Lysander at Aegospotami and was the Theban delegate that called for destruction of Athens in 404) had lost influence sometime between 400 and 397. This old guard though seems to have been well supported by cities other than Thebes, such as Orchomenus, and may have represented a looser federal tenancy, uncomfortable not just with the class direction of their supposedly more democratic rivals in Thebes, but also opposed to what they saw as an increasingly centralising tendency.

Though the new Boeotian power brokers' policy motivations were complex, it was Spartans battening their control around the Malian Gulf that got them really going. Other things that happened at the end of the Great War counted too, but it was surely this that had finally alienated much of the Boeotian elite and induced them into provoking the Spartans into a Phocian war – but only after they had searched for allies amongst old enemies. At Athens the Theban ambassadors, after first making an unconvincing fist of trying to slide out of having proposed Athens be devastated only a few years before (blaming it on an unrepresentative delegate) worked on their host's undoubted desire to win back some of their past power and influence. This resonated much more now Conon had reappeared backed by the Great King. In addition, the ambassadors could also point to the aid Thebes had provided to support the revolt against the Thirty, and their refusal to have any part of the Spartan campaign against the democrats at Piraeus. They even painted a picture of a world where Athens, rising on a wave of anti-Spartan hatred, would head a new league of, not just her old tributaries eager to return to old allegiances after the experience of Lysander's harmosts, but places like Elis and others too who had suffered from Spartan bullying. In joining up they would make a plethora of new friends from old enemies like the Corinthians, Arcadians, Achaeans and more, all brassed off at their failure to get much out of their efforts in the Peloponnesian War.

Athens had already shown an inclination to flex old imperial muscles in 397 when they had sent men and equipment to Conon, and an embassy to the Great King. These had not got through a cordon of Spartan-held places without some difficulty, but it showed a willingness to tread the great power road again. In the winter of 396/5 Demaenetus sailed with one of the twelve ships allowed by treaty to join up with Conon. The city's rulers were in two minds: there was a desire to face off the Spartans, but many worried they just did not yet have the military chops to attempt it; Thrasybulus for one thought this tweaking of the Spartans' nose was far too premature and denounced it to the harmost at Aegina. The impression of Thebes as a ravening wolf eager to consume the carcass of Athens must have been a memory hard to forget. There was no question that Thebes' recent good offices made the difference, and as time passed the opposition to Sparta became sharper. Thrasybulus eventually came on board and was able to declare Athens' commitment to a defensive alliance, despite the fact that the long walls and defences of Piraeus were far from fully rebuilt. It was a show of unanimity that indicated that both democrats and the rump of the oligarchs had made enough of an accommodation to allow them to direct their belligerence out against foreign enemies rather than at each other. This showed a remarkable preparedness to forget grudges from the gruesome days of the Four Hundred and the Thirty and would soon show benefits in returning a recrudescent city to a central place on the Hellenic world stage.

The Attic-Boeotian confederacy was duly consecrated and soon after Haliartus it was joined by another extraordinary adherent: Corinth, the very city which had kicked off the Peloponnesian War with her ship building programme to take on the navy from Corcyra and her inclination to help a Potidaea under attack by Imperial Athens. They had fought for generations; it had been Corinthian ships that had been Athens' significant rival at sea for most of the war. Now another city that a few years before had wanted to see Athens annihilated was prepared to stand alongside her, a transformation certainly eased by the Persian money pocketed by their leaders Timolaus and Polyanthes. An extraordinary turn around almost akin to the eighteenth century climactic when Prince Kaunitz of Maria Theresa's Austria turned the whole of European diplomacy on its head in a bid to gain revenge on Frederick the Great of Prussia. Money had also found its way to Cylon and his party in Argos and they also soon joined a confederation that was a more natural fit for these inveterate and long time Sparta haters (a dislike not in the least mollified by both peoples claiming descent from Heracles). Now these incongruous collaborators set up a council at Corinth and from there sent envoys to any place they thought might give them a hearing to propose ditching the Spartan yoke. It did not seem so difficult now to detach old allies of the Spartans. The embassies were generally well received and Euboea, Acarnania, Leucas, Ambracia and the cities of Chalcidice all came on board. Others like Eretria joined later – they were probably allied with Athens by 394/3. In the Peloponnese however there had been few defections: there the big boss with the big stick was too intimidating to mess with.

The first decisions made at the allied council showed where many of their concerns rested. A Sparta-dominated Peloponnese was perhaps a fact of life but when she looked set to become the main player in Thessaly and the north that was something else. The Boeotians had already made inroads in Thessaly after the victory at Haliartus, making friends at Crannon, Pharsalus and other places, but now a major expedition was sent in that direction to prise the Spartans out of where they had dug themselves in over the last few years. Thessaly and the road to the north were key because of timber, silver, gold and control of the grain routes. Coin and calories: key issues that explain why the Corinthian War began there. Two thousand hoplites under Ismenias went to help Medius of Larissa who was fighting Lycophron, tyrant of Pherae (a city that would soon produce real players of the likes of Jason). With this support he took Pharsalus from the Spartans, a place they had garrisoned after the Peloponnesian War and then sold the population into slavery. Apart from digging out these intruders the confederates hoped their efforts would encourage the local Thessalian cavaliers to put a block on Agesilaus coming through overland from Asia. Then in late 395 or early 394 the force helping Medius broke camp and moved south against Heraclea and took it by subterfuge. They had prepared the way by lining the pockets of some locals and were let in the walls by these turncoats. They cut down any Lacedaemonians they found but apparently let other Peloponnesians go. They still had high hopes of some of Sparta's peninsular allies jumping ship and did not want to alienate them needlessly.

Exiles that had been expelled by the Spartans were part of the force attacking Heraclea. They now took over this key strongpoint, with Argive troops left as a garrison to ensure they stayed loyal. Ismenias also did good work on the diplomatic front persuading the Ainianians and Athamanians to ditch their alliance with Sparta and join up with the Boeotian forces. These new friends brought the available army to 6,000 men and with these kinds of numbers their generals could contemplate another attack on that other great enemy in the region, the Phocians. So they marched down through Thermopylae and from Epicnemidian Locris on towards the borderland of Phocis making base near Abae (a place famous for another oracle to Apollo with plenty of famous names in its visitors' book and considerable fortifications that can still be seen today). Their presence there stirred up an immediate response and the whole Phocian levy was pulled out and led into the fray by a Spartan called Alcisthenes. There are no details of the fight, only that the Boeotians won and, intent on exploiting the victory, pressed on in pursuit of the routed enemy until darkness brought an end to the slaughter. Nearly 1,000 Phocians died – a huge butcher's bill as it must have amounted to over a quarter of the army they brought to the field. The Boeotians lost many men as well, possibly as many as 500. Both sides bloodied and exhausted pulled apart. The defenders went home to nurse their wounds and bury their dead as the invaders pulled back along the road they had come and most left the colours to return to their home cities.

Sparta had not precipitated the war but welcomed it as much as anybody else. Now, after having been struck a very serious blow by the events that had occurred around the Malian Gulf and Boeotia, they understood the conflict they found themselves involved in would be a major one not some walkover, like at Elis, as some may well have anticipated. The region where the first blood, including Lysander's, had been shed was not to be where the war developed next: the arena of conflict moved south. It was April or May by the time things came to a head. The Corinthian leader, Timolaus, had an ambitious plan, and he had the credentials: in the last war he had been a victorious squadron commander up near Amphipolis crushing an enemy fleet and subverting Thasos from her Athenian alliance. Now he encouraged his partners to take the war into Sparta itself, arguing that it was best to set fire to a wasps' nest when the occupants were still in the hive. But the very complexity and friction attendant on getting an allied force up and running were always going to put obstacles in the way of such rapid action. In Athens particularly many people had regained so little of their pre-defeat confidence that they were avoiding the recruiting officers as much as they could. As Timolaus had warned, the Laconian stream was in full spate by the time the allies were battle ready and it would be on Corinth's doorstep not Sparta's that events would play out. The confederate leaders' intentions were still offensive however. The army had moved south to Nemea intent on heading down the road to Sparta when they got news that the enemy were not far off.[7]

In this spring of 394 the Spartan invasion army was led by Aristodemus, regent for King Agesipolis, the heir of Pausanias, who was then too young to command. After the problems that monarch had experienced, he had been determined not to go off half cock. First bringing out the Spartan levy he had marched north to Tegea to pick up the allies mustered there before travelling the road over the plain of Mantinea where more regiments of allies awaited him. Sicyon, near the shore of the Gulf of Corinth, had been the target and by the time the town was reached he learned the confederate army had taken up a position on the hills around Nemea. From his base near Sicyon, intending to take the fight to the enemy as soon as possible, Aristodemus marched his men over the road through Epieicia where high rough ground rose on the right hand side. The confederates, who had travelled west from Corinth along the coast before turning up the valley towards Cleonae,

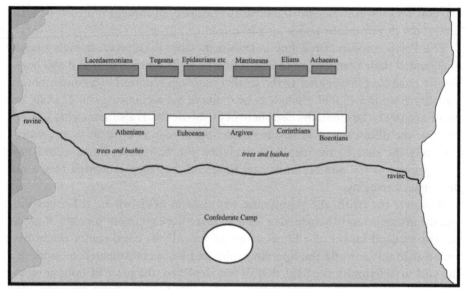

The Battle of Nemea 394 BC.

were now not far away. Though their main force was camped near Nemea, they had moved forward a good number of light troops, peltasts, slingers, archers and javelin men to guard the road the Spartans were taking. Now these agile warriors were able to do considerable damage, with missiles discharged down onto the troops below them. The Spartans, after suffering some casualties, managed to debouch onto the coastal plain between Sicyon and Corinth where the main combat took place.

The confederates also moved their main army down from Nemea to position themselves between the enemy and Corinth. The river to the east of which they camped has not been identified beyond doubt but most probably was the dry, steep-sided watercourse of the Rachiani that runs to the sea near the hamlet of Perigiali on the east and to Kato Assos on the west rather than the actual River Nemea that formed the boundary between Sicyon and Corinth. It is only about two miles between the hills and the sea so the battle lines would have filled the bulk of this fertile plain though if the sea was not far off (on the day of battle to the right of the Boeotian hoplites and on the left of the Achaeans on the other side) it is never mentioned in any of the accounts. The rival armies camped opposite each other for some days, the Peloponnesians a mile or so to the west of the river, before it came to fighting in this great hoplite contest. Most men on both sides carried spears sharp at butt and tip, with shields of oak covered by bronze and wore leg, head and as often as not body armour each occupying a front of about one yard. This panoply with a short sword or single edged sabre weighed about sixty pounds and cost between 100 and 300 drachmas to purchase, an amount represented at the time about three months wages for a labourer.

The Peloponnesian battle line is known in some detail even though rumour exaggerated their numbers on the day of battle to 23,000 infantry and 500 horse. Reality must have been closer to the smaller numbers reported by a contemporary, something around 15,000, though as he omits in his accounting the Tegeans and Mantineans who he mentions elsewhere in the battle this is also somewhat suspect. Even so the difference of something under 9,000 men is difficult to rationalize. Certainly the first figure may have included the light troops that could have been present to the number of several thousand, but even accepting this, a real discrepancy remains.

Whatever the truth, the positioning was clear in fields where, it being spring and the grounds recently turned or seeded, there were plenty of touches of green, not the parched brown of a Greek summer yet. All the contingents would have armed themselves while the Spartan leader and his seers prepared to sacrifice a she goat to Artemis on the field altar. When deployed, the place of honour on the right went to the regent Aristodemus, with 6,000 hoplites from Laconia – full Spartiates fleshed out with *perioeci* heavy infantry and enfranchised helots as well. This was a good turnout, with no significant enemy naval forces threatening, little in terms of coastal defence needed to be left behind back home. Left of them came the Tegeans; next were 3,000 spearmen from the coast of the Argolid, from Epidaurus, Troezen, Hermione and Halieis, perennial rivals of their overbearing neighbour Argos, just come in after something of a march from the country east of there; in the middle of the phalanx were an unknown number of Mantineans and other Arcadians; then 3,000 from Elis, Triphylia, Acroria and Lasionia; and the far left was held by Achaeans. Fifteen hundred were of the local hoplite levy just picked up from Sicyon. Notably absent were the Phliasians (a people from just west of Nemea) who did not join up because of a sacred truce. They would not have provided many troops, but their failure to come through for a battle so proximate must have been a worry for the Peloponnesian League leadership. On top of these heavy infantry, 600 cavalry are reported present, as well as light troops including 300 Cretan archers and 400 slingers from Margania, Letrinia and Amphidolia places near Triphylia, that had all recently been violently de-incorporated by Sparta from the Elean League. Opposed to them were an enemy drawn up but not visible, with a brush and tree covered riverbed in between. Here the four major powers in the confederacy standing against Sparta were in force – Corinth, Athens, Argos and Thebes – and with them contingents from many other smaller places and peoples who had sent men to fight.

What we get on tactical discussion from the command tent of the confederates comes from Xenophon and it cannot be taken uncritically as we know he had a particular distaste for Thebes, so that these people come out of this looking pretty shifty should not be a surprise at all. He contends that, as the command of the army was rotated and with it the position of prestige on the right, they refused to join battle until it was scheduled that they would command, and so not end up facing the Spartans. This explanation is difficult to credit as surely the dodge would have been completely transparent to their allies who could have come up with some bad chicken livers of their own if they had not been happy with their place in the formation. The more probable explanation is that the confederates intending to force their attack on the right agreed to the Boeotians deploying there as the best men for the job. This also makes sense of the other strand of the debate about how deep the different contingents should deploy.

Since the battle of Delium in 424 the Thebans had been experimenting with 25-man deep formations and wanted to do so on this occasion as well. The problem with this was it left their partners with more enemy frontage to cover with their more traditionally formed lines. It is asserted that there was an agreement to deploy up to sixteen men deep rather than the usual eight to twelve, but that when they brought on the battle the Thebans reneged and drew up 'excessively' deep, which meant the rest of the contingents needed to move to the right so the Athenians on the far left found themselves outflanked. This last swipe, like the first, emphasised to his audience that these Thebans were folk happy to renege on a previous agreement. But again it is far more likely this was an agreed tactic; after all they had been successful with the deep formation before and it is surely possible their generals had persuaded their allies to follow this practice so profitable in the past.

That all this was prearranged is made more probable as we hear that the rest of the army 'also veered to the right in leading the advance, in order to outflank the enemy with their wing'[8], which may be a description of what would develop into the classically Theban technique of oblique advance. The deployment of the whole line certainly sounds like more than just the normal hoplite shuffle to the right. It was an intentional move and done with the understanding that the rest of the army should deploy in sync with the Thebans whose job was to deliver the Sunday punch on the right.

Whether agreed or by sharp practice, the Boeotians were holding the command on the right. These men, renowned for stolidity, were probably weighted 25 men deep, opposite the weaker left of the enemy line, leaving the Athenians to face the strongest enemy the Spartans themselves. The compact Boeotian force, easier to manoeuvre because it was less broad, occupying a front of about 200 yards, was intended to outflank and crush the enemy in front before the Spartans had been able to bring their full force to bear on the weaker parts of the confederate line. A victory on this right side would cause a hesitation in the enemy mass and they would break and run, or if not the victorious Boeotians would be free to come to their allies' assistance and turn the fight that way. These warriors, designated as the cutting edge, had turned up in numbers though they must have worried about their northern borders with word of Agesilaus being on the march from Asia. They fielded 5,000 hoplites – down on numbers with the men from

Orchomenus, recent friends of Lysander and garrisoned by Sparta refusing to muster – and on top they brought 800 cavalry, beefed up by 600 more from Athens, 100 from Chalcis in Euboea, 50 from the Opuntian Locrians. Next, on the left of the Boeotian hoplites, came the Corinthians to the number of 3,000, for so long Sparta's stalwart allies and Athens' bitterest enemies, but now all was changed and they were ready to put up their city's life blood in gallons in the lottery of battle, fighting as the confederates of ancient foes. After them came the Argives: 7,000 of them, poison deep rivals of the Lacedaemonians for centuries, with memories of Spartan-driven helots burning 6,000 of their fellow citizens in a sacred grove after the battle of Sepeia almost exactly a century before. Local boys, they had picked up their kit and marched the short road to the fight taking place virtually on their home ground. After them 3,000 more hoplites were stationed; Euboeans who had long been and would become again a bulwark for the Athenians, partnered with men from Locris, Malis and Acarnania. The Athenians, with Thrasybulus at their head, fielded 6,000 hoplites on the far left, very recognisable with their officers still wearing the Corinthian helmet as against the Phrygian type with better vision and hearing worn by the rank and file. And their generals with gaudy clothes and splendid armour – Alcibiades' shield on another occasion was so conspicuous it warranted a description that is reminiscent of Achilles in the Iliad. There were 24,000 hoplites reported all told, apart from light troops, who had come from Malia, Acarnania and Ozolian Locris in considerable numbers.

When the whole army moved forward there was that typical shift to the right as each hoplite looked to get cover from the shield of the man on that side. For all contingents (except the Athenians on the far left) this posed no great issue – if they inclined right they would still be covered. But for the Athenians it was different; they knew any such move might leave their own flank in the air and likely to be overlapped by the enemy opposite. Yet considering this a lesser evil than allowing a large gap to develop in the line if they stayed put, they too edged to the right. The whole phalanx that was ordered forward had been camped behind what in parts was a very defensible *wadi*, but they decided to cross it to get at their adversary. This feature would have been the one element that might have ruled out an equal trial of strength, but the confederates decided to give up the advantage. In this resolution we find a parallel with that made by the Greek mercenaries during their *Anabasis* when Xenophon, the commander, had to gee up his men to cross a ravine and attack the Persians and Bithynians drawn up on the other side. So now, on a grander scale, the confederates faced a choice whether to give up the initiative and retain the defensive benefit of the dry bed of the Rachiani in front of them, or to go for broke, cross over, and with the momentum of advancing, hope to roll over the Peloponnesians in front of them. They had decided on attack and this movement forward occurred even before the Peloponnesians saw them. Rough ground and brush obscured their view, and only very late did the confederates' war cries alert them they were under attack. By the time the Peloponnesians had a good view of the brazen line approaching they had also shifted in typical style to the right, and so overlapped the attackers' left even more. A good part of the men on the extreme right of the Peloponnesian line had only a wide open space in front of them; these were Lacedaemonians – part of the 6,000 that presumably comprised at least five of the six citizen regiments (*morai*) as well as the Sciritae from the high border country to the north of the Eurotas valley. And more than the normal move to the right, it appears they too had deliberately advanced obliquely just like the Boeotians and 'extended their wing so far beyond that of the enemy that only six tribes of the Athenians found themselves opposite the Lacedaemonians, the other four being opposite the Tegeans.'[9] Only two thirds of the Athenians ended up in front of the Spartans. Whether because of the natural hoplite tendency in battle or through a move decided on in Aristodemus' public tent, with the lines less than 200 yards apart, and easily visible it became clear that according to one calculation a 275-man wide section of the Spartan line was extending beyond the enemy flank.[10]

If the shape of the two armies was clear, once the confederates had crossed over the riverbed the manner of the Spartan outflanking is less so. It might have been an orderly process with the Lacedaemonians split in two and one half hinging so that it was at right angles to its comrades and on the extreme flank of the Athenians. This is just believable, because of the Spartans' fame for practising battle drills, but it still seems a little too formulaic. Perhaps it would be better to imagine the overlapping Spartans marching into the space in front of them and breaking formation, with looser groupings going in on the enemy flank and rear. Without being faced by a shield wall but only a vulnerable flank, they would not have needed to keep formation so much themselves and could have fought almost as individuals, cutting at and striking down their enemies on their exposed backs and sides. The Athenians had their shields carried on the left, but if this allowed some defence all they could have really done would be fend off blows and, assaulted on the flank and rear, they could not have held together long. What is apparent in all this is that there were no cavalry or light troops on duty to guard the Athenian phalanx's vulnerable flank. So these people who had haemorrhaged fighters' blood on the fields of Sicily and the waters of Arginusae and Aegospotami not long before, now again faced the best soldiers in Greece coming at them from all sides. They had no real answers to offer. The men of Attica fought, defending themselves and their comrades as best they could, but from the rear ranks those not engaged soon began to slip away, and it was not long at all before the Spartans had nothing to see through the eye slits of their helmets but a litter of discarded shields and spears and Athenian backs fleeing in front of them. Though Thrasybulus was on hand at this moment of despair and tried to rally the fleeing men, it was to no avail.

The men of the other four Athenian tribes that did not have Spartans to contend with found themselves facing hoplites from Tegea and there it was very different. They attacked with vigour, sweeping these opponents away in the first charge. Nor were these Athenians alone in scoring success on the confederate side. The

25-deep Theban phalanx with their Boeotian comrades alongside carved through most of the Achaeans in front of them; the Corinthians had little trouble with the Eleans; and the Argives drove over the Mantineans, the Euboeans and the men from the east Argolid.

The most poignant episode of the first phase of the battle included a people who suffered from the tendency when sections of any battle line were drawn from one particular community that if there was especial carnage in their sector it could have ramifications for that people out of all proportion to the overall casualties. This event has been described as the third holocaust to strike the little town of Thespiae.[11] Seven hundred Thespians fell to Persian spears and arrows at Thermopylae in 480 alongside the Spartan 300 and there was also a massacre of their forces at the battle of Delium in 424. At Nemea there is a description of the Thespians and their opponents from the Achaean town of Pellene fighting and dying where they stood; they 'fought and fell in their places'. Something that is difficult to credit quite as it is described. It is a truism that casualties in battle virtually through the ages and certainly in ancient times come mainly after one side had routed, in the pursuit when the defeated have turned their backs in flight. Not when prepared, feet braced, shield forward and ready to fight face to face. And this was particularly the case with the Greek infantry phalanx, armoured virtually from head to toe. It was not easy to get at one of these warriors as they stood tight in formation with a neighbour on their right shielding their vulnerable side. It is just difficult to imagine how with both sides, steady and fighting on, with neither turning to run, that casualties could have been that high. Even if they battled for long hours, virtually impossible without taking breaks to rest, the slaughter would still surely not have been so total. This encounter marked for the Thespians one of the few times they lined up in battle with their Boeotian neighbour, in future they are generally found allied with the enemies of Thebes. It is noted the Spartans helped rebuild in 378 the city walls that the Thebans had knocked down after Delium despite the Thespians' suicidal efforts on their behalf. The upshot for them always seemed to end tragically though, and eventually the whole community was extirpated when Thebes took top dog position after the battle of Leuctra.

Apart from the men from Pellene who encountered the Thespians, all Sparta's allies showed poorly in the first phase of the battle and either before the front rows clashed or soon after took to their heels showing a tendency to fail in support of the Spartan cause that would not be untypical in years to come. This might have indicated that a people who might have put up with Spartan failings when they had a joint enemy to fight found them increasingly difficult to tolerate once a dominant power. And this was nothing new. A case can be made that at Haliartus Lysander had not been well supported by his allies either. What for so many of these Peloponnesian soldiers, now on the run, must have seemed like the deluge were saved by the masters of war who had led them onto the battlefield. The Spartans, under their regent, had either planned or taken advantage of circumstance as they overlapped the Athenians opposite and attacked and dispersed them, and now they showed the benefit of years of training. Not for them an undisciplined chase after a defenceless foe who had broken in blood: they looked round over their left shoulder and saw that the rest of their army had dissolved and that what they had done to the Athenians had been done to their own allies. These veteran commanders and men also saw that the victorious elements of the enemy army had regrouped from their pursuit and turned round in good order preparing to march back the way they had come. This procedure meant that on the return march they would expose their right unprotected side to the Spartans who in these circumstances did not hesitate.

As the Argives began to move across the Spartan front it was shouted, not as an order by an officer but as a spontaneous idea 'let their front ranks pass by' allowing the head of the marching column to pass in front of them before they attacked. The result was that their blows 'struck them on their unprotected sides'. Presumably if they had kicked off the attack too soon, the front ranks approaching them might have turned and been able to contrive a shield wall. By letting them go by they ensured the Argives were defenceless when the Spartans hit, crashing through, spearing and hacking against unguarded necks and torsos. The Argives could only try to turn and fend off blows, unable to form for defence. With no retort to this assault they routed, throwing down their shields and spears and running for their lives while the Spartans calmly reformed and prepared to repeat the manoeuvre against the Corinthians. They too were bowled over with tireless Spartan arms wreaking mayhem amongst men who not long before they had fought alongside. Now in front of the Lacedaemonian phalanx were the Boeotians and Thebans again with their right unshielded side exposed and expecting no threat after they had overrun all the enemy hoplites facing them. No warning seems to have been given – no one noticed what was happening. When their turn came they too were driven off in rout like the rest in a storm of flesh, iron and bronze that once it had concluded its course left many of these men from central Greece dead on a peninsular battlefield.

A conundrum is how exactly the attack of the Spartan wing against the returning Argives, Corinthians and Boeotians came about. What is described seems extraordinary but is the attestation of men who were soldiers themselves. Most literate Greeks of the time, anybody able to write a history, play or poem probably served their term in their city's army. We certainly know Xenophon, our main source, was a commander of great experience, though he was not present at this encounter and his account is extremely brief. Still the question that comes to mind is first why the allied troops were returning in such a manner? Why when victorious on the wing did they not either turn to make a flank attack on the enemy to their left, or on turning back from pursuit and realising the allies facing the Spartans had fled and that their own flank was in the air, why would they not naturally have turned to form up in that direction? – perhaps more easily said than done, but surely there would have been some attempt to make a front against the Spartan phalanx bearing down on them? Instead they marched back, right side exposed across the very front of the victorious and threatening enemy. An explanation might be that the dust of battle made the position of their enemy unclear. It may have been that the heavy units of Corinthians, Boeotians and other allies, realising their Athenian allies had been driven off, decided to pull back to find a safer position but were blind to an enemy who were perfectly positioned to fall on them when they attempted this manoeuvre. If it was not the dust (being early in the year) perhaps in the pursuit they had completely lost order and just did not have the discipline to adjust their formation.

The fighting, including the victors herding the defeated army off the battlefield, may well have lasted most of the day. The first phase – deployment and movement to combat – could have taken a number of hours, and then the fight and pursuit on both flanks of the battle has to be accounted for, as well as the reordering of the Spartans to be ready for their attack in the second phase, and the time it took for the Corinthians, Boeotians and Argives to regroup after pursuit and return the way they had come and into the brutal arms of the waiting Spartans. Our knowledge of how long combat lasted in ancient battles is inexact, but the organisation and moving of these great blocks of men was bound to be time consuming. What might be described as a swift assault would probably have included a considerable time period getting the soldiers dressed and into position before any swords were crossed.

What the roles of the other arms in the battle were, apart from the familiar armed hoplite, is not recorded. The many light troops do not get a mention in the actual battle even though the terrain was such where they might have been utilised effectively. As for the cavalry, who were quite numerous for such a classic phalanx action, we know nothing and there is no suggestion of what they did to affect the fight. They must have been involved to some degree as there is an extant tombstone of an Athenian horseman who died in the battle; perhaps they pursued the broken enemy heavy units which allowed the victorious troops on both sides to pull up from the chase and reorganise. Or maybe the horsemen of both sides were on the wings in sufficient strength to occupy each other and allow the infantry to face off unmolested across the battlefield. But this is all speculation and there is nothing to tell us what the noble cavaliers did to earn their corn.

When the main event was over, the victors who had maintained their reputation as battle winners seem to have been well placed to continue the pursuit but on seeing the rough tree covered country split by a dry watercourse between them and the enemy camp they decided against it. They must already have been dog tired and their officers no doubt worried what would happen if they became disorganised and vulnerable to an enemy who might rally and turn on their pursuers. The final act for the victors was the stripping of the enemy fallen and preparations to set up a trophy at the place where the epicentre of the contest had been. As for the beaten army they had suffered much, but at least on the final trudge back to camp they were no longer harassed, and once there were able to pull off their armour and find some rest, even those of them who had initially tried to find refuge behind the walls of Corinth itself but discovered the gates closed against them by those inside. Their generals would now have organised the dispatch of a herald to ask for the traditional truce to collect their dead; an act that formally acknowledged their defeat.

Nemea has been maintained as one of the largest hoplite battles of all time in terms of numbers involved and as befitted an encounter on such a grand scale the casualties were considerable, the victors suffered as many as 1,100 and on the confederate side up to 2,800 men fell. But as for actual Spartiates the body count was very low. Agesilaus was told that only eight had perished in the battle. The only confederates to have escaped lightly seem to have been the four Athenian tribes who had seen off the Tegeans. We know specifically they had not returned when the Spartans came at right angles taking the confederate troops in the flank. So the Spartans must have moved behind them while they were still involved in chasing the Tegeans and when they saw what was happening they made no attempt to aid their comrades but withdrew as quickly as possible out of range of the savage rampaging adversary. Thus they suffered little apart from just a handful lost in the initial clash with the men from Tegea.

Of the sequel to the battle, despite the supposed disparity in bloodletting and the apparent triumph of the Spartan war machine, the Battle of Nemea did not decide anything and in just a few months the beaten enemy were fielding an army against a Spartan king in a different corner of the country. The Spartans, realising dimly at last how hated they had become, saw that they could not afford to have some of their best men swanning about miles away in Anatolia. 'When the Lacedaemonians saw that the greatest cities of Greece were uniting against them, they voted to summon Agesilaus and his army from Asia.'[12] Ephors and generals would soon be visiting Agesilaus in numbers on the road, showing just how important he was considered to be for the war effort; not just because of the army he was bringing, but also because of the treasure he had taken in Asia which was much needed to beef up Sparta's war chest. The need for a leader was great; Lysander was dead, Pausanias exiled, Agesilaus had to be recalled. The Great King of Persia was already seeing dividends from his outlay to line the pockets of the great and good in the cities of Greece.

Chapter Six

On Land and Sea

If Agesilaus in spring 394 was deep in thought planning a further great Asian campaign of invasion he was to find, like so many before and after, that it would in the end be extraneous events that would carve out his path rather than any dynamic of personal intellect or will. The Spartan authorities had found Greece was far from submissive so the king had to come back and there was no gainsaying this imperative. But before Agesilaus could impact, the tough crowd he was leading had to be got on the road and presumably the Greeks of Asia reassured; they must have been deeply worried at the prospect of their protector being about to disappear over the western horizon. The practicalities were already in hand; while hobnobbing with the Paphlagonians earlier, Agesilaus had been in contact with the commander of the small squadron guarding the Hellespont. But while he was well on top of events on the road to Europe when the call came, it took all his ingenuity to prise his men away from the rich pickings of Anatolia to fight fellow Greeks; to battle against the tough and steady hoplites like themselves with much less in the way of goods to pillage even in the event of victory. But Agesilaus knew his men and got them out of Anatolia and over the three miles of water to Sestos on the European shore of the Hellespont by promising prizes for the best soldiers on arrival. Once there we do not hear of any resistance to moving on, so perhaps he sold each stage separately, offering initially a handy and facile campaign against the Thracians with easy loot to be had. He fought one of these people almost as soon as he got across from Asia, the Trallians; the other tribes having responded well to Agesilaus' offers of friendship. These belligerent locals harboured long memories of gifts given by Xerxes when he passed by in 480 and expected silver and women from these latest voyagers too. To get through it required a real stand-up battle but this went wholly the way of the Peloponnesians.

In this new situation a pair of old associates briefly teamed up. Agesilaus was near Amphipolis intimidating the inhabitants when Dercylidas, the very man whose army he had taken over in Asia, stepped off a boat with news of what had happened in the fields between Sicyon and Corinth. The general agreed with the king that it was crucial to get the news of the victory of Nemea to their friends in the Hellespont and Asia to discourage any sympathy movements for the confederate Greeks in those regions. This mission was very much to the taste of this globetrotting bachelor who clearly enjoyed the esteem he got abroad rather than the stick he got at home for being a non-procreator. But if Dercylidas was required to fight any fires out there in the far flung empire, the king himself had the means and the instructions to crush the Boeotian viper in its nest. With the seaways less safe Agesilaus had been required to walk all the way from the Hellespont through difficult country and threatening people. But there was more; the Macedonians, initially prevaricating, were overawed by Agesilaus beefing up his cavalry arm by mixing in mules, asses and baggage mounts, and allowed the army to pass without let or hindrance. So following all the way the route taken by Xerxes, all those years before, they pressed on swiftly, taking hardly more than a month, eager to get to Greece before the war could be decided without them. After passing through Archelaus II's kingdom the men from Asia penetrated the Vale of Tempe and onwards as the country spread out into the wide plains of Thessaly.

To keep up his pace Agesilaus tried at first to stay on good terms with the Thessalians, but when they demurred, making it clear they favoured the confederates, the impression given is that he was not too distraught. As a Spartan king he loved a fight and his combativeness was rendered only more intense when his two ambassadors to the city of Larissa were dragged off to the lock up and kept prisoner against all the custom of war. It did put him in a quandary: Agesilaus must have been sorely tempted to stay and teach these impious, impudent folk a lesson, and some of his officers and men wanted to lay siege to Larissa, but he also knew the real war was down south and time was of the essence. 'But he declared that the capture of all Thessaly would not compensate him for the loss of either one of his men, and made terms with the enemy in order to get them back.'[1] Honour satisfied, he determined to march on. The country he was now passing through was one of two open plains, the eastern one dominated by Larissa and the western by Pharsalus, which would be a cockpit of conflict all through ancient times. Two battles would be fought by Cynoscephalae – a range of hills known from its shape as the 'Dog's Head' – in 364 and 197, and others at Crannon in 322 and Pharsalus in 48; decisive conflicts in a Macedonian and a Roman Civil War respectively. Agesilaus found that many a Thessalian city was already committed to the Boeotians and the confederation whose troops had done good work there in the very recent past. So with the governments at Larissa, Crannon, Scotussa and Pharsalus on board, only the exiled factions were pro-Spartan, and there were plenty of men in war gear prepared to contest the passage of Agesilaus' army.

The people of these plains were natural horsemen; their beasts raised on the rich alluvial soil 'where haughty barons in wide brimmed sunhats raced their horses over serf tilled fields.'[2] Fighting in square formations these men, born to ride, had a reputation hard won for being the best cavalry in Greece; only Macedonians could perhaps match them. And they were hardly really Greek anyway, more akin to the barbarian Getae or Scythians from whom many of the techniques of horsemanship they excelled in had been learned. So with a country of nimble horsemen up against them the invaders, already footsore from marching hundreds of miles, found themselves required to adapt some of those practices that the 10,000 had utilised when they discovered themselves in a similar situation. Fortunately for Agesilaus he had a good few of the survivors of that campaign with him, including Xenophon himself. These veterans who had held off enemy horse and barbarian peltasts in the heart of the Persian kingdom were no doubt not backward with their counsel. It was a tactic they had used before when the army of Agesilaus moved off in a hollow square, with half the cavalry in the front and the other half protecting the rear.

The Thessalian cavalry (a grave stele shows them in helmets, body armour and flowing cloaks) called up from their cities and farms, came on hard, harassing the intruders who had entered their country without invitation. Hovering around Agesilaus' military caravan they repeatedly charged, jabbing or throwing their javelins, and then reformed to go in again, giving the cavalry at the rear of the square little rest at all. Already tired after a considerable march the rearguard came under such pressure that Agesilaus had to send all the horsemen from the front of the square back to help, except for the few men in his own personal guard. A mounted guard is not heard of before for a Spartan king so we can presume this was an innovation he had taken up in Asia, hardly surprising in that region where war was so often conducted from the back of a horse. When all these troopers arrayed themselves to defend the rear of the formation the Thessalians took pause; they had less of an advantage in numbers now and were concerned that if a general action developed so near the hoplites these infantry might intervene and turn the tables. In the circumstances the Thessalian officers gave orders for their men to discontinue harassing the enemy column and pull back. When they did so the veteran Asian horse followed them up, though initially not with great aggression, for the moment apparently content to just shoo their tormentors away.

Now though with this Thessalian hesitation the Spartan king saw a chance and sending for his own guard from the front gave instructions to his cavalry commanders to prepare all the troopers to make as fast a charge as they could against the enemy falling back in front of them. The manoeuvre was a complete success. The first horsemen, steadying themselves by holding the horse's mane as well as its reins to compensate for a lack of stirrups, reached the Thessalians before they could get back into formation to receive them. On their enemy advancing at the charge the Thessalians did not panic but tried to turn and form up to face them. But, Polycharmus of Pharsalus, their leader, could not get everybody turned around before contact was made. Some rotated in time and made a fight of it but others were taken flank on, gave up the ghost and fled. Their leader was made of sterner stuff and he and his comrades fought hand to hand, spears broken and swords unsheathed, but numbers overwhelmed them in the end. The Pharsalian general was killed and most of those around him too, and without the gaudy presence of their leader the Thessalian horse began to waver. Fewer now rallied to return to the fight, more and more took to their heels when the opportunity arose with a break in the fighting. Eventually the Thessalian squadrons disintegrated, everybody turned to flee, and many were captured or killed in the pursuit. Indeed a number did not pull rein till they reached the safety of Mount Narthacium, where the pursuers, like all Greek cavalry troops good for open ground, would have become disordered in the rough terrain and vulnerable to counterattack if they continued to chase them further.

Mount Narthacium is situated south of Pharsalus so the fight must have occurred between there and the town to the north. Thus it is clear the army had marched most of the way across Thessaly in their square formation. It is remarkable that these horsemen of Agesilaus could best the expert Thessalian cavalry and it showed how far they had come on. No longer so much the gilded youths of earlier times these were almost professional warriors and it showed. The king was very pleased with these troopers after what they had achieved; they were very much his own creation, trained up at Ephesus in his first winter in Asia. In most places the cavalry trained when hoplites did not, despite them generally being the richer men, because to be effective some such formation riding was required. There were coaching competitions in a way there was not for the infantry, but these men led by Agesilaus had clearly been prepared to a degree that was uncommon for the time.

A few days later there was a visit to Agesilaus' camp. The ephor Diphridas had arrived from Sparta and the message he brought was one urging the king to hurry, to press him on to attack the Boeotians at the earliest opportunity. This man carried clout not just as ephor but also as an experienced military man who would see action in Asia Minor in a few years. His prompting seems to have given urgency to the king's plan to invade: before his arrival he had been hoping to have time to halt and recruit more men, but the new instructions allowed of no such lack of celerity and he marched on briskly with what he had. Importantly these soon included a regiment or two of warriors from Laconia which had shipped in from the Corinth front to join the army and fifty volunteers from Sparta who had mobilised and travelled from Sparta itself for special service with the king. The army, now pretty free of enemy interference, had to cross the mountains that ran as an obstacle north of the Malian Gulf down past Lamia and into the pass at Thermopylae. But if the king pressed on to get there before it could be defended against him, once through he surely rested. It had been a very long road from the Hellespont through country by no means friendly and equipment must have needed mending, animals rested and the other normal maintenance of paraphernalia. A day or two was not going to matter now; the enemy had had plenty of time since Nemea to collect themselves, and however much he rushed he could not catch them on the hop. There was no other task force on the way from Sparta that he needed to coordinate with, and for the first time for a long time until he reached the Boeotian frontier he would essentially be with friends – a welcome change. The stronghold of Heraclea was near and the Phocians would provide markets and support for an army on its way to crush their perennial regional rivals who had only months before been ravaging their lands.[3]

Once refreshed the army took the main road past Elatea, making the most of all that was on offer from friendly villages discovered along the way, knowing they would soon be faced with enemy strong points and hostile people. On reaching the frontier of Boeotia on 14th August 394 BC there was an eclipse: 'the sun was shaped like a crescent'. This occasion surely brought a halt in the march so the auguries might be studied. This meant not just more rest and relaxation for the men, it also allowed messengers to catch up bringing news to the high command that the Spartan fleet had been crushed at the battle of Cnidus. Agesilaus' brother in law Peisander had died as his navy was thoroughly trounced by the squadrons of Conon and Pharnabazus. To keep up his troops' spirits before encountering the enemy the king did not let the real intelligence get out but instead claimed their navy had triumphed despite the death of their admiral. 'He himself also came forth publicly with a garland on his head, offered sacrifices for glad tidings, and sent portions of the sacrificial victims to his friends.'[4] This subterfuge seems to have had the desired effect, as in a skirmish down the road the men showed well: 'so that when a skirmish with the enemy took place, the troops of Agesilaus won the day in consequence of the report that the Lacedaemonians were victorious in the naval battle.'[5] But now it would need more than chicanery, as the army's route lay inside enemy territory. Passing Chaeronea where, in the future, blood would stain the soil in wars between Macedonians and Greeks and Rome and the armies of Mithridates, they pressed on under the walls of Lebadeia where the locals must have doubly cursed these latest invaders, hardly having had time to recuperate from Lysander taking and sacking their town a few months before. But the place where Agesilaus' enemies were waiting to contest his passage was a few miles further on at Coronea, a town where the Thebans and Athenians had clashed in 447 in another war. Along the route Agesilaus had been picking up reinforcements from garrison towns like Orchomenus, where both allies and Spartan soldiers billeted there joined up. There are brief notices in Polyaenus and Frontinus that may relate to this campaign, which suggests Agesilaus needed to get the authorities at Orchomenus to close their gates to allied troops to avoid their deserting. This, like the need to feed them disinformation about the naval war, may suggest morale was not all it could have been amongst some of the king's men. But whether there were some weak links or not it was still a formidable army that swung down the road by the waters of Lake Copais and got news of an enemy clearly determined to bar their way. The invaders marched over the River Cephisus, a watercourse that passes Delphi on its way to the Boeotian plain before draining into the lake.

A rayless sun was probably just up as the invaders crossed the river. The Acropolis of Coronea was seen on their right and in front the scouts thrown out at the head of the column began to have evidence of the enemy debouching down from high on Mount Helicon into the parched August fields in front of them. This arena was the only real route for anybody moving south towards Thebes, over the flat country crowded between the high ground around Coronea and Lake Copais to the north east. The invaders, now the enemy was in sight, showed no inclination to want to avoid a fight. There is nothing here of the king who had reportedly agonised over the death of 10,000 (sic) Greeks at Nemea who he felt could have been better employed fighting the 'barbarians' of Asia. Agesilaus knew he must confront the confederate army somewhere and this place was as good as any – indeed he must have been pleased they had not dug themselves in at some impregnable defended site. When his whole force had come up, he deployed them in battle order. There were probably about 20,000 men present, a similar number that Agesilaus had had at the battle of Sardis. If he had left 4,000 to garrison Asia under Euxenus, he seems to have recruited a similar number on the march. They were a formidable band, certainly the equal of those facing them, these men Agesilaus had welded together coming down on the defenders. 'Their eyes told them that the opposing lines of battle were exactly matched in strength, and the number of cavalry on both sides was about the same.'[6] The battle line the king drew up is generally well attested. The men from Orchomenus held the left while he took the place of honour with the Spartans on the right. These were at least one and a half Spartan regiments who had either shipped over from the Corinthian front or were from the Orchomenus garrison left behind to succour local friends after Lysander had died and King Pausanias left. The men were dressed in red tunics, bodies oiled, armour burnished, and their officers recognisable by the transverse crest on their helmets. None of these actual Spartiates or *perioeci* hoplites had gone to Asia, it had been enfranchised helots who had won the victories there and were still with the army, though reduced by the attrition of campaigning. Then in the centre there were those called the foreign contingent that included the remnants of the old Cyrus hands who had marched east as part of the 10,000. Brigaded with them were the veteran hoplites from the Asian allied cities, all under Herippidas, a Spartan officer we already know. Xenophon himself was present too; about to do what would define the rest of his life, getting exiled for being found in arms in the ranks of the enemies of Athens. Also in the line were recently joined men from mainland Greek cities, allies raised on the journey through central Greece and Phocis, though the number they came in was probably less than the year before, not just because of casualties from that time but because their enthusiasm was surely still blunted from reverses under the walls of Haliartus.

The tactical intentions of the Spartans are not discussed, but the auspices were taken, and the plan of the king and general leading the invaders was the old, simple and tried ploy of winning the battle on the right with his own invincible compatriots from the Eurotas valley. These awe-inspiring combatants were silent to begin with as they moved off, but when within about 200 yards of the enemy a

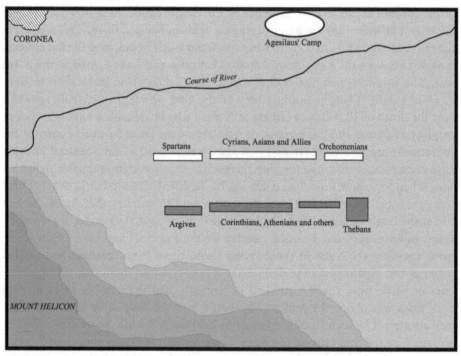

The Battle of Coronea 394 BC.

paean was raised and they rushed forward in an undulating line of armoured men of the very type we know from the *Anabasis* when the Greeks charged the Persians at the battle of Cunaxa years before.

The confederate force had descended the slopes down to the plain of Coronea to wait for the enemy army, kicking up a storm of dust as they marched to the attack. As at Nemea their forces were made up mainly of warriors raised by the big four: the Boeotians, the Athenians, the Corinthians and Argives, though others were present too, Ainianians from west of the Malian Gulf, Euboeans and Locrians as well. The battle line Agesilaus saw facing him had the Thebans, old allies turned enemy whom he loathed for what they had done to him at Aulis, on the right nearest to Lake Copais. They were in the place of honour, and holding the left with Mount Helicon close on their left and rear were the Argives. In between the two were the allied hoplites from all across central Greece, men who had had such a bellyful of the Spartans that they were prepared to stand up against a people whose reputation of warrior prowess was still second to none in the Hellenic world. Even disaster at Sphacteria in the Peloponnesian War in 425 had done little to dent the image of these iron hard fighters. It had been a long time since that occasion when Athenians had put up captured Spartan shields in their temples. They, like their allies to right and left, contained many worried warriors standing to arms in the confederate phalanx to oppose men considered fearfully irresistible.

The confederates had had time to get well ordered as they lined up facing north with Mount Helicon at their back. Between the Thebans and Argives were the Euboeans, two divisions of Locrians (Opuntian and Ozolian), Ainianians, Corinthians and Athenians; a phalanx comprising 15–20,000 hoplites all told. Some of the army would have been left to defend Corinth, but like the Boeotians the Athenians came in strength; after all they also would be directly threatened if the Spartans were not stopped, particularly as the long walls and defences of Piraeus were still not fully repaired. We learn that not all the conscripts called to fight from Attica were eager. Some felt they had done their bit at Nemea and resented having to face danger again so soon. The Salpinx, a bronze horn, would have already been blown to call for all these men to get into their armour and assemble in formation. We have images of this unwieldy instrument, up to five feet long, shrill and warlike that was called the 'public rooster'. It was also used to give the command to lower spears and charge and could sound the retreat as well. Now as the harsh musical accompaniment petered out with blood up and adrenalin pumping the enemies of Sparta advanced.

The Thebans on the right and in command on home soil took precedence; there was no rota arrangement as had operated at Nemea. They probably deployed 25 deep again and were the key strike force. When the order was given they first advanced at the walk and when the lines were 200 yards apart started to run. The rest of the army, with somewhat less enthusiasm, followed their lead and moved forward hunched down behind the shields hoping as much for survival as anything else. The Peloponnesians responded almost at once, Herippidas' men are picked out, the foreign brigade, Ionians, Aetolians, Hellespontines and old Cyrus hands as the first to spring forward in the centre of the line when Agesilaus ordered the charge. With less than a hundred yards between the opposing front ranks, these men clashing their spears on shields to intimidate those waiting for them fired themselves up for the fight with a war cry and set off at the run.

With summer dust choking every throat, sweat cascading down armoured torsos, the noise of paeans and the clash of metal, this was no place for the faint hearted. But our evidence is that there were plenty such present. The sight of enemy veterans rushing towards them was too much for the men in the centre of the confederate line who fled almost out of hand even before they reached a spear's length. It seems there was no collision of shield walls at all in this part of the line. The Argives on the left opposite the Spartans did not even wait for them to get that near 'but fled to Mount Helicon' stampeding through the undulating foothills desperate to get away. If the bruising assault was too much for these men, they were not alone. Athenians and others did no better. Like the rest of the line they broke with little or no contact required to sunder formations that looked unlikely to be restored. But as at Nemea this was to be a game of two halves and things were far from over for Agesilaus and his men.

This was because on the right of the confederate line it had been a completely different story from their defeat on the left. 'The first impact, it is true, did not meet with much resistance, nor was it long contested, but the Thebans speedily routed the Orchomenians, as Agesilaus did the Argives.'[7] These were Spartan allies from the city of Orchomenus, not the Spartan garrison, as if they had been bowled over so easily it surely would have been highlighted by someone, though perhaps not the man on the spot who was partial to airbrushing his Lacedaemonian friend's failings. The triumphant Boeotian regiments then hallooed after these local rivals hacking at exposed backs all the way to the camp where they found Agesilaus' Asian loot kept under light guard.

We get a picture now of this moment when the leaders of the victorious wings on each side, peering through the murk as the sun was blocked by the dust of tens of thousands of feet, realising the risks and opportunities that were theirs. Both left sides had crumbled, but the confederate leaders could see they were the considerably worse placed. They had been cut off from behind and forced to look back to their encircled rear, and this while some of their number were showing more interest in discovering Spartan treasure amongst the braying pack animals, grunting camels, and carts left in the camp, rather than sticking with the fight. Most of the rest of the confederate army was fleeing up over the grass and rocks to the protection of high ground. Thus the initiative lay with the Spartan king. The Thebans knew they were vulnerable, and while still in reasonable fighting order were bound to be mainly interested in finding safety with their friends at the earliest opportunity.

A battle had been fought but it had not been decisive. Agesilaus himself had had little enough time to enjoy his triumph. 'Some foreigners' had been trying to crown the king with a victory wreath when word reached him that the Thebans had dispersed the troops on the left of his line and reached the baggage train where all the booty from the Asian war was stored, money key to funding the mother city's war. As in any encounter victor and vanquished were both in disarray after the confusion of combat, but now some order was beginning to be constructed and Agesilaus realised he needed to act. Amongst the murk and muddle one crucial movement was decided upon. Rallying his victorious divisions he redeployed them and moved by counter march to block the Thebans and the rest of the Boeotians who were already marching back towards Mount Helicon. So in the wake of Agesilaus' prompt manoeuvre the problem for the Boeotians was that there were thousands of warriors, Spartans, veterans of the Asian wars, and others in arms between them and their goal. This may not have immediately been clear – in August the amount of dust kicked up would have made visibility very difficult – but it became apparent soon enough when they perceived in front of them the extent of the barrier they would need to get through. There were still hours of light left on this summer day and to withdraw from the contest could only be done by hard fighting. These combatants who thought they had won a great victory would have to labour again to get through to allies they could see desperately in search of a bolthole or trying to rally high on Mount Helicon ahead.

But though on the king's side order and formation had been established, there was much still to decide on. The commanders in the Spartan ranks knew they had the option to manoeuvre the army to allow a sufficient passage to let the Boeotians march back through. This would have meant that once the enemy had passed they could take advantage and attack them in the rear and flanks. But they decided against this and the Spartan front remained unbroken forcing a contest against the head of the Boeotian column which, with no option, showed a disciplined front as they determined to break through to the other side: 'although the victory might have been his without peril if he had been willing to refrain from attacking the Thebans in front and to smite them in the rear after they had passed by, Agesilaus was carried away by passion and the ardour of battle and advanced directly upon them, wishing to bear them down by sheer force.'[8] So the king and his men disdained an easy win and the result was a second brutal battle that raged far more evenly than the first fights had on either wing. There is a hint that the Spartans' tactical choice had some sense in it, that they thought by striking quickly they would be able to overwhelm the enemy in front of them, before others distracted by the pickings in the baggage train came on to support their comrades.

The axis of the battle had altered, with the Spartans facing to the northeast and Mount Helicon over their left shoulder, as they braced themselves for the shock of the enemy's desperate charge. This second affray was much harder fought than the first; it was no Nemea where the Spartans cut through the unprotected side of their enemies like a knife through butter. Agesilaus' men marching forward to the tune of flute, and attacking with a hymn to Castor and Pollux on their lips, were a dreadful sight to behold and hear, but still the enemy did not flinch.

The encounter was so brutal and difficult and the Thebans so stubborn that Plutarch claims 'Xenophon says that this battle was unlike any ever fought, and he was present himself.'[9] This is not only impressive corroboration of its ferocity but is also interesting in that this comment is sometimes held to prove this part of his history was penned before the battle of Leuctra (371 BC) took place.[10] In any case the Peloponnesians now began to undergo real concern for the outcome; Agesilaus, far from anticipating setting the seal on his victory, realised the battle was once again in the balance.

The bronze stitched line of shields Agesilaus' men were disputing with was at least 5,000 strong, made up of all the Thebans and most of the rest of the Boeotians. That number had gone to Nemea and now they were fighting on home ground. Boeotia is about 1,000 square miles in extent and at the time home to well over a quarter of a million people. Thebes itself may have had a population of 25,000 adult males and they could really show strong on their own doorstep. Agesilaus, amongst his own fifty personal guards picked peers fresh from home (rather than his old horse guard we hear of in Thessaly) like a hero at the centre of the line took the brunt of an assault by these formidable hoplites.

'But they received him with a vigour that matched his own, and a battle ensued which was fierce at all points in the line, but fiercest where the king himself stood surrounded by his fifty volunteers, whose opportune and emulous valour seems to have saved his life. For they fought with the utmost fury and exposed their lives in his behalf, and though they were not able to keep him from being wounded, but many blows of spears and swords pierced his armour and reached his person, they did succeed in dragging him off alive, and standing in close array in front of him, they slew many foes, while many of their own number fell.'[11]

The report almost has the ring of Leonidas' guard fighting to protect his bloody corpse at Thermopylae but this time in contest with other Greeks. In years to come these Thebans would repeatedly show what they were made of and it is claimed they owed their tutelage to Agesilaus because of the number of campaigns he fought against them, allowing a honing of their skills against the best soldiers in Greece. Even now, in this his first fight against them, he suffered for it as both sides tore into each other, receiving wounds from spear and sword, only kept alive by the ring of chosen men about his body. This was an unyielding affair with corpse piled upon corpse and the Boeotians battering as at a locked gate. And it would have been even bloodier if the Peloponnesians had not adapted double quick.

The king was a good commander, if rash at times, and still well in control of his men. Despite fighting for his life, he was apparently able to order them to open their ranks and give an avenue for the enemy to escape. 'Since it proved too hard a task to break the Theban front, they were forced to do what at the outset they were loth to do. They opened their ranks and let the enemy pass through, and then, when these had got clear, and were already marching in looser array, the Spartans followed on the run and smote them on the flanks. They could not, however, put them to rout, but the Thebans withdrew to the end of Mount Helicon, greatly elated over the battle, in which, as they reasoned, their own contingent had been undefeated.'[12]

Only once they had gone through, without an enemy in front and with escape in their eyes, did the Boeotians descend into disorder and Agesilaus again ordered his men to follow and attack them. Quite how the Spartans let the enemy through their files is not clear but what is notable is that this action essentially forced on Agesilaus has come down as a stratagem of great cunning particularly associated with his name in the how-to-do military manuals of later centuries.[13] Though Xenophon, always willing to inflate Agesilaus' talents, in his two versions of the battle does not report this as a great master-plan but only that 'finally, some of the Thebans broke through and reached Mount Helicon, but many were killed while making their way thither.'[14]

Whether forced upon them or a great piece of generalship the Spartan chase was halted as soon as the Boeotians reunited with their comrades on the slopes of Mount Helicon. Extermination was against the spirit Lycurgus was originally supposed to have instilled in the warrior state. 'When they had conquered and routed an enemy, they pursued him far enough to make their victory secure by his flight, and then at once retired, thinking it ignoble and unworthy of a Hellene to hew men to pieces who had given up the fight and abandoned the field. And this was not only a noble and magnanimous policy, but it was also useful. For their antagonists, knowing that they slew those who resisted them, but showed mercy to those who yielded to them, were apt to think flight more advantageous than resistance.'[15] Moreover, the Spartan system depended on having people still alive to exploit rather than a pile of useless corpses. If the pursuit failed to kill or capture many more of the fleeing enemy, at least the Spartans held the field and had regained their camp and treasure. They would leave alone a foe that now had the advantage of higher ground and the support of their allies who had been rallying and reforming there for some time.

It is easy to castigate Agesilaus for his decision not to let the Thebans through at the start rather than forcing them to fight head on. But perhaps it is no surprise; the whole ethos of the hoplite battle was about settling things face to face and seeing which 'best man' won. To somehow steal a victory by taking the enemy when he was unprepared was not the point, it did not satisfy the desire to win a victory that was accepted by all concerned. These contests still harked back to an older time when that quick decision by battle was necessary for men who could not spend long under arms and both sides required an agreed procedure for seeing who had prevailed. Life had become more complicated since then with larger political entities, leagues and empires not just simple city states. These polities had budgets and organisations that allowed lengthened campaigns; wars of attrition where professional soldiers could be hired to fight all year wherever the employer demanded; where even militia hoplites might be under arms for much longer, leaving the farm in trust to family members. This was something very different from that farmer soldier who left his plot to fight for a few days of marching and battle before returning to weed or harvest as the agricultural calendar demanded.

At Coronea Agesilaus commanded a large force of peltasts, many more than his enemy, and an equal number of good cavalry to face the Boeotian and confederate horse, but there is no mention of them pursuing as the confederates rallied on Mount Helicon and the battle drew to a close. Indeed the use of light troops in formal battle is hardly at all noticed in this war, though we know from Thucydides that these troops could start combats by skirmishing between the lines of heavy infantry. The first battle, in front of the walls of Syracuse in 415, commenced in just this way. But the only mention of cavalry or light infantry in this encounter is at the tail end when some troopers rode up to report that eighty enemies were hiding in a nearby temple. This is one of the few places that can be identified on the field of combat as it has been convincingly linked to the site of a local church.[16] The precinct was near the Spartan camp behind their battle line, and those trapped there must have been Boeotians left behind when their comrades broke out in the second phase of the battle.

The king, though just emerged from a fight to the death, trodden down in combat with desperate enemy hoplites and weak from loss of blood, was holding to his post despite his companions pressing to carry him back to his tent for treatment. Hanging on to his guards for support he struggled over to the other men who had been wounded or killed to ensure they were cared for or their corpses collected back at camp now the battle was over. And it was when involved in this that the horsemen informed him about the trapped enemy. Blood was up and the temptation must have been to kill these adversaries still in their power. But Agesilaus was going to be pious in victory, no reason to risk upsetting the heavens by despoiling the sacred precinct of a temple, after such a great day. So weary and wounded 'he ordered that all of the enemy who had taken refuge in the sanctuary should be dismissed.'[17] It was evening by now anyway and probably few men were interested in the task of keeping an eye on this group when there was an evening meal and liquid celebration on offer.

To Xenophon's partial eye, Coronea was a triumph for the organisation of the Spartans over the arrogance and indiscipline of the Thebans. But a postscript to the fighting suggests that the extent of the victory was perhaps not as apparent to those present as this man, always eager to blacken the Thebans' reputation, claimed. The next morning it seems Agesilaus was eager for another round and attempted to goad the Thebans into fighting again by having his pipers celebrate and his soldiers wear wreaths on their heads while they set up a victory trophy. It could be argued this taunting incendiary behaviour shows that the battle the previous day cannot have been that much more than a draw, if he wanted to go at it again so soon. There is even a feeling that there was some bravado here; was the calling out of what was claimed as a defeated foe an attempt to overawe the enemy into backing off rather than the other way round? That Agesilaus placed the confederate dead in a separate pile inside his armies' lines rather than leaving the corpses as usual on the field of battle which might draw the enemy on to fight to get them back, may suggest this. In any case, it soon became clear the confederates had had enough: they refused the invitation to duke it out again and sent a herald to ask for a truce to collect their dead.

Back on the battlefield the Spartans did not linger. The army pulled out on the road it had come by and the bruised and battered king got his bones to Delphi where he found tourist crowds attending the Pythian Games then under way. The visit was part convalescence but mainly piety, and once there he offered a tenth of his spoil from Asia that came in all to 100 talents. This was a huge amount but perhaps less surprising when we hear that Phylarchus, a deep source for many others who wrote in the third century BC, says Spartan kings received a third share of any booty his army won. The amount laid down by the king himself showed the whole of his share amounted to around 1,000 talents. This was the equivalent of the entire annual income of the Athenian empire at its height and emphasises both the value of loot from a successful campaign and the amount that could be received by the commander in chief. Agesilaus could well afford his largesse at Delphi, but while he convalesced in these attractive surroundings it must have bruised his ego that the task of invading Boeotia that had been laid upon him by the ephors had been essentially a failure. His army had retained the field but it had hardly overrun the land and after the fight they had had to retire back the way they had come rather than triumphantly march through the heart of enemy country. This makes his next move revealing. The orders he shaped for the polemarch Gylis who took over command in the field clearly reveal the frustration felt at this strategic reverse.

It was Gylis who had arranged the victory celebrations and indeed organised for the invalid king to be taken to Delphi. Now quick to strike, at the king's orders he initiated a punitive expedition into Eastern Locris. But where an easy success was expected danger took another turn. The local villagers were not having these bandits who took their goods and food getting off scot-free. They followed the intruders along country routes they knew well and as the sun went down attacked them from the rear with javelins, stones and anything else that came to hand. The Spartans tried to get back at them but with little success, only making the attackers more circumspect and aiming their missiles from higher ground. When the Spartans tried to attack these gadflies in the dark they became confused, fell off rocks and into ditches and lost more and more men to accurately flung missiles. Gylis himself, and another Spartan officer, Pelles, already grazed and wounded from projectiles, were cut down in this running fight and eighteen full Spartiates died altogether. More would have fallen if other troops already in camp and enjoying an evening meal round their cooking fires had not dropped everything to come to help. This was a real bloody nose for the men who had claimed a great victory at Coronea and an interesting precursor to what organised light infantry would soon achieve in the war around Corinth.

The context of Agesilaus' endeavours, that ended with so little decided on terra firma, had been a naval campaign of the most decisive kind. The man whose name would be associated with it was an Athenian. While Thrasybulus had been the man of the hour in both the struggle against the Thirty and the recent war against Sparta, he was not alone in trying to muscle his way into the pantheon of Attic greats in the 390s. Conon was just about to make not a bad fist of getting himself acclaimed as a second Themistocles. The first Athenian empire had gone down amidst a wreckage of oars, spars and planking on the beach of Aegospotami and was buried to the sound of Lysander's flute girls and the demolition of Athens' long walls. But now there would be a successor state, midwifed by Conon, who was last noticed scuttling away from the same beach in the Hellespont, and this subsequent dominion would ironically be sponsored by a Persian, a man from the very people who the first Athenian empire had come into existence to confront.

Pharnabazus, so long a key figure in the Aegean world, started a process in 397 that would lead to changes almost as significant as when his compatriots started feeding money to Lysander and his cohorts in the last decade of the fifth century. Always it was the Persians who pulled the important levers. They may have lost at the momentous battles of Marathon, Salamis and Plataea, but the difference in potential and resources was always bound to show in the long run.

Pharnabazus had been pushing matters by first badmouthing Tissaphernes, for paying off Dercylidas rather than fighting him. He, as Justin puts it, 'irritated the king against Tissaphernes.'[18] With his rival undermined and pull at court assured he now found a tool to hand in the Athenian commander Conon. This veteran in his forties had experience of command going back to when he led a squadron at Naupactus, when most of the rest of the Athenian navy was mired in the harbour of Syracuse. He had also shown his prowess in battles at Chios and was the one Athenian to come out of the Aegospotami debacle with any credit. Well worthy of encomium he turns up in a Roman source lauding military cunning, organising ambushes against himself to impress allies about how well informed he was or confusing enemies by dressing up triremes and servants as decoy flagships and admirals. He had been active in Cyprus for his host Evagoras, king of Salamis, and not a few Athenian exiles had joined him to boost his navy in exile over the years. Conon is described as being a Persian admiral as things warm up and in the service of the Great King's vassal, Evagoras, as in a sense he was, as were other Athenian officers with him. After Aegospotami he had been too afraid of being made a scapegoat to return home, yet when he pitched up in Cyprus he had far from completely cut the cord with the mother country.

In 397 Athens tried to send men, equipment and an official embassy intended to sustain Conon and his sponsor Evagoras. The exile was still clearly an Athenian at heart and the people at home knew it. Indeed both Conon and the Cypriot monarch would have statues put up next to each other in the Athenian *Agora* once it became clear how crucial their contribution had been to the city's revival. Conon had been a fixture in the Persian maritime world for some time. Indeed if we believe some, his leadership, funded to the tune of 500 talents, would save the Persian presence in Anatolia from crumbling in the face of Spartan aggression: 'if Conon had not been there, Agesilaus would have taken all Asia, as far as Mount Taurus.'[19]

This material, from later poorly reputed sources, is probably too much, but certainly during this period he and other Greeks who had joined him had climbed to significant command in Persian naval service. These new players did not have an easy ride of it, as they found they were facing a Spartan admiral called Pharax, installed at Rhodes with 120 well equipped triremes. The context of this impressive presence included an alliance between Sparta and the Egyptian pharaoh Nepherites I who had given his new friends the means to equip 100 triremes (which is odd considering the Nile kingdom was never a source of ship timber) and a huge quantity of grain.

Ruins on the Cadmeia, the acropolis at Thebes, which housed the Spartan garrison after Phoebidas took over Thebes in 382. (*courtesy of Nefasdicere from en.wikipedia.org*)

Lion monument from Cnidus erected to commemorate Conon's naval victory, now at the British Museum. (*courtesy of Wikimedia Commons*)

Examples of hoplites of this era from the Nereid Monument from Xanthus, in the British Museum. (*authors' own photographs*)

Picture of Salpinx, the long horn, the 'public rooster' used to relay orders to soldiers in battle and camp. (*courtesy ©Marie-Lan Nguyen/Wikimedia Commons*)

Coin of Pharnabazus, satrap of Hellespontine Phrygia and partner with Conon, in the Athenian naval rebirth of the 390s. (*courtesy of livius.org*)

Thessalian horseman, typical of those who attacked Agesilaus' army on the march from Asia to the battle of Coronea, now at the Louvre, Paris. (*courtesy of macedonian-heritage.com*)

Epaminondas, the Theban commander, at the battle of Leuctra. Copy of an eighteenth century statue at Stowe House in Buckinghamshire, England. (*courtesy of Wikimedia Commons*)

Looking down on the Eurotas River from the Menelaion on the outskirts of Sparta. (*authors' own photograph*)

Chasm just outside Sparta that is proposed as the place where Spartan babies deemed imperfect were cast to die. (*authors' own photograph*)

The Acrocorinth, the dominating citadel of the city of Corinth. (*authors' own photograph*)

Sixth century temple to Apollo at Corinth. Near here took place the massacre of pro–Spartans in 392. (*authors' own photograph*)

Funerary monument of an Athenian cavalryman who was killed at the battle of Nemea in 394, found at Athens' Kerameikos cemetery. (*authors' own photograph*)

The acropolis at Sardis near where Agesilaus fought and defeated the army of Tissaphernes. (*courtesy of livius.org*)

Coin of Tissaphernes. Becoming satrap of Lydia before c.415, he was the leading Persian official in the Anatolian provinces up to his death in 395, brought on by his failure to deal with the invasion of Agesilaus. (*courtesy of livius.org*)

Xenophon, Athenian historian, soldier and Laconophile; one of the main sources for the period. (*courtesy of Wikimedia Commons*)

With the opening of the sailing season Pharax was found on the move from Rhodes to Caria and when there, he heard news that Conon had come west with forty ships and was basing himself at Caunus. In response Pharax moved directly to Sasanda in Caria, a fortress about twenty miles away and, using the facilities there, set up a blockade. But though the Athenian was only in place with an advance guard the main body of the fleet was nearby under the command of Pharnabazus and Artaphernes. These two launched their ships, set off and drove Pharax away back to Rhodes and, rendezvousing with Conon, established their conjoined forces on the mainland over from the island with the intention of dealing Sparta's Aegean hegemony some heavy blows. 'He laid waste the enemy's country, stormed their towns, and bore down everything before him like a hurricane.'[20]

This also may be a considerable exaggeration but even so once opportunities in the Rhodian towns had allowed the pace of events to speed up, the eventual outcome almost makes the hyperbole justifiable. Resistance at Rhodes to the Spartans had been encouraged by the news of activity in Persian controlled shipyards, and now local dissidents 'revolted from the Lacedaemonians' and contacted Conon and his partners who came at the fastest pace to the island. Their fleet was let into ports on Rhodes Island and besides the obvious benefits to Conon of this initiative by the local democrats the lack of awareness of the change of control was going to reap a world of pain for the Spartans. They had a large convoy coming from Egypt loaded with grain that intended to take a break at Rhodes, assuming the government there was still favourable to their side. The whole lot was seized on arrival and, with the warehouses bulging at their new base, the Athenian-Persian axis was looking in solid condition. Particularly since a busy season of shipbuilding and crew hiring meant there were now ninety ships to press the campaign, comprising some of Conon's Greek vessels, those from Cyprus, veteran Phoenician ships, 'under the command of the lord of the Sidonians', and ten others from Cilicia.

After this a journey is reported and clearly one that boded something pretty significant. Two Athenians Hieronymus and Nicodemus were sufficiently trusted to be left with hands on command as Conon himself was called away to attend the court of the Great King. The exact timing of this is unknown only that he sailed north 'along the coast of Cilicia, and when he had gone on to Thapsacus in Syria, he then took boat by the Euphrates River to Babylon.'[21] Explanations vary as to whether he was the main player whose plans outlined on this occasion kick started the great anti-Spartan maritime effort or was he just an instrument? Or indeed if the trip was mainly a response made because the men building and manning the new fleet were on strike, that they had not received the pay local bureaucrats had been siphoning off and it was necessary to importune the Great King to make up the difference. Certainly once at Babylon it seems to be Conon leading the agenda, urging that the investment of more Persian money and support would allow a real challenge to Spartan thalassocracy in the Aegean. This was a winter residence so the time of year is clear though what is not is whether Pharnabazus was with Conon. In fact Diodorus Siculus has it that the Athenian made the journey off his own bat and only co-opted the satrap once his project has been agreed but this is not very credible. What is most likely is the two went together and the Persian proposed to the imperial administration the policy that would strike at Spartan sea power and raise up Athens again as a makeweight to them in the Aegean. And that Conon stood respectfully at his shoulder, introduced as the fixer who could move this Achaemenid enterprise along. It is also of course more than possible this scheme was already in the mind of Artaxerxes and Pharnabazus had brought Conon to court to audition to see if he was the man to carry it out.

Whenever Greek heroes met Great Kings there were stories about the freeman refusing to prostrate himself to the despot. *Proskynesis*, an inclination of the body that Greeks considered only a god merited, would be a cultural divide for Hellene and Persian down to Alexander's time; but on this occasion the issue was fudged by ensuring the two sides communicated in writing, and so Conon never had to actually confront the great panjandrum. Another version of Conon at court has him assisted by Tithraustes (who disposed of Tissaphernes and stoked the Corinthian War, but now is described as captain of the guard). This man, showing improbable sympathy for some foreign petitioner's disinclination to show what surely he would have regarded as normal respect, offered to act as go-between with the Great King. These tales may be fanciful, but what is undeniable is that Artaxerxes either proactive or not, was brought on board and the treasury door was opened. Of course the Greek was not going to be given *carte blanche*; there had to be supervision, and Pharnabazus, that old Aegean hand, was hitched to the Athenian condottiere. These two now returned to their forces with the kind of finances and authority that could make a real difference. 'Money and other supplies' were promised and Conon was weighted down with rich gifts from a beneficent monarch. At the same time the order went out for 'the Cyprians, Phoenicians, and other maritime people, to furnish ships of war.'[22]

Nothing happened at a stroke; if it was around 395 when Conon and Pharnabazus returned to take up command in the Persian navy the climax did not come until the following year. In the time in between if there was manoeuvring and fighting we do not hear of it and no doubt mostly it was a case of Persian and Greek officers thoroughly utilizing Artaxerxes' uberty to bulk up an Achaemenid navy that had deteriorated in recent years. By 394, with the mainland Persians and the island allies on board, it was not long before Conon and Pharnabazus at Rhodes got word of the whereabouts of the enemy. The Spartan admiral Peisander, it turned out, was not far off at Cnidus with 85 triremes, and to get in his face, the anti-Spartan combination sailed their vessels across to Loryma on the peninsula twenty-odd miles north of Rhodes Island. Loryma, which has its atmospheric citadel walls still standing, possessed a sheltered harbour capable of containing all the allied ships, and with an entrance narrow enough to be easily defended.

The two sides were staring across at each other from the Rhodian to the Carian Chersonese, now that the new fighting season had brought a fresh commander on the Spartan side. Peisander's instructions must have included encouragement to fight the enemy if opportunity arose and, though the details are sparse, it is clear the aim of his manoeuvres was to regain control of the island of Rhodes which both sides had long seen as crucial. Exactly what transpired in the run up to the decisive encounter is open to dispute but it seems likely that Peisander's first move was to sail down the coast to Physcus, near modern Marmaris. This would have taken him past his opponents' base and must surely be seen as a challenge.

Conon and Pharnabazus took it up eagerly. They knew this was what they had been working towards; that finally they must confront the Spartan navy that had been not just the top but almost the only dog in the Aegean for virtually a decade. Their boats and crews were mint new. They had no recent experience at fighting but the man in charge was a veteran and his whole career shows him possessing confidence enough both for himself and all his men to boot. They may also have had word that Sparta's allies had become restless under a brusque and intrusive hegemony that many were feeling was no real improvement on that which they had suffered under the Athenians. So it was with considerably more than blind hope that they dumped their masts and rigging and launched in battle order.

Once they were out at sea Peisander matched their belligerence with all the war ships he had, and set out to face them. Quite how the combat started is not abundantly clear but it is said they 'fell in with each other', which suggests it might have been an encounter affair. If that was the case it is unlikely either side would have been properly deployed at the beginning, no doubt reacting as best they could as their ships came up. The Athenian and Persian fleet was most likely spread out in column just a few abreast when the Peloponnesian vessels began the day by falling on the head of the file, and initially gave them a very testing time. It was trepidation all round amongst Conon's men when battle commenced, with his smaller number of Greeks trying to deploy into line in front, as a sort of advanced guard and the rest of the fleet much further back. Peisander pressed the attack despite the fact that the ships under his immediate command were few in number; indeed the first in line to engage are reported as being outnumbered by just those warships Conon had in hand, which must mean that at first contact most of his 85 vessels were strung out behind and not able to take part in the original onslaught. Or it is possible that this is a matter of terminology, that the reference to his numbers 'he had far fewer ships than the Greek contingent under Conon', should be understood as applying only to the Spartan bottoms rather than the bulk of the task force that were provided by the allies. Initially Conon's Greeks were receiving hard blows from an eager enemy, but when most of both sides' full complement of triremes had come up and deployed, everything changed. Orders and exhortation consumed lots of time, transmitted by shouts or signals between bobbing warships, but eventually the broken lines of triremes were restored on both sides as Sparta's allies formed the left, with Peisander and his own vessels on the right.

When the two sides drove at each other with oars out and bows cleaving the water, Sparta's allies quickly showed they had no heart for the fight. They did not even make it to contact: 'his allies on the left wing immediately fled'. Peisander, though, was a Spartan still, and he instructed his trumpeters to order the ships left to him to attack. His captains directed their triremes at Conon's line, many of them Athenians with memories of Aegospotami eleven years earlier to erase. It was a bitter struggle, evenly matched. Bronze beaks bit into shattered planking and oars, broken like matchwood, floated on a placid sea. But the fight did not remain even for long, as Pharnabazus and his ships entered the contest ensuring the deserted Spartans were considerably outnumbered. The Phoenician and Cilician ships, manned by some of the most skilled seamen in the Mediterranean world, had a clear run getting in around the flank and rear of an enemy unable to take defensive action because they were already held in combat by the Greek division of the allied fleet. The fighting was close and brutal but numbers were bound to tell, and the Spartan ships that remained afloat and could still make way had no option but to try to find refuge at Cnidus port or any beach nearby, while Peisander and the men in the triremes around him fought for their lives. Eventually, after the flagship had been rammed several times, they were driven ashore. Herded by their pursuers few could escape, and most died like the admiral who perished fighting on the battle platform of his own trireme.

'But Peisander turned his own ship against them, believing ignoble flight to be disgraceful and unworthy of Sparta. After fighting brilliantly and slaying many of the enemy, in the end he was overcome, battling in a manner worthy of his native land.'[23] Like predecessors at Cyzicus and Arginusae, another Spartan commander had gone down fighting with his fleet, this time butchered in his red Spartan cloak on the decks of his own ship. Now for those triremes still left, nothing remained but ignominious retreat. This was no orderly manoeuvre to build a defensive perimeter on the beach, it was blind panic, and the Peloponnesian crews on feeling the sand under their keels jumped ship and scampered off in the direction of Cnidus or any other town they thought might take them in.

Spartan losses are claimed at 50 out of 85 warships captured with 500 men of their crews, while the rest made it to the safety of Cnidus either rowing their triremes back or taking the fugitive road overland and leaving their vessels to be captured by the enemy. Despite the suspicious roundness of these figures, the result was not in question. It was not just the loss of Peisander and the destruction of so much of his marine; it was what the victors did with their success. Activity that turned out so decisive in the Aegean and Greek world that it would have been difficult to conceive of such an impact just a few years before. Conon and Pharnabazus, once they had patched up their ships, tended their dead and wounded and replaced them with new recruits, sailed to Cos where the people eagerly dumped their old friends, and joined the winning side. The same was true in the other key island of Chios. There the locals had, off their own bats, flung out a Spartan garrison in their eagerness to join the victors. The same pattern was followed at Nisyros, Teos and Ephesus as well as with the Mitylenaeans and the Erythraeans. These had been stalwart fighters against the Athenians and Persians in the past, and though it would be easy just to see them as turncoats jumping ship because of Cnidus, there was more to it than this. These of course were the very allies who had failed to fight with any resolve in the battle, and it had been an experience of some years of Spartan supremacy that made the difference.

'Something like the same eagerness for change infected all the cities, of which some expelled their Lacedaemonian garrisons and maintained their freedom, while others attached themselves to Conon.'[24] As well as expelling the Spartans and their harmosts out of the islands and coastal cities the newcomers won hearts and minds by not leaving their own garrisons; action advised by Conon and taken note of by his Persian sponsor. From the scene of their triumph they decided on a strategy that utilised their potency both on land and sea. Pharnabazus disembarked at Ephesus and sent couriers to the Athenian officers still established around the Hellespont. He called them to meet him at Sestos, in his home satrapy, to organise steps against his old enemy Dercylidas, while Conon sailed north with forty triremes to blockade Sparta's Asian remnant. The Spartan general, hot from his meeting with Agesilaus on his way to Coronea, had managed to stop the rot at Abydos when the rest of the communities in the region had shrugged off Spartan control. With his base secure he collected together the ousted governors and anybody else in the area who had stayed loyal. Even after Cnidus there were some such people around, like those in the Thracian Chersonese who still remembered Dercylidas for building the defensive wall against their Thracian tormentors a few years before. The determination of the Spartan resistance in these enclaves seemed to have nonplussed Pharnabazus, or the weather may have made life difficult, as for the rest of the year he and Conon did little but secure their position and hoover up any available warships that might be crewed to boost their fleet.

Nautical verities had been dramatically altered and Lacedaemonian thalassocracy would find it difficult to survive this crumbling. Apart from Abydos so much had been lost, and these were places that had provided most of the ships for the Spartan led navy. That state itself had no great maritime tradition and was not able alone to field anything substantial in the way of a fighting fleet. The Aegean had overnight ceased to be a Spartan pond and the forces deployed by Conon and Pharnabazus could go pretty much where they pleased. The first targets they chose in the New Year, after hiring mercenaries and refitting their ships, were the Cyclades, those islands that acted as stepping stones from Anatolia to mainland Greece itself. Once these were secured they prepared to enjoy letting their enemies know how much things had changed by sailing onwards from Melos, the most south westerly of the Cyclades islands. This was a fine jumping off point to hit at the enemy homeland

and, landing at Pherae on the Peloponnesian mainland in what is south Messenia, the Persian, eager to give the Spartans a taste of what his lands had recently suffered at the hands of Agesilaus, spent happy days ransacking the countryside and after that coasting along the shore laying waste to everywhere on Spartan soil that was within their reach.

But they could not stay long. Anchorage was not good along that coast and equally local provender was soon all used up, while there was always the danger of being pounced on by Spartan defence forces. Good reasons that led them elsewhere, this time to attack Phoenicus on Cythera, a large island just off the south eastern tip of the Peloponnese. They turfed out the soldiers they found there, and an extra detail is that Pharnabazus repaired the walls of the town after the Spartans left; it was already a cruise of wall building even before the big project got going. There was fighting in other places nearby as well, indicated by the finds on the smaller island of Anticythera of slingshot with the name of the Persian king on them which most likely were deposited at this time. When they decided enough was enough a garrison was left under an Athenian, Nicophemus, at Phoenicus to hold the place as they cast off and cruised north to Corinth. There they would find the leaders of the anti-Spartan confederation that had been fighting the 'good fight' on land, just as they had most successfully been doing on water.

It is almost a surprise how decisive the battle of Cnidus had been; indicating the shallowness of Spartan sea power particularly compared with the Athenian version before it. The Spartans were not natural mariners and once they had destroyed Athenian maritime pre-eminence they had no natural inclination nor resources to replace it with anything anywhere near as robust; Conon and Pharnabazus had been punching a paper bag and it had burst on the first blow being landed. But if what had occurred is understandable, this in no way took the edge off the happiness of the group of leaders from Corinth, Argos, Thebes and Athens who greeted the victorious arrivals in council at the isthmus, bringing as they did the wreaths of a great victory, Persian money in abundance, and promise of more in the future. Pharnabazus 'exhorting the allies to carry on the war zealously and show themselves men faithful to the King, he left them all the money that he had and sailed off homeward.'[25]

Pharnabazus headed for home, but Conon did not accompany him and most of the fleet remained too he would be in the position to keep the conduit of contributions from allies open in the new maritime empire they had established, ensuring it was not just Persian money that funded the anti-Spartan endeavour. How long the triumphant fleet remained at the isthmus is unknown but the next move is pinned down to 393 as 'at this time Aeropus, the king of the Macedonians, died of illness after a reign of six years, and was succeeded in the sovereignty by his son Pausanias, who ruled for one year. Theopompus of Chios ended with this year and the battle of Cnidus his *Hellenistic History*, which he wrote in twelve books. This historian began with the battle of Cynossema, with which Thucydides ended his work, and covered in his account a period of seventeen years.'[26] In this year Conon pulled into the bay of Piraeus with eighty-odd triremes, the first occasion for a good long time that port had witnessed the presence of a substantial friendly fleet, though it was part foreign built and manned and wholly Persian funded. Many of the officers and men on board would have been long exiled natives like their leader, eager to enjoy the plaudits of family and fellow citizens who had not seen them for years. Everybody was aware that these returnees were part of a force that was vital for the revival of the city's fortunes. The smiling Jacobins of the port town were particularly ecstatic when they realised the ruined defences of Piraeus and the long walls to Athens, overgrown and crumbling, a constant reminder of the humiliation after Aegospotami, were what the returning admiral Conon had come to do something about. In this his Persian backer was fully behind him, contributing not only fifty talents of his own but also monies raised in their recent cruise through the islands.

It is extraordinary really that Pharnabazus did not consider that a revived Athens might be far more of a threat to Persian influence in the Aegean than the land lubbers of Sparta. But he was a short termist; Sparta had hurt and offended the Persian Empire after they had part-funded her triumph and they were going to get back at her with whatever tools were to hand. With plenty of money, and left with most of the fleet, Conon hired up every skilled worker, mason and carpenter available, made the crews of the ships help as well, and set to work on those ramparts that had always been an emblem of Athenian power and imperialism. It seems some work might have already been in progress on some parts of the defences before Conon arrived but still there can be no doubt on the decisiveness of his contribution. The Persians were not the only ones happy to help old enemies if it hit at Sparta, the Thebans sent 500 skilled labourers and stone masons too. The confederates at Corinth also did their bit by holding the walls at the isthmus to ensure no Spartan army could push through and intervene before the work was successfully completed.

This was a coming home in style. Apart from walls, a temple to Aphrodite was constructed in Piraeus to commemorate the epochal triumph at Cnidus, and it is probable that this period of plentiful money saw the recruiting of the force of peltasts that would make such a name for themselves under Iphicrates. Conon, whose bronze statue would soon be on display for all to see, and whose body would be buried cheek by jowl with Harmodius and Aristogeiton, the tyrannicide lovers who were the ultimate symbols of Athenian freedom, was now a real celebrity, a ghost from the bloodbath of Goat River who now stood at the pinnacle in his home city and with only Thrasybulus anywhere near in his class in terms of popular standing. As the new man just arrived, he not only had exotic glamour but also had not been around long enough to make enemies. His return was comparable to that of Alcibiades years before; they had both come back from being significant figures in foreign courts, but Conon had come back with his pockets full of his sponsor's gold, not chased out by a cuckolded king.

The first Athenian Empire had suffered and been lost under nutcracker pressure from both west and east. Syracusans and other Sicilian and Italian based Greeks had sent their ships, soldiers and sailors to fight in the great battles around the Hellespont while the Persians had opened their chests of treasure to fund the whole effort. But now the western powers with their resources of manpower and staples were out of the game. The Carthaginians had used the opportunity of the same quarrel between Segesta and Selinunte that the Athenians utilised previously, to start a new Great War in 409. Before the turn of the century there were battles and sieges fought at Gela, Himera and Acragas, and the 390s saw first Carthaginians losing their great base at Motya and then embarking on another epic siege of Syracuse itself. So when the Spartans asked their old allies led by the tyrant Dionysius I to give them succour after the disaster at Cnidus they got no joy. The threat from one direction had been nullified and would remain so for the first half of the century; and from the other side the Persian moneybags were on the side of Athens now. So in a new world Athens was now capable of truly independent and significant action. She could, with her long walls rebuilt and a victorious navy on call, dream of a Periclean past, and fantasise of an imperial future.

Athens now had two leaders, but the evidence suggests that they did not see city policy going in the same direction. Conon, considering the experience of his last few years, saw a future for Athens where sticking firm to his Persian friends would make possible a very real Aegean resurgence. This despite the fact that many of even his partisans found it difficult to swallow this cosying up to a power who had twice gutted their city only three generations before. Thrasybulus saw things differently, he had an idea of Athens that harked back to the Delian League where contesting the Great King's control of Western Asia was again the keynote. He and his remembered only too well what Xerxes had done and this outweighed any favours they may have done in the very recent past. In years to come Thrasybulus would show that if Sparta had sold out the Greeks in Asia for Persian lucre he did not intend to and was prepared to confront, struggle and finally bleed to push his version of this Athenian future. But this was for the future; immediately matters on the city's doorstep would attract attention.

Chapter Seven

A Corinthian Revolution and an Athenian General

We think of great seaway canals like Suez and Panama as the products of modern times, redolent of turbine engines and high explosives but the idea of them goes back virtually to the dawn of history. Indeed the most famous, the Suez Canal, was a project, albeit an abortive one, on the in-tray of at least one Egyptian pharaoh. Some were even accomplished, like that built through the peninsula of Athos by Xerxes when he invaded Greece in 480. If the Greek infantry in this war showed the Great King something about battlefield fighting, there is no doubt lessons were learned the other way as well about the logistical dimension of grand campaigning. The isthmus where the Peloponnese joins mainland Greece had been, like Suez, a prime candidate for canalling since man took to the seas, cutting out, as it would, a tiresome journey around the peninsula to regain the Gulf of Corinth from the west. Local potentates had had a go at it from archaic times but without success only achieving the less efficient but more attainable alternative of a stone built overland ramp called the *Diolkos*, a construction of the sort most famously built by Mohamed II during his siege of Constantinople in AD 1453 to get his navy into the Golden Horn that had been blocked off at the mouth, an occasion that has left to us a memorable description of the sight of his battleships apparently sailing over land as they were pushed and pulled on rollers to their destination.

The community where that isthmus road went and the canal does now was legendarily founded by the son of Helios and actually occupied as far back as the fifth millennium BC. It was a Dorian establishment from around 1,000 BC with a rich traditional history, allegedly visited by many of the great names of myth and fable. Its position at the neck of land connecting mainland Greece with the Peloponnese was exceptionally advantageous and added to this was the wonderfully defendable Acrocorinth, with its spring of fresh water that made it virtually impregnable. The usual round of kings and aristocratic coups are attested in the archaic period in the city, as was an impulse to colonisation that led to the settlement of places like Corcyra and Syracuse. They were early in the fashion for tyrants when in the seventh century a successful general called Cypselus, who had made a reputation fighting the Argives with the support of his soldiers and the mandatory Delphic backing, set himself up in power. These Corinthian autocrats were long-stayers with the dynastic founder claiming a thirty year stint and his son Periander ten years longer than that. Under these tenacious despots colonisation went out at a pace: the east coast of the Adriatic became dotted with Corinthian foundations like Ambracia, Epidamnus and Apollonia. Then these adventurous folk went east as well, setting up places like Potidaea in the Chalcidice. It is even asserted they contributed to settling towns in Egypt including the great trade emporium of Naucratis.

A nephew of Periander went down to an assassin's knife but the end of the dynasty by no means meant the end of Corinth as one of the great cities of Greece. The corollary of colonisation was naval power and Corinth bossed the local Greek waves well before Athens took to the waters, and remained, until the later years of the Peloponnesian War, the only power who could contest with the Athenians at sea. It is claimed the trireme was developed in Corinth's shipyards and certainly they were a people inventive in naval warfare. There were ample docks for warships at both the ports of Lechaeum and Cenchreae on the gulfs to the west and east of the isthmus, and the first sea battle in Greek history that gets anything of a mention was fought in the seventh century between Corinth and Corcyra, a colony that had by that time grown significant enough to challenge the mother city. It is reckoned to have been one of the first communities in Greece to use coinage, and Corinth's holding of the Isthmian Games meant that plenty of tourist cash could be depended on to arrive in the city coffers every two years.

It was a place notoriously expensive to live in and loose enough in the morals department for Strabo to claim at a later date totally erroneously that there were 1,000 temple prostitutes housed on the acropolis. It was a town of merchants, many making their money in exporting the black figure pottery they originated before Athens got in on the business in the sixth century. Our aristocratic writers who we depend on for most of our information of course were quite prepared to believe anything of this kind of new money. Like Venice in a later age, debauchery, intrigue and treachery clearly had to be the hallmark of people who made their money in the market place not in the proper way through raising animals and crops on wide estates. The Corinthians though had little option in how they made a living, the city was not only perfectly placed as a trading emporium, but hemmed in by Sicyon, Argos, Megara and other places it just did not have the wide open spaces of Sparta or Thebes who in land hungry Greece could be counted as truly blessed in the extent of their agricultural acres.

It is perhaps this commercial bent that explains the dominance of oligarchic government at the city. There were aristocrats and landless poor but not in the same way as in many places. A much greater proportion of the people were dependent on trade and so a somewhat different class balance existed to that in many other cities. Hatred of her neighbour Argos meant that the sixth century saw these city fathers cosying up to Sparta, Argos' other bitter peninsular foe. Cooperation with the taciturn folk to the south had continued in the struggle against Persia, a war summit was hosted at the isthmus in 480 while 400 Corinthian warriors marched to aid the Spartans at Thermopylae and 40 triremes joined the navy at Salamis. Finally a huge force of 5,000 hoplites were mobilised for the decisive encounter at Plataea the following year. But the oligarchs who dominated after the tyrants departed were very far from a monolithic grouping, and if the Corinthian establishment had been pro-Spartan for a long time, it had been far from an even commitment. The peace of Nicias in 421 had already led to real divisions between Corinth and Sparta, with the former prepared even to march in tandem with Argos to undermine that peace arrangement. And then the failure to receive what she considered her due after the war against Athens was won had brought a sea change in their attitudes.

The new controlling faction were much more Sparta-phobes, and the likes of Timolaus and Polyanthus showed themselves eager and willing to pocket the Persian money sent by Tithraustes to fund the war they were anyway inclined towards. They had a different attitude to their nearest neighbour Argos too. They were happy to cooperate with men like Cylon and his party in that city, who had also been eager to get their hands on money to pay for the contest with Sparta they longed for. Spartan ineptitude in foreign relations seemed capable of achieving almost any unlikely outcome. Not only had she managed to force Argos and Corinth into each other's arms but would even make bedfellows out of those previous mutual haters Athens and Thebes.

Corinth was one of the cities around which recent tides of combat had violently washed. Nemea and Coronea had been epic affairs when large numbers of hoplites, the quintessential Hellenic warrior, had squared off and fought it out. These two encounters had gone to the formbook in that the Spartans, the masters of war, had been victorious, yet they had been far from decisive. After the second great confrontation, Agesilaus had showed due appreciation to his gods, convalesced at Delphi, and then sailed his army back across the Gulf of Corinth; local allies had dispersed to their homes and much the same was true on the confederate side. Sufficient soldiers under arms remained to hold up their ends in this continuing contest, but from now on the war of great set piece land battles subsided. Long wars between these Greeks would usually drop a gear after an initial attempt to decide the question with a head on battle or two. This had been the case in the Peloponnesian War as well when the number of full throttle hoplite affairs were far less numerous than more minor fighting in Thrace or the edges of the peninsula itself. Land campaigns would for some years be conducted on a smaller scale while decisive events had already begun to happen at sea. The Corinthians were certainly throwing their all into expanding the conflict on an element where they had long felt at home. Pharnabazus, the Persian plenipotentiary in the west, had soon after the year of battles arrived with Conon at the isthmus and part of the money he brought had sponsored a naval dimension to what had for the Corinthians so far been a terrestrial war. Sparta had not been tested yet in the Gulf of Corinth. She had been able to transport her troops across it into Phocis and Boeotia without let or hindrance and had blocked the normal trade routes west for the city merchants, but now the Corinthians intended to alter that. A commander called Agathinus was delegated to take the ships recently fitted out at Lechaeum to try to establish a footing in the western gulf.

Success here would have huge benefits. It would be bound to distract the Achaeans, key Spartan allies on the north coast of the Peloponnese, and perhaps any other locals who were not a hundred percent committed to the war. It would also allow strategic and mercantile links with those states to the west that might make a major contribution if their resources could be brought into play. Acarnanians, Aetolians, and even Epirote peoples could be contacted in the hope of opening a western front to test the Spartans and their Peloponnesian friends where they had previously felt pretty safe. But the move was not destined to be uncontested; the Spartans had not completely lost their maritime nerve due to Cnidus. In 393/2 an officer called Podanemus was in command of a Spartan squadron in the gulf and he took the intruders head on. We have no details of the encounter but it is clear he was outclassed; these Corinthians had been wet water sailors when the Athenians were landlubbers never mind the Spartans. This admiral was killed and Pollis, his deputy, wounded and though many of their vessels got away, a new commander Herippidas had to be appointed. This steady man, who had done well under Agesilaus in Asia as well as at the battle of Coronea, was made of sterner stuff than his predecessor and soon knocked his men into shape. A renewed contest began when the Corinthians on the annual changeover of admirals sent out Proaenus to take over. He turned out a weak link and when forced to face Teleutias, Agesilaus' half brother, who had in his turn taken over from Herippidas as admiral, he floundered, gave up the key post of Rhium and withdrew back to Lechaeum leaving the Spartans again in firm control of the gulf.

This was a significant reverse and it just piled on the Corinthians stresses that seemed out of proportion to those suffered by their allies. Other worries were surfacing too: it was all very well that Piraeus was defended again but if Athens was an ally her port was still a trade rival and while alliances fluctuated, commercial competition always remained. Secondly, there were issues of internal politics. Corinth had been subject to oligarchic rule for a very long time; in the Peloponnesian War this had fitted well. Alliance with Sparta had meant the interests of the government thoroughly matched that of the major partners, ideology and policy fitted neatly hand in glove. But when Corinth had become a key player in the anti-Spartan confederation tensions had come to the fore. There had been indications of fractious inclinations before when the gates were closed to the fugitives from the battlefield of Nemea. This had not been behaviour indicative of a people with one thought going in one direction. Amongst the better off, whether in the government or just well connected, there was always a residual sympathy with Sparta and a concern about how the poor in the city might be contaminated by influences from the democratic Athenians they were now aligned with. Always on the outside were extreme oligarchs excluded from government who hoped a reversion to a pro-Spartan policy would allow them to get back in the power seat. Thirdly, there was the matter of land. The farmer class, the hoplites, were discontented that the war seemed to be settled almost permanently on their land and the Athenians' and others' property remained virtually untouched. It was their fields that were ravaged every year and it is no surprise they baulked at this unpleasant attention. Though Corinth was a trading town, like every city in Greece or any part of the ancient world it was still bound to the land. A commodity, of which there was never much from the start, was getting squeezed. Indeed since the war against Sparta had begun, the land to the west of the city and the walls that reached across the isthmus had had to be abandoned. Goods and cattle were sent east to the region on the road to Megara and in that part there was not much acreage to go round.

The city leaders were feeling the strain, as were their allies, deeply worried about them dropping out of the confederation, which would have been a disaster considering that the city itself comprised the heart of the defensive front line of the war at the isthmus. In these circumstances they decided on the most radical of actions to cement their hold on power. Dissidents of almost any stamp were identified and groups of armed men assigned to murder them in one job lot. The massacre was planned for the day of the festival to Artemis when most people would be gathered in the market place. Such was the impiety of the assassins that when they struck, as the celebrations continued, they even cut down those who had taken sanctuary at temples and altars. The whole affair has more complicated roots than one of those strictly oligarch-democrat spats that pepper the politics of the period but nonetheless it turned out a hugely traumatic and bloody business. When bodies were counted it transpired, to the exasperation of the assassins, that the carnage had been largely restricted to the older men, 120 had died and 500 driven out of town, the younger people tainted with pro-Spartan inclinations were apparently alerted by a man called Pasimelus and kept out of the way. Quite why the older set had been allowed to go to their deaths without notice is unclear but the outcome was that when the warning was shown to be spot on many of the younger, vigorous potential victims hightailed it for the Acrocorinth. From there some slipped down the walls and into exile over the border while others, encouraged by their womenfolk, believed the assurances from the authorities that they would not be touched and returned to their homes. A telling postscript is that when these desperate young refugees had been tearing up the steep path to the safety of the Acrocorinth they had been set upon by Argive soldiers who it seems were billeted in the city and presumably were in on the plot.

It had been February or March 392 when the blood flowed, but any celebrations by the instigators were premature: it had by no means resolved matters. The extent of disaffection amongst the well-to-do in Corinth was still such that the administration saw that the only way of ensuring the city remained stalwartly anti-Lacedaemon was by mortgaging their autonomy to their neighbour and oft times rival Argos. Our sources are meagre and obscure and it is not clear when all this happened: the merger may not have finally been completed until 390.[1] But in any case boundary stones from the fields on the border were removed, key matters in these land based societies and the city was amalgamated into the polity of Argos.

Extraordinary matters; this was radical and controversial in a way difficult to conceive of for a modern sensibility. The nearest parallel in our football obsessed age might be the combination into one of two great football rivals like West Bromwich Albion and Wolverhampton Wanderers and the trauma this would cause to the feelings and devotion of the fan base. Though it should be remembered that the move must have had some popular support or it could not have been attempted. This was not joining a League or a takeover by a different faction or foreign garrison which was not unusual in any city; this was civic demise and, as Aristotle contends, that was very real death to many Greeks. It is not something that happens much in the pages of the Greek story: towns might be moved like Sicyon, from an inland hill down to the coast, or even dissolve into constituent villages (Mantinea would soon suffer this) but for one great city to subsume another, that was an event of cosmic significance. This was an event of the magnitude such as when the Spartans conquered Messenia and determined for centuries the direction of the economic and social organisation, and the culture of the victor as much as the vanquished.

Though the chronology is confusing – some move towards merger was certainly underway in 392 – what is undisputed is a subsequent episode involving both a man we have heard of before and the Spartan forces encamped to the west of the city. This blockading army was still based at Sicyon commanded by Praxitas. No great battles had been fought nearby for almost two years, but if they had become a little complacent with the passage of time, still they would have been aware of what was happening in Corinth. Greek intrigues were about as porous as such processes can be, with exiles no doubt in contact with families and friends in Corinth itself; gossip spread freely during the frequent festival truces. But the Spartan in charge did not make any move to take advantage of his enemies' discomfiture until certain news arrived in his camp. It came with two men emerging wet from a river crossing who on arrival claimed they were prepared to open a gate to him in the walls stretching from the city to Lechaeum, the port on the Gulf of Corinth. The leading spirit in this conspiracy was Pasimelus, the Cassandra who had warned of the recent bloodbath, and his co-conspirator was Alcimenes. Neither could stomach what had happened in the city and had stolen out of town and swum a swollen watercourse to outline their proposition. They were both already known to the general and the trials they had been prepared to undergo convinced him of the veracity of the offer.

This bored besieger ordered up his troops from their camps, and the two men returned to the city to prepare their act of treachery. Praxitas got everybody under arms as quickly as possible even calling back a regiment that was just then marching away. At a time proposed by the plotters these forces marched through the summer night reaching a place described to them in the long walls that they knew well, as by it stood a trophy set up for a previous Spartan triumph. There they discovered the two men who had contrived to be put on guard duty at the right time. The Peloponnesians found that what had been promised had been done, and the gate was gaping wide open for them. But Praxitas was careful; the Spartans were men for ruses themselves and so expected it of others. To ensure no ambush was planned he sent forward an officer who was shown round the gate by the two Corinthians; only after he reported back that all was well did Praxitas lead

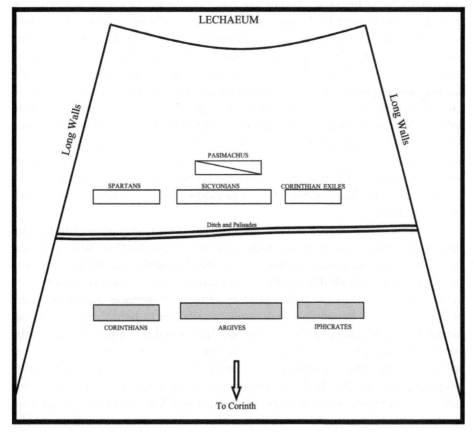

The Battle of Lechaeum 392 BC.

his main force forward. He knew he did not have long; the coup would surely be discovered soon, and if he was to take full advantage of the opportunity he must complete the introduction of his own troops from Sicyon and get the Corinthian exiles with him into position to defend what the sneak attack had won.

The Corinthian long walls descended steeply down to the coast and at the place they entered were quite far apart, something around 1,400 yards, giving more than ample room for the men Praxitas had brought to form up in phalanx formation between them.² Once inside they became jumpy about how short on numbers they were: probably no more than a couple of thousand altogether, comprising a few hundred Spartans, perhaps most of the 1,500 we know the Sicyonians fielded at Nemea, and the 150 Corinthian exiles we hear of. These numbers, if deployed in the usual eight-deep formation, would not have covered much of the distance between the walls, so for greater safety they dug a ditch and built a palisade across between the walls, while messengers were rushed back to their allies with instructions to send all the men they could muster. The position of these daring intruders was realised to be even more precarious when they learned not only of the presence of major confederate forces in Corinth, but also a garrison of Boeotians at Lechaeum as well. If things went badly they could end up caught between two fires. As it turned out they ended having at least a full day to prepare their defences. The folk in Corinth might have been abuzz, like a wasps' nest poked by a stick, but the officers of the local levy and their allies in town had been caught off guard and needed time to get in combat order. Once weapons were got down and men and animals accoutred a real set piece affray was going to develop between the long walls of Corinth. Facing towards the city the Spartans held the right of their line up against the wall in the direction of Sicyon, while the allies from that city were on their left in the middle of the line. The far left, tight up against the eastern wall, comprised 150 Corinthian exiles baying for the blood of the men who had so recently cut down their fathers, uncles and elders in the gory day of assassination around the temples.

The home side gathered at last. They posted the Corinthian hoplite levy up against the Spartans on their left while their new Argive brother citizens formed the centre. Right up against the eastern wall and facing the Corinthian exiles was an Athenian general called Iphicrates, with a corps of mercenaries, almost certainly the peltasts he would soon make his name with. With defences dug between the walls the intruders hoped they had numbers sufficient to hold their position but the ditch and palisade turned out not to be effective and the impression is that the numbers the Peloponnesians had just could not cover the whole length of it. When battle was joined the Corinthians and Argives in the centre leapt forward, first jumping down into the ditch and pulling out the wooden stakes. Then, making good use of their numbers, both the Corinthian and Argive levy hoplites pressed on against the Sicyonian shield wall in the centre. These men were intimidated by the attackers and surprised to see them get through the defences so easily. They proved not up for the contest and gave way at this determined assault by so many and fled down between the walls to the sea hotly pursued and losing many men in the process. Their bacon was almost saved by a quick thinking Spartan officer called Pasimachus who dismounted his handful of cavalry men, tied their horses to trees and, picking up the shields the fleeing men had dropped, formed a line against the rampaging Argives. The attackers thought they were just more Sicyonians facing them and, not fearing this foe as they would had they recognised them as Spartans, took them on, bowled them over and cut down their leader.[3] On the right of the confederate line however, where Iphicrates commanded, things definitely did not go so well. The Corinthian exiles were in do-or-die mood, despite their small numbers, and Iphicrates' men were squeezed against the wall with little room to throw their javelins and then get out of range of the heavy infantry. The exiles routed the men opposite and chased after their retreating backs almost to the walls of Corinth itself. To push so far may suggest they hoped supporters within the town might let them in, but if so they were out of luck and with no gates opened or ropes dropped down to them they turned back to the main action.

Back at that fight it seems that because the Corinthian citizen levy had concentrated against the Sicyonians, the Spartans had a free hand with no organised force in front of them. Seeing this they crossed the wooden wall and ditch unmolested and lined up with their left against the palisade, at right angles to their original line, and repeated what they had done at Nemea on a smaller scale against the Corinthians and Argives who had driven off the Sicyonians. These men were now coming back, realising enemy soldiers were still behind them, and showed their shieldless right side to the Spartans. Staggering back over the temporary defences between the walls, and disrupted by combat, they were cut down in numbers and those not butchered ran, crowding most of the rest of the confederate army into a huddling mass against the eastern wall. Apparently the casualties in this continuing disorganised contest were very large indeed, with the piled up corpses likened later to heaped cords of wood, stone or grain. Slaughter had been particularly severe where some of the Corinthian levy were so constrained that friend was treading on friend and comrade crushing comrade.

But instead of getting out of harm's way as quickly as they could when they saw the Corinthian exiles coming after them, faction bile trumped self preservation and they turned again to fight these bitter foes. This led to an action by the eastern wall where the defeated Corinthian hoplites tried to climb up onto the parapets to fight the enemy off but were caught and hacked down on the steps, some even leaping to their death down the other side of the wall. Others were crushed and trodden down by their companions in the press of battle. Then, when they had seen off the confederates sent against them, the Peloponnesians led by the Spartans turned north and marched between the long walls down to the port of Lechaeum. Once at the port they massacred the Boeotian troops who tried to defend the outer fortifications, before falling back to a final redoubt on the roofs of the ship sheds. The upshot of all this was the Spartans and exiles were in control outside Corinth itself and took advantage to throw down the long walls creating a gap big enough for the whole of the army to advance through. And that is exactly what they did, taking the road to Megara, capturing Sidus and Crommyon on the coast along the way. These places were left garrisoned while Praxitas turned his men around and returned to Epieicia and threw up ramparts round this town that seems to have been well situated to help defend Sicyon. Then, deciding they had done enough to ensure the isthmus defences were well and truly breached, the Spartan commander let the allies go and prepared to return to Laconia, no doubt to give thanks to the gods who some believed had a direct hand in encompassing the downfall of the impious murderers from Corinth.

Diodorus, though, has the battle fought differently; that a force of Spartans and their Corinthian friends in exile marched at night directly into the port of Lechaeum and on entering took over the dock yards. In this account it is suggested that once in the town these commandos found a formidable foe waiting for them. Iphicrates was in command of the confederate garrison and he took the attackers on. His men, fighting hard, suffered a considerable number of casualties but, though a good number of these Athenians were cut down, they at least bought some time. This brief window allowed the rest of Boeotian and Athenian forces, and the men of the Argive and Corinthian levy, to arrive from their camps and houses, bleary but determined. Finding the enemy in command of the defences of the port and lining the walls they began to set up genuine siege lines to take back this crucial place. But though the confederates were now present in large numbers and seeming to have the initiative, this was something of an illusion. The men they faced were in determined mood and forming a solid phalanx. Shields forward they drove out against the enemy, pushed them back uphill between the long walls, and soon routed them. Crushed in spirit, drowned in blood, having suffered altogether 1,000 or more casualties, and with all discipline gone, the confederates all fled back to Corinth leaving the intruders to occupy the field.

If there are two descriptions of what happened during this battle by the Corinthian long walls, some things are definitely established. The first is that the Peloponnesian triumph was sufficient and the situation in the countryside so secure that it allowed their protégés, the Corinthian exiles, to put on the Isthmian Games that were calendared for just that time. And the other is that whichever of these two battle reports has veracity, in both Iphicrates is unveiled as a coming man, a fascinating character whose long life would take him to Macedonia, Thrace, Persia and Egypt apart from the normal stomping grounds of any Greek soldier or mercenary; he was still fit and fighting forty years later. He would show himself even more cynical than most, intimidating Athenian law courts with armed supporters and happy to openly declare his massaging of augurs' findings. With a propensity to learn from his own mistakes that some would see as plebeian and this may even explain Plutarch's suggestion that he was the poor son of shoemaker and explains why it is reported a descendant of the tyrannicide Harmodius, reviled him for his low birth to which he replies 'My nobility, said he, begins in me, but yours ends in you.'[4] All this is surely fable as he must have been very young at the Battle of Lechaeum as he was still fit and fighting forty years later. Generals anyway were almost always wealthy men and to reach such heights so young must have meant he had money behind him. It is just another echo of Lysander and his *mothax* roots, these storytellers always loved a rags to riches tale.

Whatever the truth of his antecedents, now Iphicrates, this Athenian general who had tasted defeat with the rest between Corinth's long walls, picked up the pace, demonstrating that cunning and dexterity for which he and his men would soon become famed. Unprepared to be constrained by his enemies' recent success, once he heard most of them had demobbed he decided on action. He took his men over the hills and marched south west down the road into the country around Phlious intending to catch this enemy at a disadvantage. These were the people who had failed to muster with their neighbours at Nemea, but on this occasion, if we accept an account that probably refers to this campaign, they turned out the local armed levy and chased after the invader, following him over a defile near the town. 'The enemy were pressing on his rear; he ordered his troops to march through the pass as quickly as possible. Meanwhile he took a body of his best troops and fell back to the rear, to cover the others. With these troops he attacked the enemy, who were scattered and disordered in the eagerness of their pursuit, and killed many of them.'[5]

After this the locals were much more circumspect and Iphicrates needed to delve further into his box of tricks. Laying up most of his soldiers in an ambush, with the rest as bait he started to plunder the fields and villages. The locals had still not fully realised how dangerous was this man they were dealing with and came out to attack what they thought was just a raiding party. But once they were outside the protection of the city walls the main part of Iphicrates' force emerged, and attacked and killed a very large number of them. This was enough to put a real scare into the city fathers; fear was the spur as they sent agents speeding off to Sparta to ask for help. This showed how shaken they were: relations with the head of the Peloponnesian League had been cool since they had claimed celestial authority to get out of the bloodletting on the shore between Sicyon and Corinth. When the help arrived, sent by the authorities at Sparta, they even handed over the citadel to their saviours. Though previously they had refused to allow troops from Sparta to even come inside their walls because they feared they would take advantage and reintroduce exiles, many of whom in the past had shown themselves more committed to their Spartan friends than to their community's autonomy. As it turned out, on this occasion the Spartan soldiery came only to protect, and when the emergency was over and Iphicrates pulled out of their territory they went away again without attempting at all to interfere in the city government.

Iphicrates, the Athenian peltasts' chief, was still on a roll and despite the arrival of troops from Laconia depriving him of his immediate prey, he kept straight on down the road into Arcadia. Here he plundered the country and even attacked some walled places where the local hoplites were too frightened to come out and face him. This was rugged terrain with small plains and steep hills: an ideal working environment for the troops that the invaders were using. The movement was all south, threatening friends of Sparta who had not heard the clash of war for a long time. We do not know the names of the places the Athenians trashed, but the fact that Xenophon alludes to the possible involvement of some hoplites from Mantinea at this time suggests they may even have got down to near that city. The aim of these razzias was to deepen the perturbation of the authorities in the places visited in the hope that they might either see the error of their ways in supporting the enemy or at least be hog tied by the demands of the population that their armed men were kept for the defence of their home fields. This was what warfare was about in Greece at this time, the contestants did not generally have the resources to occupy the land and cities of their foes; it was all about intimidation. Indeed it was rare that even after a complete victory a state would impose officers to take control; Sparta with their harmosts were somewhat unusual in this respect. To intimidate those around as the Spartans did in the Peloponnese and the Thebans tried in Boeotia, this was the strategy. It was only a maritime empire that could do more and be really effective over distance as naval might could be deployed quickly and extensively in a way that land forces could not.

Clearly Iphicrates in this period, though the general chronology and sequence is misty, had been moulding the troops he had come to command into a very efficient and effective fighting machine. The specie Conon and his Persian paymaster had made available when they arrived at Corinth after Cnidus, had allowed a special force to be kept under arms to be trained and inculcated in tactics and manoeuvre in a way that was not usual up to that time. Peltasts had been around for a long while and during the Peloponnesian War this troop type had been increasingly used in rougher country where hoplites were at a disadvantage. The mercenary version had shown the way the wind was blowing having as they did the advantage of being more flexible than citizen warriors who needed to return to city and farm regularly to make a living. These un-armoured javelineers, named from their small, light, rimless shield or *pelte*, had had successes on various fronts but particularly in the north where they were easily raised, and in nearby Thrace where they were the typical form of infantry. Over time they had become more respectable and effective, losing the tag applied since Homer, to missile men as being of less worth than real stand up battlers whether Achilles-like heroes or regular hoplites. The Greek attitude to such fighting was always somewhat ambiguous, even in the Iliad. If archer Paris was portrayed as a bit of a wimp the same could hardly be said of the 'great bowman' Philoctetes. The peltasts' style also fitted very much in with the sporting culture of Greece: throwing javelins and nimble running were key skills in both peltasts' fighting and athletic games. Yet still such warriors were not regarded as quite the proper thing. Indeed the kind of war they excelled in was considered as approaching bad form. Ruses and clever tactics could be considered the sphere of the coward; though equally on other occasions this kind of tricky intelligence was admired. It depended on the context and perhaps that is true of most military cultures, where the acceptability of what you did depended on where and when you did it. At the time of the Corinthian War the attitude to peltasts certainly seems ambivalent. The ones now plaguing Arcadia were regarded with contempt by some, while others found them terrifying. Spartan hard men remembered them as poor opposition, very diffident when it came to taking on their hoplites because they had frequently been found out by the nimbler younger phalanx men who had caught up with them and hammered them in past actions. Indeed they were particularly contemptuous of some Mantinean hoplites that had fled from peltasts during action round Lechaeum's walls, like children afraid of bogeymen. Iphicrates was soon to do something to the Spartan heavy infantrymen of great reputation that would turn this world view upside down. This Athenian general won lasting renown, apart from his victories in the field, for developing a particular type of soldier with longer spears and smaller shields than normal hoplites, and sturdy boots that became named after himself. This reformed peltast is often claimed as a forerunner of the Macedonian phalangite of Philip and Alexander, but nothing suggests anything like this had been achieved yet by the still very young Athenian commander. The days when he would become an adopted brother of Philip were still to come. What he had accomplished up to now was to train the traditional peltasts in his command to a pitch that would make them very effective against even the fearsome Spartans when the opportunity arose.

An opening soon arose but not before other events had occurred around the city. Praxitas' achievements in taking Lechaeum and throwing down Corinth's long walls had stirred up an Athens very conscious of how vulnerable she had become, with the road from Sparta now open and their defences hardly completed. So they responded with all the ingenuity, alacrity and energy for which they were known. Late in 392 or early in 391, probably with support from a force of Boeotian warriors, they marched down to the isthmus in very considerable numbers. Despite the presence of at least one unit of Lacedaemonians entrenched in siege works round Corinth's defences, they stormed directly into Lechaeum, took over the place completely, and linked up with their friends in the city itself. The next task was to throw up what Praxitas had cast down, and they rebuilt the long walls in only a few days. Despite their speed they were careful, bringing down the whole army from Athens to protect the thousands of workers and masons brought along to accomplish the rebuilding. Then after this rush job, in more leisurely fashion they went to work on refurbishing the ramparts that led down to the port of Cenchrae on the Saronic Gulf. Once again an extravagant outlay of perspiration and currency seemed to have blocked up the only land route for Peloponnesian invaders to come at Attica or Boeotia.

But this was a tit for tat war and the Spartans responded. Agesilaus, particularly, was having none of this confederate wall building and little encouragement was needed to crank him up and set him off. The news was treated with gravity as he speedily mobilised the whole Spartan levy and, to make it a family affair, his half brother Teleutias launched the gulf fleet to really put the squeeze on the coalition forces trying once again to re-stop up the isthmus bottleneck. In May or early June 391 the king was over the Parnon range and crossing the plain of Mantinea before marching further on along a north east road to take a swipe at the Argives. The country round Argos had suffered little so far and was ripe for plunder, but the attack also functioned as a feint as the Spartans, after filling their knapsacks with looted victuals and valuables, were soon back on the road that went through Tenea. This was the most direct route from the Argolid over the mountains north to attack the walls that the Athenians had just built. It had clearly been a deep laid plan, as when they reached the waters of the gulf they found Teleutias with twelve triremes from his fleet on hand to back them up. The Spartans attacked and captured the walls, the ships and the dockyards at Lechaeum, the whole lot; though no great struggle is suggested, so it is possible little in the way of a garrison had been left to defend the place.

Despite the relative ease with which this success was achieved, still it all must have made the kinfolk proud as these active siblings, now for a second time, flung down the long walls of Corinth. Before leading their Spartans home to enjoy some well earned rest and recuperation eating blood broth in the comfort of the communal messes. These fraternal accomplishments once again allowed the contemplation of movement of Peloponnesian forces into the areas east of the Corinthian line in a campaign where as it turned out it would be the qualities of the new force of militant peltasts under Iphicrates that would be highlighted. The sequence began in early 390 when again Agesilaus was in charge of an army that entered Corinthian territory to support the men who had been left there to hold the regular front around Sicyon. Sometime after the Spartans arrived and took up post alongside their allies, contacts from amongst the Corinthian exiles brought intelligence that very much interested the king. It was reported that a large number of Corinthian cattle were being grazed at the Piraeum, on a headland north of the city. Agesilaus could not resist the opportunity, and getting his men under arms he distributed rations and marched them towards the isthmus. This bellicosity was not strictly in season as the Isthmian Games were underway at the time and the Argives, expecting the protection of a holy truce, were conducting sacrifices to Poseidon. They fled when they heard the Spartans were coming, leaving sacrificial victims and a ceremonial meal untouched. With everything in place and with Corinthian exiles accompanying his cavalcade, Agesilaus did some hearts and minds work. Organising the bemused athletes who were still hanging around, they held their own Games under the aegis of men who, though driven from their homes, could still show they were far from a spent force. It was a brave moment for the exiles and, as it turned out, would lead to some interesting sports statistics in the future. When Agesilaus left the area the Argives came back and held their own interrupted version of the Games, so that some competitors ended running and winning the same race twice.

After this interlude the Spartan king got back to business and approached Piraeum which he found well defended. To deceive the garrison he feinted back as if to attack the Acrocorinth, and Iphicrates, who the Corinthians had called up for help, followed and unknowingly passed by him during the night, allowing the Spartans to turn back and get a hold of the heights above Piraeum on the flanks of Mount Geraneia. The drovers there with the herds of cattle were so frightened when they saw the Spartans on the hills above them they ran their charges into a temple precinct on the point of the promontory. There was also a fort called Oenoe nearby but it could not offer the refugees any protection as Agesilaus' men came rushing down the hill, overran the walls and captured it. Realising the game was up, the people left in the temple surrendered unconditionally to the king. Here was not just the satisfaction of bags of booty but they also found amongst the prisoners they took some of the very people involved in the murders during the coup of February or March 392 who were handed over to the Corinthian exiles for what presumably was less than gentle treatment. They also in the trawl took captive some ambassadors from Boeotia who were discovered travelling on the road to Corinth. Some people even suggest these envoys constituted peace feelers from enemies reconsidering what benefits were accruing from their contribution to the confederate effort. But this is hardly supported by the facts: there is no suggestion they made any attempt to instigate any such discussions once they found themselves in the presence of the Spartan king.

But if this seemed a happy moment for the Spartans it did not last long as the king heard of the disaster that was the defining moment of this war of outposts. A horseman arrived in a lather while Agesilaus was parading his looted pickings and the prisoners he had scooped up. While everybody asked the rider what the news was, not until he found the king would he divulge it. Then he reported the debacle that had transpired near Lechaeum while the main army had been cattle rustling on the Piraeum. The king called everybody to arms and, without even waiting to prepare a meal, marched them out. Passing some hot springs, close to the shore at the base of a south westerly spur of Mount Geraneia, they pushed on towards the plain of Lechaeum, there hoping at least to get their comrades' bodies back. But three more riders arrived with the information that these had already been retrieved under truce. With no need now to hurry back, and perhaps feeling a little exposed, he returned towards the Piraeum to ensure the whole campaign might not be a waste by putting under the hammer what beasts, men and goods had been seized.

The disaster that Agesilaus had found dumped in his lap had been the first great triumph of the Athenian Iphicrates. The episode was initiated when that general decided to rain on the parade of some Spartan holiday makers. The men from Amyclae, a *perioeci* community a couple of miles south of Sparta, by tradition always went home to celebrate the festival of Hyacinthia, a three day bash in early summer with music and dancing, horse races and a parade of carts. The man in command at Lechaeum, after Agesilaus had left for the Piraeum, arranged for the allies to defend the walls while he escorted the celebrants on the first part of the road home. He had hoplites and cavalry when he started out but a few miles before they reached Sicyon he left the tourists with just the cavalry, with orders to return when the travellers were in safe country, and took his 600 hoplites back the way they had come on the road to Lechaeum. Iphicrates was at his alertest, having just a few days before broken in blood an attempt by a force of Corinthian exiles from Lechaeum to get into Corinth itself with the night time assistance of their friends still inside the walls. Now he and another general, Callias, saw the enemy movements from the ramparts of Corinth and the sight of only 600 hoplites marching not at all out of reach with no cavalry or peltasts for protection was too tempting.

Callias may have been the sprig of a plutocratic family who made their money leasing slaves to work Athens' silver mines, but he was no dilettante. He acted with great energy and rounded up every hoplite, Athenian and allied, that he could lay his hands on, and formed them up outside the city walls while Iphicrates headed his peltasts into the attack. They poured out of the gates pushing across country to reach the Spartans. Then, rushing to within short range, they started scoring hits with their needle sharp javelins immediately. Soon the helot servants of the Spartan hoplites were having to carry the wounded down the Lechaeum road in an effort to find assistance for the casualties, as the main body of Spartans prepared to defend themselves. They tried to react; the men of the twenty to thirty age groups were delegated to chase the attackers off. These men were no doubt lighter armed than the older soldiers: during the Peloponnesian War there had been a tendency to reduce the hoplite's defensive armour. Not infrequently men from this period are depicted with no greaves, a light helmet and no body armour at all, defending themselves just with the great hoplite shield. It seems likely these would have been the younger men and perhaps helot or *perioeci* hoplites without the wherewithal to afford fancy protection. Whoever they were, they ran forward to try to catch the peltasts that were tormenting them. But Iphicrates had coached his men well. They pulled back not allowing the breathless Spartan warriors to catch up to them. The hoplite shield, which could not be ditched as it would have been both shaming and render them defenceless, meant that despite their being little armoured they were still too encumbered to catch their nimble attackers. When the pursuers, tired, panting and winded, fell back Iphicrates' peltasts halted, turned themselves and threw at the Spartans again. Clearly slingers were also employed in amongst Iphicrates' men, as when the Spartans rushed out pellets from them hit and disabled nine or ten of the front rank as they came on. We also hear that the peltasts, when the main body of Spartan hoplites tried to march away, ran along their right flank to throw javelins in at this undefended side. While Spartan soldiers were famous for being the only Greeks who trained in infantry drill, it must be assumed that the movement of swopping the shield over to the other arm during combat was not part of their coaching manual.

With the young men a busted flush, the somewhat more experienced warriors, up to their mid-thirties, now tried their luck. But their attempts to catch the peltasts were also of no avail. The only result was that even more were isolated and killed. At this point the cavalry, who had left the pilgrims, finally arrived and now surely many must have felt the tables had turned. But these troopers were badly used, it seems they did not chase the peltasts down but only kept pace in a continuous front with the hoplites when they charged forward and came back with them when they retreated: a poor performance that does give some credence to an old prejudice that pre-Macedonian Greek horse were pretty feeble operators. At this point the Spartans were still a couple of miles from Lechaeum itself, but only a quarter of that distance from the sea, when the whole force began to disintegrate. Many could not take any more while some tried to make a stand on a nearby knoll. But this was no impenetrable bronze stitched line of shields but more a spavined beast, and when they saw the Athenian hoplites under Callias leaving the city walls and advancing towards them most seem to have panicked and fled. The cavalry and a few hoplites made it to Lechaeum and some got off in boats sent by people from the port who saw what was happening while others ran into the sea and drowned. Two hundred and fifty all in all were recorded as fatalities; altogether a success that is a nice example of the initially hyperbolic but eventually very effective simile used by Serge Yalichev in *Mercenaries of the Ancient World*: 'The damage inflicted by light troops was achieved by repeatedly attacking and then yielding quickly, much as the constant crashing and subsiding of the ocean waves gradually wears down the hardest of rocks.'[6]

Agesilaus when he realised the extent of the debacle understood there was little he could do to effectively turn the tables on these active adversaries lurking behind the walls of Corinth. Still, he determined to minimise as far as possible the impact on the spirits of both his own men and, just as important, the allies they now even more needed to keep committed to the cause. He resolved to try to demonstrate that the military verities had not significantly altered and that he was still decisively in the game. To achieve this he marched for Corinth ravaging all the way, cutting down trees, destroying crops and buildings, emphasising that whatever Iphicrates had accomplished he and his army could still march where they liked and that no enemy was prepared to come out and face them in a stand-up fight. When he reached Lechaeum itself he put his men into camp to show he called the shots there too.

But if it was a bold bluff front around Corinth; when fighting petered out and the army was homeward bound it was very different. Then he knew that, whatever impression was intended, it was bound to seem to many that they were skulking home with the remnants of a beaten regiment. Now the king's priority was to avoid embarrassment, so they only entered the cities on their route after dark and left before dawn. Orchomenus and Mantinea were passed like this; they did not want the humiliation of vanquished Spartans being observed by people they kept in subjugation. Nemea and Coronea might have seemed to bolster the old certainties about Spartan invincibility in the field, but there was another strand developing now where the disaster at Lechaeum could be added to that suffered at Pylos back in the old war.

As the Spartans completed the walk of shame Iphicrates made hay. He took back Sidus and Crommyon that had been garrisoned by Praxitas and Oenoe, the fort taken by Agesilaus only a few days before, with no great apparent effort. The impact of these confederate victories made a real difference. However much Agesilaus might parade through the country, in the key isthmus area the ramifications of the defeat of the Spartan hoplites and the concomitant augmentation in reputation of Iphicrates and his men, were such that they clearly now held the upper hand. As for the exiles they were too scared to travel overland from Sicyon: if they needed to make a journey they went by sea. Even so some raids were still managed from Lechaeum, reinforcing how important it had been for the Peloponnesians to retain control of the Gulf of Corinth.

Diodorus adds much to what happened during this part of the war but it is very confusing. It seems on occasions that he is repeating himself, as twice he describes a battle involving Iphicrates around Lechaeum, either of which might be that fought between the long walls connecting Corinth and its port described in detail by Xenophon. The sequence is the only thing that might give a clue, as Diodorus' first affray is recorded as having been just after the massacre, which fits with Xenophon, while the second is described as being a few days before Iphicrates' Lechaeum battle, which is usually considered to have happened some time later.[7] But this poses further difficulties, as he places the Athenians' descent on Phlious after rather than before the Lechaeum triumph, which clearly contradicts our contemporary source. He is also alone in talking about a combat fought with a Sicyonian force outside that city's walls where his men inflicted 500 casualties on warriors reckless enough to leave the shelter of their battlements to face Iphicrates' men. Although the timing of these triumphs might be dubious, there is no doubt that the anti-Spartan leaders in congress at the isthmus were considerably bucked by these successes and are afterwards recorded as acting with real energy, accord and ambition.

Early in 389 an offensive was decided upon along the north coast of the Gulf of Corinth. If the Spartans controlled the waters they could at least try to batten control on the coastline and at the same time hit at the interests of a key member of the Peloponnesian League. Calydon town west of Cape Rhium, where the gulf crossing was shortest, had been taken over by the Achaeans a while before, despite it having been originally an Aetolian community and was held by an Achaean garrison. Now a joint Acarnanian, Athenian and Boeotian force was mobilised to try to remove these peninsular intruders who looked all set to absorb more places outside the Peloponnese. It was a long march for the confederates through Phocis and Locris Ozolis but certainly safer than trying to ship out over waters controlled by a hostile marine. On arrival the army began to besiege the place, but the soldiers there stood out well against them and it looked like a long blockade might be required to take it. But when things became desperate, the defenders begged Sparta for help with none too subtle hints that if they did not come up trumps the whole of Achaea might fall away and exit the contest. It was an effective ploy that would work, but the effect of this intervention – whether it would interrupt the confederate advance – would not be revealed until later in the year.

Chapter Eight

Attempts at Peace and War

The Corinthian War that her gold had facilitated brought valuable returns for the Persians. The people who were tearing up her Anatolian provinces when the conflict started had been badly knocked back and their Aegean primacy shown to be frangible enough. But divisions at policy level were a given in most polities. For every proponent of a strategy there was almost always a rival pushing the opposite. Such division can be assumed as the default situation anywhere but with a large and rickety ancient empire where the distances between headquarters and outer limbs were so great, it was even more likely. So though the victory at Cnidus, the ravaging of coastal Laconia and the reconstruction of Athens' walls were lauded by many in the Persian hierarchy there were also powerful people with different perspectives. If Pharnabazus was backing Conon all the way there was evidence that others in the Persian ranks were not so convinced of the strategy. We learn of a key official called Tiribazus, 'who commanded the land forces in Asia, was envious of Conon's successes.'[1] Xenophon had a history with this man as Tiribazus had been the satrap of Western Armenia at the time of the *Anabasis*. Indeed Tiribazus was deemed so important by the Great King that no one else was allowed to help him mount his horse when he was present. Now in control of Ionia, he would have much to lose if Athens began to reassert her influence over the Greek cities of the Asian coast. From the other side, even before the first battle at Lechaeum when Praxitas burst into the long walls of Corinth, the thinking men back at Sparta had been trying to even up the odds against a coalition that remained very menacing. Alarmed by the achievements of the Athenian admiral and Persian satrap they realised the key strategy they needed to pursue was to dislodge the Persians from amongst their enemies. So when they heard reports of this officer Tiribazus, who might be a very different Persian, who not only hated them much less but also realised the drawbacks of a recrudescent Athens, they decided he was very well worth approaching. The agent they dispatched in 393 or 392 was called Antalcidas.

Antalcidas seems to have been something of a professional envoy. This was not normal though of course the Greeks in general were very far from unskilled when it came to arts of diplomacy. They had to be adept in a world where the natural state of intercity relations was war. You were fighting unless an agreement confirmed you were not, so a plethora of arrangements were required to ensure normal intercourse without recourse to bloodshed. Equally it was crucial to supply protection for representatives when they travelled into hostile lands. Envoys were not themselves considered sacrosanct, but certain specified heralds were, and these could offer protection for the ambassadors who came with them. Even with these sanctified go-betweens there could be breaches. Heralds had been known to be killed, imprisoned or at least refused to have their accreditation accepted. Rules in this age were as bent as in any other, yet to depict a conflict as a truce-less or herald-less war was to describe a particularly brutal conflict to the knife.

There were treaties that ranged from those that just declared an intention not to make war on each other, through to defensive pacts and offensive alliances. Truces were frequent but never watertight; there could be plenty of argument and disagreements on the details, and if the opprobrium of breaching them was real it did not mean it did not occur. Accords were usually limited to a generation or two though there is one example in 420 of Athens, Argos, Elis and Mantinea entering an agreement for a hundred years; but it probably makes sense to see this as more a statement of seriousness of intent rather than any sort of realistic expectation. Covenants were carved in stone or inscribed on bronze pillars and hedged round with religious ceremony to underpin what had been agreed; the Peace of Nicias of March 421 was recorded on stelae in temples at Delphi, Amyclae in Laconia, Olympia and the isthmus. Yet solidarity of recording material was often not matched by the permanence of the content. Agreements were almost always broken and as often as not the monument itself smashed or the pillar pulled down.

Antalcidas, on receiving his credentials, shipped out to meet Tiribazus. His task was to convince him that Sparta was far less a danger to Persian interests than the Athenians they were currently building up with their money. This bad-mouthing in such a key quarter could not be kept quiet. There were networks of *proxenoi*, citizens of one place who acted as a kind of consul in the interests of another. This complex of relations spread over the Aegean as well as the mainland, as did trade links, and even old school tie camaraderie between pupils of the great teachers. Information gathering might have been haphazard – they did not have a spy service like the Persian Empire – but there was enough to ensure this kind of secret negotiation was very hard to keep quiet. When word leaked out about Antalcidas' mission the confederates worried about their rival getting sole access to these vital Persian ears, and it was not long before there were envoys from Athens, Corinth, Argos and Thebes shipping out and dancing attendance on the busy satrap. We know the names of the Athenians who crossed the water: Hermogenes, Dion, Callisthenes, Callimedon and the man of the hour, Conon. Soon others showed up too, and what had started as a dialogue instigated by Antalcidas at Sardis in 392 turned into a sort of peace conference with almost all the belligerents trying to have their say.

Antalcidas got straight to the point, proposing that the Spartans drop any claims to the Asian cities, leaving them under Persian authority, and that the islands and cities on the Greek mainland should be autonomous after peace was made. Tiribazus was interested in this but the Athenians made it clear they would not countenance any such beginning that included autonomy for all the islands. They wanted to keep their paws on Lemnos, Imbros and Skyros, their ownership of which went back to the days of Miltiades and Cimon and were crucial in securing the northern grain routes and maintaining Athenian influence in Thrace. The Thebans were equally worried that autonomy meant them losing influence over the Boeotian communities they controlled; and the Argives were apprehensive it would end their recent arrangement with Corinth. Tiribazus was able to build up a sort of auction between the parties knowing he could only win from such a competition, but despite an apparently commanding position as power broker he did not have full authority to conclude terms and could not make definite commitments on anything else before he had gone back to Susa to consult the king. Some progress had been made but when it looked like differing bottom lines had resulted in an impasse, the delegates began to drift off home to test the response of their various constituencies to what had been discussed. But if the convention dissolved, the participants were still sufficiently hopeful to ensure it would only be a hiatus and a pretext for a change of venue. Arguing the toss in the shadow of Persian spears was perhaps anyway too stressful for the egos on parade at the conference table. Whatever the reasons for things falling apart in Sardis, soon most of the same ambassadors reconvened in Sparta itself in the winter of 392–1 to see what it would be possible to thrash out in that different environment.[2]

But while hot air was being exhaled in Laconia to, in the end, no great effect Tiribazus, though no longer directly involved, had not changed his mind about the dangers of a revitalised Athens. Secretly giving money to Antalcidas so he could collect a fleet of his own to boost Spartan effectiveness, hobbled since Cnidus, he also, recognising how crucial an actor Conon was, arranged to have him arrested and imprisoned, claiming jurisdiction against a man he only recognised as a Persian officer rather than an accredited Athenian. Conon's fate is unknown. The veteran admiral may have perished while under lock and key either at Sardis or the Great King's court, whilst some report he escaped. If he did break out it was not back to power and influence, but at most to his old exile's billet in Cyprus where he died soon afterwards. That Tiribazus kept his payments to Antalcidas secret indicated he was treading on eggshells and knew he still needed to get court approval for his support of the Spartans. With this in mind he travelled up the royal road to Susa not long after the crowd of contentious Greeks left Sardis in the other direction. On completing his journey upcountry and his report given at court he found that his audience was decidedly captious. The king and his ministers were not about to just rubber stamp the reversal of the policy of supporting the anti-Spartan cause and Tiribazus found himself unceremoniously replaced by an officer called

Struthas who was pro-Athenian to the core. All this showed the official Persian line was still strong against those who had taken their gold in the late war and then turned against them, and been instrumental in wreaking a trail of destruction and rapine from Sardis to Paphlagonia.

It would not in fact be long before Tiribazus was back in charge but, for the moment, the arrival in Anatolia of his replacement Struthas motivated the Spartans, who realised a dangerous enemy had arrived to replace a friend. This, on top of the fact that the talks at Sparta had petered out and the route to peace closed off, caused the dispatch of Thibron, rehabilitated now and returning to his old stomping ground to raise a new Asian war. So it was over to Ephesus again in the spring of 391 for another Spartan expeditionary force. It is claimed there were 8,000 of them, and Thibron also raised more men when the army arrived, and then set up bases in the Maeander valley preparatory to ravaging the country. 'Thibron seized the stronghold of Ionda and a high mountain, Cornissus, forty stades from Ephesus.'[3] The response by Struthas was impressive: he raised a large force of cavalry, 20,000 light armed locals and even got 5,000 mercenary Greek hoplites on the payroll. These troops and their commander, resentful at another intrusion by these rapacious foreigners, marched to confront again a Spartan threat that had only allowed a few years breathing space since Agesilaus had been evicted by the investment of 'ten thousand archers'. It had taken time to mobilise his forces and it was late summer 391 before he was ready, but then Struthas was lucky. Thibron and his officers were slapdash. This general, though something of an intellectual, (he apparently wrote on the Spartan constitution) was not proficient in army command and had faced trial at Sparta for failure to keep his troops in hand after his previous Asian escapade. Now he showed he had not learned any lessons, and when the Persians sent out some raiding parties of cavalry to act as bait, Thibron headed out with a response force without even informing the officers left at the main camp that he was leaving. Once exposed in the open plain, and clearly not at all alert, he was caught by the whole Persian army. When they struck there can hardly even have been a watch kept at all as Thibron was caught apparently dallying in his tent after breakfast with a flute player, a muscular fellow who was a local celebrity and we are told aped Spartan ways. This final incompetence was fatal, as he and the soldiers with him were cut down; one report even suggests Struthas slew him in personal combat. A few Greeks got away to a nearby fort whilst the rest of the army was left stranded in the main camp.

There were not going to be many rushing to stitch battle honours of Lechaeum and Thibron's campaign on the regimental colours of Sparta, yet in the years after the failure of the peace talks it had not been all disaster. In the summer of 391 Agesilaus had had success in the Argolid and Corinth, while his half brother Teleutias had retaken Lechaeum. But the war had moved even further around since its beginning in 395, from Phocis to Thessaly, from the isthmus to Arcadia, as well as Rhodes, Asia and the Aegean, but now another country would be added to the list of battlefields: Arcanania. An appeal for assistance from a beseiged Achaea, with its implicit threat to the unity of Sparta's League, the ephors took very seriously, and with the assembly all in favour they decided to reinforce this other war in Acarnania. Their preparedness to act may also have had much to do with the fact that the conflict fought around the isthmus had not been a source of good news for some time. So the Spartan elite were not unhappy to redirect their efforts.

So it was there that events unrolled when in 389 Agesilaus was again in command. He took charge of two regiments of Spartans, the same number of allies and the whole Achaean levy, making a large army indeed. The immediate objective of the thrust was to sustain Sparta's besieged Achaean friends, but when the king crossed the Gulf of Calydon, the siege of the city had in fact already been lifted and the confederates including the Acarnanians pulled out. Typically this success did not satisfy Agesilaus. If his enemies would not stay to face him he would track them down. He and his men, with their Achaean friends secure behind them, were able to follow north-west through Aetolia and back to the Acarnanians' own country and there scoop up the goods and chattels the populace had not been able to get under cover. This west flank of central Greece was a land of lakes and rugged mountains rising to over 4,500 feet in places – difficult country, apart from the plain of the Achelous, that the intruders would not have been as familiar with as their normal campaigning grounds of the peninsula, Megara, Attica, Boeotia and Phocis. To make war here they no doubt had itineraries to let them know what communities and landmarks there were on their routes of march, on top of what the locals would have told them more or less willingly. The activity in this country was intended as pressure, and to accompany it Agesilaus sent ambassadors to the assembly at Stratus urging them to leave the confederation and instead join up with the Spartan side. The kick in the tail was that if they declined the offer he would completely despoil the country. When no response came he was as good as his word. Only moving a couple of miles a day his men concentrated on deep and efficient wreckage. They also had a bit of good fortune, as after they had withdrawn some distance away, the people around Stratus and Lake Trichonis brought out their cattle and took up working their fields again. Agesilaus, after leaving fifteen days to lull them into a sense of security, pounced. He set off at a great pace, covered the twenty-odd miles to that region, and bagged most of their cattle, movables and slaves. But after this, with the people roused, what had been a cakewalk turned into something very different.

These western Greeks were well known as efficient light infantry and they collected in good numbers and climbed up onto the high terrain above the Spartans' camp. From there they began pelting them with slingshot and stones to such effect it forced them to move their camp site down onto lower ground. Agesilaus, after auctioning the ample spoils already taken, decided he would gain little more from remaining in the region and attempted an orderly withdrawal. But when the army was marching, stretched out in a long vulnerable column, along the road by the lake, they were attacked again from the hills that squeezed the path in against the water. It was becoming difficult and a bit too reminiscent of the Lechaeum affair as they tried to drive the enemy off, but as on that earlier occasion they were unable to catch them as they ran away, making good use of local knowledge of tracks and country. They could not get at the men who had been harassing them and, when their pursuit came to a halt, back came the Acarnanians again, almost bringing the invaders' column to a standstill. The sense of the account we have suggests that the Spartans had stopped and spread out in a battle line with their backs to the lake and their front facing the hills. In this circumstance Agesilaus took stock and appreciated the left of his line was where his troops might make best headway as the terrain was more accessible and more of the enemy were pressing in there. Once decided where he would attack, and the diviners on board, the horns blared, the paean raised and the intruders, who had been suffering under the slingshot and javelins of the Acarnanians, now bounded forward. The less experienced men 'the fifteen year class' (20 to 35-year-olds) led the way, but crucially this time the cavalry played their part, and when the enemy fled before them they chased them up the hill until they reached the top where many of the Acarnanian hoplites and peltasts were drawn up. The cavalry took some losses in this melee but critically they pinned the defenders in place until the main force of Agesilaus' heavy infantry came up. When the full phalanx hit it was decisive. At 'close quarters' these bloodthirsty warriors from Laconia and their Peloponnesian allies were unstoppable and their victims routed soon after the first impact with a loss of three hundred dead.

It had been a useful victory in a place where it looked as if the Spartans were in difficulties, and Agesilaus had plenty of armour stripped from the enemy dead to put up a trophy to victory before he led his army onwards. For the larger picture of the campaign, we are specifically told he had taken no towns, though he did try assaults on some. Despite their Achaean allies' continued worries over Acarnanian reprisals, autumn was coming on and the Spartans determined to go home. A force of Athenian triremes based at Oeniadae to the west meant the direct route from Calydon they had come over by was too dangerous and so they had to detour, returning back across the gulf at Rhium, the shortest crossing point.

In the following year, spring of 388, Agesilaus again bristled, making a great play of organising another expeditionary force and sending to the allies to meet him on the road to the gulf. This time the menace was enough. The Acarnanians, still bruised from what had befallen them the year before, kowtowed. Tough these highlanders might be, but their enemies had made it abundantly clear they had the wherewithal both to destroy the provisions they produced in their own country and cut them off from any their friends might try to send to them. So having reaped the whirlwind the Acarnanian leaders decided the war going on between Sparta and the confederate Greeks was not truly central to their interest. They made peace with the Lacedaemonians and sent some amenable men to sort out their problems with the Achaeans, the confrontation with whom the whole business had begun.

So the men from Laconia had one enemy the less, but that did not at all mean an end to the war. In the fighting season of 388 it was another old enemy. This time the tormenter in chief was, Agesipolis I, who had been too young to command six years before at Nemea. Now presumably in his early twenties, he pushed forward for a war against Argos. It is probable the establishment at Sparta was having concerns about the dominant position Agesilaus had achieved over the last few years and wanted the other king to gain experience and reputation to prepare him to act as the counterbalance their dual system intended. Argos was always a likely target, standing as it did threatening the right flank of the route up to Corinth. The new commander of the army was a true Spartan, pious to the fingertips with a fetish for getting the gods onside. The Argives were claiming that a holy truce made any attack on them sacrilegious, so the young monarch first went to Olympia to ask if he could disregard these claims. He got a yes, but that was not enough. He continued on to Delphi, the 'navel of the world', and got the same answer. So he joined his army at Phlious where it had been mustering and from there it was on to Nemea and over the hills to ravage the Argolid, despite heralds draped in garlands claiming the sacred truce was still on. After only one day of pillaging, when the weary looters had returned to camp for their dinner, the area was struck by an earthquake. The king decided to interpret this as an omen from Poseidon giving the invasion the go ahead. This says much for the men's mood: if they were shaken and expecting to retreat just as Agis' invasion of Elis had in a similar situation, surely he would not have taken this confident line. Incidents and responses like this are revealing about the ancient Greek attitude to religion. Belief was genuine and deeply felt but equally whatever happened was eminently open to interpretation and manipulation.

After all this the Spartans drove for the city of Argos itself, looking like they wanted to abolish one of their most desperate foes for good, and with the young king intent on bettering the destruction done quite recently by his veteran colleague Agesilaus. The invaders got so close to the walls that some Boeotian cavalry, allies of Argos, who were caught outside, desperately called to be let in but were refused to ensure Agesipolis' men could not follow in after them. Instead these traumatised blue-bloods had to cower under the lee of the walls depending on the defenders above to keep their tormenters off with slingshot, javelins and arrows. They would have been in even worse trouble had Agesipolis' Cretan archers not been on detached duty ravaging Nauplia a few miles further south on the coast. The Spartans had started well, but before any sort of proper siege could be got underway the heavens again took a hand. This time a thunderbolt is reported falling in the Spartan camp, killing some men. This sequence of celestial strikes was getting to everybody by now, and the invaders decided they had best get out before worse followed. They set off home with such celerity that they even abandoned the construction of a fort they had planned to build just west of Nemea, justifying their lack of resolution by some conveniently faulty divination. A good haul of booty was from all accounts the best of it for the invaders. The people in the country had been taken by surprise at the incursion and had failed to hide or get their movables into shelter.

But buffering about in the Peloponnese was not really going to bring home the bacon. That would be accomplished in two other places: the court at Susa, and around the corn lanes of the Hellespont. Defeat at Cnidus had set Sparta back in a big way but naval warfare was always about balance and though it had swung against them after that encounter it was very possible the scales would soon enough tip their way again. The opportunity to make this comeback was offered by those inveterate mixers from Rhodes. The local oligarchs, exiled in 395 when Conon arrived, had put in hand a coup, eager to get back their power and property and to do some damage to their domestic rivals. They had some success in killing or driving out a decent number of the democratic party, but things were still on a knife edge so they dispatched some of their cleverest talkers to ask for aid from Sparta.

The crisis reported by the Rhodian oligarchs had the Spartan authorities concerned, and as the summer waned in 391, despite normal worries over seafaring at that time of year, they decided on the need to show some muscle in the south Aegean. Ecdicus, an officer hanging around the *agora* looking for employment, was co-opted to take action. It was no massive effort – more of a feeler – with the commander given only eight ships to back his intervention in favour of Sparta's Rhodian friends. But the effort on the Asian shore was to be resuscitated too. Another military man called Diphridas was shipped out on the same boats to take charge of what remained of the dead Thibron's army. This general gets high marks for being active, resolute and eschewing the hedonism of his predecessor, and once landed he showed talent and vigour, managing to recoup the army's strength, beefing up the disillusioned rump by hiring extra mercenaries.[4] In addition, Struthas' son in law, and others of his family, were discovered on the road to Sardis and very profitably ransomed back to their distraught *pater familias*.

The other watery arm of this double push had some early success when the small fleet under Ecdicus detached Samos from her established Athenian connection before heading to find winter shelter in the harbour at the old Spartan base of Cnidus, scene of their defeat not long before. Any inclination to carry on to Rhodes had been shelved when news came in that the anti-oligarchs there were well dug in and had disposed of a local maritime force well in excess of their own, possibly even twice their number. Not that this front was about to go to sleep. In the spring of 390, when Spartan hoplites were about to get a drubbing near Corinth, Teleutias, Agesilaus' half brother brought his own twelve-ship gulf squadron all the way round the Peloponnese to the Aegean and joined the small fleet already there. With Samos on side and providing seven ships of their own, he landed there to rest and feed his men before sailing on to take over the whole navy at Cnidus; so this experienced and able officer now disposed of 27 warships. Confident in his resources Teleutias felt in a position to press the Rhodian mission and so manoeuvred his navy out into the seaways on the way south down the Anatolian coast en route to the island. On the way he struck lucky. Philocrates, an Athenian with ten triremes, was sailing to help his allies on Cyprus and presumably anticipated little danger at this early stage of his cruise, but the unlucky soul bumped into a Spartan force well tuned and eager in anticipation of sorting out the Rhodians. They were no match and the whole squadron was seized and sailed in short order back to Cnidus where the spoils were disposed off. After this triumph the whole, now presumably boosted to 37, sailed once more to Rhodes. This incident, apart from adding to the growing fame of the king's brother, also indicates a confusion of loyalties at this stage. Athens had been discovered sending help to a Cypriot prince who was fighting Persia, their ally whose money had been absolutely instrumental in her revival, while the Spartans were stopping succour getting to that same prince whose activities might have been vital in doing down those very Persians whose support was so crucial for the Greek coalition they were fighting.

What Teleutias did when he reached the theatre of war at Rhodes is unknown, but the impact of this interruption on the high command in Athens was profound. They had not been very proactive since the end of peace talks at Sparta. It is possible, but not absolutely established, that the arrest of Conon and Attic support for the rebel Evagoras were all part of a deep breach with Susa. If this was the case, or even if the Athenian Persian relationship was only beginning to be strained, a threat to the flow of Achaemenid money was bound to make the funding of viable naval forces far more difficult. With the peace summit long folded and Rhodes become again a storm centre, there was real pressure to get back in the game. In the city of Athens itself, and Piraeus the port, the generals and officials were deeply alarmed at the turn of events and determined to release their big guns. Thrasybulus was now demanding that the people act, and nobody was going to gainsay the father of reborn democratic Athens. He was given command of a fleet, the best they could come up with: a new armament of forty ships that the people hoped would be sufficient to confront the forces the Spartans had posted to the south Aegean. Thrasybulus sailed with confidence, intending to make the kind of difference he had made so often before in recent years. But when he got near to Rhodes, most probably at Halicarnassus, he learned what the state of play was on the island. Though Teleutias was known to be still around, and his oligarch associates held at least one important fortress, most of Rhodes Island was well held by the democrats who had recently even won a stand-up battle against their rivals. So the Athenian champion realised his allies did not really require his help and that the danger he had been dispatched to counter had virtually evaporated. There was no need now to risk taking on the enemy in a head-on fight the outcome of which, with near parity in numbers, could not be absolutely predicted. This was almost certainly taking place late in the year 391 and probably Thrasybulus, with the sailing season virtually over, was confident Teleutias could not be reinforced sufficiently to make headway against Athens' Rhodian allies until the next spring.[5] On the strength of these ruminations, and strongly disinclined to allow his campaign to end as a damp squib, he decided to use the tail of the sailing season to head for the Hellespont.

There were beginning to be echoes of the end of the Decelean War, a reversion to old patterns, Rhodes and the Dardanelles were becoming the key centres of action with the corn lanes again the heart of the matter. The importance of these always remained and the Athenians constantly tried to ensure against their disruption. In years to come the city fathers even attempted to tie up the producing end; we know they set up a statue in the market place to the Thracian king of Bosporus, Satyrus, and later made a commercial treaty with another king, Leucon of Bosporus, who in 357 gave them the first option on corn supply and an exemption from export duty as *quid pro quo* for he and his sons getting Athenian citizenship.

But on this occasion before reaching these crucial Hellespontine roadsteads Thrasybulus' squadron cruised along the Ionian coast picking up what *specie* they could from their allies, laying under contribution as many communities as could be reached whether on the islands or the mainland. The Athenians, once in northern waters, used their clout to some purpose. They established peace between two Thracian warlords; Seuthes, who controlled the coast of Thrace, and Amedocus, king of the Odrysians, getting on board useful clients for the future who would be able to exert pressure on the local Greek communities in Athenian interest.

Thrasybulus not only busied himself making pals with Thracian bosses, he also sailed to the island of Thasos. Thasos, which he had liberated during the days of Alcibiades and after a further spell under Spartan rule at the end of the Great War, was now free once more. The descent on the island throws some light on the economics in this new Athenian set up. Since 413 the old tribute was not demanded but the Thasians were required to pay the five per cent tax, an amount recorded as well at Clazomenae, which Thrasybulus visited in either 390 or 389. After this showing of the flag in Thrace and around, the Athenians sailed for Byzantium and Chalcedon, all the old places, where they threw out the oligarchs and put democratic friends in charge. Here they revived the ten per cent duty, first imposed in 410, on all goods coming from the Black Sea. Thrasybulus' people are also recorded filling their coffers selling contracts to grain trade tax farmers. The local satrap Pharnabazus' attitude to all this was not vouchsafed, but it is probable he was still friendly. His policy at this time seems to have remained consistently pro-Athenian whatever the concerns of others in the Persian establishment either in Anatolia or at the Great King's court. So with the corn lanes safe and with ready money to pay the oarsmen, sailors and soldiers, in spring of 389 they directed their prows south for Lesbos.

The Athenian fleet got to Lesbos without incident and dropped anchor near Eresos. It was early in the year and the Athenians were playing with fire campaigning at this time. It cost Thrasybulus 23 ships as a storm hit and he had to try to find shelter in places that he hoped had thrown over their masters and would turn out to be friends in time of need. The people of Mytilene did ditch the Spartans and joined him, but they were the only ones who did and at Methymna, an important place on the north of the island and Mytilene's main rival, he had to fight the locals under their harmost Therimachus. By collecting 400 heavy armed marines from his ships, together with exiles and the Mytilenaean hoplite levy, he triumphed, killing the enemy general and defeating his men, though many got back to the protection of the city defences. Despite the satisfaction of erecting a trophy and burying another Spartan commander, Thrasybulus could neither reinstate the exiles as he had promised nor make the Mytilenaeans undisputed leaders on the island of Lesbos. But the success was certainly part cause of others coming on board, and we hear that on departing, some places including Eresos and Antissa had changed sides and that Thrasybulus' flotilla had been fleshed out with ships from allies on both Lesbos and Chios.

From Lesbos they sailed south past Rhodes, coasting down the Anatolian shore where Lydia bulges out, to arrive near where the Eurymedon River reaches the sea. Rhodes was still the main objective but this was a necessary detour to drum up funds to pay the men. This estuary had seen and would see the likes of both Cimon, son of Miltiades, and Hannibal, the Carthaginian, in their time fighting battles there, but now it was where Thrasybulus and his men beached their ships. The citizens of Aspendus, the most important town nearby, paid up under pressure, but still camping casually in the country the intruders began to ransack the farms and estates around. This was a fatal underestimation of the martial qualities of these people who deeply resented being bilked twice over. When the freebooters retired to sleep the Aspendians got their weapons out, put on their armour and attacked the snoring and slackly guarded men. The effect was immediate: officers and men hot footed it back to their ships, raised anchor and pulled off in the direction of their friends on Rhodes. On counting the cost they found that amongst the dead was Thrasybulus himself, a miserable end for such a character who had been the greatest man in Athens since leading the men of Phyle against the Thirty a decade and a half before.

The grieving officers and men arrived at Rhodes to find the oligarchs had driven their allies out and that the popular remnants were holed up in 'outposts' outside the city, and there they joined them in the continuing Rhodian civil war. When news of the loss of Thrasybulus reached Athens itself the inclination to lose themselves in mourning did not stop them from attending to practicalities, sending one Agyrrhius, a man with an illicit financial past but who had made himself popular enough to be elected general by upping payments to assembly attendees, to take over the fleet at Rhodes. The passing of Thrasybulus by an unknown blade is not noted to the extent that might be expected. A contemporary comment that he 'was esteemed a most excellent man'[6] was laudatory but brief – not much for the second founder of democratic Athens.

What is unclear at this time is what exactly Athenian policy was towards Persia. That Thrasybulus had been trespassing on what is clearly Persian territory suggests not just that the peace talks had floundered, but that the Attic city considered itself at war with the Great King. This also fits with their involvement with Evagoras, now in deep dispute with his Persian overlord, and the Egyptian rebels. Yet it is still very surprising the Athenians pursued actions that seemed bound to push Persia back into Sparta's arms. An argument can be made that there were different factions, one pro-Persian headed by Conon, and one more bellicose in respect of the old foe led by Thrasybulus. What cannot be shocking is that the Persians, even ones who been sponsors of Athens before, started to reconsider their options with these untrustworthy people, whose behaviour hardly seemed much friendlier than the Spartans they had been supporting them against. These were considerations that would soon bear significant fruit when Tiribazus returned to his old bailiwick.

In just a short time both Thrasybulus and Conon, two remarkable men, important naval officers in the final phase of the Peloponnesian War and in their different ways joint founders of the new Athens, passed from the scene. But if these two had gone there were others with talent and ambition to carry the flag. Iphicrates was just beginning his career and it was the next Spartan move that gave him his opportunity to show again what an outstanding general he was. The Athenian push in the face of Teleutias' presence had of course caused concern in Sparta but it was the presence of the old enemy back in the Hellespont and Bosporus that triggered the greatest shockwaves. To rectify matters now became the highest priority in Laconian councils, to deal with an enemy who now seemed able to mulch the corn trade, and despite other Persians' disquiet still had Pharnabazus looking like a staunch ally. Determined to act, Dercylidas might have done enough when he held the line at Abydos and Sestos when Pharnabazus and Conon were on the offensive; they now wanted somebody to do more. The man dispatched was called Anaxibius who had made a strong pitch to the ephors, that with slim resources he could still trouble the enemy around the Hellespont. Xenophon had a history with this man as well; he had fallen foul of him over a decade before at Byzantium when he failed to produce the pay promised for his soldiers as the 10,000 campaign was winding down. So now when he took over from Xenophon's old friend Dercylidas we are not hearing things from an unbiased informant. The implication that he bribed the ephors to get the command at Abydos and promised much more than he could realistically deliver should be taken with a pinch of salt. Furnished with only three triremes and money to hire 1,000 mercenaries he nonetheless seems to have had an impact on his arrival. Securing Abydos he also got some other towns to come over, while ravaging the lands of local rivals. He also refitted three other triremes he found in the dockyards and so soon had under hand a neat little squadron of six warships that might at least contest control of the waters around the town.

In Athens it looked like what Thrasybulus had achieved had already started to unravel, but at least to plug this particular hole in the dyke they had the very man they needed. With the Corinth front pretty quiet Iphicrates could be spared – in fact the general and the men were back in town unemployed. He was given eight ships and took 1,200 peltasts, enough to overtop what his antagonist was known to field. Reaching the Dardanelles after a short and uneventful cruise they entered what had become something of a small war. Both Spartans and the Athenians seemed to be scrimping at this time; just enough resources and the talents of the man in charge were meant to make the difference. Any fighting looked like it was going to be carried out in a pretty desultory way. Both sides got in a bit of plundering, but it did not seem anything decisive was likely to occur.

Iphicrates decided to disabuse those who had decided this had become a quiet front, though first he intended to lull the enemy into a false sense of security. He gave the impression he was afraid of Anaxibius by building an unusually strong wall around his encampment. But the young fox was just waiting for his opportunity to pounce. His now complacent antagonist decided to take a swipe at the Antandrians on the south coast of the Troad. Anaxibius marched there with his Spartans and 200 hoplites from Abydos, and with these intimidated the city fathers onto his side. This was spritely stuff so far but the problem was getting back home. Anaxibius left a small garrison in place and gave orders for the remainder to pack up their kitbags for the return journey back to base. Iphicrates must have had a very decent spy service as he soon knew exactly what was happening and moved to take advantage. He was based on the north European side of the Hellespont channel, but got his ships to ferry the men over during the night. At first light he sent these craft up the Asian coast in clear view so his enemies might think he was off raising contributions from the coastal communities, while with his soldiers he was marching hard down a little populated part of the country round Abydos to the mountains south of what is modern Canakkale to set up an ambush.

The Spartans were almost saved by an iffy sacrificial outcome but, like Claudius Pulcher at the battle of Drepana in 249 BC with his chickens, Anaxibius disregarded the gods and suffered for it. In the face of a known enemy he might not have moved without favourable omens, but he assumed the whole of the Troad was friendly and marched anyway. But friendly Iphicrates was certainly not. He had hidden his peltasts on the slope that led down to the river valley of the Rhodios. This plain was the home stretch for Anaxibius' men and when they reached it they were not in good order. Part of the column entered the valley while others were stretched out behind still in the high country above. Now Iphicrates struck and, with the hoplites from Abydos way up ahead and too far off to help, the Spartan leader knew he was lost. The heavy troops that might have won the battle could not climb back up in time and the rest, strung out, would be bound to fold on the impact of Iphicrates' men. Anaxibius may have been lax but he had integrity. Taking his shield from his shield bearer and lover and grasping his spear he prepared to sell his life dearly. Twelve other Spartan officers, harmosts from local cities that had thrown them out, were also with him and they did the same telling the remaining men to run for safety as they recognised they were anyway too unnerved to fight. They died weapons in hand under a hail of javelins, though their sacrifice did not save all their men. Many fell including fifty of the hoplites from Abydos. Either they had got up from the plain too late to help but not too late to die, or perhaps they were the rump who had not reached the plain when the ambush was sprung. Once again a Spartan commander had died in battle; but he and his party had certainly shown that Thermopylae spirit. Iphicrates, happy from the hunt, with more Spartan shields as spoils, and once again very content with how his peltasts had showed, returned to his ships to cross the water back to his base.

After this satisfactory Hellespontine scrap matters began to develop more ominously much nearer home for the Athenians. Eteonicus, an active and experienced Spartan officer, if not a popular one, once military governor at Thasos, and who had led the land attack on the Athenian camp at Aegospotami, had been posted harmost at Aegina, and now he returned to take up his command. Intercourse between Athens and this old rival from ancient times had been relatively peaceful for some years but would not stay so for long after his landfall on Aegina. Once on this triangular island, the remains of an extinct volcano poking out of the sea, seventeen miles from Athens, under ten miles across, less than seven up and down and rising up to 1,300 feet, with direct orders from the ephors he encouraged the people there to retake up the old tradition of raiding Attica. The resuscitation of this front was clearly disquieting to the Athenian authorities who reacted, sending a man called Pamphilus with hoplites to the island to build a fort to pin the Aeginans down on land as they blockaded them from the sea with ten triremes of the home fleet. Unfortunately for the men from Athens, Teleutias, the veteran regal sibling, was back from Rhodes and on hand with a Spartan force just starting out on a revenue cruise. A timely arrival, he drove off the blockading fleet, though he was not apparently able to winkle out Pamphilus or destroy the fort. This was probably around 389 as a new admiral called Hierax soon arrived to replace Teleutias who handed over the command. As he departed he was lauded by his men, garlanded like a winning athlete for his achievements at Rhodes and capturing a whole Athenian fleet of ten ships (though as half brother of Xenophon's idol Agesilaus perhaps it is reasonable to take some of this hero worship as less than gospel). Hierax did not remain on Aegina but headed again for the other battle front at Rhodes leaving only twelve ships under his lieutenant Gorgopas to take care of the Athenian fort. But Pamphilus was not left to swing in the wind. His compatriots got down to business and in four months fitted out a goodly fleet, rescued their hoplites and brought them back home. If this saved the soldiers, the downside was that the raiders from Aegina were free again to harass the coast of Attica, and in response the Athenians now deployed thirteen ships under Eunomus to take care of these pests.

This Aegina war was far from spent and Gorgopas, called away to escort Antalcidas to Asia, had to be swiftly re-dispatched with his twelve triremes back to the action. It was not an easy run home and he only managed to re-enter Aegina port by dodging the fleet of Eunomus who was trying to cordon off the town. This little place was finding a big role in the war. Dominating the Saronic Gulf as it did, forces there could almost impose a blockade against the Athenians if they were minded and had the ships to do it. It was beginning to be a real problem; Spartan control of Aegina was emerging as a sort of Decelea in the water, a mote in the eye that something had to be done about. It is no coincidence that Athens' first maritime rivals were the merchant princes from that island and that when Themistocles needed a rationale for fleet building he found it in the power of this water-girt rival.

Now Eunomus, with his enemy having eluded his watch and entered the harbour, decided to return home and as night came on sailed north towards Cape Zoster east north east of Aegina. But the Spartans, despite having just arrived, were active and observant and followed the light of Eunomus' rearmost boat, but far enough behind not to be noticed. The Spartan boatswains kept time by clicking stones and the oarsmen sliced the water to avoid making a noise. It was silent running until Gorgopas saw that the enemy had beached and were going ashore. Then he ordered the trumpet sound to initiate the attack. The battle was fought under moonlight and the Athenians were at a great disadvantage. Some of their crews were on the beach, others half disembarked, and only a few fit for fighting. It took crucial minutes for oarsmen to get back to their benches, steersmen to their oars, and marines back on board and in this time the Spartans had captured four ships. Only with great endeavour and enterprise did the rest get off the beach and out of the Spartans' clutches to the safety of Piraeus.

It was summer 388 by now and it looked as though Aegina, as a Spartan thorn in Athens' side, was up and running again. But at this moment Chabrias took a hand, an Athenian destined to be thirteen times a general and who in the future would best both Agesilaus and Epaminondas in battle. Like Iphicrates he was an accomplished military trickster. The mission was to get 800 peltasts on ten triremes to Cyprus to boost the cause of Evagoras who was trying to carve a little Levantine empire out of the body of the Persian state. But when his new orders came he took his own force, with some other ships and a number of hoplites made available, to try to finally resolve the Aegina war before taking up the original task he had been given. Arriving on the island during the night the crafty Athenian slipped over the sides of his beached ships with his peltasts and found a convenient hollow near a temple to Heracles to wait out the night and let his plan unfold. As arranged, when day broke the hoplites from the rest of the fleet under Demaenetus disembarked as ordered and marched a couple of miles past the hollow where the peltasts were hidden to a hill where they took a stand. Gorgopas, hearing of the intruders' arrival, reacted immediately. He was accompanied by eight other Spartiates, his own marines and some local hoplites, and also mobilised all the freemen from his triremes' crews to act as light infantry. This heterogeneous group pushed on to get at the invaders but, as the column passed the hollow, the ambush was sprung. The peltasts threw javelins and stones while the Athenian hoplites from their hill advanced down on Gorgopas' men. They were spread out along the road and not in fighting order at all. The vanguard including Gorgopas and the other Spartiates were quickly eliminated. The Spartan commanders were dropping like flies, brought low by tricky Athenians, and in addition 150 Aeginan hoplites and 200 foreign resident aliens and sailors were also killed as they fled for the protection of the town. Chabrias and his men had done well in cowing their enemies and freeing the sea lanes into Athens. Indeed after these reverses the sailors refused to man the Spartan ships. Morale was sagging badly; the Spartans not only seemed incapable of organising a passable defence of their island base but had exacerbated matters by failing to get the crews paid, a contractual bottom line more important even than the prospect of victory.

This had become a key front and it was not going to remain quiet for long. The Spartans were going to get right back in the ring and now they wanted success. Their most recent champions had unfortunately died in glorious defeat; now the man they turned to was Teleutias, dispatched as a popular officer who could get the fleet back in working order. His arrival certainly did make a difference and despite bringing no money with him he at least got the men fed and made promises of what they would get in the way of loot. The revitalised crews and soldiers boarded their twelve ships and sailed straight for Piraeus where Teleutias expected to find the enemy vessels unmanned. Informants had told him the officers usually would spend the night at their houses when in home port and that the sailors would be spread about in billets. Half a mile out at sea he stopped and let the men rest on their oars for the night, and at dawn he attacked. His orders were to concentrate on disabling the warships first and only after that to secure the merchant vessels: rich prizes that might distract his unremunerated crews. The raiders, after gaining control of the harbour, even entered Piraeus itself and kidnapped traders from their booths on the western quays as they were setting up to show their wares. The locals in Piraeus and Athens itself were soon woken by the commotion in the port. Hoplites rubbed sleep from their eyes and grabbed down spears and shields from their house walls while cavalry troopers bridled their horses and gathered themselves into their units. They stumbled into formation but before they could get at the intruders Teleutias was underway sending his prizes off, escorted by three triremes, back to Aegina. With his other nine he slipped anchor before turning to scoop up the small fishing boats and ferries discovered entering Piraeus from the islands at their routine time of appearance in the morning. It had all been gravy so far, but the Spartan admiral wanted more and turned his ships prows south towards Cape Sunium where, waiting on the grain route, he was able to detain merchant vessels in some numbers. Then it was back to Aegina to offload the booty and sell it to eager profiteers. So Teleutias was able to make good on the promises he had made when he arrived and we hear no more of mutinies in the fleet while he remained in command.

Chapter Nine

The King's Peace

The Athenians had felt the pain when Agesilaus' half brother made a wreck of Piraeus. Not only did his piratical activities make the war more self supporting for the Spartans but it brought the kind of pressure that had many citizens lobbying their leaders to approach the peace table, pen in hand. It was almost becoming an Aeginan War just as the end of the Peloponnesian conflict had been known as the Decelean War, and indeed the island was functioning not unlike that fort when Agis had sat like a toad foursquare on the Attic landscape drawing runaway slaves and oligarchic exiles into his orbit.

If Spartans had a reputation of being reactionary militarists unwilling or unable to see any other point of view there were always those who broke the mould. The Spartan diplomat Antalcidas had been the prime mover involved in the abortive negotiations of 392. He was the obvious choice to lead in the new quest for a settlement in 387, the choice of a people who wanted peace and saw in this firm friend of Tiribazus someone who might conjure up a treaty that was to their advantage. This Achaemenid official was back from Artaxerxes' court, re-established in power, and when this news arrived the Spartan leadership formulated a plan. The idea was as a minimum to get the Persians out of the game, but if possible bring them back onto their own side. To do this they were prepared to do some reshuffling in their command structure. Despite it not being the usual time of year, Antalcidas was made admiral to replace Hierax in the crucial Aegean War. Antalcidas raised sail, and on the way to his new command picked up Gorgopas and his fleet as escort to Lysander's old base of Ephesus. Once there he ordered that officer back to Aegina and his date with Chabrias and death, while he himself made contact with the Persians at the highest level. It is possible he travelled to Artaxerxes' court as on his return to the Anatolian shore it is specified he 'came down to the coast', though this could just mean he had come back from Sardis, an alternative perhaps more feasible in terms of time frame.

Whether face to face with the Great King or in discussion with his agents, he had found he was dealing with people eager to listen to what he had to say. This is hardly surprising once it had become common knowledge that in spring 388 the Athenians had made an alliance with the rebel Hakor (Acoris) in Egypt. They had been dallying with anti-Persian types for years. Evagoras, king of Salamis, had had statues put up to him in the city and that princeling had been at daggers drawn with Susa at least since 391. He, who liked to style himself descendant of Teucer, son of Telamon and half brother of Ajax, hero of the Trojan War, had had a long and chequered career, even suffering exile, before securing his position at Salamis in about 410. By this time though he had got control of most of Cyprus, captured Tyre, cut up rough in Phoenicia, stirred up the people in Cilicia, and made friends with Hakor in Egypt. It is claimed he intrigued with Hecatomnus, a Carian leader, and even an Arabian king. The Persians had become very wary of him after a honeymoon period at the beginning of Artaxerxes' reign when they pushed in tandem the anti-Spartan crusade that led to the battle of Cnidus. Now relations had completely fallen down, so Athenian support for Evagoras was the cause of tension enough with Persia, and the Greeks' latest diplomatic initiative in the Nile Delta was looking like the last straw. Egypt, congenitally seditious and enormously wealthy, always worried the Achaemenid administration as no other place did, so when Athenian dealings became known Artaxerxes determined to redraft his government in Asia Minor, withdrawing Pharnabazus, the friend of Conon and Athens, and sending back Tiribazus and Ariobarzanes, Laconophiles of long standing.

Antalcidas arrived back with Tiribazus in tow in spring 387 with proposals from the Great King to settle the Greek war, and this time the Persians were prepared to use coercion against those disinclined to accept the conditions they had cooked up. But for the moment he was faced by another problem. Nicolochus, the man he left on the ground in Anatolia, was in trouble, besieged and blockaded in Abydos by considerable Athenian forces commanded by Iphicrates and Diotimus. Nicolochus had got there with 25 ships after ravaging the small island of Tenedos, but had allowed himself to be bottled up by an Athenian fleet of 32 ships that had been cruising round Samothrace and Thasos which had been alerted by Tenedians fleeing from the Spartan raiders. To retrieve his subordinate's irons from the fire Antalcidas quickly marched overland and entered Abydos city, which was clearly not being very effectively blockaded, as he was able to man the ships in the port and sneak out at night past his enemies' beached boats and the sleeping camp of an unusually unvigilant Iphicrates. Sailing up the straits to Percote on the Asian bank, a little down from Lampsacus, the Spartans anchored themselves while the Athenians under the command of four generals – one of whom, Demaenetus, had had a hand in the downfall of Gorgopas – chased after them towards the Sea of Marmara and actually passed by allowing them to turn about and take their ships back to Abydos. The reason for this was the news that another fleet of twenty Syracusan and Italian triremes under Polyxenus was on its way to a conjunction that ought to have given the Peloponnesians a chance to face the enemy with superior numbers. This was the profit end of continuing Spartan diplomacy in the west that had been kept fresh at the highest level over the years. Lysander had even visited Dionysius of Syracuse some time after the fall of Athens to ensure that a friendship burnished in the fire of the siege of Syracuse was kept alive. More practically, in 398 or 397, the Spartans had facilitated that tyrant raising mercenaries in the Thracian Chersonese for his ongoing Italian and Carthaginian wars.

As things were boiling up around the Hellespont a familiar name entered the fray even before the ships from the west arrived. This was another Thrasybulus – not the great man of Phyle, Piraeus and Nemea fame, their home districts in Attica are specified as different and the other one was anyway probably a year dead. This Thrasybulus had eight triremes in his squadron and was hoping to connect with the rest of the Athenian fleet when he found he was facing not just a smooth diplomat but a vigilant commander as well. The twelve triremes Antalcidas could fully man against the enemy eight meant the odds were good, so soon after receiving news of their arrival he sailed at once to intercept. The Hellespontine coastline is littered with promontories and inlets and a small squadron could easily conceal itself. So the Spartans laid up in ambush and once their prey sailed past, the trap was sprung and they emerged from hiding, with decks cleared for action against the Athenian vessels. Antalcidas chased them down, catching them at a disadvantage with masts, sails and rigging still hoisted, and ordering his men to concentrate on the lead ships. His thinking was good: when these were overtaken, rammed and captured the slower vessels surrendered anyway and all eight were bagged and escorted in triumph to Abydos. Now when the Sicilian and Italian vessels sailed into harbour as well, the Spartan supremo found himself with the core of a grand navy. Sufficiently boosted, he felt himself on the verge of a decisive stroke; but he wanted to be sure and looked round to augment his strength even more. With the Persians onside he called on support from a large number of maritime communities in Ionia with warships of their own that were controlled by Tiribazus. He also appealed to places in Hellespontine Phrygia, including Aeolis, that Ariobarzanes had taken over from his kinsman Pharnabazus. Ariobarzanes would have a long career that included a role in the Satraps' Rebellion in a few decades time. Now the tapping of his maritime resources was made easier by the coincidence of his being a guest friend of Antalcidas from back in 407 when he had travelled to Greece as an Achaemenid envoy.

The fleet which assembled in the summer of 387 was eventually eighty triremes strong – much larger than anything even a revitalised Athens could mobilise, and with it Antalcidas was able to put a stranglehold on the Pontic corn trade just as Lysander had done to such effect in the earlier war. With the post-Aegospotami era being recalled, and the difficulties on their doorstep emanating from Aegina, the people in Athens now were forced to think seriously about a cessation of hostilities. This was a more fragile city than it had been twenty five years before; it just did not have the sinews to fight and fight again as it had after the Sicilian debacle. They also now knew that the deal Antalcidas and his Persian cohorts were offering was nowhere near as bad as that which had been proffered on previous occasions. It was clear that Athenian retention of the northern islands had been accepted and what was being demanded, even if it included leaving their friends in Asia and Africa in the lurch and a break with Evagoras, did not hit at their core interests. Fidelity to the king on Cyprus was never a bottom line for Athens, but it was a key factor for the Persians who wanted both to isolate this island rebel and to be able to hire Greek infantry freed up from their wars to serve in their army. It is no coincidence that the very man pushing the project from the Achaemenid side was that same Tiribazus who would very soon end up commanding the Persian fleet sent to crush the ruler of Cypriot Salamis.

Spartan motivation for a cessation of strife was more complex, but sufficient even after the prospect of Persian support had emerged as a factor. As the first decade of the fourth century had shaded into the next, her position had distinctly changed. The Spartan empire that had touched all edges of the Aegean was no more, indeed only a few isolated strongholds were left by the Hellespont and the Bosporus and even old stalwarts like the Rhodians were now undependable. In the Peloponnese it was the same old story – not loved but feared and followed – but opposition combinations north of the Gulf of Corinth had not by any means been suppressed. Indeed the isthmus line held with neither side looking capable of properly breaching it. There had even been intrusions deep in Sparta's backyard inflicted by the likes of Iphicrates and Chabrias, making trouble in Phlious and Mantinea, with the latter even reaching Sellasia on the edges of Laconia itself. It is also probable that islands off their southern coast were still occupied as we do not hear of them being retaken from the garrisons left there by Pharnabazus and Conon after Cnidus. So for Sparta, despite the apparent promise of Persian support, the desire for peace was the very rational response of a leadership that realised the demands made on their stretched military resources were becoming too much. Protecting friends and overawing enemies was draining their economic and human capital in a worrying way. Even providing two regiments as main garrisons at Lechaeum and Arcadian Orchomenus had become a stretch. With the Spartans feeling they lacked the military muscle to completely dispose of their foes, a more subtle and less belligerent alternative forced itself on the Lacedaemon elite.

For the other powers too there was much sense in a move to peace. The confederates east of the isthmus line were not a happy monolithic entity; it would have been a lot to ask for people who had so often been enemies in the past to continue in problem-free cooperation for long. We hear of intrigues involving Iphicrates that suggest serious tension. In 390 or 389 apparently driven by concerns about increasing Argive presence in Corinth, he tried a putsch of his own to get control of Corinth for Athens. Likewise for Argos and Corinth the stresses of fighting their powerful Peloponnesian neighbours were proving very great. It always seemed to be their territory that ended up as the battlefield. Inevitably people who had suffered despoliation became vocal on the subject of a termination to the conflict. The peace terms the Great King had proposed to the combatants began to look acceptable to many of the delegates who gathered at Sardis.

The terms of the peace Antalcidas had arranged were stark. 'King Artaxerxes thinks it just that the cities in Asia should belong to him, as well as Clazomenae and Cyprus among the islands, and that the other Greek cities, both small and great, should be left independent, except Lemnos, Imbros, and Scyros; and these should belong, as of old, to the Athenians. But whichever of the two parties does not accept this peace, upon them I will make war, in company with those who desire this arrangement, both by land and by sea, with ships and with money.'[1] The central principle of the treaty was a guarantee of autonomy, and every city that signed up was bound to respect the independence of all fellow Greeks. The acceptance of Persian control in Anatolia might be seen as selling out Hellenes in Ionia and confirm Athens' weakened position in places that had followed her lead under the auspices of the Delian League. In fact many of these communities had been controlled by the Persians for some time and Cyprus had been a tributary of the Great King for much of its history. But the upside for many looked clear: that apart from specified north Aegean islands, the rest of the Greeks were to be left autonomous.

Autonomy and its implementation were bound to be difficult for some. How would it be interpreted when it came to those confederacies where one city dominated less powerful neighbours? In reality it was always going to be pragmatism not principle. In Sparta's case the outcome not only emphasised her influence in drawing up the treaty but gave her virtually everything she could wish for. There was no attempt to impinge on her long standing occupation of Messenia or even over her position as hegemon of the Peloponnesian League, both of which were clear cases of infringements of autonomy. Sparta would continue to speak for her Peloponnesian cohorts – no one argued that – but the same privileges were certainly not going to be extended to the Theban envoys when they demanded they should sign any agreement on behalf of the whole Boeotian League. The settlement gave the Spartans a chance to break up the Boeotian federation and they were going to take it. Agesilaus, in bullying mood, threatened Thebes would be excluded from the peace and that he would be on her borders with a Spartan army in double quick time unless they complied. Indeed he was already at Tegea inspecting his regiments when the Theban envoys crumbled and acceded to the other Boeotian towns' autonomy. The Argives and Corinthians were caught in the contradiction as well. Their incorporation was always going to be interpreted by the Spartans as a denial of autonomy whatever the wishes of their leaders. Eventually they buckled too with Agesilaus threatening war if they did not; it was also required that the Argive garrison of Acrocorinth would be withdrawn. The establishment at Corinth were the real losers in this, who knew what to expect when exposed to the return of Sparta sponsored exiles. Putting survival before office they packed up their movables and took the road to exile where at least they found that old allies at Athens were prepared to offer refuge of a sort.

For the Greek envoys travelling the road to Sparta it was their whole world they were reordering. These delegations to the conference in 386 chaired by Agesilaus were grand enough comprising higher-ranking men. The Athenian group was ten strong and though they were paid a subsistence allowance it was little enough to make a splash in these high status affairs and expending private funds was usually expected. Amongst such egos, despite being part of the same mission division was not unusual. This tendency is highlighted years later, when an emissary called Andocides, a Laconophile eager for peace and tainted with association with both the Four Hundred and the Thirty, was hauled before the courts by Callistratus for the line he had taken during the negotiations six years earlier in 392. Sparta though had the sense to minimise these kinds of problems by usually entrusting their negotiations to only three delegates but this was unusual and most states came far more mob handed.

On arrival they found Sparta a kind of ancient Westphalia in the 1640s, Vienna in 1814, Geneva in 1954 or Paris in 1968. While in those places the issues had been the fate of Germany, Europe or East and South East Asia. Over 2,000 years before, envoys crowded the streets under spring sunshine in 386 BC to decide on how their world would be constructed. The agreement on which oaths were taken and libations spilt was something special, a Common Peace, often cited as the first 'multilateral peace treaty in history'.

This was a universe that now clearly functioned under the sway of the almighty daric. The accord was largely dictated on the terms of the Great King of Persia, Artaxerxes. But it has an alternative name often still used: the Peace of Antalcidas. This is fair, it may have been built on Persian power but to make the settlement stick, this Spartan's influence was crucial, because with the *realpolitik* of Greece at that time he could ensure that the treaty not only acknowledged Persian power and interests but also the reality of Sparta's predominant position. So the tribute to this man's contribution is proper and secures his place in history, and also fittingly seems to set the pattern for the rest of his life. He spent almost the whole of his time on diplomatic missions trying to maintain Sparta's cordial relations with the Persian Empire and apparently became a great favorite of Artaxerxes himself who once 'took a wreath of flowers, dipped it in the most costly ointment, and sent it to Antalcidas after supper; and all men wondered at the kindness'.[2] This familiarity with a wider world certainly gave him an alternative view from many of his Spartan brethren; for instance it is reported by Agesilaus' biographer that he was an enemy of the king and critical of his policy towards Thebes. A long career ended when in 367, once more on a mission to negotiate peace with Persia, his efforts ended in failure. Fearful of the consequences he decided to starve himself to death.

The agreement this interesting man had done so much to engineer was supposed to last forever and bind all Greeks who signed up for it whether on the mainland in the Aegean or in Asia, and was guaranteed by the involvement of the power of Persia. Many though undoubtedly experienced something of a bad taste in the mouth that the concord was being formed under the shadow of a great barbarian king. It was almost an acceptance of tutelage, recognising as they all did terms both laid down by the king, and in the end guaranteed by the Persians' preparedness to support Sparta against those who would not sign it. Reactions to the agreement have been extreme. Later luminaries like John Adams, the second president of the United States have seen the treaty as one of the most shameful events in Greek history, bringing to nothing all that the Greeks had so epically struggled for against the Persians over a hundred years before.[3] Even in Sparta not everyone loved the outcome. It has been argued that Teleutias for one was deeply unhappy with Antalcidas' policy of accommodation with the 'Mede'.[4] That Agesilaus was happy to push around the Thebans to accept autonomy for the Boeotians did not mean he was joyful to be tied up with the people he had declared a crusade against ten years before, though he consoled himself to a degree when the view was put to him that 'alas for Greece, now that the Spartans are medising,' by replying, 'Are not the Medes the rather spartanising?'[5]

Unpalatable facts though could not be ducked because Artaxerxes' envoys in gorgeous robes and unmanly trousers were there waiting in the wings when the pledges were made. Armies and navies were disbanded, though this was of less significance in an era when every citizen was a soldier, with spear and shield on the wall or oarsman with a bench pad in his luggage. No full text of the peace has come down to us so whether the Spartans were assigned any formal role as its executive is open to doubt yet the reality was they alone had the clout in Greece to interpret it as they saw fit. But if it was to a great degree Sparta and Persia's treaty it was not a peace of victory, the other participants in the war would not countenance that. Still, rivals like Thebes had been significantly humbled and Corinth unpicked from her Argive entanglement, and the only real downside for Sparta was that her long time foe Athens had become an important player again hardly two decades after her complete demise at the end of the Peloponnesian War. She had returned to the ring in terms of sea power. Athens was not a twelve-ship state anymore but something much more worrying. Access to the Achaemenid purse had allowed this change and even if the tap had been turned off, Athens as a significant rival would remain.

But if autonomy was the ideal the truth of the post peace world was very different. The Persians had sponsored the negotiations and the Great King Artaxerxes had ensured that he was the major beneficiary. He had settled the status once and for all of the Greek colonies of Asia Minor that had been a source of contention for centuries, putting them firmly within the Persian sphere of influence. This would not seem at all unreasonable for most inhabitants of the east Mediterranean world. That it seems a kind of aberration to us is to do with the partiality of our information that comes from peoples who were really minnows in the world. But because it is their story that we are left with, this perspective takes on a magnitude it objectively did not warrant. It again emphasises the obvious, that history depends on the survival of evidence. Here the spotlight shines on the edges, for most people in the world, what happened in the heartlands of the Achaemenid state would have been what affected them, but the details of this bigger picture do not remain very much at all. If, for example, all our third century AD sources were Germanic, then we would get detailed narrative of intertribal conflicts with the Roman empire involved as an important, intrusive but outside presence that would not at all reflect the real balance of the respective world significance.

The Greek world now seemed to be Sparta's oyster. The King's Peace had left her by far the strongest power, a position she could arguably have maintained with a more moderate policy. She did not choose to take this road but instead acted in a manner so highhanded it seemed designed to stir up trouble against her. The pattern is not dissimilar to what happened after the defeat of Athens that ended the Peloponnesian War. With no power standing who might weigh in the balance against her, the Spartans settled old scores in a very hard-handed style. Elis had been made to pay for her shilly-shallying during the conflict just ended and this time it was going to be the same again but with different targets in their sights. Typical was her treatment of Mantinea. Long an irritant and bulwark against her in the Peloponnese, Sparta was determined to destroy her. Less than fifty miles away she had been formed by a *synoecism* from four or five villages to form one political unit around one hundred years before (the date is disputed). It had often enjoyed a fractious relationship with Sparta; for one thing it was a democracy, and for another it was surrounded by walls, neither of which Sparta had or wanted for themselves, nor much liked in others. During the Peloponnesian War Mantinea had sided with Sparta's enemies and been defeated along with Athens, Elis and Argos at the battle of Mantinea in 418. Soon after, a thirty year treaty between Mantinea and Sparta had been concluded though it seems one that neither side paid that much attention to. During the Corinthian War Mantinea had fought somewhat halfheartedly on the Spartan side and had on occasion refused to take part citing religious reasons. After the defeat at Lechaeum in 390 Agesilaus reputedly led his defeated troops back past Mantinea in the dark 'so hard, he thought, would the soldiers find it to see the Mantineans rejoicing at their misfortune.'[6] Since then they had been accused of supplying corn in 388 to Sparta's enemy Argos. All this gave Sparta reason to flaunt her new-found power and ensure that they be once and for all humiliated and destroyed. She was ordered to take down her walls but not unnaturally refused and prepared for the inevitable consequences – a Spartan attack.

Agesilaus who was no doubt calling the shots knew that the destruction of Mantinea would bring opprobrium on the heads of the perpetrators so thought it prudent to excuse himself from the actual deed, citing the somewhat specious grounds that the Mantineans had been a great help to his father during the war against the Messenians in 464 nearly eighty long years before!! So the young and still inexperienced co-king Agesipolis was designated in command instead even though his father, the ex-king Pausanias, in exile at Tegea since 395, was known to be on good terms with the democratic faction in Mantinea. It is also thought that his grandfather Pleistoanax was in large part responsible for the drawing up of the thirty years truce.

The Mantineans, well aware of their likely fate, not unnaturally looked for help elsewhere. Ambassadors were dispatched to the Athenians but they declined to send assistance giving the reason that any such action would be in contravention of the King's Peace. Presumably they were still too war weary to want to enter into another confrontation with the Peloponnesian power, as Sparta's own blatant infringement of the treaty by her threats against the Mantineans would surely have given them grounds for offering aid. Following the rejection of another appeal to Argos, Mantinea prepared for the inevitable.

To attack Mantinea under the terms of the King's Peace was likely to be difficult to justify so the authorities at Sparta instead mustered an argument around their failure of these people to do their duty as members of the Peloponnesian League. The obligations of members of these sorts of associations at this period are problematic and this is certainly true of this one, formed in the sixth century BC with no permanent institutions and only meeting when Sparta wished it. Clearly from the fact that it is often called the Spartan alliance, subservience to the policies of its Laconian hegemon was expected, despite the fact that the days of combining against a common enemy during the Persian and Peloponnesian Wars were long gone. The Mantineans' commitment to Sparta and the League of allies she led had clearly waned during recent years, so it was not unreasonable for the Spartans to claim a cloak of legitimacy by taking the lead in punishing a recalcitrant member. Thus Agesipolis was at the head of an army mobilised from the Peloponnesians as he marched to bring Mantinea to its senses and then its knees.

Agesipolis led this force into Mantinean territory and proceeded to lay waste the surrounding countryside. He then tried to storm the city but without success. During the campaign the epicentre of the conflict was always around the town, though it is alleged an open battle took place in which the Thebans, Pelopidas and Epaminondas, fought with great heroism on the losing flank of the Peloponnesian battle line before being rescued by the Spartan king himself. What all however are agreed upon is that Agesipolis' most significant act was to dig a trench all around the city walls, a feat he achieved by having half the army dig the lines of circumvallation and the other half stationed in front of the workmen to protect them. Once the ditch was completed a rampart was built to enclose the city walls. However, though success now looked likely, the harvest that year had been good and the Mantineans had plenty of corn and could therefore expect to withstand a long siege. Wishing to obviate the need for this Agesipolis now took decisive action and dammed up the river which flowed through the city. The effects of this were catastrophic as water levels began to rise above the foundations of the walls and towers. Cracks started to appear in the mud-brick defences that were absorbing the water and before long there were indications of collapse. Attempts to prop them up with timber proved ultimately futile and the Mantineans realising that discretion was the better part of valour agreed to surrender and demolish their walls as the Spartans had originally demanded.

But Agesipolis was not so easily satisfied and now insisted that the Mantineans should break the polis up and reconstitute their original villages – four or five depending on which source you follow.[7] But if the Spartans justified this dismemberment by the demand for autonomy of individual settlements in the King's Peace, observers saw this as really stretching things. Most judged that they were just persevering with what had long been the secret of their success in the Peloponnese to ensure the abolition of any un-subservient communities in their peninsular bailiwick. The democratic faction at Mantinea who had been the long standing foes of Sparta and had led them in their defiance now had every reason to fear for their lives. But help was at hand, as Agesipolis' father, the exiled Spartan king Pausanias, intervened. Coming from Tegea he was somehow able to persuade his son that their lives should be spared and they should be allowed to leave in peace. This is a curious episode as Pausanias was still technically a fugitive from Spartan justice so it is difficult to see how he would be allowed so much leverage. The family connection must be at the bottom of all this and it is conceivable the reason Agesipolis accepted the mission against Mantinea at all was just so he could be in a position to defend these long time family connections in *extremis*. In any case the sixty democrats involved left with spear-armed Spartan troops lining each side of the road. It is implied that this was to prevent their domestic rivals from attacking them, though they themselves would normally have had few qualms about joining in brutalising people they had just conquered and indeed the fact that they didn't is recorded as 'a striking example of good discipline.'

Now with this episode of Mantinea's chequered history ended, and having got rid of these accursed democrats, the local aristocrats welcomed developments that meant that, living now in their village mansions, they were much nearer their estates and could govern like feudal squires of old without having to compete for power with their city rivals. For the Spartans too the benefits were real: the villages now provided hoplites as required for the Peloponnesian League army right up until Leuctra, not long after which Mantinea was to rise like a phoenix from the ashes once more.

Events were now to take Sparta much further afield from the parochial politics of the Peloponnese. Ambassadors arrived from Apollonia and Acanthus in the Chalcidice, and in addition no less a personage then Amyntas III of Macedonia also made an appeal for help to Sparta at around this time.[8] Their concern was the Chalcidian League or more specifically the city of Olynthus. This League had been formed just before the outbreak of the Peloponnesian War in 432 and indeed played a large part in instigating it. Potidaea, a colony of Corinth on the Chalcidice peninsula, paid tribute to Athens as a member of the Delian League. But its connection with Corinth (which supplied its chief magistrate) always rendered it suspect in Athenian eyes. After the battle of Sybota in 433, between Corinth on one side and Corcyra and Athens on the other, the Athenians demanded that Potidaea take down its walls, expel its Corinthian magistrates, and send hostages and increased tribute. Potidaea decided on revolt. They allied themselves with Perdiccas, king of Macedonia, and sent ambassadors to Sparta who eventually agreed to help in the rebellion. Other cities in the Chalcidice joined in most notably Olynthus the largest and most powerful settlement in the area. As a result the Chalcidian League was formed as a bulwark against Athens, dominated from the outset by Olynthus.

The League affiliates adhered to a shared foreign policy and had developed a common currency (several coins have been found) and though dominated by Olynthus, the members retained their individual citizenship and ordered their own internal affairs. A form of joint citizenship had been proposed to allow intermarriage and the interchange of property rights throughout the league, but without any loss of privileges. If this had been implemented the League would have become much closer to a Chalcidian 'sympolity', a far more integrated state than most other such associations in north and central Greece. Under the terms of the Peace of Nicias in 421 which ended the first part of the Peloponnesian War, it had been agreed that the League should be disbanded, but Athens apparently did not have the wherewithal to achieve this. There were obviously more pressing concerns for the two wild beasts of Greece as nothing further is heard of the League for over twenty years, though in 404 following the end of the War a defeated Athens relinquished control of Potidaea. But in 393 Amyntas of Macedon had suffered defeat at the hands of the Illyrians and was driven out of his kingdom. These northerners looking for land and plunder under King Bardyllis the Dardanian would intrude into northern Greece for some time to come causing shockwaves that would not just bring Spartans to this area but to Epirus too. In Macedonia though, Amyntas was reinstated after a year with the help of the Thessalians. He felt unable to defend some of his frontier lands and to try to fend off one wolf at the gate he employed another. He took the extraordinary decision to hand control temporarily to the Chalcidian League who he hoped would offer the protection a fragile Macedonian polity could not. In 385 this Macedonian king had felt sufficiently able to reclaim his loaned-out country but found the Olynthians were not cooperative. War was the result, with the king in the end losing even more of his country, right up to and including Pella itself. Needing friends and knowing that the Chalcidian League was on good terms with Thebes and Athens and had supported them in the Corinthian War, Amyntas now sought Sparta's aid.

The particular concerns of the envoys from Acanthus and Apollonia were that Olynthus was now trying to coerce them into joining the League. This, and the fact that the League was known to be on friendly terms with both Athens and Thebes, led the ephors to allow the ambassadors to address 'the Lacedaemonian Assembly and the allies'. The ambassadors gave dire warnings of what the consequences would be of Olynthus' seemingly unstoppable rise.[9] 'Again, we left ambassadors both of the Athenians and of the Boeotians already there. And we heard reports that the Olynthians on their side had voted to send ambassadors with them to these states in regard to the matter of an alliance. Now if so great a power is to be added to the present strength of the Athenians and Thebans, take care lest you find that situation no longer easy to handle.'[10] They urged the Spartans to act quickly before it was too late. 'We, then, men of Lacedaemon and of the allied states, report that such are the conditions there; it is for you to deliberate as to whether they seem to deserve attention. But you must understand this also, that the power which we have described as great is not yet hard to wrestle with. For such of the cities as share in the citizenship of Olynthus unwillingly, these, I say, will quickly fall away if they see any opposing force presenting itself.'[11]

After hearing all this, the Spartans gave permission for their allies to speak and advise on what they should do. Predictably the vote was for an army to be raised and each constituent state of the Peloponnesian League to send a proportionate amount of men to form a force of 10,000. If a member of the League did not want to contribute men it could give money instead. The going rate was three Aeginean obols per infantryman but for those states which sent cavalry each was assessed at twelve obols per trooper, four times as much – an interesting guide to the relative worth of the constituent parts of an ancient army. Furthermore if any member was remiss in sending its proper share of men it could be fined by the Spartans at a rate of two drachmas a day per man (one drachma was the equivalent of six obols). Whilst this might all seem somewhat lucrative for the Spartans it indicates that enthusiasm in the League was not all it should have been and that some members were no longer willing to waste manpower on what they saw as Spartan imperialism attacking a state a long way from the Peloponnese and their immediate interests. Thebes, understandably worried by the intrusion of Spartan power, decreed that no one from the city should join this specific foray. As for the particulars of Amyntas' embassy we have no details and only know that the expeditionary force, after garrisoning those Chalcidian communities that asked for them, and winning back the Potidaeans from the Olynthian fold, linked up with a Macedonian army.

The decision by the Spartans does seem to indicate a determination to entrench and extend their authority over as much of mainland Greece as possible. Around 395 they had lost control of their military colony of Heraclea Trachinia near Thermopylae, and this campaign would give them an opportunity to try to reinstate it. They were also aware that if a solid alliance was formed between

Olynthus, Thebes and Athens it would have serious repercussions for them. This was also about coin and calories: there was gold in the Thracian and Chalcidian hills and anybody gaining control in the region could also threaten a choke hold on the Pontic corn routes. And more than this, the Chalcidice was awash with timber particularly suitable for ship building. The idea of a renascent naval power at Athens having access there would bound to have loomed large in Spartan thinking. A far from unreasonable fear when it is remembered it was the exploitation of this area that allowed the growth of a militant and all-conquering Macedonia in a couple of generations' time.

When the decision had been made the ambassador from Acanthus stood up and sensibly pointed out that this was all very well but a force of 10,000 men would necessarily take some time to raise and that some action was needed immediately. What he proposed was that an expeditionary force set out as soon as it could be feasibly assembled so those states havering about whether to ally themselves with Olynthus would pause for thought and that her other allies might reconsider their position if they saw Sparta and the League taking action. This proposal was passed and it was agreed to raise a force of 2,000 consisting of emancipated helots, *perioeci* and men from Skiritis. The whole force was to be under the command of one Eudamidas.

Before setting out Eudamidas made an unusual request of the Spartan ephors. He asked that his brother Phoebidas be allowed 'to gather together all the troops assigned to him which were left behind and to follow after him.'[12] It is unclear whether this means the rest of the 10,000 or the original 2,000. In the latter case it is difficult to understand the need for two expeditionary forces but anyway for reasons that we will see Phoebidas never met up with his brother.[13] Eudamidas reached the Chalcidice with whatever troops he had and based himself in Potidaea harassing the enemy as best he could. As we hear nothing of a journey which if overland would have taken them through all of Greece, Thessaly and Macedonia it is reasonable to assume this advance force would have gone by sea.

Phoebidas eventually set out from Sparta with his men in 382 BC. Frustratingly little of the route is detailed, whether it was partly by sea across the Gulf of Corinth or dry-shod up through the isthmus. Whatever route they took, Boeotia had to be crossed and after what must have been a journey of some days the army encamped near Thebes. What happened next was to have momentous consequences. In Thebes there were two factions fighting for control, one anti-Spartan led by Ismenias, and the other pro-Spartan led by one Leontiades. The latter approached Phoebidas in the Spartan camp and made an extraordinary offer to him. 'Phoebidas, it is within your power this day to render the greatest service to your fatherland; for if you will follow me with your hoplites, I will lead you into the Acropolis. And this once accomplished, be sure that Thebes will be completely under the control of the Lacedaemonians.'[14] Phoebidas not surprisingly agreed and a plan was put in place.

On the appointed day the women of Thebes were holding a religious festival in the *Cadmeia* on the acropolis and although the council sessions were normally held there, because of the celebrations the meeting had been convened in the portico of the market, ensuring the streets would be empty. Phoebidas, giving the impression he was marching his troops away from the city, continued as arranged until Leontiades riding up led the Spartans back into Thebes and up to the acropolis. Having given them the key to the citadel's gates he then went straight to the council, informed those present what had happened, and while assuring them that the Spartans had no hostile intentions to those who had none to them, ordered the arrest of Ismenias. Many of those assembled must have been in on the plot as Leontiades' speech was well received and Ismenias arrested whilst the rest of his faction fled the city or retreated to the safety of their homes, three hundred eventually landing up in Athens. Having ensured the election of a pliable chief magistrate, Leontiades set off for Sparta to explain his actions, and to try to win official support from that quarter.

The ephors and a large majority of the citizens were unhappy with Phoebidas' unauthorised actions, and were fully aware that their reputation in the rest of Greece might suffer from such a violation of another community's sovereignty. Agesilaus, however, was having none of it and argued that Phoebidas had only shown initiative and was to be applauded because the results were an extension of Spartan power and influence. This begs the question of whether Agesilaus had secretly authorised the seizure all along. Indeed it is difficult to reach any other conclusion. Phoebidas and Eudamidas were of royal stock and therefore probably related to Agesilaus. As Phoebidas was supposed to be marching to the Chalcidice his decision to camp at Thebes is puzzling as it is not on the direct route, suggesting that the decision to camp there was preordained. Perhaps the clinching evidence is the attitude of Xenophon, a known confidante and friend of Agesilaus. He describes Phoebidas as 'a man with a far greater passion for performing some brilliant achievement than for life itself, although, on the other hand, he was not regarded as one who weighed his acts or had much practical wisdom.'[15] This suspiciously sounds like an excuse for Phoebidas' behaviour to deny any involvement from Agesilaus.[16] Furthermore Plutarch actually mentions the possibility (as does Diodorus) that Agesilaus had planned the whole coup from the beginning, whilst in his life of Pelopidas (who fled from the city when the Spartans took the *Cadmeia*) informs us that Phoebidas was fined a hundred thousand drachmas – a detail Xenophon somehow manages to omit. Phoebidas' subsequent career also suggests a close relationship with Agesilaus, as the latter personally appoints him harmost of Thespiae four years later. All in all from what we know of Agesilaus, a man whose cunning ensured a long career and one able to outwit such as Lysander, his hand in the seizure of Thebes is all too clear.

Leontiades meanwhile was all too busy cranking up the anti-Theban feeling in Sparta. He reminded them of Theban hostility in the past and that they were about to embark on an alliance with the Olynthians well aware that Sparta had already started a military campaign against them. Now an occupied Thebes could no longer pose a threat. Perhaps bowing to the inevitability of the course they had embarked upon, the Spartans voted to maintain a garrison at the *Cadmeia* and have Ismenias, in prison at Thebes, put on trial. To give the proceedings a veneer of respectability judges were recruited, one each from the member states of the Peloponnesian League and three from Sparta itself. Not surprisingly the trial was a foregone conclusion. Ismenias was found guilty of being in cahoots with the Persian king, having received money from him and, together with Androclidas, a fellow leader of the democrats in Thebes, of being 'chiefly responsible for all the trouble and disorder in Greece'. They were dragging up stuff from the Corinthian War now and it was no surprise that despite an apparently spirited defence he was found guilty and subsequently executed. All this shows what a dead letter the autonomy trumpeted in the King's Peace had become in just a few short years. However muddy some of what had been understood in that accommodation was, Sparta could in no way justify her actions as conforming to its spirit. They had taken over by guile and treachery a great city with no justification at all, and one that not only had been at peace with Sparta at the time but was actually now a member of the Peloponnesian League. This not only did the Spartans' reputation an awful lot of harm but perhaps more importantly ensured that any possibility of a rapprochement between Sparta and Thebes was forever dashed. Such a cooperation might have been the basis of a not too unstable future for the Greek world; instead she had started a train of events that would eventually have catastrophic consequences.

Sparta's main force left for the Chalcidice in 382 BC. The choice of leader of the force shows clearly Agesilaus' grip on power for it was none other than Teleutias his half brother. Knowing the campaign would be a long one he did not hurry north but stopped to collect troops from their allies. Thebes now contributed both hoplites and cavalry. He also contacted Amyntas and directed him to hire mercenaries and bribe rulers in the area to provide assistance. Derdas, Amyntas' neighbouring king in Elimia, a region just north of Thessaly with its capital at Aiane, was also contacted and warned of the dire consequences for his small kingdom if Olynthus was not checked having, as it did, control of much of Macedonia. Derdas, willingly or not, decided to join forces with Teleutias and by the time he reached Potidaea, where he presumably rendezvoused with Eudamidas, he had a very considerable force.

Teleutias now decided to advance on Olynthus itself. Setting out his troops in battle order, he did not tarry, refraining from burning crops or destroying shipbuilding timber. This was in the first case so as not to make it difficult for his troops to move back and forth if they had to, and in the second so they could later chop down the trees as obstacles to stop any enemy from following and attacking their rear. At a distance of about a mile and a half from Olynthus' walls he halted and, preparing for battle, took command of the left wing which was stationed directly opposite the city gates, thus ensuring he had his best troops to attack the main body of the enemy. On the right were posted the allies: the cavalry from Sparta and Thebes and the Macedonian contingent. Next to Teleutias were Derdas and his 400 cavalry. The reason for this posting is given as that Teleutias thought most highly of them and wished to show his appreciation of Derdas for having joined the cause. An alternative reason is that he might have wished to keep a close eye on such new and potentially untried allies. Or indeed perhaps it was a combination of both.

The Olynthians did not ignore this threat and came out and lined up in front of the city walls. Battle duly commenced and initially the Olynthians had much the better of it. Their cavalry charged down upon their Spartan and Theban counterparts and succeeded in killing the commander of the Spartan horse. Soon the Spartan right wing was in flight, but catastrophe was averted by the action of Derdas and his Elimians. They charged against the Olynthus city gates and Teleutias followed them with his troops still in good battle order. Whether they were trying to get into the town is not clear but they certainly were now threatening to cut the Olynthians off from there. Understanding the real danger they were now in, the Olynthian cavalry abandoned the pursuit of the enemy horse and rushed back to the gates suffering severe losses from Derdas and his troops as they did so. Although the infantry managed to retreat in better order to the city and did not incur many casualties, what had promised to be a victory for the Olynthians now turned into something very like defeat. That is certainly how Teleutias interpreted it. He set up a victory trophy and then steadily withdrew, cutting down the timber as he did so. Although there are reports of further activity during the summer, the suspicion must be that the campaigning season was well advanced as it is otherwise difficult to understand why Teleutias would have withdrawn from the city at this moment. In any case further fighting did take place, with the Olynthians having some success, but the situation as bad weather approached was clearly one of stalemate as Teleutias dismissed the Macedonians and the Elimians for the winter.

Derdas was back for the start of the next season and his forces were resting, just arrived at Apollonia, when the Olynthians began pillaging that city's territory. Derdas made no immediate move to attack them – he was eating his morning meal – but put his troops on battle alert. When the Olynthians were outside the city gates he charged them. No doubt astounded by this sudden apparition the Olynthians turned and fled all the way back to their own city walls, Derdas killing eighty of them in his pursuit. But this proved only to be a prelude to the main action of the season. Teleutias was intent on ravaging the Olynthian countryside, and he was engaged in this near the city walls when their cavalry sortied out, crossed the river which flows past Olynthus, and appeared intent on confronting him. Teleutias, irritated by their audacity, ordered his peltasts to charge at them, but the opposing cavalry retired in good order back over the river. Now things took a more serious turn. Just as the peltasts crossed the river the Olynthian cavalry suddenly turned about and charged them causing severe casualties, more than 100 men, including Tlemonidas their commander. Teleutias, furious, now readied his hoplites and led them into battle, whilst telling his remaining peltasts and horse to pursue the Olynthians back to the city. What happened next is slightly unclear but it appears that not only did the Olynthian cavalry get back behind the town walls relatively unscathed but their compatriots managed to inflict considerable damage on the Spartan army by means of missile fire from its towers. Indeed the Spartans suffered such that they were forced to retreat in some disarray when the Olynthians rode out again from the city gates, this time supported by peltasts and hoplites. Falling upon a disorganised Spartan line, the Olynthian hoplites beat them in a stand-up fight and even managed to kill Teleutias himself. At this the whole Spartan army disintegrated and fled for their lives in all directions, some to Apollonia twenty five miles to the north, some towards Acanthus about the same distance to the east, and some for Potidaea less than half that to the south, with the Olynthians killing a considerable number in the pursuit. It was a major triumph and a complete disaster for the Spartans, not only losing their esteemed commander but in effect their army was now no more.

The disaster gave Xenophon a fine chance to moralise on the importance of generals not acting in anger. It is worth quoting in full: 'From such disasters, however, I hold that men are taught the lesson, chiefly, indeed, that they ought not to chastise anyone, even slaves, in anger – for masters in anger have often suffered greater harm than they have inflicted; but especially that, in dealing with enemies, to attack under the influence of anger and not with judgment is an absolute mistake. For anger is a thing which does not look ahead, while judgment aims no less to escape harm than to inflict it upon the enemy.'[17]

Whatever one may say about the Spartans they were certainly indefatigable. As soon as they heard of the disaster and Teleutias' death their response was to fit out another force to teach the Olynthians a proper lesson. This time the king Agesipolis was to be in charge. Again Agesilaus declined to lead the army and it may well be he was afraid of ultimate failure in the Chalcidice which, if he was associated with it, could well undermine his reputation and position, and perhaps he was also reluctant to be too far from the centre of power in Sparta at a difficult time. Agesipolis was certainly not kept short of resources. Agesilaus had had a band of thirty Spartiates to accompany him to Asia back in 397 BC and Agesipolis was granted the same number in 381. In fact it seemed a very popular venture as a number of well heeled men from the *perioeci* communities volunteered to join up, as well as a body of foreigners who had been brought up in the *agoge* (Xenophon's own sons went through the system). Also recorded as signing up were some 'bastard sons of Spartiates' who had been brought up with much the same advantages as peers (*homoioi*) but presumably were not entitled to full citizen rights, the same sort who we have heard of as inferiors and who some suggest were always an important source of recruits for the army.[18] On top of this well equipped force from Laconia his army picked up contingents from allied cities, as well as some local cavaliers when they passed through Thessaly, and on arrival at the front Amyntas and Derdas came contributing their troops too. Though we are given no numbers it must have been as impressive a force as Teleutias had commanded that Agesipolis arrived with for the third year of campaigning on the Chalcidian front.

In the years before the Olynthian adventure the Mantineans had not been the only community whose recent conduct had been put under the microscope. In about 384 it is reported 'that the Lacedaemonians were investigating to see what sort of friends their several allies had proved to be to them during the war.'[19] This was clearly something different from the assault on Elis after the end of the Peloponnesian War. That was an angry response to one particular backsliding ally. This time there was a sort of institutional arrangement put in place; a body determined that, now she had the muscle, Sparta was going to bear down on any who had not done their duty in recent years. It turned out very soon after this audit was put in place that Phlious became next on the list. Phlious, a city in the north western Argolid, occupied a strategic location. Though geographically close to Argos, she had been a member of the Peloponnesian League since its inception. At the time of the King's Peace she was run by a democratic faction and exiled oligarchs, seeing their chance now that she was acting as policeman of the Peace, approached Sparta and asked whether they could be restored from their exile. Their case was based on the claim that while they had been in power they had always supported Spartan policy and had willingly sent their levies to join the Peloponnesian League's campaigns whereas now the city was not only refusing to help Sparta but was not even allowing her citizens to enter at all. In reality the truth was a little more complicated. In 394 they had refused to send a contingent to help the Spartans at the battle of Nemea on the grounds that they were keeping a holy truce due to a religious festival – an excuse the Mantineans also used from time to time. In 392, after suffering defeat by the Athenian Iphicrates, the Phliasians had handed over their citadel for the Spartans to guard as insurance against further attack. The Spartans had left things as they found them when the danger had passed. They had not interfered in the city's internal affairs and had refused to force the restoration of her oligarchic exiles. Relations indeed had remained sufficiently cordial for King Agesipolis to use Phlious as a place of rendezvous before his invasion of the Argolid not long before the King's Peace.

But this time the appeal did not fall on deaf ears and the ephors decided to send to Phlious asking them to restore the exiles implying it was better to do it voluntarily than by compulsion. The city in its turn, recognising a thinly veiled threat voted reluctantly to readmit the exiles, restore their property, and settle any issues which may arise from the admittance in court. The problem of Phlious seemed to have been settled to Sparta's satisfaction but it was not to remain that way for long.

Sparta's war in the Chalcidice had been going on for nearly three years since this Phliasian interlude, and now Agesipolis was in charge, advancing speedily on Olynthus. Without any apparent reaction by the enemy he laid waste again to their territory and also took Torone by storm, an important ally of Olynthus and a rich and strategically significant place at the rugged end of the middle leg of the Chalcidian peninsula. Unfortunately that would be as good as it ever got for Agesipolis for he was now laid ill by a 'burning fever' in the height of summer. He was taken to the shrine of Dionysius at Aphytis which he had seen earlier and now felt a strong desire for the 'shady resting-places and its clear, cool waters'. He survived for seven days before dying outside the sanctuary and in the Spartan tradition his body was embalmed in honey and transported back home for a proper royal burial. Thus ended the life of Agesipolis, after a reign of fourteen years, an apparently malleable and hapless younger king.

That is not however the way Xenophon wishes us to see it, though it gives some insight into the relationship between these Spartan kings, part competitive, part complementary. For Agesilaus 'did not, as one might have expected, rejoice over it, as over the death of an adversary, but he wept, and mourned the loss of his companionship; for the kings of course lodge together when they are at home. And Agesipolis was a man well fitted to converse with Agesilaus about youthful days, hunting exploits, horses, and love affairs; besides this he also treated Agesilaus with deference in their association together in their common quarters, as one would naturally treat an elder.'[20] Reader, we do not believe this was the only sorrow Agesilaus felt. Surely he wondered whether he would ever get a co-king as compliant as Agesipolis?

But in any case a replacement was needed for Agesipolis and one was promptly found in Polybiades who was sent out to Olynthus to take charge. Though information is meagre in the extreme he apparently won several pitched battles and managed to put the Olynthians under siege. The very fact that he was away with such a large force gave other cities in Greece pause for thought on how they could take advantage. The first to do so was Phlious, still smarting from reluctantly admitting the oligarchic exiles. They had refused to restore any of their rights, though to be on the safe side they had donated a considerable sum of money towards Agesipolis' force. The exiles for their part demanded that their legal cases concerning their rights be put before an impartial court, not internal courts where some of the disputants formed the jury. The ruling Phliasians refused this demand. The exiles, not willing to accept this, once more came to Sparta and appealed their case. In turn they were fined by Phlious for going to Sparta. The exiles remained where they were and forcibly expressed their views. Agesilaus, a known friend of the exiles, was not displeased at this development as it gave the Spartan state an excuse to intervene in Phlious and hopefully extend their power and influence even further. With the approval of the ephors Agesilaus set off, no doubt this time confident of a quick and easy campaign.[21] Despite several embassies from Phlious begging him and offering him money to desist, Agesilaus would not be stopped. He demanded that they hand over their acropolis to him which they had done in 392. However that was because of the pressure they were under from Iphicrates. This time the circumstances were very different and the Phliasians could see no advantage in succumbing to Agesilaus' demands. Retreating back to their city they soon found themselves under siege as the king built a wall of circumvallation around them and submitted it to a siege.

Even in such a tightly controlled state as Sparta there were not a few who ventured to express their doubts about Agesilaus' latest imperial adventure, pointing out that 'merely for the sake of a few individuals they were making themselves hated by a state of more than five thousand men.'[22] The Phliasians themselves also added to his difficulties by brazenly holding their assemblies where they could be seen by the Spartans. Agesilaus, with his usual low cunning, saw a way to counteract both these problems. The exiles were told to encourage friends from the city to come and visit them, subsequently to set them up in the famous common Spartan messes (how they got out of a city under siege is not clear), essentially bribe them into training in army discipline, and provide them with all necessary arms until they were fit enough to join the Spartans. By such methods, according to Xenophon, a force of 1,000 Phliasian auxiliaries was quickly raised, and thus were the objections undermined, at least to some extent.

So both sieges ground on; the Phliasians, who were remarkably spirited for such a small state up against the mighty Spartans, put themselves on half rations thus lengthening the siege to twice its expected duration. A man called Delphion emerged as leader of the resistance. He arranged guard duty, put any one who wanted to make peace under arrest, and made several sorties from behind the walls inflicting some casualties on the Spartans. But ultimately, as he must have known, it was futile, as eventually the city ran out of food. The Phliasians now approached Agesilaus and asked for safe conduct for an embassy to Sparta in order that they may surrender unconditionally. It is difficult to see why they made this request. Agesilaus would have been well able to deal with the matter of Phlious' surrender. He granted the request, but sent to Sparta at the same time asking that he be given full powers to deal with the matter. Predictably the answer soon came back giving him complete authority. Annoyed by the Phliasian insolence he now imposed harsher terms than would have otherwise been the case. His conditions were that fifty of the exiles and fifty of the men who remained (Delphion had apparently escaped during these negotiations) should form a commission to decide on who should remain in the city and who should be put to death, and also to draw up a constitution. In order to make sure these terms were complied with Agesilaus left a garrison in place for six months. In fact they were not to leave till everything had been sorted out to the king's satisfaction. The rest of the army now dispersed and Agesilaus led his forces back to Sparta; the whole siege had lasted a year and eight months, and it is difficult to believe Agesilaus was there for all of what had been an extremely time consuming episode.

The end result was to Agesilaus' satisfaction, and more good news arrived from the Chalcidice from where the Olynthians had sent an embassy to Sparta asking for terms. The Olynthians 'were in an exceedingly wretched state from famine, inasmuch as they got no food from their own land and none was brought in to them by sea.'[23] How long the siege had lasted is a matter of some debate but the whole campaign in Olynthus had lasted over three long years; years which had seen the Spartans lose many troops as well as a king and one of their best generals. But still the result must have been pleasing to Agesilaus for without becoming personally involved in the campaign he had got what he wanted. The Olynthians agreed to the same conditions as any other member of the Peloponnesian League, to pursue the equivalent foreign policy as Sparta and join any military expedition if so requested. The embassy returned to Olynthus and the siege was lifted. But the Chalcidian league had essentially been dissolved.[24]

Now Sparta seemingly was at the zenith of her power. She had garrisons in Phlious and Thebes while her long time enemy Athens was quiescent and no longer a major naval power; Mantinea had been effectively destroyed; Corinth and Argos were still licking their wounds from previous wars; and the Peloponnesian League remained a constant bulwark with most of its members now ruled by oligarchs committed to Sparta. *Force majeure* had proved effective and Sparta's capacity for seemingly endless military campaigns had paid off handsomely. There was now no doubt who was the major power in Greece. The sky may have appeared to be the limit for Sparta and in particular Agesilaus' ambitions. But in her quest for power she had already sown the seeds for her destruction.

Chapter Ten

Theban Campaigns

In about 380 an Athenian orator, a sophist and follower of Socrates called Isocrates professed his views about his world in a pamphlet called the *Panegyricus*. He was said to lack confidence to address large audiences so made a living by providing court room speeches for other people to read out and later set up his own exclusive school of rhetoric. During his career he published large numbers of speeches that were distributed widely and had some considerable influence on public opinion. Born in 436 he lived until 338, an amazing survivor who was thus witness to the Peloponnesian War, the Spartan supremacy and the rise of Macedon. The *Panegyricus* was the kind of thing that might be read at festivals like the Olympic Games, but the retiring Isocrates is unlikely to have been up to this and its impact came from written distribution. In this address, which it is claimed he took ten years to write, he called for Athens and Sparta to drop their wars against each other which he attests were not only damaging to both of them but also undermining the fabric of what was great and to be cherished in Greek society. In his view the real enemy was Persia and that all the Hellenes should unite against this age-old enemy who, exactly a hundred years before the publication of the *Panegyricus,* they had combined against in the great defence of Greece at Thermopylae and Salamis. It appears to have had little direct impact at the time despite the fact he sent copies to important men like Agesilaus, whose history of anti-Persian crusading made him an obvious target. But still it is often said that his vision inspired Philip II to attack Persia and thus would have been an important if indirect influence on the career of Alexander the Great.

Yet if Isocrates deplored the infighting that rendered the Hellenes chaff in a world of Persian wind, Sparta's actions in Boeotia was part of what would ensure it continued. An extension of conflict that saw the coming to the fore of a group of men at Thebes who would drive much of the story of the next few years, characters of considerable talent only coming to prominence in a Theban elite that had been driven by Phoebidas' coup into a hard line anti-Spartan stand. The two most famous of these Thebans, Epaminondas and Pelopidas, had already entered the picture once during the harrying of Mantinea in 385. On that occasion there are no details of the composition of Agesipolis' invading army, but in this pan-Greek force there was a Theban contingent which included these two men who were destined to have an almost fatal impact on Sparta.

They marched with the army into Mantinean territory that proceeded to lay waste the surrounding countryside. The invaders tried to storm the city without success, and then both Pausanias and Plutarch mention a battle which Xenophon omits. What is remarkable about this alleged affair is the part the two aforementioned Thebans played in it. Pelopidas and Epaminondas were stationed together fighting on the wing of the army which was defeated. Locking their shields together they fought on whilst their colleagues either fled or were killed. Fearlessly they supposedly drove back their opponents, but in doing so Pelopidas received seven wounds and eventually collapsed on a pile of corpses. Epaminondas, his lifelong friend, unwilling to leave him, even in death, stood guard over the presumed corpse defying all comers. Inevitably he began to have difficulties himself and it was not too long before he received wounds in the chest and arm. However he was rescued by Agesipolis coming from the other wing who saved him, and then miraculously Pelopidas was discovered to be still alive, and indeed both were to recover completely. It would have been far better for Sparta if both had been left for dead.

These two were part of a new generation that would eventually replace the old guard led by Ismenias. He had risen to power after the Peloponnesian War and suffered fatally for his anti-Spartan inclinations after Phoebidas' regiments had secured the Theban Acropolis and put Leontiades and his oligarch junta in power. Most of those who survived did so by slipping out of town and escaping arrest. After the hundreds of people exiled by the coup settled in Athens they were initially given direction by Androclidas, Ismenias' old partner, but he did not last long and while in the Attic city fell to the blade of an assassin sponsored by his enemies in Thebes. With his removal, space was made for a younger generation of activists to come to the fore. There was Pherenicus, whose father had sheltered Athenian exiles when the Thirty were at their bloody worst, whose significance is illustrated when liberation was embarked upon: it was he who led on the main body of the émigré army. Pelopidas, Melon, Damocleidas and Theopompus are others also mentioned as key men in the refugee community, but whether old hands or newer blood these banished leaders had ensured they did not lose contact with their comrades who had remained in Thebes.

Some of these who had kept their heads down at home we know of too. There was Charon who would be elected boeotarch (of the Boeotian confederacy) in 378 and once again to high office in 375, is recorded leading a cavalry raid on Plataea, and remained a figure of political significance at least down to the 360s. There was Galaxidorus who, like Ismenias and Androclidas had taken money to kick off the Corinthian War, so might have been expected to be a target of Leontiades but had been allowed to survive and remain at liberty in Thebes and probably had a part in the winter revolution. There was Gorgidas, Epaminondas and even his brother, who were all deep in it too if we believe some questionable evidence from Plutarch. These would all become, with Pelopidas, the mainstay of a Theban military leadership that would attempt to challenge the supremacy that the Spartans seemed to be have secured for themselves with success at Olynthus, Mantinea, Phlious and Thebes. There were others also who had not only stayed at home when the exiles slipped away but were sufficiently untainted by anti-Spartan reputations to gain positions of influence with the junta in power. Phillidas was the key name here and he turned out not just a resourceful intriguer but a man of action who was central to the success of the uprising that was coming.

On a winter's day in 379/378 it was set in motion. The main body of exiles was led out of Athens by Pherenicus and gathered in the Thriasian plain where they were ordered to await developments. Meanwhile twelve men were handpicked for the attempt on Thebes itself, including not only Pelopidas but others related to the city's leading families and led by Melon.[1] The plan had been carefully thought through with little margin for error, the twelve setting out disguised as hunters complete with hounds and nets so no one who met them on the way from Athens would have their suspicions aroused.

Back at Thebes, Charon prepared himself for their arrival. However another conspirator, Hipposthenides, apparently got cold feet and panicked and, feeling that the whole enterprise was doomed due to lack of adequate resources, he dispatched one of his friends to Melon and Pelopidas urging them to postpone their plans. This man duly made his way to his house to find his horse but could not find its bridle which his wife had lent to a neighbour. A furious quarrel ensued with both of them cursing each other and ended with his journey being aborted on the grounds that these delays indicated the gods meant it was not to be. In any case the intrepid twelve were now near the city where they swapped the garb of hunters for that of peasants and separated in order to enter the city from various different directions to ensure that their presence would raise no undue alarm. The weather was also on their side as though it was still daylight snow began to fall, meaning that most Thebans had retreated indoors, so the conspirators could remain for the most part unobserved. Eventually they all gathered at Charon's house where they were joined by other sympathisers, which brought their numbers to 48 in all.

Meanwhile Phillidas, secretary to the oligarchs, was playing his full part. He had arranged a drinking party that night to celebrate the festival of Aphrodite with plenty of women to ease the festivities along. The intention was to get them so drunk that the coup could proceed unhindered. But these best laid plans soon began to go wrong when rumours of exiles being in the city reached the drinking party before it had really got going. Phillidas tried in vain to distract his guests, but Archias, the pro-Spartan leader, duly alarmed, sent for Charon. When the messenger reached his house Charon had no option but to obey the summons but, fearing the worst and worried the fully armed conspirators who were prepared for action might believe he would betray them, fetched his son and handed him over to Pelopidas telling him 'that if he found any guile or treachery in the father, he must treat the son as an enemy and show him no mercy.'[2] This move apparently had some of the conspirators in tears, urging him not to involve his son as they did not doubt his resolution for a moment. But Charon 'refused to take his son away, asking if any kind of life or any safety could be more honourable for him than a decorous death with his father and all these friends.'[3] Offering prayers to the gods, he proceeded to obey the summons and went to Archias' house. On arriving he found Phillidas on hand to obfuscate and orchestrate the conversation and reassure Archias who it soon became clear had no specific information. Charon agreed to look into the matter, while Archias was led back to the party by Phillidas and suitably plied yet again with wine, women and song. Disaster had narrowly been averted. Charon, no doubt his heart pounding at such a perilous escape, returned but chose to tell only Pelopidas how close a shave it had been. To the others he merely said that Archias had talked of 'other matters'.[4] But unbeknownst to all of them the most harrowing threat to their enterprise was being acted out at that very moment elsewhere. Now more accurate information about the coup had come Archias' way. An Athenian priest who was both his namesake and friend (his suspicions aroused by the exiles' activity and the mobilising of Athenian troops that looked set to intervene in the north) had sent precise and accurate details of the plot then underway. Archias was implored by the messenger to read it immediately as it contained urgent business, but Phillidas had done his job well and the magistrate was now so drunk that he merely replied 'Serious business for the morrow'.

There was now not a moment to waste and the conspirators split into two parties, one led by Pelopidas and Damocleidas to attack Leontiades, whilst Charon and Melon were to lead the assault on Archias. The latter party now changed their attire once more: over their breastplates they put on women's clothes and wore thick garlands of pine and fir to obscure their faces. In the confusion they hoped to fool Archias and his drinking buddies into thinking that more women had arrived to join the merriment, and notwithstanding this broad hint of Brian Rix farce, the ploy succeeded. In the general confusion and hoped-for debauchery the disguises were soon whipped off and Archias promptly killed.

Pelopidas and his compatriots were not quite so fortunate as Leontiades was a more formidable and indeed sober target. He was asleep by the time Pelopidas and the other assassins arrived. His servants eventually opened the door and were immediately knocked out the way as the conspirators rushed to the bedroom. The intended victim drew his dagger and managed to kill one of the invading party before Pelopidas, who was right behind, grappled with him and an almighty struggle began in the narrow doorway over the dead body. The intruders eventually prevailed and killed the hated Leontiades. Then they all rushed to the house of another enemy Hypates only to find he had fled to his neighbours, but it was to be of no avail as they soon caught up with him and he was also soon on his way to Hades.

All was going to plan and next Pelopidas and Melon reunited, sent messages to Pherenicus in the Thriasian plain informing of their success, and asked them to march immediately to link up. They were now also joined by Epaminondas and like-minded Thebans, while Phillidas, not content with his key role in the attack on the lead oligarchs, killed a jailor and managed to free and arm the political prisoners kept in custody. Understandably the rest of the city was now in complete uproar and turmoil, but though Pelopidas, Melon and their followers had succeeded in killing a few of their most significant enemies and taken over the town, the Theban Acropolis, the *Cadmeia,* was still in the hands of the Spartans.

They themselves were by now fully aware of events since some oligarchic sympathisers had during the chaos fled to the citadel seeking refuge. Inexplicably the commander, despite having 1,500 men to hand, chose to do nothing apart from sending for help from Plataea and Thespiae and of course Sparta, when prompt action might have squashed the coup there and then. In the city the people endured the rest of the night in a state of chaos, though the local hoplites and cavalry had been called out and political prisoners freed and armed to defend against any counterstroke by either the garrison troops or Spartan supporters in the town. In the morning Pherenicus arrived with the rest of the exiles from Athens and the new leadership felt confident enough in their control of the city to summon a general assembly of the citizens. In a well orchestrated move Epaminondas and Gorgidas led forward garlanded priests, along with the rest of the twelve, and acclaimed them as liberators and saviours of Thebes. Pelopidas, Melon and Charon were duly saluted, installed as the chief officers of free Thebes, and a siege of the *Cadmeia* was immediately initiated. But it was not all plain sailing; before they could try to take the fortress there was news that help for the Spartans was about to arrive from Plataea. However, the Thebans had assembled a considerable number of cavalry who came out of the city to meet them, and a melee ensued in which the Thebans were victorious slaying more than twenty of the enemy.

Expecting that aid for the people on the *Cadmeia* would soon arrive from an alerted and alarmed Sparta, Pelopidas, Charon and Melon deployed their men, surrounded the citadel and sent ambassadors to Athens asking for aid. In fact there is evidence that there were two Athenian generals already waiting on the border, though as they were subsequently put on trial by the Athenian Assembly it must be assumed the forces were there in somewhat of an unofficial capacity. Whatever their status the Athenian commanders swiftly brought their troops into the city to help with the attack on the citadel. An official and very considerable response is also reported by the Athenian Assembly, who voted to send a force of 5,000 hoplites and 500 cavalry under Demophon who was dispatched the following day with all haste.[5] When all these were counted, as well as troops who came in from Boeotia eager to expel the Spartans, they reached in total an army of 12,000 foot soldiers and more than 2,000 cavalry, and with these the *Cadmeia* was well and truly besieged.

The Spartan troops with their allies in the *Cadmeia* were 1,500 strong and initially put up an energetic defence. They threw back the assaults, but it was hard fighting: 'they held out stubbornly against the attacks and slew and wounded many of their besiegers, supported by the strength of the citadel.'[6] But the lack of provisions soon became urgent and with no sign of immediate help from the motherland the besieged fell to arguing amongst themselves. The allies who outnumbered the Spartans felt they should capitulate, though the latter wished to adhere to the Spartan discipline of fighting to the death. Under this pressure the commanders appear once again to have lost their nerve. Just as they failed to act decisively against the insurrection, now they meekly surrendered on terms of safe conduct out of the city. This agreement did the allies little good, as many of them were massacred on their way out, the Thebans even slaughtering the children. Those who survived only did so with the help of, of all people, the Athenians.

At Sparta the response to the news of the revolt had been predictable. If there was gloom at the setback there was also determination, though it does not seem to have been enough to engender great urgency, 'the Lacedaemonians, occupied in mustering forces, were long in coming.'[7] A mobilisation was ordered, but we know of a debate over command that would not have made for speed. Agesilaus was offered but declined pointing out that it was more than forty years since he had reached military age. Advanced years though may not have been the real reason, 'because he well knew that if he was in command the citizens would say that Agesilaus was making trouble for the state in order that he might give assistance to tyrants. Therefore he let them decide as they would about this matter.'[8] This however seems doubtful in the extreme; a more likely explanation is that Agesilaus, fearing defeat in this venture, did not want to be associated with it.

So Agesipolis' successor Cleombrotus was sent on his first military command to relieve the garrison – an expedition starting in the cold of midwinter that was fated for ultimate failure. He had got no further than Megara when he met the thoroughly chastened Spartan contingent on their way back home from Thebes. Getting the garrison out of the *Cadmeia*, though a great achievement for the new Theban leadership, was a serious blow for the standing of the Spartan military. That the relief column had been a little tardy was no sort of excuse and 'they put on trial the three officers of the garrison, sentenced two to death, and inflicted so heavy a fine upon the third that his estate could not pay it.'[9] This was harsh and immediate justice showing just how disgusted they were by the behaviour of the three officers. The actual proceedings seem to have been carried out on the spot with no suggestion that the accused were hauled back to Sparta for the trial, as would be the case with another transgressor not long in the future. It was the public tent of Cleombrotus in Megarian country that witnessed Herippidas, a veteran who we have heard of so often before, summarily condemned and executed, a swift and radical disposal of an officer who had been a great man for a long time and probably had many friends in the Eurotas valley elite. Executed with him was another general called Arcissus while a third, Lysanoridas got away with exile.[10] But it was all too late; it did not get back Thebes for them, and from a highpoint, Spartan hegemony looked on the slide.

Cleombrotus now pushed on with a winter war. The need for quick action was indicated when it became known the Thebans had made an attack on his allies at Thespiae. On his way he found Chabrias, the distinguished Athenian general, with a force of peltasts guarding the borders of Attica, and so barring to the Peloponnesians the road that led by Eleutherae.[11] Not wanting to fight the Athenians as well, Cleombrotus adroitly avoided this route and took another over Mount Cithaeron that led directly to Plataea. But though this nimble manoeuvre looked to be effective in neutralising the Athenians, it did not allow him to steer clear of the enemy defences altogether and at the summit, over 4,500 feet high, he found himself confronted by a force of 150 Thebans comprised of inmates released from prison after the coup. Their freedom was to prove of brief duration as the Spartans sending forward their peltasts made short work, killing most of them. They then descended to the still friendly Plataea and thence on to Thespiae. Still seemingly untroubled Cleombrotus advanced into Theban territory and camped at a hill called Cynoscephalae, four miles from Thebes, for sixteen days. Quite what he was hoping to achieve is somewhat perplexing as he then returned to Thespiae before deciding to go back home to Sparta having accomplished remarkably little. As for his men they were not at all happy having marched so far for so little, and indeed many suspected that their leaders did not really have their heart in this war against Thebes.

It was not just blows to his followers' morale. The callow Spartan king was to suffer even more ill fortune on the way back along the mountain coast road from Creusis. His army was struck by a ferocious wind storm that raged with such fierce power that pack animals were thrown into the sea. Even more incredibly it is related that such was the strength and direction of the squalls that soldiers' shields were blown off the ragged crags they were traversing and into the water and that they had to resort to weighing them down with stones and leaving them to be retrieved after the tempest abated. Whatever the exact truth, it was a thoroughly disheartened Cleombrotus who eventually reached safety and was finally able to disband his men. But before he had called an end to the campaign he had made a fateful decision which was to turn his mission from one of little moment into one of far reaching consequence. He left a certain Sphodrias behind as governor of Thespiae, an appointment that would turn out to have an enormous impact on future relations between Sparta, Thebes and Athens.

The Theban establishment, if immediately relieved at the removal of many of the enemy, could take little long term comfort from the discomfiture of the invaders. They knew well how much the odds remained stacked against them. Their enemies still had a number of strongholds in Boeotia with garrisons at Plataea, Thespiae, Orchomenus and Tanagra, places ringing Thebes where the oligarchs in charge continued in bitter opposition to the democratic-leaning authorities there. They could also call on the resources of the Peloponnesian League to come back and do what this year they had failed to. There was even a danger that the Athenians might join their enemies against them. After all the assembly there had chosen to condemn those who had helped in the Theban coup. They needed to do something quickly as the prospect of both Athens and Sparta in arms against them was too awful to contemplate. The ploy used to coax Athens back into a Theban alliance, though it is attested to in virtually all the sources, still at times seems suspiciously like a good story.

Sphodrias, the newly-appointed Spartan governor of Thespiae, had been left with a third of the allied troops as well as all of Cleombrotus' war chest and instructed to use it to hire more mercenaries. He now involved himself in an adventure that was destined to drive Thebes and Athens together in a combination that would give his country much trouble in the next few years. He is attested as a pretty feckless person and what happened next does not challenge this conclusion. Not long into his tenure of office in 378 some Theban representatives had travelled the twelve miles of road to Thespiae with an intriguing proposal that may have been dreamed up by Pelopidas and Melon. It was suggested to Sphodrias that he could replicate the action and fame of Phoebidas when he had seized Thebes in 382. But this time the target would be in Attica, the plan was for the Spartans to seize the Piraeus while the Athenians were off guard. The envoys hoped to force a wedge between Sparta and Athens, and trusted that the prospect of easily snapping up this prize might be sufficient enticement for a Spartan general eager to make a name for himself. We do not know if he saw through the Thebans' intentions, but even if he had, the danger of his forcing Athens into war might seem worth risking, knowing that if he succeeded they would be bound to start any conflict at an immense disadvantage, deprived of the use of Piraeus. There is also a suggestion of money changing hands between the Theban envoys and the governor of Thespiae but, while other people's gold was always catnip to these Spartans, it was surely dreams of glory that trumped cupidity in his decision making.

Sphodrias made some nice calculations to cover the fifty odd miles to Piraeus. The route would be past Plataea over the Cithaeron Mountains and into Attica near Eleutherae and the Spartans intended to march all day and all night to catch the Athenian defenders before the morning sun had risen. Sphodrias had information that the port town's gates had not yet been hung and hoped that he would be able to march right in while the watchmen on the walls were still rubbing the sleep from their eyes. The 10,000 men of the task force (either plenty of money must have been spent on judicious mercenary recruitment to reach this number or it was just the frequently deployed code in our sources to indicate so many) were given a good early dinner before they stepped out as they were not going to be able to stop to eat once the hike had begun. But if the preparations seemed promising, either the commander had miscalculated or his men let him down because when dawn broke the column of invasion was only at Thria, fourteen miles north of the Piraeus in the same plain where the Theban exiles had gathered preparatory to winning their city back. Apart from this crucial mistiming, some of the troops deserted and warned the Athenians that a massive force was approaching. The damage was done and with Eleusis nearby, dawn arriving meant the locals would have seen the intruders and sent warnings to the sentinels at both Athens and Piraeus who put their cavalry and hoplites on full alert. Sphodrias knew the element of surprise was gone and with it any chance of taking his objective; disheartened he engaged in some desultory looting and made his way back to Thespiae.

It so happened that three Spartan ambassadors were at the time staying in Athens and they were immediately arrested as implicated in this attack on their host. When it became apparent the coup had failed and the ambassadors were able to make their case, they not unreasonably pointed out that if they had been party to such a plot they would not have been so stupid as to remain in the city. And they assured their audience that the renegade and unofficial character of Sphodrias' venture would soon become clear as they guaranteed that he should be put on trial back at Sparta and condemned to death for his foolhardy and dangerous gamble. The Athenians, as befitted such a philosophic people, could not fail to recognise the logic in their arguments and, sufficiently appeased by their assurances, released the ambassadors to return home to Sparta. When there, in contrast, they seemed disinclined to follow logic or common sense and did no such thing. Sphodrias was impeached though he never appeared, allegedly being too frightened and clearly thinking he would be found guilty, and the trial went ahead without him. Remarkably he was eventually acquitted – apparently the only known instance in all of Greek history where a defendant defied a summons to judgement but was still acquitted.[12]

How this happened needs some explaining as the sources leave us much to ponder. Sphodrias was not the first to jump bail before he was brought to court; King Pausanias had done it not long before but when dealt with in absentia it turned out that there was actually no real will to deny what the man had done. There is an account that Agesilaus' son Archidamus (later to be Archidamus III) entreated his father to help the accused because Sphodrias' son Cleonymus was his lover. Agesliaus was clearly not a friend of Sphrodrias: 'Now, there was a certain Lacedaemonian named Sphodrias, of the party opposed to Agesilaus.'[13] He initially proved resistant to his son's blandishments for several days saying he could only act and vote in Sparta's best interests, but eventually changed his mind. We learn of the new attitude from one of his friends Etymocles (who was one of the three Spartan ambassadors arrested in Athens) who quotes Agesilaus' words to a friend of Sphodrias. 'Agesilaus, for he says to all with whom he has conversed the same thing, that it is impossible that Sphodrias is not guilty of wrong-doing; but that when, as child, boy, and young man, one has continually performed all the duties of a Spartan.'[14] While the idea of a good record may well be part of it, an even more telling comment made after, 'it is a hard thing to put such a man to death; for Sparta has need of such soldiers,'[15] earned a reprieve for the runaway. This effort of a king on behalf of a man he would not have sponsored in normal times is a good example of how it is so difficult to tie these Spartans down to exact parties or factions. Alliances changed, nothing was necessarily solid or forever, an Agis and a Pausanias might take up an unusual arrangement to bring down a Lysander but it did not infer permanency.

Notwithstanding the outcome of Agesilaus' intervention, there is clearly more going on here than meets the eye and perhaps relates to who really was behind the attack on Piraeus. It is possible Sphodrias was just a loose cannon although to act so without permission would have gone against all Spartan military training. There is also a contention that King Cleombrotus had encouraged the coup and this put forward by Diodorus, using a reliable source, cannot be dismissed out of hand. But if he was involved how this would have been possible without Agesilaus, who had been king for over twenty years and surely too dominant a figure for such a thing to be planned behind his back. This king had not always been at the head of the page since he had bullied the rest of Greece to kowtow to the King's Peace of 387. Apart from an outing against Phlious we do not hear a lot about his contribution in those years when much had been achieved at Mantinea, at Olynthus and indeed in Boeotia itself. But if his involvement had not been central; if he had not been leading armies or driving policy directly there was the compensation that his young co-king Agesipolis, who had ravaged Argos and ended dying in fever in the frontier lands near Thrace, represented little in the way of a rival focus of power. But that had changed now with another monarch becoming his stable mate and this man was far from a confidante and supporter. Cleombrotus was in fact a policy rival, part of a group less enthusiastic about the war in Boeotia than Agesilaus; these opponents of the veteran king saw efforts against Athens as likely to be more productive of the general good, an attitude that may have been supported by many of their main Peloponnesian allies. And the death of Teleutias around this time could not have been anything except a blow to Agesilaus' position. They had worked in tandem and his half brother had had a terrific career on land and at sea, his reputation with his men was very high. There had been no hint of sibling division and his death at Olynthus was a real hit to the veteran king's power base. What is less easy to ascertain though is if the policy difference between the two kings held any kind of echo of those that had pertained in the days of Pausanias, Agis and Lysander. Whether there was still a hangover around the division between the imperialists who had stood behind Lysander and the old traditionalists of the Pausanian bent is not knowable. But what can be recovered from these latest tensions is that they could not but be affected by old fights that had not gone away or been resolved. And, if there were now two monarchs who were acting as intended in being something of a constitutional brake against one getting too powerful, in the matter of the project of Sphodrias perhaps both of them had seen sufficient advantage in the venture to egg him on.[16]

While the gestation of Sphodrias' Attic adventure remains enigmatic and puzzling its impact is clear. Athens had been trimming while the recent drama played out at Thebes, Chabrias was on standby up in the hills on the border to keep out any who might try and cross but as yet the city was still at peace with both sides. The people resented certain Spartan actions, worrying about those old enemies increasing clout where Athens herself had traditionally been influential. To Athenians the expansion of Sparta's grip beyond their usual stomping ground of the Peloponnese towards Thrace and Macedonia in the north and increasing involvement in central Greece would have been enough to put the wind up, but now Sparta even had garrisons in most of the large Boeotian cities, meaning a powerful and dangerous rival was active uncomfortably close to Attica itself. In the light of this, fear was the dominant imperative. It should not be forgotten there were still many Athenians left who found it difficult to forgive what damage a powerful Thebes had done her in the Peloponnesian War; at the end of that conflict with Athens on her knees a Theban delegate had pushed for her absolute extinction and the transformation of the city into sheep pasture. Indeed some Athenians had been instrumental in supporting the Theban revolutionaries, but now there was a *volte-face*. The assembly chose to condemn those who had participated in the Theban coup. The two generals who had aided Melon and Pelopidas were put on trial and sentenced to death (though one managed to escape into exile before judgment was given). This is the context within which the whole Sphodrias affair occurred, the coup itself and the forensic aftermath. In the end it was bound to look to Athens like the actions of a man who had invaded their country in peace time and had been at least condoned if not the whole enterprise cooked up by the authorities in Sparta. In the light of this they could really only jump in one direction. The attempt on Piraeus had changed everything, and when the Boeotian war rolled out the Athenians had little hesitation in joining with the men from Thebes.

They pulled out all the stops. Their best officers, Timotheus, Chabrias and Callistratus were voted into office with a levy of 20,000 hoplites and 500 cavalry; a very formidable effort once the decision to fight had been taken. It had been a fraught peace since 387 with Sparta not just riding roughshod over her neighbours in the peninsula but with red-cloaked regiments taking control of Boeotia and infesting the long roads north to Thessaly, Macedonia and Chalcidice. So Athens, almost a generation after Lysander crushed the Delian League incarnation of the city, had been forced into a corner. She had either to accept a life constrained under Spartan hegemony, or fight.

Now the contestants were lining up it was not just the Athenians who looked to beef up for the challenge. To streamline their military shape the Spartans too, in a new war, swept away the cobwebs in a league that had stood them in good stead for a long time. The Peloponnesian League was of considerable antiquity; Sparta's alliances with other peninsular powers had transmogrified into a permanent organisation by the end of the sixth century and, in the years after, even incorporated non-Peloponnesian communities too. Megara, looking for insurance against her dominant neighbour Athens and the Boeotians, came on board. Indeed the post-King's Peace years had seen places way up in the Chalcidice joining too. Sparta's hegemony over the members was never absolute, but because she controlled the convening of meetings it was difficult for others to drive the League in a direction that she did not like. As for what was demanded of the membership, with Sparta's reluctance to get much involved in a cash economy it was natural she eschewed imposing any sort of tribute in money. It was the blood of her allies that had been required as their side of the bargain, though that had changed recently, after the war against Mantinea had commenced, when a sort of scutage alternative had become available to those sick of sending their men off to die.

Ensuring that the governments of the constituent states of the League remained congenial was far more crucial than any sort of procedural detail. Rules and regulations could not stop members on occasions becoming ex-members and even enemies, as had happened with Corinth and Thebes recently. The need to keep her allies happy was well understood, and it is noted with the new war about to open that the Spartans took measures to renew the sinew of the whole organisation, to strengthen the axis that contemporaries referred to as 'Sparta and her allies' that had been and remained so central to their great power status. 'The Spartans, perceiving that the impulse of their allies to secede was not to be checked, put an end to their former severity and began to treat the cities humanely.'[17] The proof of the rearrangement was military reform that spread the martial burdens much more equitably. 'In fact they divided the cities and the soldiers that were levied for the war into ten parts. The first part included the Lacedaemonians, the second and third the Arcadians, the fourth the Eleans, the fifth the Achaeans. Corinthians and Megarians supplied the sixth, the seventh the Sicyonians and Phliasians and the inhabitants of the promontory called Actê, the eighth the Acarnanians, the ninth the Phocians and Locrians, and the last of all the Olynthians and the allies who lived in Thrace. They reckoned one hoplite to two light-armed, and one horseman as equivalent to four hoplites. Such was the organisation.'[18]

When it came to action with this new model army it was an Attic-Theban alignment that faced King Agesilaus in 378 as he marched to invade. This was the first time since Coronea that the veteran king had faced the Thebans, but if he had pleaded old age in the recent thrash at them he was not going to now, and in the coming showdown would demonstrate he had lost nothing of the skill and energy he had shown against Persians, Argives, Acarnanians, Thracians and Thessalians in the past. But he would find ranged against him an opponent in the end more dangerous than any of these in a war that is extraordinary in its intensity and almost as crucial as the great battle of Leuctra fought seven years later that is normally considered the key moment in the unravelling of Spartan hegemony.

But as the war began there was no thought of failure. Intent on ensuring his road was clear for the expedition Agesilaus intended to occupy the passes of the Cithaeron Mountains north of Attica, and purely coincidentally he found assistance to hand in a manner he could not have expected. The people of Cleitor, up in north Arcadia close to Achaea, had raised a band of mercenaries in a local spat with the Arcadian Orchomenians and these soldiers were on hand at the town when the king's officers arrived giving them a month's pay and directing them to dump their current war and march north over the isthmus. While the Orchomenians were intimidated into not taking advantage of the absence of their enemy's soldiers, these troops for hire took over the passes that would allow the Spartans trouble-free ingress to the Boeotian plain. Agesilaus intended going mob handed, 18,000 men are claimed with five regiments of Spartans who alone would have amounted to 2,500 men. More than 1,500 horse came too. After penetrating the Cithaeron passes they bivouacked round Thespiae, Sphodrias' old base, a safe place still held with a Spartan garrison.

By the time the invasion army had made this town its advanced base the leaders at Thebes had prepared against what they knew was going to be a very considerable enemy endeavour. To counter it they constructed ditch and palisade defences round much of their agricultural country, to ensure the predictable invasion tactics of wasting the arable land was not going to be as straightforward as usual. We do not know exactly what territory the ramparts covered but probably it utilised the escarpment rising to a good few hundred feet that runs east-west from Thespiae to Thebes and on to Tanagra. Somewhere west of Thebes the works must have traced a line to the north and the shore of Lake Copais but this would have left much of the rich land to the south in the Asopus valley unprotected. To fence that in too would surely have made the circumference too extensive to be effectively secured. This was not a usual strategy. To rail in such a large area was a policy for which it is difficult to find antecedents, but dealing as we are with men with the engineering skills of the Greeks (apart from works of civilian construction that still dot the modern country of Greece they are known as military wall builders from the sieges of Plataea to Syracuse in years not long gone) the grandness of the project should not surprise us at all. Nor was this the only mural extravagance undertaken at this time. The Athenians had also just built the Deme wall, blocking the main route into Attica from the west. A substantial stone tower-studded barrier, the remains of which can still be seen today, that probably was one reason the Spartans never tried directly to attack the Athenians overland during this war.

Having marched out of Thespiae and arrived to find a ditch in their way and a bank and palisades rising above them, the somewhat dumbfounded Spartans moved around looking for a place to enter. But the defenders shifted their armed men too, mirroring them inch for inch. At each place, by the time the aggressors had made any headway in throwing down the works, the defenders had had sufficient time to come up and show them a serried barrier of unassailable spear points. Agesilaus tried to break his way in at not a few locations along the line until it seemed he was almost completely stymied by these extraordinary and effective preparations.

The Thebans, when they built the wall, had left specially constructed sally ports to allow egress for their horsemen to be unleashed, to raid out and attack the forces besetting them. On one occasion their troopers galloped out to take a thrash at the peltasts, soldiers less able to face up to them in a fight than their hoplite brethren. Some of these men were disarmed and eating their dinner when the riders descended on them, while others were about to settle down to eat. There was soon another target as well; certain units of cavalry that again had clearly just come off duty 'some of them still dismounted and others in the act of mounting.'[19] The Theban horse scythed through them all and the peltasts lost severely. With their javelins and small shields they had little enough to defend themselves with against horsemen who, with spears and chopping swords, could rain down blows from high in the saddle. If nimble peltasts had shown on other fields that they could easily avoid heavy armed hoplites they certainly could not get away from this teeming mounted enemy. The invaders' cavalry lost men too including two Spartan officers, one of whom was Epicydidas, who we know from before for going to recall Agesilaus back to Greece from his Asian crusade at the commencement of the Corinthian War. *Perioeci* troopers suffered as well, as did some blueblood Theban exiles accompanying their Spartan friends, cut down even before they could get up on horseback.

But this was just the first act. Agesilaus reacted fast enough and was soon on hand with support from the rest of the army he had been about to lead off further round the ever present palisade. His Spartan cavalry and the younger hoplites were sent hotfoot to get at the Theban horse who in their joy at overrunning the first foe they encountered had not kept in hand at all and 'acted like men who had drunk a little at midday.'[20] It is difficult to understand the fighting method these Theban cavaliers tried out but when the enemy approached it consisted of waiting for them to get close before throwing their spears. Anyway, everything went awry as none of their volleyed darts reached as far as their targets and the Spartan cavalry, neither discouraged nor taking any casualties, bowled them over with ease, catching and killing twelve in the chase before the rest could get back to the protection of their defended line.

This seemed to be something of a typical encounter for the campaign, with the Thebans popping up to attack the men prowling the circuit of their defences. But after a time it was noticed by the harassed Spartans that these alarms and skirmishes almost always took place sometime after breakfast. This encouraged the old king in a ploy to catch out his active enemies. With the break of day, after his bleary seers had done their divination and well before the hour for the first meal of the day, he marched his men as rapidly as they could go and found an unguarded part of the stockade. Before the Thebans knew what was happening or had time to organise or deploy their men in an effective defence he got his soldiers over the ditch and flung down sufficient of the palisades to allow the whole army through. Now with no obstacles in front of them the Peloponnesians could let loose, showing that skill in demolition and devastation they had honed by years of practice. Farms and orchards, barns and olive trees went up in smoke at the hands of the peltasts, horse and other light troops, while the hoplites stood guard beneath a pall of black smoke that spread from the improvised wooden ramparts to the very walls of Thebes itself.

A telling fact in all this fighting is the star part given to the Thebans which is extraordinary for a reporter who usually tends to downplay the doings of these combatants. This in itself should incline us to giving it credence despite another account that highlights to a much greater degree the part played by their Athenian allies in the fighting. This account makes it clear the target in the invasion had not been inactive on the diplomatic front. The Thebans had quickly been in contact with friends, who had not let them down. The Athenians had reacted to the plea for help by sending an army of 5,000 foot, hoplites mainly, and 200 cavalry, through the Parnes Mountains on the road that ran below Aphidnae into Boeotia, passing by Tanagra and onto Thebes staying well east and out of the way of the road they knew the much larger force led by Agesilaus would take. A prologue to a description of Agesilaus' first invasion of Boeotia that is quite different in detail if not in outcome and does not include the extensive 'Limes' which were central to the first explanation though certainly some battlefield defences are mentioned. The nub of this version has Athenian reinforcements arriving at the start of the campaign and finding Thebes abuzz with the local levy called out in force and led by Gorgidas, who seems in the first years of the newly free Thebes to be the leading military man. Nor was this all they discovered; a defensive line had been built on the crest of an oblong hill about three miles along the road to Thespiae down which the Thebans expected their enemy to advance. The defenders dug this 'into a bastion' and from there were preparing to fight despite what they clearly realised was a considerable disparity in numbers and the enemy now being led by a veteran monarch of great military reputation, and being too overawed to take on the Spartans on the level in a stand up phalanx confrontation.

The Spartans, once they reached the looming hill with its well manned defences, sent forward peltasts and other missile men to stir the defenders up, hoping the annoyance of flying spears, arrows and slingshot might encourage them to emerge from their bulwark. But the impact was limited against men standing behind wooden walls on higher ground and who when the light armed attackers came close could easily sally out and drive them back out of range. Then Agesilaus deployed his main body into phalanx formation and ordered them up the hill in an effort to terrify the Thebans into retreating. In this place near Thebes, Chabrias, in command of the Athenians, was deployed, about to bear the brunt in command of a mixed corps. Of these, the mercenaries were not steady and when Agesilaus approached with his red garbed, long haired spearmen they evidently felt whatever they were being paid was not sufficient compensation for facing this mangling machine. From the rear ranks they began to slip away until the whole lot were in flight almost certainly before they ever came into contact. But Chabrias was not fazed. He had the citizen hoplites with him and they were rock solid and confident. Ordering these men to stand their ground as the mercenaries swept by them in retreat he now called for a manoeuvre that became something of a trademark for the man in the rest of his life. He directed his men to kneel down 'with the knee placed firmly against the shield and the spear stretched out,'[21] thus showing contempt for the attackers by having his men rest their shields against their knees rather than holding them ready for protection. The Spartan king, seeing his enemy so well placed and ordered in such a disciplined manner, despaired of the prospect of an attack up an incline and over the ditch. In fact this solid bank of armoured men seems to have thoroughly unnerved the attackers, and through the noise of trumpets the king had to bellow out the order to halt. He fell back and once more offered battle in the plain, but the defenders, no fools, stayed where they were. So the invaders pulled their heavy armoured infantry back to their base at Thespiae, only leaving the cavalry and light troops to wreck the country around.

This rearward stuff was not carried out without comment. What are called advisers were far from ecstatic that their superior force had drawn back from an enemy position and they blamed it on the king. Agesilaus can be imagined being on the defensive when we hear him responding to questions, saying he had achieved his strategic goal by being able to go where he liked and leave a country of burned farms and orchards without the enemy being able to stop him, and that he had done all this without having to risk a battle. After this the whole campaign drew to a close, and after building fortifications for their faithful friends in Thespiae (un-walled since the King's Peace) the main army left for Megara on the way home to demobilise. But once this fighting had cooled the problem for those remaining was having to contend with the Thebans, who were not about to let lie people who had aided their hated enemies, particularly as Phoebidas, the very man who had violated their community's heart back in 382, had been left in charge at Thespiae with orders to reprise his previous impact and look to keep up the plundering of the Theban *chora*.

Thespiae was slated to suffer. The Theban forces, led again by Gorgidas, began well, catching an outpost of two hundred men on the road and extirpating them. But when they got to the city it was different. They attacked again and again, charging the walls in attempted escalades but to no avail. And when they accepted defeat and began to withdraw they found themselves exposed to a slashing attack from Phoebidas who harried them so fiercely with his peltasts that the Thebans almost buckled into rout. He kept after in pursuit dreaming of defeating these people, who had nullified his great coup of 382, in open battle and called up his hoplites and put them in battle order. However the pursuers found when they got near the Theban cavalry that they were not going to prove a mere passive prey. They had in fact already been forced to turn about to face their enemy as they discovered an 'impassable ravine' blocking their front and now, with no option but to fight, they charged the force coming after them. This is not the only explanation: Polyaenus has it that the retreat was a stratagem by the Theban cavalry under Gorgidas to lure Phoebidas on. 'Gorgidas ordered a retreat, as if he was unable to withstand the attack of the peltasts. The enemy continued to pursue him closely, until he had at last drawn them into an open plain. Then Gorgidas, by hoisting a helmet on a spear, gave the signal to his troops to turn around.'[22] It is not clear whether Phoebidas had any cavalry with him. They are certainly not heard of, and none acted to protect the Spartan peltasts who were soon put to flight, or to save the general who lost his life in the ensuing melee, his dreams of glory crumbling into dust. A good beginning had ended badly, and got worse as the hallooing cavaliers kept on to roll over the Thespian hoplites coming after the peltasts who were not in the least in formation when they were struck. Greek cavalry could be feeble, but the Thebans had been training good troopers in recent times; and anyway hoplites in march formation unprepared were very vulnerable and might be cut down almost with impunity. But if for the survivors retreating back to the Thespian city walls it had been a salutary experience, for their conquerors it had been exactly the opposite. They got back their motivation and returned to attack Thespiae again. Something in which they were mightily cheered on by Boeotian democratic exiles from those places where the Spartans had put oligarchs in power. Partisans encouraged by the news that the military back-up left to support their rivals had taken such a drubbing. At the end of the whole combat it turned out to have been an expensive hit with the general himself and 500 soldiers falling in the fight that he had brought on which sufficiently alarmed the Spartan authorities they decided to ship over another polemarch and regiment to reinforce the garrison.

But this battling round Thespiae was always going to be marginal and both sides knew it would be the spring to come that would bring the real test. The defenders took up an initial position near the Asopus River at Scolus, south of Thebes, hoping to block off the road that way, but were gulled into changing their plan. Back again, Agesilaus' first move was to send to the new polemarch at Thespiae to occupy the passes at Cithaeron even before offering sacrifices for safe passage of the frontier for his own army. And more than this, misinformation was disseminated as well. 'When Agesilaus heard that the Thebans had secured the pass at Scolus, he ordered all the embassies from Greece to remain at Thespiae; and commanded the supplies for the army to be stored there.'[23] So hearing of the market being prepared in the town for the arrival of the invasion army the Thebans moved their whole host and prepared defences as before along the road from Thespiae to Thebes. Expecting the blow to fall in the same place would have seemed reasonable from past experience anyway, apart from the news coming in about the attackers' intentions. 'The Thebans, informed of this, marched their forces from Scolus to Thespiae, in order to intercept the enemy there. Meanwhile Agesilaus, after two days' march, found the post at Scolus deserted, and passed through without opposition.'[24]

So Agesilaus, having put one over on his foes by advancing from the direction of Erythrae further to the east of the Cithaeron passes, and by forced marches into the country south of Thebes, suddenly debouched behind the line of stockade at Scolus. Once there his army destroyed everything they could find east of the city up as far as Tanagra, a pro–Spartan place, and then with that town on their left tried to march back out again. The Thebans meanwhile had not been idle and, recovering from the initial shock at Agesilaus' manoeuvres, drew themselves up in battle order. As a result the Spartans found them posted imposingly on a hill south west of Tanagra. The problem for the Spartans was that the stockade ran along this hill too and made it an extremely good defensive position. 'When Agesilaus was ravaging their territory, the Thebans occupied a hill, called the Seat of Rhea, which was almost inaccessible by nature. He could not attack them there except at a great disadvantage, nor could he penetrate any further into the country, without dislodging them from there.'[25] Pulling back, he slipped away to the west in the direction of Thebes, knowing that if he lunged there the enemy would almost certainly follow him and leave their secure location. 'Therefore he made a feint of drawing away his forces and marching directly against Thebes, which was at that time quite undefended. The Thebans, afraid for their city, abandoned their advantageous position, and hastened to the defence of their homes.'[26]

Decamp the Thebans did and headed west, forced to remove at a run along a road to Potniae that seemed safe. Though it took them near the Spartans they could always remain above them on a ridge. When in fact some of the Spartan troops tried an offensive, they flung down their spears on them from the heights killing amongst others the polemarch Alypetus. But that was not the end of the fighting; when the defenders got near home and had to come down from the high ground they found themselves exposed. On their tail came some Sciritae who had been frustrated by this enemy keeping out of their reach. These were top notch warriors from a hill region in northern Laconia. Claimed as battle winners, 600 of these picked men were usually either positioned on the extreme left in the battle line or fought alongside the king, who kept them ready to shore up any parts of the line that came under pressure. They also were expert sentinels and scouts, which supports the contention made by some that they were some form of light infantry. Now, accompanied by cavalry, they managed to catch up with the enemy rear guard and chase them to the very shadow of Thebes' defences. Cheekily, once the Spartans withdrew, their Theban foes put up a trophy despite hardly having enough in the way of stripped off armour to construct it, as we are specifically told that none of the Sciritae lost their lives in the clash.

But again this is not the only account. There is an alternative albeit truncated version of Agesilaus approaching the Thebans who would not face him in battle but, occupying 'certain new obstacles', stopped him from having free range to despoil the countryside around. This is followed by an encounter with the Spartans advancing against Thebes' bastions and the defenders coming out piecemeal to engage them. In this long drawn out and bloody fight Agesilaus' men first had the upper hand, but when more Thebans marched out from the city the Spartans found themselves outnumbered and the king ordered the trumpeters to play the retreat – the occasion when 'the Thebans, who found themselves now for the first time not inferior to the Lacedaemonians, erected a trophy of victory and thereafter faced the army of the Spartans with confidence.'[27] This success and the trophy may not have recorded a great decisive triumph but was still not unimportant in the psychology of war. It was all a progression allowing the Thebans to begin to see themselves as something like the equals of the masters of war from Laconia.

After this confrontation under the walls Agesilaus led his army back the way they had come intending to exit the stockade at the hill called the Seat of Rhea, before turning to re-find the route back to their base. But they were still not home free; even on the road to Thespiae they found themselves followed and harried by both mercenary peltasts and Chabrias' men as well. It was still rough action in a war the Spartans were finding very difficult though these Boeotian paid peltasts had to encourage the Athenian led men who they considered a bit too dilatory for their liking. These antagonists harried them all along the way before the appearance of the Spartans' mounted Olynthian auxiliaries, brave and active warriors who had shown what they could do in the northern war and now served according to the oath made when forced into submission after Polybiades' siege. They came up and drove the enemy off back up the hill they had been attacking from and caught and killed not a few in the process.

This rescue allowed some respite for Agesilaus' tired troops though on reaching their base they found conditions less than unruffled amongst the people there. At Thespiae while the army was away there had been faction fighting and now the pro-Spartans were impatient to eliminate their rivals for good and all. They wanted the opposition leader dead and plenty of his followers too if possible, but to their chagrin found Agesilaus to be less than compliant with their ambitions. Even if there is an intent to underscore the Spartan king's aplomb and humanity it still made total sense that before he withdrew for the year he wanted peace between the rivals knowing another internecine atrocity now would only store up trouble for the future. So the locals dependent on his protection had to consent when he demanded they reconcile under binding oaths, and the old king piloted his army back home again to the Peloponnese.

The Thebans however were to have more success before the season ended and a vitally important one at that. The Spartan battering they had suffered had been having a deep impact and unable to gather their crops for the past two years a lack of decent harvests meant stomachs were getting very empty. They had no Piraeus with long walls and a fleet to guard supply lines so the Spartan strategy of wasting her country could be effective in a way it had seldom been in Attica. But though in desperate straits their authorities were not without resource in attempting to circumvent their adversaries' best endeavours. Agents had managed to agree with suppliers to buy corn at Pagasae, a town situated in Thessaly on the bay of Volos, and it had been agreed the desperately needed foodstuff would be shipped down through the Euboean channel with a small escort of two triremes.

But the long island of Euboea that held tight to the waist of central Greece was a troubled place. A pro-Athenian tidal wave had brought many places from there into her confederation but still there were those that had not been included. Of these exceptions Oreus was controlled by the Spartans. They had unusually made themselves popular there by getting rid of a tyrant so when Chabrias had arrived they did not admit him even though most of the other cities on the island had been more amenable. And the vessels carrying the corn to Thebes had to pass by this place that sat on the route round the northern tip of Euboea. The harmost, Alcetas, had heard of the Theban venture so himself fitted out three triremes and duly intercepted the convoy, and not only got a booty of 300 prisoners but a full load of grain. But this seizure was far from the end of it. The Thebans, captured on the ships and kept in prison on the Acropolis of Oreus, were able to take advantage of the negligence of a lovelorn governor who spent all his time pursuing an attractive local boy. They broke out of jail, escaped their guards, took over the town and with the help of the locals who came over to the Theban side the corn was reshipped and got through to assuage the hungry bellies back in Boeotia.

It was 376 as the time for campaigning came round but this time Agesilaus was not to lead the charge. On returning from the year before's fighting he overdid it climbing an acropolis in Megara, bursting a blood vessel in his leg that with some rough doctoring by a Syracusan surgeon left him in poor shape for some time, though this might have been a convenient malady to allow him to get out of commanding in this war that was getting so difficult to win. The next campaign was entrusted to King Cleombrotus. Again under his orders peltasts were sent ahead to get control of Cithaeron but found Theban and Athenian troops there who rushed out and killed forty of the attackers as they came up the road. The king apparently saw this as making the whole enterprise unsustainable and retreated demobbing the army back home.

In the following year 375 worse was to follow. It saw the Spartans attempt to once more attack by reverting to the plan of shipping an army across the Gulf of Corinth into Boeotia and thence to Thebes. But their putative victims' friends were having none of it and the Athenians, in their capacity as head of the Second Confederacy, sent a fleet around the Peloponnese to prevent the invasion. Now the Thebans were no longer under threat, they had the possibility to take up the cudgel in the old Boeotian game. With a veteran military well tested in the last few years, they had the prospect of utilising the absence of the main Spartan field army to impose her hegemony on any recalcitrant limbs of the Boeotian League. It was not just deep policy. Greeks did things that were in their blood, as their forefathers had done before, and fighting between two particular Boeotian rivals came very much in this frame. Orchomenus, which was near the border with Phocis and on the north shore of Lake Copais, had stayed a thorn in Thebes' side during the whole of the Corinthian War, and nothing had changed as sides took up weapons again in the last few years. Spartan troops had been billeted there for years ensuring their local collaborators were able to both keep domestic rivals quiescent, and ensure the Thebans were kept well away from their property. These were neighbours and rivals watching each other day by day, but if this meant an amount of vigilance it also could mean an amount of complacency. But Pelopidas was very far from smug. He had kept his 300 Sacred Band spearmen well up to snuff on the off chance of the enemy letting down their guard. This elite corps had been formed by Gorgidas and kept by the state to allow them to train and be mobilised permanently. This was not so revolutionary; the Argives had recruited and maintained such a 1,000 strong force years before but these Theban professional fighters were going to get a reputation in the period second to none. Billeted in the *Cadmeia*, it is claimed they were made up of pairs of lovers, 'since the lovers are ashamed to play the coward before their beloved.'[28] Others talk of the unit having its roots in an era of two man team fighting chariots; but both could be part of its development and don't have to be contradictory.

Pelopidas had some bluebloods doing cavalry service with him available too, so when messengers arrived with news that the men in command at Orchomenus were about to set out to have a swipe at the East Locrians he was ready. Ordering his command out onto the Orchomenus road they set off immediately so that any observers would not have time to give warning of what was underway. It was a decent march north out of the city round the east side of Lake Copais, a distance of at least forty five miles. Approaching from the east, Pelopidas was probably hoping dissidents amongst the citizens would open the gates to himself and his men or that a swift escalade against poorly defended walls might force an entry, but it was not to be. When they got near their objective they found that replacement troops from Sparta had arrived and were manning the walls, and any decisive coup was no longer going to be on the cards.

No doubt deflated, Pelopidas began to make his way back to Thebes by way of Tegyra hoping to avoid the water logged swamp that made up so much of the shore of the undrained Lake Copais. His army travelled along the circuit at the foot of mountains where it was difficult to avoid an inundated river that spread out into marshes and lakes substantial enough for boats to cross. They pushed on passing a temple to Apollo with a defunct oracle, and by two springs where sweet cool water drained from a nearby mountain called Delos. Pelopidas kept his men in column with the lake on their right and their horse in the rear to check any audacious spirits from Orchomenus who might sally out to stalk them on their route home. But just before they could reach the town of Tegyra they became aware it was not just those behind they might have to worry about. In front were seen another enemy emerging from a defile between the high ground and the water into a wider plain where considerable bodies of troops might deploy for battle. These were two Spartan divisions either 'consisting of five hundred men, according to Ephorus, of seven hundred, according to Callisthenes, [or] of nine hundred, according to certain other writers, among whom is Polybius,'[29] those same who had gone off to attack East Locris and were now returning in the opposite direction. When these men, recalled by news of Pelopidas' raid, appeared it looked like the Thebans might be caught strung out in column, but still Pelopidas determined to give them battle despite the shock of their arrival unmanning some of his men. These weak links were vocal enough. 'Someone ran up to Pelopidas and said: "We have fallen into our enemies' hands!" "Why anymore," said he, "than they into ours?"[30] So full of confidence he ordered his cavalry to come from their rearguard position to the front in order to lead the charge whilst the Sacred Band closed their ranks into an unusually tight cluster. The horse that had been protecting the rear now moved straight away to threaten the enemy phalanx, to harass and pin it down, and allow time for the Thebans to properly deploy. The 300 men of the Sacred Band drew up in very close order as their general, eager to lead the attack, set himself in the front ranks behind his great hoplon shield.

The evidence is that both sides pressed the charge, but it was the sheer savagery and abruptness of the Theban assault that made it so demoralising. The Spartan generals at the front of the phalanx found themselves caught up in the spreading disorderly melee as Pelopidas himself led his picked warriors hacking into their ranks. 'The onset being made on both sides particularly where the commanders themselves stood, in the first place, the Lacedaemonian polemarchs clashed with Pelopidas and fell.'[31] The Spartans fought with their accustomed valour but were soon in a state of some panic having lost their two commanders cut down. The quality of the Theban warriors really began to concern them. They found it impossible to make headway in the way they were used to doing in this kind of contest, so almost in desperation, whether under orders or just as a natural reaction, they left a lane open for the enemy to push through. It was just like at Coronea, an action fought not that far away over the other side of the lake, and the Spartans presumed that the Sacred Band would be quite content having inflicted these losses just to push on through and escape back to Thebes. But Pelopidas was not like his compatriots in that encounter. He did not just want to get away. Once the enemy had divided into two halves he led his bellicose lovers back into the attack against any of the enemy who were still in formation and fighting on. Those maintaining orderly ranks were taken on the flank or rear and did not stand for long. Soon the whole of the Spartan force was getting away from their ferocious assailants as quick as they could, dropping shields and spears, careless of their reputation, and only interested in saving their lives. The Theban cavalry, who had been initially threatening the Spartan phalanx, even if they may not have actually driven at the enemy in the first assault, now took advantage and turned on the fugitives, exploiting on horseback what their infantry had begun. The Spartan soldiers, whose very reputation had been the terror of their neighbours for centuries, had become a mob of pale and terror stricken men running from the shambles of the battlefield. It was an extraordinary triumph, but Pelopidas chose not to pursue the fleeing Spartans back too far, afraid of a counter attack from the 'Orchomenians, who were near, and the relief force from Sparta'. Having accomplished so much he also did not want to push his luck.

It is not known how many Spartans perished at the battle of Tegyra in 375 BC, though Plutarch talks of 'great slaughter', and those that remained must have been very worried that they had not yet experienced the worst of it, that the blood thirsty Sacred Band might have another go at them as they tried to make their way away, particularly as the Thebans were still between them and safety at Orchomenus, the nearest place they could expect to find refuge. But as it turned out the victors had their own worries and were happy with the way things had gone so far. Their enemy had left plenty of dead men in armour on the field and so Pelopidas stripped them, set up a trophy and returned in some triumph to Thebes.

This action was barely more than a skirmish and had little military significance, but its psychological ramifications were great indeed, for this was the first time in the whole of Sparta's history that they had been defeated in a stand-up phalanx fight by an enemy of inferior or even equal number, though it should not be forgotten that the Thebans were the only ones with cavalry support present. The morale boost to the victors must have been substantial and the blow to Sparta, concomitant with several reverses both at sea and on land; it had been a disastrous last few years. Antalcidas' jibe at Agesilaus that he was teaching the Thebans to fight seemed to have a real ring of truth about it now. 'This is a fine tuition-fee which thou art getting from the Thebans, for teaching them how to fight when they did not wish to do it, and did not even know how.'[32] Indeed the defeat at Tegyra was too much for the Laconophile chronicler of the period to report it at all.

The Boeotian League that had achieved the feat of fighting the mighty Spartans to a standstill was a different project from the ones that had gone before. Previous political groupings in this Greek heartland had generally been conglomerates of local oligarchies with the establishment at Thebes more or less dominant. This had certainly been the case for the one dissolved in 387 where the leadership had been drawn from a ruling Theban elite organised in aristocratic clubs of the sort we are familiar with from Athens and who shared little power with middle and poorer people. There had been different factions led by the likes of Leontiades or Ismenias. The former's commitment to his Laconian friends we know of, while the latter, though himself very rich, had preferred a linkage with democratic Athens. But those that survived the Phoebidan takeover, whether driven into exile or not, found themselves forced together and committed to opposing the position peddled by Leontiades and his quisling oligarch friends. After the liberation the new administration installed a fully fledged democracy with the whole citizenry of Boeotia meeting in assembly at Thebes and electing directly by one man one vote the key community executives, the boeotarchs, and deciding on League policy, arrangements that seem like a specific bow in the direction of Athens. In Attica the smaller towns had long been constitutionally subsumed into the city at the heart of the country. Now in the new Boeotia too the secondary places retained no great say as individual communities, with political power coming through the assembled citizens attending the *damos* on the *Cadmeia* at Thebes.

Many of the individuals at the fore in Thebes who adopted this model of an Athenian type democracy had themselves experienced exile in that city. It is probable during their sojourn they had discovered a pattern that could be followed to their advantage and even those originally of an oligarchic bent had observed that, in what was apparently an egalitarian setup, the rich and influential would continue to monopolise most of the key positions. They saw a system where the social elite they belonged to could thrive both economically and politically as their equivalents at Athens did. Thus these Theban rulers in exile became less resistant to a democratic mechanism, seeing that it might offer their own city a way to effectively energise and dominate a new Boeotian League.

The level of commitment and vigour the new arrangements released was soon to become apparent in military muscle but still for some places there remained problems. The key factor was that the assembly met on Thebes' Acropolis which of course over time made it inevitable that the citizens of that city had more ability to regularly attend and so control League policy. And it was not only geography that meant not every Boeotian was the equal of each other, history counted too. Once their cities were suppressed, the people of Plataea, Orchomenus and Oropus who had so frequently stood up in battle against their Theban neighbours could hardly have been surprised when they did not receive the benefits of full enfranchisement but had to be satisfied with some sort of *perioeci* status. The Thebans' ability to keep the populations of such important towns in a subservient position was not just a factor of there no longer being Spartan garrisons to defend them or that the Theban army was organised and potent, it was other things too, particularly the fact that each of these places had in their own bailiwicks smaller communities historically oppressed by their bigger neighbour and these were eager to help Thebes draw the teeth of places that had kept them down in the past; mini rivalries were as potent as their larger equivalents and meant where Thebans had enemies they almost always also had potential allies. Lebadeia and Haliartus could usually be depended on to help against Orchomenus and Thisbe; and Eutresis and Chorsiai had in the past been oppressed by Thespiae. Thebes' partiality to and confidence in these communities is well illustrated by the fact that while old enemies' walls might be thrown down these others kept theirs and were sometimes refortified.

The achievements of a recrudescent Thebes had been great since the Spartans had been unceremoniously evicted from the *Cadmeia*, but it was soon clear that there were limits. Their next move was the invasion of Phocis, a natural enough strategy to crush this bitter enemy on the north and western border that had so often served as an entry point for Peloponnesian invaders. But the response when the alarm was sounded in the Eurotas valley showed the people there were far from out of the game. Such was Spartan concern when they received the Phocian appeal for help that they responded immediately and Cleombrotus in late summer 375 was dispatched with a decent force; four Spartan battalions, two thirds of the Spartan establishment though many would have been *perioeci* hoplites and an equivalent force of allies. Shipping across the Gulf and landing in Phocis it did the trick. The Thebans, facing now the full Phocian levy mobilised to defend their homeland in conjunction with a larger Peloponnesian army, decided not to push their luck and withdrew back to Thebes to prepare to resist any possible invasion of Boeotia itself.

The presence of two veteran armies facing each other in the rugged highlands where Phocis and Boeotia meet did not lead to the bloodbath that must have seemed likely to those in the ranks of the two sides. Instead of more fighting, in the year of 375 peace was made, and the train of events that led to this agreement seems to have been initiated by interventions from two different places. It was either or perhaps both Jason of Pherae and Artaxerxes of Persia who were behind it. While Phocis had been the centre of military attention, at Sparta itself an embassy had arrived led by Polydamas of Pharsalus, a man who had been vouchsafed autocratic powers at his home town to resolve a particularly nasty bout of civil strife. There had long been links between the two places, before the Corinthian War a Spartan garrison had been stationed there and once more the pro-Spartan tendency seemed to be in power. Polydamas came to the Eurotas valley with warnings about the ever increasing power of Jason of Pherae, tyrant of a city about twenty miles to the north east of Pharsalus. This man had lofty ambitions even claiming to possess an army of 6,000 mercenaries; he talked of acquiring a fleet greater than Athens, of possessing Macedonia, and then having acquired a pan-Hellenic force, even of invading the Persian Empire. Also around this time there are suggestions he was taking over places in Euboea, an island that any big player in central Greece was likely to try to get control of. Polydamas was in town in 375 requesting aid from the Spartans in order to unite the rest of free Thessaly in halting the juggernaut progress of this warlord.

His audience took matters seriously, making a complete stocktake of their forces and where they were posted to see if they had spare capacity to help out their desperate friends. The verdict was not one to make their visitor happy. It was decided they had far too much on their plate with Theban and Athenian wars to consider aid for Thessaly at that point in time. So reluctantly they refused and Polydamas was sent back empty handed, though he reportedly thanked them for their candour. Jason was going to reappear and the picture painted by the visitor turned out only too accurate; the free Thessalians forced to cooperate with the tyrant of Pherae became part of a northern vision of power that for a time seemed likely to change the face of Balkan politics. The new threats enunciated, and the audit undertaken, forced on the Spartan leadership an understanding of how overstretched they had become in a world full of dangers. This realisation tipped the balance. Sparta's next move towards a successful military outcome would not have been at all obvious.

If the north buzzed with worrying developments, another significant outside influence, it is suggested, came from the east. Artaxerxes, the Great King of Persia, intervened and sent ambassadors to Greece to help forge a common peace. He was about to embark on a campaign to recover Egypt for the empire so was keen to acquire mercenaries for the enterprise. Greece was one of his most fertile recruiting grounds for good heavy infantry so it looked now to be in his interests to put a stop to their petty squabbles and free up plenty of these troops for hire. When his agents arrived with letters to the Greek powers they found people more than ready to listen.

Ambassadors from the combatants were soon covering the miles to Sparta and as negotiating parties pitched up in Laconia some important things rapidly became clear, particularly that the Spartans were at least tacitly prepared to recognise Athens' hegemony at sea. A preparedness to face reality is shown here that is telling about how things had changed since the King's Peace of 387. The dangers of Sparta's Theban policy had also been championed by Antalcidas for some time. He had talked of the need for peace since the naval defeat at Naxos and now people were listening. Sparta was realising she could only really stay top of the terrestrial pile; to try to achieve hegemony on both land and sea was beyond her.

But if Sparta was having to face harsh realities it was not all rosy for their enemies either. The Athenians were more than ready to listen to armistice proposals, fed up as they were with having to stand duty as home guard and suffering the depredations of pirates from Aegina who were up to their old trade again. Also many Athenians were beginning to resent Thebes' failure to keep up her contributions and that she apparently preferred to build up her own fleet rather than contribute to the confederacy. According to the Athenian ship lists for the era virtually no new ships were being built. Many of the existing fleet were in poor repair and the Thebans had not paid a drachma towards the cost of the navy for a very long time. This was bound to cause problems, with the Athenians giving their all to provide a fleet that Timotheus was required to use to defend the shores of an ally who was not contributing her fair share. Athens also appears to have had been suffering from other financial woes at the time, her citizens having to pay 'extraordinary taxes', and there is little doubt people were becoming weary after years of war.

If Antalcidas was already familiar as a peacemaker Athens' delegation was fronted by another man who would also become noted for trying to find a non belligerent way forward, he was called Callistratus. He and his colleagues brought the Thebans along as members of the Second Confederacy and these allies, though basking in their triumph at Tegyra, still did not feel sufficiently confident to confront the Spartans in open combat. Their withdrawal from Phocis when threatened by King Cleombrotus proved this, so they were also prepared to discuss a non-battlefield alternative.

There are no real details of what went on involving the diplomats shuffling between their lodgings and arguing their corner for the cities that sent them. Perhaps there was tacit agreement regarding Sparta's hegemony on land, though presumably the autonomy clause of the King's Peace was, at least, notionally the context of this. Our sources are poor, brief and confused; one sails through it in a sentence whilst another muddles up the two treaties of 375 and 371.[33] But the signs are the great players ended in some form of accord. The Athenians welcomed peace with an enemy who had seemed to have essentially withdrawn from the maritime contest that was closest to her heart and Sparta's other great enemy Thebes acquiesced too, happy for a breathing space in a war that had sat like an incubus on her territories for many of the last years. When Thebes eventually if reluctantly signed up it is not clear whether they took their sacred oaths on behalf of just the city itself or for The Boeotian League as a whole, and indeed what implications her membership of the Second Athenian Confederacy had for what was agreed. But eventually consensus was reached. Again the clarion call was for autonomy, the condition that all cities should be independent and free from foreign garrisons, and this was to turn out to the great advantage of one of the participants.

The Theban establishment, produced by the trauma of enslavement and the adrenalin rush of liberation, was peopled by decisive and talented characters who had shown already they could carry out a notable *coup d'état* as well as warfare of both the spade and manoeuvre sort. And now to make Thebes a major player in Greek interstate relations they prepared to entrench their hegemony over all Boeotia by reducing those communities that had previously acted as Spartan strongholds. It was after the failure of the Spartan invasions, actual and attempted, that started in 378 and lasted until 375 that it is reported the Thebans 'subdued the cities in Boeotia.' The how and the when of this decisive imposition of the new order on the army-ploughed fields of Boeotia is difficult. It was a process not an event. Certainly the Thebans had been moving towards a hegemonic conclusion even before then. In a life of Pelopidas, the slaughter of the Spartan garrison and the death of the harmost at Tanagra are reported quite early on but the chronology is suspect and a Spartan army passes that town still clearly occupied by a garrison not long after. The reality seems that this reference was to fighting outside these places rather than to their takeover. A considerable cavalry combat was also fought near Plataea with Charon in command of the Thebans, which may have occurred at this time and was sufficiently significant for a domestic rival of Pelopidas and

Epaminondas many years later to try to overegg its impact in an attempt to put the achievements of those two in the shade.

Once the agreement was completed, Sparta, under the eye of officials duly appointed, withdrew her garrisons from Thespiae, Plataea, Tanagra and the rest. Now these towns, which had been for some years on the front line, were bound to be exposed without the Spartans there to protect them. Unsurprisingly the Thebans grasped the opportunity to complete the eradication or the absorption of these long-time regional enemies, and the process was started pretty quickly as they made war on Thespiae and Orchomenus. We have no details of this conflict only that during the fighting the Theban horse gained the kind of experience that would put them in very good stead for when they were fully tested in battle in 371. It is probable that by as early as spring 373 they had successfully taken Thespiae, as just before we hear of those people begging Athens for succour. At about the same time, the Thebans also recovered that other old Spartan stronghold Tanagra, and in both these places they pulled down their walls; without outside backing these places were turning out very vulnerable.

Another plank of this offensive we do have details on. Pausanias tells us it was again in 373, two years before the battle of Leuctra, that Plataea was finally dealt with. The Thebans had not taken long to decide to harass this old friend of Sparta causing them to also look for protection from Athens. They sent an appeal for help but before there could be a response the Thebans had acted; it may have been hearing about these negotiations that hurried them up. The details made a famous story. The Plataeans were on their guard and only went outside the walls to tend their fields when they knew the Thebans were attending the League Assembly, taking advantage of what would be the long debates held by these wordy participants. But a boeotarch, called Neocles, who is not heard of before, noticed the pattern and when next an assembly was called he got the citizens to attend in full war kit. When he judged the Plataeans were busy with their crops he prorogued the meeting and led the armed men of Thebes to the attack. Neocles led the pumped up citizens in a roundabout route east past Hysiai and Eleutherae through the Cithaeron highlands and actually into Attica. This avoided them being noticed by the Plataean lookouts watching the direct road, though it did mean hard climbing. Once over the passes they turned right, marching under the cover of the mountains, and then back through, approaching undetected from the south east. The plan was to get to the city by noon and by rushing along this circuitous route and sending the cavalry on ahead the Thebans caught many of the Plataeans out in the fields and detained them with ease. Some made it back to the city but realising the impossibility of resistance without help the best they could negotiate was permanent exile with what movables they could carry. Told in no uncertain terms to collect their property and leave the city for good the occupiers then razed the place to the ground. The only consolation was that the refugees found the Athenians waiting with welcoming arms; hosts who, with memories of the Plataeans' aid at the battle of Marathon, ended up giving full citizenship rights to the escapees. So the Thebans solved the problem of this city which had been a perennial thorn in her side and for any enemy a key strongpoint that guarded the invasion road out of the Cithaeron passes. A violation of the peace of 375 it undoubtedly was but one that must have given the Thebans huge satisfaction considering the number of times enemies had come there on the way to wreaking destruction on her countryside. This was a policy of Theban hegemony with a vengeance – they now only had Orchomenus left in Boeotia to absorb.

Chapter Eleven

A Maritime Confederacy

Struggling in the shadows of the Cithaeron hills and on the shores of Lake Copais had not been the only recent endeavours of the laconic inhabitants of the Eurotas valley. Campaigns in Boeotia, peace conferences in Sparta, all had gone on concomitant with another struggle in the waterways around Greece. The other side in this contest was the old antagonist Athens, but an Athens clothed in new constitutional raiments. This was the Second Athenian Confederacy. A league of city states headed up by Athens purportedly for mutual defence against in particular Sparta and a resurgent Persian empire (though of course the latter was never explicitly stated: it was in no one's interest to get on the wrong side of that great power). We are fortunate enough to have a copy of the charter of 377 inscribed on stone found in Athens' *agora*. Called the decree of Aristoteles it goes into the detail of the mandate of the Confederacy, the rules, the oaths taken by the constituent members, and the names of the affiliates themselves. As if having learnt from the folly of its high handed behaviour as head of the Delian League in the fifth century, the decree shows how much ground Athens was prepared to give in order to keep everybody on board.

The Confederacy's members were to be totally autonomous. Athenians were not allowed to own land in any of them nor could they impose any garrisons, and each was free to choose its own form of government which did not necessarily have to be a democracy. The League was to be run by two conventions, one of which was the Athenian Assembly, the other, the *synhedrion*, a congregation of all the other members who had one vote each. No decision could be made without the agreement of both which, while it curtailed Athens' ability to direct the rest, still allowed her a final veto. Indeed there seems to be a deliberate echo of the King's Peace here, as if Athens now saw herself as the custodian of that treaty, and there is definitely an effort to not be seen to be stepping on anybody's toes. Despite all this, the substance was bound to look like she was moving towards something that looked not a little like her old empire. But this new relationship was about negotiation not *diktat*: the Athens of the Second Confederacy led by consent, needing at least tacit support from her partners delivered via the *synhedrion*. This was a real partnership and it is telling that though no Athenian was allowed to chair it, on one occasion a Theban did, clearly illustrating that the real authority resided there, as otherwise such a major power would hardly have bothered to take the chair. Issues of contributions and policy were argued out between the two bodies, and as far as it is possible to tell from the evidence, any Athenian troops active on League territory were sent by agreed arrangements, as part of her commitment to defend her friends. The decree itself is perhaps solid evidence for a charm offensive to bring in anybody prepared to fight a Sparta that both Athens and Thebes contended had made themselves outside the law by breaching the Common Peace of 387 through the actions of men like Phoebidas. The Spartan ability to swell those ranks by making enemies all around is again indicated by the presence in Athens at this time of exiles from the island of Thasos, expelled when Sparta re-installed a pliant regime there.

The original members of the Confederacy were Chios (Athens made a permanent pact with her as early as 384), Byzantium, Mytilene, Rhodes, and Methymna, but within a year or two it had expanded to include at least ten more, amongst them towns from Tenedos, Chalcedon and Euboea. The offer to join was open to all except those who were inside the Persian Empire. In one form or another it was to survive for almost forty years before being wound up by Philip II of Macedon in the Peace of Demades in 338. This new creation was clearly formed in response to Sparta and its activities. When Sphodrias tried his luck against what he hoped was a somnambulant Athens he not only forced that city into the arms of Thebes, his actions may also have been instrumental in midwifing this confederacy as well. Others postulate its very gestation may have been what provoked that act of aggression in the first place as a proactive attempt to nip it in the bud. Whatever the motivation, the end result was the same. Athens renewed their alliance with Thebes, who joined the Confederacy. They began to put up gates at the Piraeus, levied troops and began building more ships. War was at hand. But whichever was cause and which effect, the confederate structure must have taken some time in emerging. The slow growth of certain arrangements between Athens and other places put on a formal footing to give some kind of solace to people worried by Spartan behaviour.[1]

The Second Confederacy was certainly up and running when King Cleombrotus took up the baton of command from Agesilaus who had pleaded his damaged leg to get out from under the responsibility of another campaign against Boeotia in 376. The lack of aggression in this year's undertaking was difficult to explain but it undoubtedly had something to do with concerns amongst sections of Sparta's leadership and her allies about what were the long term implications of her aggressive anti-Theban policy. These divisions had been brewing, encouraged by the desultory nature of the last few years' campaigning, and were now the context of a meeting of the Peloponnesian League at Sparta where each member argued long and hard on what to do next. It may be that the cohorts of Sparta were finding the drain on their military manpower over so many years difficult to sustain and hoped that a change to a naval war might give them some respite. In addition it would be fought mainly by the coastal and island members of the League and, if the others still had to contribute, the people who would spill their blood would be the lower classes who generally provided oarsmen and sailors rather than the hoplites and cavalry drawn from the more moneyed sort. The upshot was that a real change of emphasis was decided upon and Sparta's League agreed it should cease prioritising the contest with Thebes and mobilise a navy to put the squeeze on the Athenians.

But now this target city was again the head of an association, infant but full of potential, and so very different a proposition when it came to slugging it out at sea. In the last few years much had been done, new and bigger ship sheds had been built at the Zea harbour and the other shipyards in the Piraeus to replace those trashed by the Thirty. They had been filled with triremes funded by port taxes, or built and manned by plutocrats driven by both patriotism and the reputation such commitment would win for them. The Athenians were not just building and refitting 200 triremes mandated by the new Confederacy directive; campaigns came thick and fast as well. Within a year of the Confederacy establishing itself, its maritime muscle was tested by a threat from a considerable Peloponnesian League navy. They had fitted out a fleet of sixty triremes under the command of the admiral Pollis, a man we know from 393–2 when as deputy to the admiral Podanemus he had suffered both defeat and injury in battle in the Gulf of Corinth. Now this veteran Spartan officer was in charge, and started with the tried and trusted strategy of interdicting the grain route to the city, 'learning that a large shipment of grain was on its way to Athens in freighters.'[2] His main task was to interfere with the route from the Black Sea to Athens by way of Euboea, and his forces duly entered the Aegean. Basing himself in the waters around the islands of Aegina, Keos and Andros he closed off access round the southern coast of Euboea, camping out on the sea lanes near Sunium, and effectively blockading the Saronic Gulf and, of course, Athens.

This state of affairs was not destined to last long. To break the Peloponnesian cordon the Athenians elected as general, Chabrias. Tricky and truculent when fighting on land he was to prove the same on water. Indeed he was something of a naval reformer as well, training men to row on machines set up on shore, improving his ships by new foul weather fittings, extra steering oars and thick defensive screens. His term of office was going to see the beginning of an impressive maritime revival. As first duty he responded to the immediate threat by sending an escort squadron to bring the grain convoy over the dangerous miles from Erastus in Euboea into the harbour of Piraeus despite the attentions of Pollis and his ships, to be greeted not only by people relieved their food bowls would not be empty in the upcoming months but also merchants assured of good trading profits again.

After this housekeeping, action moved south in what must have been the same sailing season. Pollis was certainly still there when events unfolded. The main

Athenian fleet sailed out from Piraeus, 83 triremes strong, some with veteran crews familiar with each other and others newly equipped and manned by trierarchs eagerly exhibiting their charges in an effort to win the crown for the best turned out of these privately funded warships. Naxos, one of the circles of islets surfacing above the sea around Delos that made up the Cyclades, became the storm centre. A well watered, fertile, hilly, strategically positioned island set in the middle of the archipelago, important for trade and with a history of self assertion going back to dealings with the Persian empire in 502 BC when she was a key contributor to the Ionian revolt. Enemies of Athens had got into government there since Conon and Pharnabazus cruised there after the battle of Cnidus. Chabrias ensured he was well prepared for this descent on the island. He had a sufficient fleet, carrying almost 20,000 men, most of them oarsmen, but many others, marines, hoplites and missile men; and his army had the wherewithal to lay siege to the city of Naxos. When he got there he 'laid it under siege. Bringing his siege-engines to bear against the walls, when he had shaken them, he then bent every effort to take the city by storm.'[3] But he had hardly got his equipment off onto the lovely beaches, well known to the modern tourist, and set his engineers to laying out the assault lines when Pollis, not prepared to take this lying down, sailed in to rescue the islanders. His fleet consisted of 65 triremes whilst Chabrias had 83. Despite this numerical difference the two fleets were soon drawn up in battle order facing each other in the three mile wide channel between Naxos city on the west shore and Paros Island nearby. Both sides were eager, though neither had had much recent experience of fighting at sea. The Spartan was taking a risk with eighteen fewer warships than his enemy who was also primed and ready having embarked on their ships as many marines as they could, only leaving ashore sufficient troops to hold the siege lines against any attempt by the defenders to sally out of the beleaguered town.

On the Spartan side when battle was joined, Pollis held the place of honour on the right and intended to take the fight to the enemy there. Opposite him was an Athenian commander called Cedon, and the impression when these two came to grips was that the Spartans had the edge in skill and quality. Although we have no absolute details of formations or tactics of the battle of Naxos from any of our sources, it is reasonable to suppose the naval tactic of the *diekplous* was used as both Diodorus and Plutarch mention ramming. The *diekplous* (breakthrough and ram in English) was where the ships would row between the enemy vessels, if possible shearing off their oars, and then come about and take them by ramming the enemy's flank or rear. It required great precision and coordination between the fleet's ships and also great speed, of which triremes were well capable. Pollis led with his flagship spearing straight for the Athenian admiral. He rammed and sank Cedon's craft and the man himself was killed. He continued in this fashion, manoeuvring in amongst the rest of the Athenian left wing, and both his and the other vessels of his command did considerable damage to their enemy's ships. They rammed, crippled and sank every one they could reach.

Disaster was staring the Athenians in the face as Chabrias reportedly made the decision that it is claimed would win the battle. Experienced officer that he was he realised what was required and, from his position of honour on the right wing, he briefed a number of his most experienced officers commanding his strongest warships and sent them to the rescue of his left wing. 'When Chabrias beheld what was happening, he dispatched a squadron of the ships under his command and brought support to the men who were hard pressed.'[4] The subordinate he chose to lead the rescue squadron was called Phocion. A remarkable survivor, worthy enough to warrant a life by Plutarch, his career would be dramatically intertwined with his own city's history down to a time when Alexander the Great was dead over fifty years later.[5] Now he was in his early twenties, a junior officer attached to Chabrias' retinue, which not only gave him a military education, but apparently Phocion's winning personality helped in taking the rough edges off the older general whose temperament was 'uneven and violent'; and more than just public relations, he had a knack of stirring up the general when he was lethargic and holding him back when he took a bipolar turn to the kind of extravagant bravery that would cost him his life when he was the first combatant on the beach in a future amphibious adventure.

Phocion materialised to command the battered left wing taking over from the dead Cedon and with his 20 new arrivals he shored up the dissolving flank. It is he who retrieved the situation and allowed the battle to be won but where exactly his initial position was in relation to his predecessor is unclear. Perhaps he was in a second line of ships behind Cedon or maybe he was in the centre and acted on his own account, certainly a case could be made that Chabrias would have had great difficulty reacting so quickly caught up in the melee and confusion of an ancient sea battle. Wherever he came from, his arrival eventually allowed a turning of the tables along the whole fighting front. With the danger point stabilised it was up to Chabrias and now he attacked leading 'the strongest part of the fleet' disabling and capturing many of the enemy facing him in the opposing battle line. This was apparently not only the impact of greater numbers; the Athenian admiral also exhibited his vaunted cunning at this high point of the combat. He had ensured his ship captains did not display the usual city insignia so when it came to duelling between the triremes the Peloponnesian captains were confused for sufficient time for the Athenians to gain the advantage by ramming anybody who was showing their colours. 'When Chabrias was about to fight a naval battle against Pollis at Naxos, he ordered the captains of his triremes, if they were ready to face the danger, secretly to lower the flags of their own ships, so that they would know how that any ships with flags belonged to the enemy.'[6]

Once the victory was won and the Spartan remnant in flight Chabrias did not push the pursuit as hard as he could, perhaps bearing in mind the lessons of Arginusae in 406 where stricken comrades had not been rescued. He chose not to chase the fleeing Spartans but go to the aid of his crippled ships so the drowning might be rescued and the corpses of their dead compatriots retrieved. Yet despite this care for his casualties the victory count was still 32 triremes against eighteen in his favour, including eight enemy boats captured with their crews. The end result was the Athenians (not in tandem with the Persians) scored their first significant naval triumph since the Peloponnesian War. The battle of Naxos took place in September 376 (the Eleusinian mysteries were being celebrated). It had been won by raw courage as much as the intelligent direction of the commander and this early autumn triumph was sufficiently significant for Chabrias personally that he stood drinks for the citizens of Athens on every anniversary of the battle in years to come.

Thus was the threat to the corn supply of Athens removed and it must also have been a significant boost to morale in the seemingly never ending wars. As for Sparta it was grim indeed, though Xenophon seeks to minimise matters only reporting, 'then the Athenians, realising the necessity that was upon them, went on board their ships themselves, joined battle with Pollis under the leadership of Chabrias, and were victorious in the battle. Thus the corn was brought in for the Athenians.'[7] Though perhaps we should at least be appreciative of this brief notice from a source who not infrequently completely overlooks events that he thinks reflect badly on his Spartan sponsors. Anyway, the Aegean looked like an Athenian lake again and there is a suggestion that it was in the aftermath of Naxos that Chabrias made his presence felt hard on the enemy home front, disembarking raiding parties on the coast of Laconia that made inroads as far as Sellasia.[8] As well as this aggressive stuff, other officers, including Phocion, kept the fiscal sinews in good condition by cruising round friends and allies of Athens to pick up crucial financial contributions. The forces of the Second Athenian Confederacy had kicked off well, but it had not been decisive and the overall enemy naval presence had far from been comprehensively disabled.

The following year 375 saw the Spartans attempt once more to attack Thebes and they reverted to the plan of transporting an army into Boeotia and thence to Thebes by ship. The Thebans and Athenians were having none of it; the former had been members of the Confederation and no doubt felt entitled to some benefits for her adherence. So the latter fitted out sixty ships under the command of Timotheus, the son of Conon, and sent them around the Peloponnese. This admiral, probably given command because Chabrias was not available, off campaigning in Thrace, sailed from Piraeus to thwart any Spartan attempt to take the short ferry route to Phocis. This new man had spent many of his formative years in exile with his father in Cyprus, but lack of familiarity with his home city did not translate into any lack of patriotism. Years later he even fought for Athens against Jason of Pherae, and that prince spoke up for him at court in some difficult days not far in the future. Reputedly Timotheus was 'eloquent, active, persevering, skilled in military affairs,'[9] an artful financial fixer on behalf of his men, and with little aroma of personal venality or corruption about him.

Now with a substantial fleet this officer, about to make a great reputation, made sure the flank of their ally in Boeotia was protected by cruising protectively around the shore of the Gulf of Corinth. Not only had he circumnavigated the Peloponnese unhindered, but the Athenian authorities who had ordered him west intended he should gain purchase in the crucial Ionian passage between the western shore of the Balkans and the lands on the heel of Italy and the island of Sicily. So it was to Corcyra, that old storm centre of the Peloponnesian War, that he sailed next. There he cemented Athens' association with the locals, but while doing so he was very considerate of the pride of these touchy people: he even eschewed the normal prerogatives of exiling enemies or interfering with the city laws, moderate conduct that not only won over the Corcyraeans but encouraged a rush of new members to the Athenian Confederacy. These included cities in Acarnania on the mainland and on the island of Cephalonia, all impressed by the young admiral and the new version of Athenian camaraderie he was peddling. It is claimed Timotheus even made Athens' enemies appreciate his qualities. A humane and rational man, even in hostile country, he stopped his men from gratuitous destruction of property so that, either when he had won the enemy over they would have the assets to stump up the funds required, or if the war continued his men could sustain themselves by coming back later for what they had left untouched. But while all this was impressive progress it soon became clear the Athenians were not about to be allowed to garner friends in the west without a riposte. The Spartans, suitably alarmed by the turn of events, could not sit by and do nothing, so a fleet was rushed out to attack Timotheus.

There is no detailed record of what happened in the rest of 375 in these waters, but there was at least one major engagement, between Leucas Island and the mainland. Nicolochus, remembered as Antalcidas' vice admiral who got bottled up in Abydos by Iphicrates in 387, was in command. A man with a reputation for boldness, he responded to Timotheus' incursions with 55 ships. Despite the absence of six triremes expected from Ambracia he was determined not to wait for battle at the time and place of his enemies' choosing. So sailing up the channel between his base on Leucas Island and mainland Acarnania he found the enemy fleet lying at Alyzeia which sits on a high ridge above a wide curving beach-lined bay on the coast of Acarnania just where the small elongated island Kalamos approaches (looking on a map as if it is about to be consumed by a gaping maw). There is also an even smaller island just to the south and the complexity of the waterways around makes some sense of what we are told of the Athenians' tactics. A lot comes from the admittedly fragmentary and at times incoherent Polyaenus about this western campaign, but he does give real colour to the scenes he describes. 'The battle was fought during the festival of Scira. In the morning Timotheus decorated his ships with myrtle.'[10]

The key to the contest is that Timotheus, before the combat broke out, had landed most of his ships and crews away from the fight while the remainder, the fastest and lightest equipped, were ordered to wear out the enemy with manoeuvre, to stay outside missile range, to advance and retreat, and to harass but not come into contact. Of this line that went out first, lightly fitted out and meant for fast manoeuvre, the twenty at the front were probably from Corcyra and they did their job well, dodging in around and about the headlands and bays between the Acarnanian coast and Leucas Island. The intention was attrition, to wear down their pursuers, and they achieved it. The Spartan warships tried to catch them, they tried to ram them, they tried to smash off their oars or board them, but the nimble quarry always kept out of the way of their rams and out of range of their missiles. Once the enemy were exhausted and disordered the order was given for the ships to draw back and pick up the men and warships that had been held quiet and rested. Thus reinforced, the whole Athenian fleet came out to face an enemy already dog-tired after the frustrated efforts of many hours. The result was a foregone conclusion, with many of Nicolochus' fleet disabled and captured.

Another incident recorded probably refers to this time of battling off the Acarnanian coast. The Athenian admiral Timotheus, with prisoners taken and ships captured, found himself exposed as more of the enemy arrived, including most likely a combination of ten newly arrived Ambracian and Sicilian triremes that looked set to take advantage of their enemies not being concentrated or in battle order. Timotheus however managed to get the ships he had in hand to take up a crescent formation, facing prows out to the attackers, and backwatering as the vulnerable prizes were kept protected and brought towards the safety of the shore.[11]

It is also in all likelihood soon after this that Nicolochus tried again and, after being reinforced, offered battle once more at Alyzeia but found Timotheus reluctant to pick up the gage as his ships were at that moment all beached in preparation for refitting. After the previous encounter the Athenian had put up a trophy and now in the light of their enemy's refusal to fight the Spartans too claimed victory and put up their own on a nearby island, though there could have been little enough satisfaction as the enemy were far from disarmed, as was soon shown. Nicolochus no doubt hoped to benefit by both the boost to his own men's morale and credit gained with the people in the vicinity; much of what these people did was about reputation. All this occurred in late June or early July 375 which suggests most of the fighting had taken place fairly early in the sailing season. After it the Athenians built up their numbers of warships to at least seventy, refitting some vessels and sending for their Corcyraean allies to bring down the rest of their fleet while dunning the authorities back home for whatever money could be raised; plenty would have been required to service a fleet of that size. This had been far from a maritime Cannae for either side, no battle of annihilation, but still the new hero, son of an old hero, had done much in taking important steps down the road to re-establishing Athenian maritime ascendancy. Following this contest round the waterways of Acarnania, though the Spartans frequently mobilised fleets, transported armies across the sea taking their agents about the world, we do not hear of them again going toe to toe with an Athenian war fleet.

The eruption of Timotheus into these western sea lanes was about to come even nearer home for the Spartans as some democrats from the island of Zacynthus had been in contact hoping the Athenians might help them out. In this place to the west of the Peloponnese, off Elis, many people had known Spartan rule long enough to resent it and some such exiled by the Laconophile government fled to Timotheus, with high hopes of this Athenian glad hander who had been showing himself eager to make friends in the region. But almost before they could make their case, any expectations from their putative sponsor seemed likely to be stillborn when word of the peace between Athens and Sparta in 375 became common knowledge. Two of the Athenian ambassadors from the peace conference at Sparta had sailed directly to inform the golden boy Timotheus (who would warrant a statue with his father in the Athenian *Agora* and a festival of peace in their honour) of their success at the negotiating table. But despite this the new accord hardly seems to have lasted at all. On his way home, probably at the end of the sailing season of 375, Timotheus put in at the island of Zacynthus and restored the exiles, as *quid pro quo* for their fighting for him at Alyzeia. Deposited back, they tried to re-establish themselves on their island home, taking a 'stronghold by the sea which they called Arcadia,'[12] and from there they made hay against the oligarchs' estates around the city. All this might suggest that Timotheus was not completely happy with a peace accord that removed him from the western front. Whatever his motivation, as night followed day the local oligarchs looked to their patrons and promptly appealed to Sparta who in turn protested to Athens that the treaty had been breached. Incensed at their erstwhile peace partner's rapid backsliding they had people on the road to complain in double quick time. But once in Athens the ambassadors soon realised the leadership there was not about to dump their Zacynthian auxiliaries. So with complete lack of a satisfactory response the Spartans as an opener dispatched a fleet of 25 ships under the admiral Aristocrates to the aid of their friends on the island. This would have occurred around the spring of 374 so at sea the peace had proved hardly more than a brief hiatus.

The fightback by the Peloponnesian power was not just limited to this island outpost either. While this was all going on the Spartans slipped another iron into the fire. Oligarchs from Corcyra deported by their domestic rivals had been in touch promising to hand over the place to the Spartans if they sent a fleet. This was too good an opportunity to counter Athenian progress. To detach the Corcyraean marine from Athens' side would be a win win, both crucially weakening the enemy and meaning with their own partisans in charge the Spartans could utilise the Corcyraeans' strong naval forces. So, knowing the strategic importance of the island, Sparta had no hesitation about dispatching in the summer of the same year a second fleet of 22 triremes under Alcidas into north-western waters, though apparently under the pretext it was heading somewhere else entirely. The new task force was not strong enough to sail fearlessly into seas the Athenians and their friends were prowling, so hoping to blow smoke in everybody's eyes, the Spartans put it about that they were Sicily bound. But this did not fool the defenders at Corcyra; they rumbled the ruse and Alcidas found the gates firmly closed against him when he arrived. But if the coup itself failed, it sufficiently frightened the authorities in the city who rushed off desperate pleas for help to Athens, friends whose help they needed in earnest. With war on again the Athenians were not going to neglect the western waters. Friends had to be boosted and rivals hit, so the Athenian Assembly voted not only to prepare a fleet for the following season under Timotheus but also immediately to send an officer out to try to provide some backbone to anti-Spartans who were holding out under pressure. A general, called Ctesicles, was dispatched initially to head up the Zacynthian exiles in that island war, but who would eventually have a decisive impact in a more important place.

When word of this very considerable Athenian response became known in Sparta, again a riposte was ratcheted up. An officer called Mnasippus would make the main Peloponnesian effort. He was provided with a major force and its components are well enumerated; the ships came from Sparta, Corinth, Leucas, Ambracia, Elis, Zacynthus, Achaea, Epidaurus, Troezen, Hermione and Halieis. With these resources his brief included dealing with any enemy established from Zacynthus to Leucas, before moving on to take charge at Corcyra. This was a great response for what was probably the 373 campaign in a complicated and difficult to understand conflict.[13] But apart from an opaque chronology other key things are not reported too. For instance we are never told where the main base for these Peloponnesian naval forces in the western theatre had been established. It surely was not Gythium on the coast of Laconia – this would have been too far off. And there were allies on the Corinthian Gulf that could have hosted the fleet, though it is clear as the war had warmed up that Leucas Island was established as the advanced western base of the Peloponnesian navy until at least the tail end of this maritime conflict. Wherever they originally called 'home' the marine authorities had now sent out a third fleet (the ultimate fates of the first two under Aristocrates and Alcidas are unknown) comprising 60 or 65 triremes and 1,500 soldiers, which substantial armament soon landed at Corcyra.[14]

They met up with the exiles, seized the harbour, and ravaged the countryside around the city before putting it under siege. The descent was sufficiently a surprise that they managed to seize four ships in the port, and only just missed acquiring three others that the defenders had beached and set on fire to prevent 'their falling into the hands of the enemy.' Everything seemed to be going well. They even caught a unit of Corcyraeans who, unable to get behind the city walls, made a stand on a hill but were 'wiped out,' though the locals who got back to man the defences were safe enough for the moment as the place itself was on a peninsula protected by water on three sides. All the invaders could do was get tight on the neck of this town of refugees, make camp outside, and prepare to wait them out until starvation broke their will or an opportunity arrived to take the place by assault. This holdup had the compensation of allowing the troops to acquire a taste for luxurious living as they 'laid waste the land, which was most beautifully cultivated and planted, and destroyed magnificent dwellings and wine-cellars with which the farms were furnished; the result was, it was said, that his soldiers became so luxurious that they would not drink any wine unless it had a fine bouquet.'[15]

Once the hug was put on the town of Corcyra the people inside were not long in feeling the strain of short rations, and in some numbers they began to slip through the lines to throw themselves on the mercy of the besiegers. But, frustrated by the resistance and realising the exodus only meant the defenders had fewer mouths to feed, Mnasippus decided to act. He first announced that any more who came over would be sold into slavery; and when even this did not do the trick he drove back with whips anyone who emerged; and as the besieged did not allow them back into town they died of starvation caught between the lines. This was a kind of Alesia in miniature and was lasting a lot longer than had been anticipated. In this crisis Mnasippus it turned out was the kind of Spartan capable of making people hate him in a spectacular way. In the middle of the siege he dismissed some of his mercenaries to save paying them and did not even reimburse those who stayed, though many believed he was sitting on plenty of money. The besiegers' camp, from being peopled by happy sybarites, was becoming a far from jovial place and the defenders on the walls began to notice that many of their assailants were going off to forage because they had no money to buy provisions at the established market.

The Athenian general Ctesicles had come up from Zacynthus during the siege and somehow slipped through the lines into the city with 500 or 600 peltasts brought on transports provided by Alcetas I, a helpful monarch from Epirus (the great-grandfather of both Alexander the Great and Pyrrhus). After giving some backbone to the citizens, rather like Gylippus at Syracuse back in 414, he even tried his hand at reconciling the city factions in the face of the foreign threat. But, if he could turn his hands to mediation, he was primarily a military man and was soon chafing at the delay in making the impact he intended. In an earlier surprise attack the Athenians killed 200 of the besiegers but the main event came at a moment when the enemy was observed to be unprepared and the whole defending garrison emerged to sortie out from the city gates. Ctesicles with his own men went first followed by the citizens armed for the fray. They made good headway at the beginning but then found Mnasippus was still capable of a response despite his rising unpopularity. Donning his war gear the Spartan general called on his commanders to get the steady men into line to fight. It was not easy: even some of his officers reported their men would not fall in as they had not been fed, and the frustrated general lost control striking out at one officer with a stick and another with the butt spike of his spear in an attempt to get them arrayed. The hoplites and some of the mercenaries were eventually bullied into ranks, but it was a reluctant and fractious phalanx that faced the Corcyraean levy marching down between the city walls and the siege lines.

It was a complicated combat that had started up. The Spartan general at the head of his best men on the right attacked the Corcyraeans who had filed out of town, and drove them back into a cemetery that was situated between them and the city walls. But once herded there the hoplites and peltasts made a steadfast resistance as the attackers' line was disrupted by the tombstones and other buildings in the cemetery. They used their surroundings to great advantage, utilising the stones raised for the dead as defences. From behind these they threw out javelins and spears, occupying their attackers and stopping them from advancing. While this was taking place another conflict raged on the left of the Spartan line. More and more troops had streamed out from the city and attacked the flank of the enemy on the other side from where Mnasippus was fighting. It had turned into a stand-up phalanx battle, but for the Spartans there was a serious danger: their left flank, arrayed eight deep, was in the air. When the Corcyraean hoplites on the right of their battleline deployed it was with the intention of exploiting this, they knew their comrades were under pressure in the cemetery and thought the best way to support them was to wreck the enemy flank exposed to them.

As the threatening formation approached, Mnasippus tried to bring men from other parts of his army to form a front to oppose the attackers; possibly the kind of movement described by Xenophon in his *Constitution of the Lacedaemonians* – the *anastrophe*. Some of the ranks in the centre of the phalanx were to face about in order to march to the relief of the distressed wing, though of course it meant a weakening of the centre. But on this occasion it all went wrong. The Corcyraeans, seeing the manoeuvre in progress, attacked in a whole body; either they thought the Spartans were in retreat, or they wanted to get at them before they could reform. Their celerity paid huge dividends. The original formation was caught in the flank and the rest in mid manoeuvre; all were overrun and dispersed. While the left collapsed the remainder were also under pressure by now as more defenders had come to the aid of the men in the cemetery. This not only meant Mnasippus could not send aid to the crumbling sector, and even where he and the men around him stood firm the fighting was bloody and casualties high. The Corcyraean battle front was constantly being reinforced as more citizens pulling shields and spears down from their house walls poured out to get in on what was beginning to look like a triumph. At some point in the fray the Spartan general was cut down and from then any cohesion in his army began to disintegrate, until the whole turned to flee with the enemy hallooing after.

What had seemed just a skirmish at the outset had turned into a full scale battle and for the Spartans catastrophe had ensued. It would have been worse with the whole army and camp captured had the victors not paused in pursuit to round up the slaves and servants to sell for a nice profit in the local slave markets. This defeat perhaps says a considerable amount about the fighting qualities of

Mnasippus' army, allowing itself to be trounced by a people more renowned for naval prowess than anything, even if, as on this occasion, led by a clearly very competent Athenian captain. It seems pretty clear there were few real hard-to-kill Spartiates in his ranks and in the quality of the rest there also seems something of a falling off. There may be a hint here of changes to the army of the Peloponnesian League that had been recently institutionalised with member states coughing up money rather than men. Funds to pay for mercenary warriors just suited for the kind of long haul, long time campaigns outside the peninsula that were required to keep up Sparta's profile in greater Greece. But mercenaries could be a double edged weapon, they were flexible and stood in when Spartan blood was thin on the ground, but they were all about the cash nexus not the steady savagery of Spartiates or the best of allied infantry. The Corcyraeans had none the less won a hard fought encounter and took great pleasure in building the trophy to celebrate it. Their feelings were matched by a corresponding despondence amongst the headless besiegers who found the tables turned, with them now blocked up in their own camp. Hypermenes, the Spartan second in command, was left to clean up the mess. He was not actually in such awful danger once he had rallied his men behind the palisades of the encampment but certainly the erstwhile besiegers had lost the initiative and were at a loss how to proceed, no longer having the strength to take the town without being considerably reinforced. In fact he had already shipped out all the goods, slaves and wounded men he could manage. The end came when word arrived that an Athenian armada was not far off. This news forced the Spartans' hand and Hypermenes withdrew with his armed remnant back to the advanced base on Leucas Island.

Around about November 372 a man stood at the dock of the law court near the *agora* in Athens facing a jury that might have numbered up to several hundred, men selected by lot and paid 2–3 obols a day to allow the participation of even the poorest citizens. It was Timotheus, who had done so much with Callistratus and Chabrias to build the new Athenian Confederacy, who was being called to account. But it was not because a strong case could be made that he broke up the putative mid-seventies peace by his actions at Zacynthus that he stood there. In fact it was for the very opposite of bellicosity that he was being brought before his peers. The brilliant admiral who had hoped to reap more fortune and glory by continuing at the head of the Confederacy navy found it had not turned out quite that way.

Desperate pleas from their allies in the west had meant Athens again had decided to reinvest in that region where previous efforts had brought dividends. An Athenian fleet of sixty ships was launched from Piraeus under the command of Timotheus, but it did not remain under his command for long. It had proved impossible to fully man all the ships, such was the state of Athenian finance and manpower, so he had first been directed to sail round the Greek islands and recruit crews. Timotheus went north as well into Thracian waters and managed to make friends of Jason of Pherae and Amyntas III of Macedonia but still could not get the financial and human wherewithal to fit out a fully functional fleet. Still unable to sail to war, or perhaps failing to see the need for urgency of action, he returned to home waters and seemed to be lying idle in the Saronic Gulf, apparently twiddling his fingers and wasting the summer winds that would assist circumnavigation of the Peloponnese, when he found some of the ever-litigious Athenians had decided to prosecute him. The official reason given was treason and the suit was led by the high placed politician Callistratus and the distinguished general Iphicrates.

These two had their reasons. Callistratus had recently worked for peace between Athens and Sparta and perhaps was still reluctant to see his recent efforts scuppered by Timotheus returning to western waters. For Iphicrates it was different: he had just returned from leading 20,000 Greek mercenaries as part of the Great King's host sent to make war on the Egyptians. The non-Greek units in the invasion army were commanded by Pharnabazus and cooperation between the two appears to have been difficult as we hear that the Athenian, while admiring the Persian's adept tongue, thought him a bit sluggish in action. Things did not seem to have improved when they met the 330 triremes of the imperial fleet at Ace from where in the beginning of summer they moved along the Levantine coast towards the Nile. There they found the slothful rate of march, with everything referred back to the Great King, had allowed the Egyptians time to prepare strong defences both along the Pelusiac river line and the whole Delta coast too. Iphicrates, learning from captives that Memphis was undefended, had proposed a direct attack by his men up the river but Pharnabazus vetoed the coup, concerned that the Greek general had plans to set himself up in power at the capital in his own right. Unsurprisingly with dissention rife the whole project ground to a halt and during the withdrawal tension reached such a pitch that Iphicrates slipped away from the army at night and took ship to Athens. Back home, with complaints from Pharnabazus winging after him, the general was very eager to find a command with which he might refurbish a heavily tarnished reputation. He needed to make an impact and was ruthless about what he had to do to achieve it. These could be venomous types when they wanted something and now he wanted command in the new war and he got it, with Timotheus forced to concede control while under threat of inquisition.

Though the fact of the trial seems certain there is another story that has Timotheus certainly removed from command but soon reinstated into his fellow citizens' good graces when they realised his recent activity in northern waters had brought not only a number of ambassadors from places looking to ally with Athens but also that he had recruited other friends for the city who had already stumped up 30 triremes. Neither account however disputes that the navy sent to the rescue in Corcyra went under new command. The suggested impeachment itself, so welcomed by these officers eager to make a name at the head of the armada waiting to go and help the Corcyraeans, is very far from a transparent process. While Timotheus was unshipped from his command in June Demosthenes suggests he did not actually face a hearing until November when his case became the centre of a fascinating trial. He was eventually acquitted in part due to the intervention of Alcetas of Epirus and Jason of Pherae, who were now both new found allies of Athens. But he was not reinstated as admiral and chose in his turn to go to Egypt and tread the well worn path as a mercenary fighter for the Great King of Persia. He was to return later.

Iphicrates' voyage to Corcyra in 372 around the hostile coast of the Peloponnese proved to be something of a *tour de force*.[16] On this cruise security for his seventy warships was always key (clearly ten extra had been launched somehow on top of the sixty Timotheus had commanded and these included the sacred state triremes the *Paralus* and the *Salaminia* and the triremes usually kept to guard home waters that were promised to be returned as soon as possible). The men would have had to eat and sleep for at least a few days with their ships beached on an enemy shore, but Iphicrates ensured they would not be caught off guard. The masts were each time stepped and a lookout kept from the top as foragers located water and the balance of the men rested. From first leaving Piraeus he kept his squadron cleared for action, with the main sails left at home and oars utilised as almost the exclusive form of propulsion. The oarsmen worked in shifts, so some rest could be got, while the fleet kept a steady, higher speed in transit and the men kept fit into the bargain. Along the way he practised fleet manoeuvres. Steersmen learned the signals to keep the ships in line ahead or in battle formation abreast, with the most adept winning extra time off by arriving first on the shore where their commander was planning to camp. The circumnavigators passed near Pylos and around the coast of Elis as Mnasippus was getting himself killed in Corcyra, and with men now joyfully seeing the end in sight they prepared to establish an advanced base at the island of Cephalonia.

Now as Iphicrates ordered the construction on the shore of defences for his ships and men, he heard not just credible news but even encountered eyewitnesses who had observed the Spartans go down in defeat at Corcyra. So the navy arrived in the war zone in tip top condition and in record time but too late to take part in any battle with the main enemy. Yet they scored a noteworthy coup all the same, for Iphicrates managed to intercept a fleet of ten Syracusan triremes sent by Dionysius to reinforce the Spartans, capturing all but one of them and ransoming the crews raising over sixty talents. In accomplishing this he again showed the cunning for which he was becoming increasingly noted. Advance news of the Sicilians' arrival allowed him to scout the high country around Corcyra Island and station signallers to give warning of when they dropped anchor. With this watch in place he kept twenty triremes on standby. When word was given and a signal beacon lighted to gull the new arrivals into believing their Spartan friends were still in control of Corcyra, the crews of this task force rushed like athletes getting underway to scoop up the whole squadron, except one prescient Rhodian skipper who had sniffed danger on the wind like Conon at Aegospotami. After warning the other captains to no avail, he kept his own crew close and was able to get launched and dart through the Athenian line of ships when they closed in for the kill.

After parading the beaks of the captured enemy vessels in Corcyra harbour, Iphicrates made friends and assuaged the perpetual need for cash to pay his men by hiring the sailors out to work in the local fields while he took his soldiers, peltasts and hoplites across the water to Acarnania attacking some hostile communities and squeezing money out of others. He also reconfirmed the island of Cephalonia in its Athenian alliance and the fleet, which now included the Corcyraean ships, was massive, well over a hundred triremes strong. Callistratus and Chabrias were both along in the armada as officers so it was a real senior effort that was being made to round out this western war. The point is made that they had come along at the request of the commander even though neither was his friend, and our informant, who is apt to go overboard in praise of Iphicrates' seamanship, suggests he probably took such high ranking men along either to avail himself of their advice or more cynically because he feared their influence back home when he himself was away.

Diogenes Laertius, a third century AD biographer, provides an epilogue from the next year for this period of intense activity on the high seas. In his life of Plato he has quite a lot to say about Pollis, who despite defeat at Naxos was one of the main men in the Spartan resistance to Athenian maritime recrudescence. His story has the tyrant of Syracuse Dionysius, like in some thousand and one nights tale, having Plato, who had shown him insufficient deference, kidnapped by the Spartan admiral and put up on the slave blocks at Aegina. But the final significance of this man Pollis for the maritime war was that he with ten triremes was swallowed up by the sea when anchored at Helice on the south shore of the Gulf of Corinth. That town, amongst a number of others, was struck by an earthquake during the night. Most of the population were killed by falling masonry as they slept while those left, including the Spartan squadron, were swept away by the subsequent tsunami.

This was the end of a doughty opponent of Athens and without him much of the sinew seemed to have disappeared from the Peloponnesian effort at sea and little more is reported before another peace in 371 brought an official termination to the conflict. A number of years of successful campaigning had been important, as had been the activities of a few Athenian commanders not only brilliant militarily but adept at winning friends and allies, all of which had ensured a bedding in of the Second Athenian Confederacy that at least for a period boosted the Attic city for a second time to a preeminent position in the Aegean. There are plenty of extant, broken and enigmatic inscriptions to allow long debate over the exact character and regulations of the Second Athenian Confederacy. Who exactly was a member is open to question, whether places like Corcyra were full affiliates to the Confederacy, or had different relationships as allies of the League, or just bilateral associates of Athens as was probably the case with Jason of Pherae and the Macedonians. But if the details may be difficult to agree on what is clear is these polities and peoples aligned themselves with Athens and her League.

Another perennial topic of debate is inevitably whether what they were part of matched up in terms of clout to the first Athenian maritime empire, a well chewed over bone that is bound to remain difficult to answer satisfactorily. This is because any comparison needs to take into account factors that had changed considerably between the fifth century combination and its fourth century heir. The Athenians of the Second Confederacy were sharing their world with an imperialistic Sparta, an interfering Persia, and a blossoming Boeotia, none of which had been quite the case with the earlier manifestation. But whatever conclusions are drawn from this comparison what is certain is that this war at sea in the seventies had not only been good for Athens, but had also shown the fragility of Spartan naval power without Persian money to fund it.

Chapter Twelve

A Plain in Boeotia

The Athenians had accomplished much they could have wished for in the war against Sparta. Triumphs at Naxos in the Aegean and Corcyra out west meant they had virtually regained control of the seaways round Greece. The Peloponnesian power had as good as given up the ghost at sea and this left few obvious flashpoints between the two old enemies. Besides this, and perhaps more importantly, the successes of Thebes in Boeotia and the threat to Phocis had now raised alarm at both Athens and Sparta. Accordingly Athens decided once more to press for an accommodation and to this end ambassadors were dispatched to Sparta after picking up representatives from Thebes who had been persuaded to join up too. It was notable that once again the council chambers in a city that was designed to produce soldiers had become the place where an end to conflict was being tried for. The peace conference thus instigated is known of in some detail. Arguments and speeches are reported and Xenophon quotes from three Athenian discourses made at the meeting, and whilst we should allow for rhetorical exaggeration it is reasonable to assume a measure of accuracy as, if not actually present, he would have heard details from Agesilaus or other of his Spartan friends.

Quite what if any involvement there was from Persia in kicking negations off is unclear, as again our sources are far from helpful. Xenophon's partiality and omissions are at times astonishing but at least he mentions the Spartan diplomat Antalcidas, and the letter from the Great King of Persia to the cities in Greece pushing accommodation based on autonomy in what he reports of Callistratus' comments, whereas Diodorus is at his most muddled seeming to repeat details from the 375 peace treaty. King Artaxerxes of Persia had problems of his own at this time. His attempt to recover Egypt had proved unsuccessful and even worse he now faced a revolt by the commander of the forces entrusted with this task. Datames, governor of Cappadocia, had withdrawn with the Egyptian forces to his home province and had joined with other satraps of the empire in an insurrection against the Great King. The chronology is unclear but with all this going on Artaxerxes would certainly have welcomed an end to the distractions caused by the endless internecine squabbling between the Greek city states.

Once business commenced the first to speak was Callias who emphasised his role as Sparta's diplomatic *proxenus* in Athens and that he was not the first in his family to be so honoured, his father and grandfather both also holding the position. Developing from this he went on to point out the common ground between the Attic and Spartan peoples and the anger felt by both over Thebes' recent actions. 'I see that you do not think one way and we another, but that you as well as we are distressed over the destruction of Plataea and Thespiae.'[1] These places had great resonance for both communities: the Plataeans alone fought alongside the Athenians at the battle of Marathon in 490, whilst ten years later the Thespians had died to the last with the Spartans at Thermopylae. Now they were suffering extinction at the hands of a people who, though admittedly had sent troops to Thermopylae, had eventually medised, taking the Persian side in that epic and defining conflict. These events had occurred over a hundred years before but the memory was still fresh, as was the pride felt in this common heritage.

Autocles, another Athenian, followed Callias to address the assembly and pursued a very different line of argument and one far less likely to be congenial to his hosts. He reminded them of how frequently they had championed the cause of city autonomy and backed the clauses enshrining this in previous treaties. But he then cited the frequency with which they had themselves contravened these agreements, in particular with their seizure of the *Cadmeia* in Thebes which had in the end spectacularly backfired on them. Unsurprisingly this tough talking was heard by the Spartan audience in stony silence.

Now it was the turn of Callistratus just released from his duties with Iphicrates' fleet in the west on a promise that he would either drum up the funds to keep these forces furbished or negotiate an advantageous peace. He took the middle line between Callias and Autocles. Stressing that both Athens and Sparta had made mistakes in the past and, while he could not resist another dig admonishing his hosts once more for Phoebidas' coup, still the main thrust of his words were that Sparta and Athens coexisting peacefully would have nothing to fear either on land or sea. Clearly here he was pointing the finger at Thebes, the only power who might, as hegemon of a united Boeotia, have the muscle to impinge on either of their interests. Finally he urged them to come to terms at once whilst they were both 'still strong and successful' and not debilitated by some misfortune that might befall them in a continuing war.

With powerhouses like Callias, Callistratus and Agesilaus present there was no real doubt that if Sparta and Athens could come to some arrangement they would make it stick. The military and naval escapades of the last few seasons had not landed a decisive blow for either side and a weary realisation had grown that they needed to live with each other. Thebes though was a very different matter. Her contribution to the conference had been considerable and we learn that her chief negotiator was Epaminondas and indeed there had arisen a furious argument between Agesilaus and the Theban, with the Spartan king trying to insist that

Thebes could not sign any agreement on behalf of the Boeotian Confederacy but only for themselves. Epaminondas came back with the riposte that in that case 'whether he (Agesilaus) too thought it justice for the cities of Laconia to be independent of Sparta. Agesilaus sprang from his seat and wrathfully bade him say plainly whether he intended to make the cities of Boeotia independent. And when Epaminondas answered again in this way by asking whether he intended to make the cities of Laconia independent, Agesilaus became violent and was glad of the pretext for at once erasing the name of the Thebans from the treaty of peace and declaring war upon them.'[2]

Of course this was always a sore point with the Spartans whose whole existence and *raison d'être* depended on their subjugation of the peoples of Laconia and Messenia. There was clearly not going to be a meeting of minds between these two camps. Neither was prepared to voluntarily retire from the positions of local pre-eminence they had won, even if this meant the war would continue. It almost seems as if each had prepared the ground for a military confrontation, one which both appeared to welcome.

The Theban delegates, as they left the conference, knew they were now facing a future without the Athenians as allies. As a Boeotian behemoth she was perceived now as threatening both to Spartan and Athenian interests and one even suspects that from the beginning a fair amount of stage management between these two had been done in order to isolate her. But this did not mean the Athenians were prepared to actually take up arms against her. The peace accord had made it clear that any action that needed to be taken against those who refused to allow their tributaries autonomy would be strictly voluntary. There are evident echoes here of the peace of 387, with autonomy always at the centre, but if much was the same, on this occasion Agesilaus' bullying did not have sufficient effect. A confident and organised Boeotia was not prepared to be rolled over, and her representatives travelled away from the valley of Eurotas well aware that it was likely to come to fighting very soon.

Athens, happy for Sparta to do its dirty work for her, withdrew whatever garrisons she had in Greece (chiefly in Cephalonia) and recalled Iphicrates and the navy from threatening Sparta's friends in the Western Peloponnese. By her actions Thebes had essentially seceded from the Second Athenian Confederacy but her old partner did not appear minded to do anything about this, preferring to withdraw from further conflict and enter a period of recuperation. Whatever her feelings about the Thebans refusing anymore to follow her lead, the Athenians were generally content with an agreement that they had instigated and would be known as the Peace of Callias, from their leading negotiator. Sparta was *not* minded to do the same however. Although she withdrew her garrisons from elsewhere, the army in Phocis under Cleombrotus remained. How long it had been there is unclear, though it would not have stayed in *situ* since the last occasion when the Thebans were poised for the invasion of Phocis. That was back in 375, and more probably the force poised on the border on Phocis and Boeotia had been dispatched in the spring of 371 when the Thebans threatened again. But whatever the circumstances of its presence there, the commander asked for instructions from home.

There are even some details of a debate in Sparta about what orders Cleombrotus should be given; a record of dissent, as a man called Prothous, who is never heard of before or again, expresses a conciliatory view. He proposes that the army be disbanded as they had agreed to in the treaty and a peace fund be set up to rebuild the Temple of Apollo at Delphi which had been destroyed by an earthquake two years earlier and that each city would be asked to make a contribution. He does though also include as part of his programme 'to call together again at that time all who wished to support the cause of independence and lead them against those who opposed it.'[3] This is an extremely confusing manifesto but what it does indicate is that councils at the highest level were at least to some degree divided when the momentous decision was taken. But Prothous and his like were in the minority and were quickly outvoted, no doubt with the Machiavellian hand of Agesilaus behind the outcome, and the army in Phocis sent down a confrontational path. Cleombrotus was ordered to attack the Thebans unless they agreed to disband the Boeotian Confederacy.

To no one's great surprise, the ambassadors who had been sent to Thebes to demand autonomy for the Boeotian cities and the repopulation of Plataea and Thespiae returned with a refusal, and Cleombrotus made his plans. The usual and most direct road of invasion from Phocis into Boeotia lay between Lake Copais and the foot of Mount Helicon near Coronea, but this way involved the passage of a narrow pass that the enemy were holding with their main army to bar the road. Cleombrotus showing considerable initiative chose another way. Setting out for Thespiae, he went south over the mountains, defeated a Theban force sent to oppose him in the passes there, and reached the Boeotian port of Creusis on the Corinthian Gulf. There he stormed the fortifications, captured the city, in the process took twelve Theban triremes, and by doing so secured his communications by sea with the Peloponnese. Then, after throwing down the port city walls, he marched north east with the army to the plain of Leuctra.

But that is only one version of events. In that of Diodorus Siculus, Cleombrotus, acting very swiftly, advanced to Coronea well before the defenders plugged the gap between Lake Copais and Mount Helicon, but then waited for some dilatory allies to catch him up. This delay would cost him his advantage, as it gave time for the Thebans, after impassioned debate over whether to fight or flee, to march their army up and block off the narrow passage in front of the Spartans. Only now, this version claims, did Cleombrotus, having decided not to force his way through, swing off to his right to find the road round the shoulder of Mount Helicon, past Creusis taking some fortresses and capturing ten triremes before moving on to Leuctra to appear in the rear of the defenders, forcing them to turn about, withdraw and face him on the plain.[4]

Whichever was true, what is not in dispute is that finding a site sloping down to the level ground with a natural ditch in front, the invaders encamped in their normal circular perimeter with the Sciritae keeping guard on the arms stacks to ensure no embittered helot servants could reach them, and the cavalry kept picket duty. Facing them over a mile away on another set of foothills opposite they could see the Boeotians waiting. This rising ground where the armies were positioned bounded a wide alluvial plain to the north and to the south, while to the east the headwaters of the Asopus constrained the country in as well. The stage was set for battle, but one in which the threads are very difficult to untangle, particularly as the report that comes closest after the event is bedevilled by an infuriating partisan approach seeing the battle only through Spartan eyes and notoriously fails to mention many of the key figures at all. Later accounts are either essentially asides, or from the pen of an often slapdash copyist. Finally a biography of Epaminondas we know was written and might have helped is lost.[5] Still, enough remains to give a real flavour of what made this such an extraordinary encounter, if not by any means to answer all the questions that surround it.

Cleombrotus' whole career up to then had not been one of great military achievement, and it seems some suspected him of even worse. At a meeting of senior officers in the public tent whilst they were camped at Leuctra old talk resurfaced that he had no heart in the fight against Thebes. His failure to advance from Cynoscephalae, years before, was thrown in his face and the comparison made with Agesilaus who had on two occasions managed to almost reach Thebes' walls, though these attempts had admittedly also ended in failure. His officers urged him to clear his name of either military incompetence or, more heinously, secret pro-Theban sympathies once and for all by attacking the enemy. There was even a threat he might be tried for treason and executed, and clearly the implication was that if he did not fight he would never see his 'fatherland again'. Either this was a hint of mutiny, or the deployment of the not infrequently used threat to bring the king to book officially back home. This was probably just Cleombrotus taking a different policy line from Agesilaus his fellow king. Indeed Polybius writing two hundred years later remarked on the fact in an excursus on Hannibal: 'and again when the Lacedaemonians were supreme in Greece, all that King Cleombrotus did was done in the spirit of friendly alliance, but it was the reverse with Agesilaus.'[6] In fact rather than just being a peace lover it may well be that Cleombrotus felt Athens rather than Thebes was Sparta's real cause for concern. Whatever was the case, Cleombrotus determined to join battle.

As for the other side there are reports that it was not a happy place either. The council of war there was divided. Their plans to hold off the enemy at Coronea had gone awry and Cleombrotus' virtuoso manoeuvring to arrive at Leuctra had given many of the senior officers pause. There were seven boeotarchs entitled to vote on command decisions. Three, including Epaminondas, were for battle, three were against, and one was absent. The arguments in favour were that if they did not fight at once their allies in the Boeotian League would revolt and they would be forced back to Thebes itself. In addition many of the leaders had been in exile before and felt it preferable to die in battle rather than endure that ever again. The three against fighting acknowledged the likely effects of refusing to engage but proposed evacuating the women and children to Attica and then trying to withstand a siege of Thebes itself, a strategy that had paid dividends before. The absent seventh boeotarch, called Brachyllidas, was guarding the invasion route from the south over Mount Cithaeron, but hard marching brought him to the camp in time to give his casting vote. It was for battle. Plutarch with the instincts of a biographer emphatically credits Pelopidas, though not boeotarch at the time, with influencing the council to poll for combat, but one must regard this as a later rhetorical flourish for literary effect.[7] There could be little doubt the Theban command had been preparing for this confrontation for some time. Epaminondas, aided and abetted by Pelopidas, would have been training the Theban troops for just such an encounter as now awaited them. If they had not they surely could not have accomplished the innovatory deployment they implemented. It had been under three weeks since the peace treaty had been signed excluding them, and the Thebans would not have gambled on a confrontation with Sparta unless they were fairly confident of facing the invasion with a chance of success. The unexpected triumph at Tegyra had been an enormous morale boost and clearly shown them that Spartan invincibility was, if not a myth, at least hopefully a thing of the past.

Even so, some doubts would have lingered on the wisdom of accepting battle which perhaps explains the plethora of portents that are described before swords were drawn. The Spartans were famously pious but whether the leaders on the other side were so god bothered is a moot point. Still there could be no doubting the propaganda value of positive signs and auguries. One such example related to events that had taken place on the plain of Leuctra itself. Here there was the tomb of two virgins who had been raped by some Spartans some time before and unable to bear the shame they had committed suicide. Their father had tried to get justice from Sparta but when this was not forthcoming had also killed himself. Now Pelopidas had a dream shortly before the battle in which the father appeared to him and instructed him to sacrifice a 'virgin with auburn hair' at his daughters' tomb. Pelopidas' dream caused great disquiet amongst the Theban high command who on the one hand was loath to take part in human sacrifice, but on the other hand worried about the consequences of not conforming to the requirements of the gods expressed through the vision. Fortunately at this time a filly then broke away from her herd, sped through the Theban camp, and fortuitously came to a halt at the officers' conference. A seer Theocritus earned his pay by crying out to Pelopidas 'Thy sacrificial victim is come, good man; so let us not wait for any other virgin, but do thou accept and use the one which Heaven offers thee.'[8] A more cynical view would be that it was all arranged in advance to encourage the troops. In any case this particular problem was now resolved.

Other miraculous portents are also reported. When the Theban army was preparing to march out of the city a ribbon from a spear blew onto the tombs of Spartans killed in one of their recent campaigns and though some Thebans reproached Epaminondas, claiming it was an omen from the gods that they should not take to the battlefield, he ignored them and pressed on regardless. Indeed the general's reply to these doom mongers is even recorded by Frontinus, the Roman historian. 'Do not be concerned, comrades! Destruction is foretold for the Spartans. Tombs are not decorated except for funerals.'[9] There are stories of Theban generals, and in particular Epaminondas, deliberately rigging proceedings to procure favourable omens. In the temple of Athena a statue of the goddess was holding a shield before her knees. Epaminondas 'sent an artist into the temple who altered the statue so that the goddess was holding the handle of the shield in her left hand,'[10] a miraculous happening that Epaminondas interpreted as Athena 'taking up her shield against her foes'. And there was more. The doors of various temples kept blowing open and the priestesses were interpreting these occurrences as proof of the gods' endorsement. Also when the arms held in the temple of Heracles disappeared it was claimed as evidence the god himself had set out for battle to fight against the Spartans. Many were quite clearly suspicious of the high command, believing they were fabricating these incidents, but still it shows with what forebodings the Thebans faced the oncoming battle, the importance of which they fully understood.

On the other side there was less of a celestial build up, only a story that wolves killed the sacrificial goats which accompanied the Spartan army, and the details here are much more to do with matters very human. It is suggested that before the battle the Spartans had not only been eating the bread, cheese, poppy seed mixed with honey, and pounded linseeds that we know made up their campaign diet, but that they had also been drinking in the middle of the day, and that the effect on Cleombrotus and his officers was that it 'helped somewhat to excite them'. This accusation of them being drunk on duty is difficult to credit amongst such disciplined men, for whom it was anyway the custom to drink wine with each meal, and smacks of an excuse for what was about to happen.

Sober or not, Cleombrotus had four of the six Spartan battalions (*morae*) with him, and in each battalion were somewhere in the region of 500–600 men, though some would argue for figures twice this size. In total 700 of the men were full Spartiates, and there would also have been the king's bodyguard of 300 knights present, but whether these were subsumed into one of the *morae* is also uncertain. In terms of allies and others, an officer called Hieron led a mercenary force, there were peltasts from Phocis, and Arcadians may have been present too. Unfortunately in no case are full numbers given of each troop type. There must have been allied heavy infantry present: Plutarch suggests there were 10,000 hoplites and a 1,000 cavalry altogether in Cleombrotus' army and his conveniently round guesstimate is the most conservative, as Frontinus claims 24,000 Peloponnesian infantry and

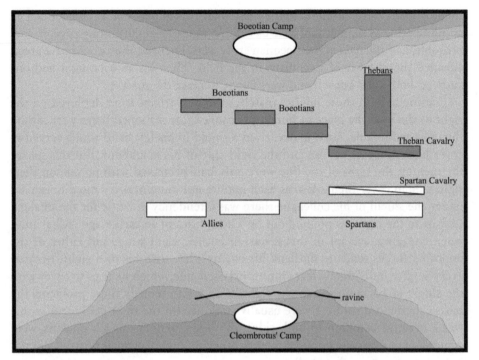

The Battle of Leuctra 371 BC.

1,600 horse, and Polyaenus gives the ludicrous figure of 40,000 Spartans against 6,000 Thebans. The only dependable information for the cavalry is that some had come from Heraclea and Phlious and there was a small force of Spartans perhaps 200–300 strong which even our horse-loving Laconophile contemporary admits were 'exceedingly poor'.

We are on slightly safer ground trying to estimate the Boeotian contingent. Nobody suggests more than 6,000 were present, a figure that gels with what we are told of Nemea in 394 when the 'Boeotians' had put in the field 5,000 hoplites and 800 cavalry, and besides that there are figures of up to 7,000 hoplites led by Thebes mentioned in campaigns fought after Leuctra. There were no other allies, apart from the Boeotians present who had signed up for the fight as members of the Confederacy. According to the Boeotian constitution as given in the *Hellenica Oxyrhynchia* there were eleven districts in Boeotia, four of which were from Thebes, each with their own boeotarch elected annually and able to provide 1,000 hoplites and 100 cavalry each. A theoretical total of 11,000 hoplites is therefore possible at Leuctra but Orchomenus did not participate and two other districts were excluded.[11] All in all for want of more definite information a total of 6,000 on the Boeotian side seems a reasonable estimate. If true, and we take the 11,000 figure for the Spartans, then the resultant victory is more believable as this means the Boeotians were outnumbered by less than two to one, not as exaggerated an outnumbering as some would have us believe. In terms of the cutting edge, if, as is probable, half the men of the Boeotian army were Thebans, they would have about equalled the number of Laconians in the field. This was an even fight and one suspects both sides knew it and were happy to make the contest.

Traditionally in these hoplite matches the best troops were deployed on the right of the line, the place of honour, because those stationed there were always the most vulnerable. Each man carried a shield in his left hand which served to cover both that side of him and the right side of his neighbour. But this meant the men on the right of the line were only half protected with no one on their right side to cover them. Also as each hoplite not unnaturally wanted to remain under the shield of his colleague there was a tendency in battle for the phalanx to drift to the right, as pointed out by Thucydides in an earlier age. 'All armies, when engaging, are apt to thrust outwards their right wing; and either of the opposing forces tends to outflank his enemy's left with his own right, because every soldier individually fears for his exposed side, which he tries to cover with the shield of his comrade on the right.'[12] To try to remedy these problems the most experienced soldiers were usually stationed on the right flank, and as this was a practice common to both sides, the best warriors in each phalanx were generally not precisely opposed to each other, and in many major battles did not come into direct conflict at all.

However Epaminondas was having none of it and decided to go for a decisive blow at the heart of the Spartan army, positioning his crack troops on his left opposite Cleombrotus who had posted his Spartans on his right following centuries-old tradition. Epaminondas' unorthodox tactic meant that the elite troops of both armies were facing each other as they deployed for action. The Thebans intended to crush the cream of the army opposite and so win the battle, a plan that was colourfully illustrated to the men when 'Epaminondas produced a large snake, and crushed its head in front of the army. "If you crush the head," he said, "you see how impotent the rest of the body is. So let us crush the head of the confederacy, that is the Laconians, and the power of their allies will become insignificant."'[13] Snakes aside, the analogy was sound: he hoped that by trouncing Cleombrotus and the Spartans the rest of the army would see that further resistance was futile.

But there was more to his tactics than the paradigm shift of deploying his best men on the left. Epaminondas also concentrated his troops in an almost unprecedented manner, choosing to order his hoplites in ranks fifty deep. In this he was following in the footsteps of another famous Theban general Pagondas who at the battle of Delium in the Peloponnesian War in 424 had fielded a phalanx twenty-five men deep, the first recorded instance of any Greek general ever changing the standard depth of a hoplite unit. It had done the trick, producing a famous victory and guaranteeing Boeotian security. In addition to deepening the phalanx Pagondas also made use of reserve cavalry and peltasts in an innovative manner. In later confrontations at Nemea and perhaps Coronea in the Corinthian War the Theban phalanx had also lined up more than sixteen deep. Epaminondas learned well from less famous countrymen who commanded on these occasions. His extraordinarily deep formation confronted an opposing Spartan phalanx which deployed in twelve ranks deep in the customary manner. The traditional depth of a phalanx is much debated although most of the descriptions of battles suggest eight to twelve was the norm. There are known exceptions, as when during Cyrus' Persian expedition mercenary hoplites drew up in a shallow phalanx four deep in a military display to show off to a Cilician queen, and though this is maintained as standard practice there is little other evidence to support the contention. No doubt it was left to individual commanders on occasions and clearly the depth could vary between different units on the same side. But if in the past they had differed considerably according to circumstance, a fifty man file was something new.

Before the main battle commenced there was some preliminary action. Epaminondas, sensing some dissension and reluctance within his ranks, assembled the men and told those who did not have their heart in the fight to go home. Perhaps unsurprisingly, considering their past history, the Thespians and some others took advantage of this offer and attempted to withdraw. These reluctant warriors were not the only ones who wanted to get out of danger's way: there were some merchants who had come to service the army and baggage carriers who felt themselves far too near the likely scene of action for comfort. As the officers and men were arming themselves these tried to make their exit, but on leaving through the gates of the Boeotian camp they were noticed by hawk-eyed foes in the enemy ranks. On the left wing of the invading army the mercenaries under Hieron, the Phocian peltasts, and cavalry from Heraclea and Phlious rushed forward to try to encircle the reluctant soldiers and non-combatants as they were exposed on the open plain. But their putative prey saw what danger they were in and, any order dissolving, they turned straight round and fled back to the defended camp, where, if we are to believe the account given, they were reintegrated into the Boeotian array adding both to its strength and depth in the coming battle. Presumably the frustrated men chasing them then returned to their original positions on the left of the Spartan battle line.

These goings on did little to impact on the first real fighting of the day as a cavalry spat unfolded. The Theban horse had been posted at the beginning of the battle in front of the strong left of the Boeotian line. This was unusual: in most battles of this era the cavalry were deployed on the wings where they might protect their own and threaten the flanks of the troops opposite, then help the pursuit or retreat after one side or the other had broken through after the clash of hoplite against hoplite. In fact, though, it is made clear that Cleombrotus was the first to range his horsemen in advance of his infantry and that the Theban command had acted in response as 'Lacedaemonians posted their horsemen in front of their phalanx, and the Thebans in like manner posted theirs over against them.'[14] This makes no real sense as Cleombrotus' cavalry was much weaker than the Thebans, a fact he was well aware of (unless of course Plutarch is accurate and he did have 1,000 troopers, so well outnumbering the opposition). Just as probable an explanation is that both sides were trying to screen some other manoeuvres and that the troopers would have reverted to their position on the wings given time, which if true suggests that the battle could have started before either side was completely ready.

What is clear though is the Theban horse now charged their Spartan counterparts opposite, and as was to be expected, given their respective quality, soon had the best of it. The Peloponnesian cavalry were physically badly out of shape and shared none of the Spartan supreme concern for gaining glory, so when the enemy closed, mounts crashing into them and riders spearing frenziedly, they were swiftly worsted, disorganised and driven back into the Spartan phalanx causing general mayhem and disorder. Trying to let the desperate troopers through their ranks must have strained even these soldiers' vaunted unit cohesion, particularly as it may have occurred just as the Theban hoplites launched their attack.

The tactical implication of the Theban formation was that Epaminondas was sacrificing width for depth. He could not now hope to match the frontage of the enemy phalanx and so his whole battle line was going to be in danger of being outflanked. Having failed to line up as usual, parallel to Cleombrotus and his army, they would appear to have been courting certain disaster. The fifty to sixty front men of the Theban column found themselves facing perhaps five times their number of armoured spearmen, many carrying a shield with the feared red V on it and with long combed locks showing from below their bronze helmets. Troops that were in the kind of numbers the Spartan authorities had not been in the habit of sending out of the Peloponnese for some time indeed if ever. With red cloaks discarded in the warmth of the day these men from Laconia must have been a formidable array, from the king's guard, to other full Spartiates, through to 'the inferiors' (*hypomeiones*), born Spartiates disenfranchised through poverty or behaviour but who still contributed recruits, to the *perioeci* hoplites, and even to those helots that had on occasions since the Peloponnesian War been armed as heavy infantry to fight in the line and usually granted their freedom as reward. How each were deployed, whether brigaded separately or mixed up, is not absolutely known. But the general rule was to have the best men at the front and rear of each file, so perhaps these positions were taken by the ferocious graduates of the *agoge* while the others occupied the ranks in between.

But as both sides charged, to the accompaniment of trumpets and war cries, the men rolling down on the Spartans had reason for confidence too. They had been contending the foe they now faced for some years and not without success. Men from the Sacred Band could show scars and trophies from the victory at Tegyra while even the soldiers of the Theban levy would have included those who had seen Laconian backs in the fighting around Thespiae and Thebes in the campaigns of six and seven years before. Epaminondas, as was expected of a general at this time, was leading from the front and this vantage point allowed him to see much. Up ahead in the dust the enemy horsemen were disrupting the ordered ranks of their own infantry as they tried to find a way through to escape the Theban cavalry which they expected to be bearing down on their retreating backs. In fact these troopers must have pulled away rather than pursued. No doubt they would not have fancied throwing themselves onto the spear points of the enemy line even if it was buffeted and shaken by passing horseflesh. So with a free run the Theban infantry had no such qualms and bravely advanced to meet the enemy.

It must have been an extraordinary press on this hot summer day as Epaminondas directed his spear-bristling column to the point in the Spartan line where he could see Cleombrotus and his retinue, on a shadeless plain with so many men behind each other, with shields pushing into backs, ensuring those in the ranks could not even think of slipping away from the fight, an inclination that was an ever present danger even amongst the best troops. Whatever the debate about the form of this hoplite fighting, whether as a great shoving match or more a linked line of duelling heroes, it was a physically traumatic experience, with sweat, terror and rage mingling in equal measure. As spears broke and shields were ripped from hands, ordered ranks became ragged and blurred. Halting for breath and falling apart at least for a brief moment would have been the norm, giving time for swords to be drawn or spear butts to be raised in place of broken and useless points.

Before the tipping point was reached the Spartans had shown their calibre and were holding their own: 'of those who had resisted some fell and others were wounded, taking all the blows in front.'[15] The Spartans fought with the kind of valour that would have been expected, but fairly early on during a savage tussle between the front rank men Cleombrotus himself was a casualty, cut down at the head of his men. 'King Cleombrotus of the Lacedaemonians was alive and had with him many comrades-in-arms who were quite ready to die in his defence, it was uncertain which way the scales of victory inclined; but when, though he shrank from no danger, he proved unable to bear down his opponents, and perished in an heroic resistance after sustaining many wounds, then, as masses of men thronged about his body, there was piled up a great mound of corpses.'[16] But while the ground was slipping away from under the king and the Theban enemy were eager to finish him off, still the guard about him resisted steadfastly: 'the heavy column led by Epaminondas bore down upon the Lacedaemonians, and at first by sheer force caused the line of the enemy to buckle somewhat; then, however, the Lacedaemonians, fighting gallantly about their king, got possession of his body, but were not strong enough to achieve victory.'[17] Even in this chaos they were still able to convey the wounded man away, showing that at least in that part of the line they still controlled the field. He does not appear to have survived very long after being carried off. Whether drunk or sober at Leuctra he had been a luckless king who perhaps has been treated unfairly by history and one whose policy instincts if followed might have led to a happier outcome for his people.

The nearest account in time is insistent that the Spartans initially held their own and more, or they could not have carried the king's body away from the forefront of the combat. But it did not last and soon Cleombrotus was not the only well-known Spartan to find a bloody end. Deinon is the commander whose death seems to have signalled the beginning of the end of Spartan resistance, and soon after him fell Sphodrias, the man whose ill-fated and ill-judged incursion against Piraeus seven years earlier had contributed to the mess Sparta now found herself in. Next to be cut down in the middle of the melee was his son Cleonymus, whose relationship with Agesilaus' son had apparently obtained the acquittal of his father, who fell along with other senior bodyguards and staff officers. So were lost any of the men who might have rallied them. As they toppled under the spears and swords of their Theban assailants the whole Spartan formation was pushed back.

The point of decision finally came when Epaminondas called for a famous last push from the fifty-deep Thebans. They utilised their greater depth to press back the Laconians on the right of Cleombrotus' line and finally broke them. In theory these armoured spearmen were the best; they should have stood but they did not. It is possible much was due to the Spartans being hit before they were ready and disordered by their own cavalry. If this was crucial it would not have been the first time. Plenty of contests before like Delium in 424 and Mantinea in 418 followed this pattern. To catch your opponent off guard and disordered was the ploy of preference at this time, even if it did not always end in victory.

Another answer to why the Spartans lost is given by a man whose interest was in seeking to present the commander of the Theban Sacred Band, Pelopidas, in the best possible light. Plutarch does not even acknowledge the disorder created by the fleeing horsemen in the Spartan ranks at all, but has Cleombrotus reacting on seeing the Thebans' unusual super-deep battle array. In response the Spartans 'began to change their formation; they were opening up their right wing and making an encircling movement, in order to surround Epaminondas and envelop him with their numbers.'[18] But then the Sacred Band, the 300-strong elite corps of homosexual couples led by Pelopidas, came down like a thunderbolt with 'incredible speed' on the Spartan spearmen out of formation in the middle of its outflanking manoeuvre. Such was their courage and discipline that they managed to disrupt the enemy completely. They were 'the first to bear down the phalanx of the Spartans.' Their impact was claimed as decisive and ensured that the shaken Spartans were not able to hold out against the pressure of Epaminondas' main column.

A question remains: where did they come from? One option would seem to be that these 300 men fought as a separate unit alongside the main Theban infantry column commanded by Epaminondas. It is easy to read Plutarch this way, as in describing the history of the Band he specifies that they had changed from being integrated into the main phalanx to working alone, and in the battle he seems to suggest the same. Yet this still seems odd, as by drawing up in the traditional eight or twelve files they would be eschewing the advantage that the deep phalanx was expected to give, while to form as an individual unit fifty deep would have given them a front of only six men, which could not be effective. Much more likely is that the Sacred Band provided the cutting edge, that they were the men who peopled the front few ranks of the fifty-deep column that did the damage. But this is to disregard that Cleombrotus' outflanking move is absolutely specified, and though seldom regarded as rock solid on military matters, Plutarch makes sense on this occasion as the Spartans, with so much wider a front, would surely try to take advantage and fall on the flank of the enemy column just as they had done in a similar situation against the Athenians at Nemea. An idea of envelopment that is even discernible in what Diodorus has to say, reporting that Cleombrotus' line deployed into a kind of crescent shape with the intention of pushing forward on both wings. Another possibility is that the Band were drawn up as part of the rear of the main attacking column and came out from there to attack the enemy who were trying to outflank Epaminondas' men. But why would a general not put his best troops at the very front of his attack, and if he was keeping them in reserve why have them posted where it surely would have been difficult to get them out and into the action? They would have had to turn to the left, march out from the column, and then turn again to the right to be in position to assail the enemy, who, being themselves in the middle of a formation change no more difficult, would have been able to respond and not be caught unprepared, as is certainly reported as crucial here. But wherever they deployed, and the meagre and contradictory source material means any debate is rank speculation, the consensus seems to be that it was, despite their paucity of numbers, the assault led by the Sacred Band's ferocious leader Pelopidas that was decisive. However whether the stroke was part of a preconceived tactic cooked up with Epaminondas or a result of his own inspired initiative is simply unknown.

What is generally accepted is that Epaminondas did have a plan in his head from the beginning. The Theban general, hefting his shield up onto his left shoulder in the front of the line, certainly seems to have been working to a blueprint, though just like his opponent, Cleombrotus, it was his first experience of command in a major battle. He had reportedly discovered the answer to the problem of all his best men being concentrated on the left by choosing to set up his weaker centre and right flank troops at a diagonal, further to the right and rear of the Thebans preceding them on the left. 'Epaminondas was drawing his phalanx obliquely towards the left, in order that the right wing of the Spartans might be separated as far as possible from the rest of the Greeks.'[19] Another account says of Epaminondas and his men, 'the weakest he placed on the other wing and instructed them to avoid battle and withdraw gradually during the enemy's attack. So then, by arranging his phalanx in oblique formation, he planned to decide the issue of the battle by means of the wing in which were the élite.'[20] But in the battle neither of these opposing wings appears to have hardly engaged, if at all.

Epaminondas' use of the echelon formation is often claimed as the first known in history and it is regularly cited that in doing this he ensured that whilst his stronger left engaged the enemy, the weaker right, by refusing battle, avoided defeat against the numerically superior left of the army opposite them. There is even a hint that the weaker wing might have fallen back, to ensure they would not engage before the outcome was decided: 'the Boeotians retreated on one wing, but on the other engaged the enemy in double-quick time.'[21] But this is to hang an awful lot on slender and problematic evidence with either very meagre material or even worse, essential details being completely wrong.

But certainly it is clear that after their initial foray to round up the Theban 'deserters' before the clash of the cavalry nothing is reported about the movements of the soldiers of the Peloponnesian centre and left, apart from the fact that they gave way and retreated once the Laconian wing did. It seems they just did not engage to any substantial extent with the rest of the enemy line. Here there is no talk of the clashing of spear on shield, or savage battling between the lines of armoured foot. And while this may have been partly because of Epaminondas' configuration, it is equally possible most of them did not want anyway to risk participation until the outcome of the furious battle between the Spartan right and Theban left was decided. The issue of the attitude of these confederates is in fact very clearly called into question: 'the allies were one and all without heart for fighting, while some of them were not even displeased at what had taken place.'[22] Pausanias gives some support to this idea as well when he states that they were discontented, gave way whenever the enemy attacked, and that not a single one of the allies died in the battle. This should not perhaps anyway be a surprise; their failure on the battlefield had been a theme of years, going back to Haliartus in 395 at least.

There is another issue that puzzles, which is why the Spartans were not able to turn and attack the right of the Theban fifty-deep column in the flank. This side too surely would have been vulnerable with the short Theban frontage showing, unless to have done so would have meant they themselves would be threatened in their own flank by the rest of the Boeotians coming up in echelon. There may even have been Theban cavalry who had not yet left the battlefield and might threaten any exposed flank offered. Leuctra is in many ways much more difficult to picture than most of these hoplite affairs where we are looking at two lines opposite each other fighting it out as one body. On this occasion there seem to be separate sections of the line operating almost independently.

Whatever the mass of conundrums on how it happened, no one contests the upshot of the fight that the invaders were forced to retreat thoroughly beaten. Though in the wake of defeat even their discipline was not completely gone and they disdained to fly in panic as so many others might have done after the hammering they had taken. The remnant stayed together and kept their ranks as they managed to make it back over a natural ditch to their camp. There they stopped and were in sufficiently good order to hold council as to what they should do in the wake of their defeat. Their camp was probably on the slopes of Gray Slope Hill on the edge of the plain of Leuctra, and it had been chosen well as a steep incline ensured that the enemy were reluctant to attempt an assault uphill against its defences. In the ensuing council there were even some who suggested they should regroup and go back and fight once more if only to stop the Thebans putting up a victory trophy, and in order to retrieve their dead. Soberer heads were to prevail however once the scale of their losses became apparent, and also the realisation that their allies 'had no heart for more fighting' and were unlikely to prove much help.

Spartan losses had been catastrophic, there are even claims of 4,000 falling. And more important than the death of the luminaries already mentioned were the other casualties: in the reek of carnage out of 700 full Spartiates fielded at Leuctra no less than 400 of these obdurate men, who had boasted they never turned their backs on an enemy, perished; a truly devastating blow for a Sparta already in a crisis of declining manpower. These numbers killed argue that there had been a large number of peers posted round the king where the fighting was particularly bloody, or at least in the front rank where most armies placed their very best men. Against this, less than a tenth of that number suffered mortally on the Boeotian side, and even this lesser bloodletting is downplayed by one reporter who claims their casualties only amounted to 47, hardly credible considering the ferocity of the fighting.[23] The disparity was such that the Spartans had little option but to ask for a truce to recover their dead and the elated Thebans were only too happy to grant it. With relish they set up their trophy to commemorate such a famous victory, a reconstruction of which can still be visited today with its stone tower hollow inside but roofed with Spartan shields taken in battle. Yet if the Spartans had to accept defeat the polemarchs who had taken charge of the defeated army did not run for it. There was no annihilating pursuit, the Spartans held the position for some days in their camp, but they could not stay there forever, and the remnants of Cleombrotus' army, of which so much had been expected, eventually slipped away at night through the hills.

On top of this account more than one informant brings in a man we have heard of before. Jason of Pherae, whose threat did much to concentrate Spartan minds in the run up to the peace of 375, crops up again. One contemporary source makes him arrive after the blood sodden efforts on the plain of Leuctra and persuade the Thebans to offer a ceasefire to the vestige of the defeated army. The upshot was the same; the Spartans withdrew back over the most direct land route to Creusis before reaching Aegosthena in Megara. When they came in sight of its walls, where the remnants of some towers overlook the Gulf of Corinth to this day, they found the son of Agesilaus already arrived to escort them the rest of the way home. He had been dispatched after news of Leuctra arrived in Sparta. Once the reality of the impossible had sunk in, the shocked and dazed folk there acted quickly mobilising the older men, and Archidamus, who would become a king and an important player in years to come, took the last two regiments of the home army on swiftly prepared ships across the gulf to the rescue.

Another source, Diodorus Siculus, has Jason play a much more proactive role in the campaign from start to finish. This account differs in many details from the one normally accepted. According to this he arrives with 1,500 foot and 500 horse while the two armies are facing each other at Leuctra and at once arranged a truce between the two parties well before any fighting had begun. The invasion army then pulled back out of Boeotia and only when they met up with another large Peloponnesian expeditionary force headed by Archidamus did they halt and then return to Leuctra and fight a decisive battle. This narrative is generally discounted and indeed there are inherently improbable aspects to it. It is for instance bizarre that the Spartans in this explanation did not want to push to a fight straight away, despite how much the Thebans were supposedly rattled by their first sight of the vast invasion army drawn up on the plain in front of them. In addition the explanation of why the invasion army came in two parts is hardly credible, in time scale apart from anything else, and while Jason is specified as a Theban ally he is not mentioned at all in the fighting, as neither is the Spartan Archidamus except at the very outset. But as we are only too well aware of the problems with the contemporary narrative perhaps this alternative should not be dismissed out of hand. The most credible explanation for this anomaly is confusion that, because Jason and Archidamus were almost certainly concerned after the battle, their involvement is shifted for effect to the main part of the action; an act of muddling which is sadly not untypical of this historian.

Leuctra had been a famous victory, shattering once and for all the ascendancy Sparta had gained over Greece since the end of the Peloponnesian War. Her military prestige was fatally undermined and Epaminondas rightly credited with the *kudos* for the achievement, a gifted general whose achievement cannot be overstated particularly as his placing of his best troops on the left of the battleline was a true innovation. There is still a statue of him in present day Thebes, Cicero called him the 'first man' of Greece and his military influence was far reaching as Philip II (father of Alexander the Great) spent some time in Thebes as a hostage and may have learnt much from Epaminondas himself. Though it should not be forgotten in this hard fought encounter of 371 he was well aided and abetted by Pelopidas whose contribution to Theban military achievement has been less credited than that of his great friend Epaminondas.

Conclusion

The battle of Leuctra in 371 was one of the epochal events of ancient Greek history, its result and ramifications were enormous. The encounter itself is regarded by many as a masterpiece of generalship, though that view has come under some scrutiny in recent times. Over two thousand years later there are literally dozens of coffee table books published with neat battle plans explaining and extolling Epaminondas' tactics and how coolly and professionally he carried them out. It is regularly cited that he innovated tactically by making his left wing stronger to engage the best men of his opponent while he withheld his weaker right, refusing combat with the numerically superior section of the enemy army opposite them, a use of the echelon formation that is claimed to have impacted on military thinking even to the present day. But equally arguments can be made that Leuctra was not simply the child of Epaminondas' genius; as has already been observed the deep phalanx was not new in itself, even if nobody had gone so deep as fifty ranks before. There are also issues about what was really happening with the oblique approach, as two of the main sources for the encounter tell us virtually nothing of the Theban formation and the one that divulges most appears to get essential details wrong. It is indeed arguable that there is really no compelling evidence as to how the right of Epaminondas' army actually did deploy. An explanation has been advanced recently that the part of the army that ended up moving diagonally did not do so as a preconceived tactic but as a response to circumstances. Seeing the superiority of their opponents they had no choice but to behave in this way to avoid being outflanked.[1]

But if his contribution to the outcome of the battle might have been over stated it would be only the very churlish who would try to deny that Epaminondas was a gifted general who showed himself capable of real tactical innovation. All this is anyway too precise and denies the chaos and unpredictability of ancient battles. Any commander would himself have been fighting in the front line making it all but impossible to exercise any real control over matters once combat had begun and the incredible amount of dust and noise generated would have made any kind of overview and unit adjustment during the fighting extremely difficult. Yet even for those persuaded by these caveats over his contribution and disinclined to be persuaded by the great man theory of history, there is evidence that Epaminondas really did make a difference. And what he achieved in the years after Leuctra certainly justifies pushing the Theban commander high in the pantheon of ancient military greats, showing a man able to envisage the big picture in a way not common amongst his contemporaries, and who could formulate grand strategies that were not only carried out, but that achieved most of what had been intended from their inception.

This individual who started as pretty much a second string player in the freeing and revival of the stricken Thebes in the winter of 379–8 certainly made his mark seven years later, coming to the fore and staying there for a decade of extraordinary triumph and achievement. Not much over a year after the battle of Leuctra in 369 the Arcadian peoples of the Peloponnese called for assistance against the Spartan enemy and Epaminondas, again elected head of the army, heeded their call. In this, the first of five incursions by the Boeotians into the Peloponnese in the 360s, the regiments when they reached the theatre found the war had subsided of its own accord. The best efforts of King Agesilaus had made little impact against a league that despite being new seemed to have been able to pull most of its own irons out of the fire. Many in Epaminondas' position would have been content with matters as they stood, in that they had not had to risk their men and reputation in open conflict far from home. The whole enterprise might have turned out a damp squib, and at the most the only advantage taken of the concentration of forces being to take a thrash at any nearby estates of any Spartans or their remaining allies. Indeed it probably seemed to observers that it would, as the Theban led military column poured south into the heart of Laconia. Fields, houses and olive trees were burned by men who had much to pay back from when years of war had sat so devastatingly on their own native soil. That Sparta's port Gythium was attacked and great damage done was no surprise, but it was what happened next that really counted. These men who had chased the Spartans back to their own homes were going to do more. Not for them a happy trek back to the motherland with cart-loads of loot to enjoy while they regaled neighbours with tales of how the vaunted Spartiates could not face them in battle even to defend their own '*chora.*'

The Theban commander had conceived a strategy back in Arcadia when he persuaded his Peloponnesian allies to accompany him and led an invasion army west over the high Taÿgetus Mountains and into Messenia where he intended to deal the Spartans a blow they would not be able to recover from. The people of this land had for centuries provided the Spartans with an agricultural surplus which enabled them to dedicate their lives and their state to war; but now they were released from their bondage. More than this they were established in a city on the very defensible Mount Ithome where defences were thrown up that would allow them to withstand the inevitable reaction of a wounded Sparta once her liberators had departed the scene. This was a blow at the Laconians' soft underbelly, well thought out and prosecuted in the most thorough manner. The trick of inspiring Sparta's Messenian helots to revolt was not new as such; it had been a key Athenian strategy in the Peloponnesian War. Taking the war to the enemy, to get at the Spartans on home turf, was hardly unique; before the battle of Nemea the Corinthian leadership had pushed just such a strategy, but then it had not been successful. In what Epaminondas achieved when he did, he surely was.

If this was the jewel in the crown of Epaminondas' achievements, it was not the only thing the Thebans did to hem their old enemy in. Also they backed the Arcadians in building their great new metropolis of Megalopolis; they sustained the Mantineans who had reincorporated their polity very soon after Leuctra despite the best efforts of Agesilaus; and they would intervene in Achaea and garrison places like Sicyon and Pellene. These were all important parts of the strategy of weakening Sparta and restricting her to a sphere of influence that would come nowhere near Boeotia again. But it was the permanent liberation of Messenia that really counted that cut at the economic base of Imperial Sparta. Epaminondas knew that deprived of their produce they could never again be a danger in the way she had been in the past. The walls that defended the liberated community can still be seen snaking up the hills round the wonderful site of Messenia today, and were in their way as important in the history of the Hellenes as the much more famous long walls between Athens and Piraeus.

That Epaminondas was the man to lead the way in this peninsular revolution should not be a surprise. He is even recorded as persuading his fellow citizens to invest in a navy to adventure into the Aegean and though this initiative did not come to much, that he was the man who sponsored the attempt says plenty about his imagination and ambition. This was a corollary of his strategy against Sparta but this time aimed against Thebes' other great potential rival Athens. Sparta without Messenia could never be a danger again and Athens without her naval hegemony would also never be able to offer any threat. The potential for the Attic city to hurt Theban interests had been shown recently enough. When Epaminondas made his decisive drive into the Peloponnese it had been against a backdrop of a hostile Athens. Iphicrates had led men against them during the first invasion, and though this had been largely ineffective, Athens had looked capable of being a useful friend for Sparta in the 360s.

Epaminondas did not have very long to last. He died in battle in 362 at Mantinea, again leading an army to victory against the Spartans. But this time the crucial factor was that this combat, though still against the old enemy, took place far from Boeotia. The Spartans that were overcome on that field of combat were a local power bloodily disputing in their own back yard, something very different from the community that had crushed Imperial Athens and bullied the Hellenic world in the years since the end of the Peloponnesian War.

It was not just the efforts of the Thebans which brought about the downfall of the Spartans. Partly it was self inflicted – it was the way they were. Nothing is more telling than the comment in the *Anabasis* that even at a drinking party if a Spartan was present he would automatically expect to take the chair. This kind of assumption of superiority was never going to be easy to take for peoples like the Greeks, never temperamentally inclined to take second place to anyone. And, of course, it was not just the impression they gave but what they did. Two events are crucially indicative. Firstly, the Phoebidas coup that led to the garrisoning of the *Cadmeia* at Thebes. This for short term advantage turned most of the elite of Boeotia into blood deep enemies who would eventually turn out a significant nemesis. Where before Thebes had been divided between pro-Spartans and anti-Spartans that act of aggression turned the whole place against her. And in Boeotia Thebes' community rivals, who had stood as friends to Sparta in the past, were incorporated into a League that ended sustaining her enemy. Secondly, the abortive descent on Piraeus that drove Athens into Theban arms forced together two places with plenty of bitter history and ensured the hostility of the former who if better handled might have become a Spartan ally or at least neutral in the coming war. Spartans just seemed temperamentally incapable of effectively playing on the divisions between the Greeks that would have allowed her a much more extended hegemony. Any Spartan leader who seemed to be displaying a modicum of subtlety in his relations with the world outside the Eurotas valley could soon find himself viewed with suspicion by his followers, as illustrated by Pausanias in his dealings with the Athenians in 403 and Cleombrotus before the battle of Leuctra. Without a leadership that might orchestrate an effective divide and rule policy the only way to have remained top dog was to have deployed the sort of military power Sparta just did not possess.

Nor was it just in relations with fellow Hellenes that the Spartans showed a self destructive tendency. After the great victory over Athens in 404, itself achieved on the back of Persian gold, they had alienated their backer by intriguing with Cyrus and interfering in Anatolia, which had backfired hugely by driving the Achaemenids into funding in the 390s both an anti-Spartan axis and a revitalised Athens. Even after the King's Peace of 387 when they seemed once more to be the beneficiary of crucial Persian largesse they did not fully learn their lesson. Although there is little to tell of Spartan-Persian relations during the next ten years there are tantalising clues. A record derived from Ephorus details a Spartan alliance with a Persian admiral called Glos who had risen in revolt against his royal master. This officer decided he was already tarnished by association with his rebellious father-in-law Tiribazus, so following his downfall also took up arms against Artaxerxes. Glos was at the time in charge of the fleet involved in the Persian war against Evagoras of Cyprus and was 'well supplied with money and soldiers' but decided to seek help from other quarters.[2] To this end he approached the king of Egypt and Sparta. He promised the latter money and they agreed to the alliance. In fact all this came to naught as the Persian admiral was assassinated and the revolt fizzled out. But this episode, though it has often been 'glossed' over by historians or assigned to a later date, still once again shows the Spartan proclivity to alienate the great power in Asia whose support they so much needed.[3] Their ineptitude in their handling of Persian relations is difficult to understand, unless again it reflects a plurality of influences within the Spartan state, with kings like Agesilaus and Cleombrotus, great figures like Lysander and Antalcidas, and even individual ephors with axes to grind, all pulling in different directions and making her overall foreign policy look inconsistent and undependable.

Also though the Spartans had always seemed a community of granite will who relished taking on anybody who contested their preeminence, there had been, since the beginning of the fourth century, an erosion at the heart, with signs showing then, when she was at the top of a slope, that she would soon find herself sliding down. The martial muscle she could flex even then was a wasting asset, and their vaunted battlefield edge under threat. Certainly there had been signs of decline showing even before Leuctra. They had been frustrated in the invasions of Boeotia and then beaten on the battlefield at Tegyra. More fundamentally, declining manpower meant the roll of full Spartiates trained through the *agoge* to be the bravest and most adept infantrymen of the day had already fallen to only a few thousand. So the numbers of armoured hoplites Sparta could put in the field was waning, at the same time as her allies seemed less and less inclined to fight and die for her cause. This also came at a time when ambition had seen her armies marching far and wide, from the traditional stomping grounds of the Peloponnese and Boeotia, into Chalcidice, Corcyra and even Asia. In the end it turned out Sparta just did not have the military chops to take on so much, to spread so thin.

In the short run this meant for Sparta, in the decades after Leuctra, a contraction back to a position as essentially a peninsular player. In the long run the result was she would not stand shoulder to shoulder with Athens and Thebes in the frontline against the juggernaut of a Macedonian future. No grizzled Spartiates fought alongside the Sacred Band at the epochal battle of Chaeronea in 338, when it is possible they might have made a difference. She would fight again, but only seven years later, and alone, to be swatted by a mere lieutenant of Alexander the Great near the very city of Megalopolis that the Thebans had encouraged as a restraint on Laconian power. An occasion when another Spartan king would die, falling at the forefront of defeat just as had so often been the case with military leaders in the years of her supremacy. Good sense could often have been in question, but heroism seldom was.

Notes

Chapter 1: Alcibiades' Return

1. See F Welsh *Building the Trireme* (London, 1988).
2. For a more favourable view of Astyochus' activities see C Falkner, 'Astyochus, Sparta's Incompetent Navarch?' in *Phoenix* 53 (1999) pp 206–221.
3. Diodorus Siculus, *Universal History V*, translated by C H Oldfather (London and Cambridge, Massachusetts, 1950) 13.38.6, has the Spartan fleet numbering 83 and the Athenian fleet 60.
4. Again Diodorus Siculus, *Universal History V* 13.39.3, has a different number, 88. One suspects this is as much due to Diodorus' notoriously bad reputation as a poor copyist than any real discrepancy.
5. Diodorus Siculus, *Universal History V* 13.39.4.
6. Though Diodorus has many faults the level of detail (*Universal History V* 13.39–40) here seems to vouch for its credibility and may be used to supplement Thucydides *The Peloponnesian War*, translated by B Jowett (London and Cambridge, Massachusetts, 1881) 8.104–6. See further D Kagan, *The Fall of the Athenian Empire* (New York, 1987) pp 218–227.
7. Diodorus Siculus, *Universal History V* 13.40.6.
8. *Ibid*, 13.45.9–10.
9. Both Diodorus Siculus, *Universal History V* 13.46.2 and Plutarch, *Alcibiades*, translated by B Perrin and included in *Parallel Lives* IV (London and Cambridge, Massachusetts, 1916) 27.2 stress Alcibiades was there by chance but Plutarch does not mention a prearranged signal only that Alcibiades raised Athenian colours. One suspects some poetic licence in these accounts.
10. Diodorus Siculus, *Universal History V* 13.46.4.
11. Xenophon, *Hellenica*, translated by C L Brownson and included in *The works of Xenophon I* (London and Cambridge, Massachusetts, 1918) 1.1.11 gives the Spartan fleet as numbering only 60. However Diodorus' account of the battle is now regarded as preferable. For further details see R J Littman, 'The Strategy of the Battle of Cyzicus' in *TAPA* 99 (1968) pp 265–72.
12. Diodorus Siculus, *Universal History V* 13.50.1.
13. *Ibid*, 13.51.4.
14. *Ibid*, 13.51.7.
15. Xenophon, *Hellenica*, 1.1.23. This same historian also suggests there were only 60 ships lost in the fight but certainly accepts that the whole fleet was eliminated, perhaps there were

ships not training in the harbour but left in the port of Cyzicus that were captured when the Athenians took the city.

16. Xenophon makes no mention of this peace offer which is reported in Diodorus Siculus *Universal History V* 13.52, Cornelius Nepos *Lives of Eminent Commanders*, translated by J. S. Watson (London, 1886) *Alcibiades* 5 and Justin, *Epitome of the Philippic History of Pompeius Trogus*, translated by J S Watson (London, 1853) 5 4. Thus there seem no reasonable grounds to doubt it and seems an astonishing omission by Xenophon for which he has rightly been taken to task.

17. Diodorus Siculus, *Universal History V* 13.52.4–6.

18. *Ibid*, 13.69.1–3.

19. *Ibid*, 13.70.4.

20. Diodorus Siculus *Universal History V* 13.71 which derives from *Hellenica Oxyrhynchia* translated by J Marincola (Stuttgart, 1993) 4 mentions Clazomenae. Xenophon *Hellenica* 1.5.11 has him at Phocaea. Just to complicate matters Plutarch *Alcibiades* 35.4 says he went to Caria to raise funds though this is thought to refer to earlier activities.

21. Diodorus Siculus, *Universal History V* 13.71.3–4.

22. *Ibid*, 13.72.1.

23. *Ibid*, 13.72.4.

24. See Diodorus Siculus, *Universal History V* 13.74.3.

Chapter 2: Lysander Triumphant

1. One current commentator (D Kagan, *The Fall of the Athenian Empire*) sees him as a peace party man and friend of Lysander's enemies.

2. Diodorus Siculus, *Universal History V* 13.76.2

3. *Ibid*, 13.76.4.

4. This is Diodorus' account *Universal History V* 13.76.5. In contrast Xenophon *Hellenica* 1.6.13 has Callicratidas take Methymna by force.

5. Xenophon, *Hellenica* 1.6.14.

6. Diodorus Siculus, *Universal History V* 13.77.4.

7. *Ibid*, 13.77.3.

8. This alternative version is from Xenophon *Hellenica* 1.6.15–18. See also D Kagan *The Fall of the Athenian Empire* pp 335–7 who prefers Xenophon.

9. Diodorus Siculus, *Universal History V* 13.79.1.

10. *Ibid*, 13.79.6.

11. These details are from Xenophon *Hellenica* 1.19–23. Diodorus' account cuts off at the beginning of the siege (*Universal History V* 13.79) and does not resume until the dispatch of the Athenian rescue fleet at 13.97.

12. Diodorus Siculus, *Universal History V* 13.97.3 numbers the Spartan fleet at 140.

13. Diodorus Siculus reports he 'dreamed that he was in Athens and the theatre was crowded, and that he and six of the other generals were playing the *Phoenician Women* of Euripides, while their competitors were performing the *Suppliants*; and that it resulted in a "Cadmeian victory" for them and they all died, just as did those who waged the campaign against Thebes. When the seer heard this, he disclosed that seven of the generals would be slain. Since the omens revealed victory, the generals forbade any word going out to the others about their own death but they passed the news of the victory disclosed by the omens throughout the whole army.' (Diodorus Siculus, *Universal History V* 13.97.6–7)

14. Diodorus Siculus, *Universal History V* 13.98.5.
15. This is from D Kagan, *The Fall of the Athenian Empire* pp 341–353 and his description of the battle.
16. Diodorus Siculus, *Universal History V* 13.98.4
17. *Ibid*, 13.99.1
18. Xenophon, *Hellenica* 1.6.33. In reality both our main sources for Arginusae, Xenophon and Diodorus, are unsatisfactory. Xenophon is sketchy while Diodorus has a fuller account but one which is at times implausible and also full of obvious mistakes (e.g. he calls Thrasyllus Thrasybulus).
19. Diodorus Siculus, *Universal History V*, 13.100.4
20. Again no source is satisfactory on the generals' trial. For an interesting account see A Andrewes, 'The Arginousai Trial' in *Phoenix* 28 (1974) pp 112–122 who, for instance, points out the association of Theramenes and Thrasybulus with Alcibiades in contrast to the generals appointed after the latter's exile.
21. No less a personage than Aristotle reports this – Aristotle, *Athenian Constitution*, translated by H Rackham and included in *Aristotle in 23 Volumes, Vol. 20* (London and Cambridge, Massachusetts, 1952) 34.1.
22. Diodorus Siculus, *Universal History V* 13.104.4.
23. Plutarch, *Lysander*, translated by B Perrin and included in *Parallel Lives IV* (London and Cambridge, Massachusetts, 1916) 9.3, suggests this.
24. *Ibid*, 9.4.
25. Once more neither Xenophon's nor Diodorus' account of the battle is satisfactory. For contrasting academic views see C Ehrhardt, 'Xenophon and Diodorus on Aegospotami' in *Phoenix* 24 (1970) pp 225–228 who prefers Diodorus *contra* B S Strauss, 'Aegospotami Reexamined' in *AJP* 104 (1983) pp 24–35 who would seek to reinstate Xenophon's primacy. For an interesting aside on the topography see further B S Strauss, 'A Note on the Topography and Tactics of the Battle of Aegospotami' in *AJP* 108 (1987) pp 741–745.
26. At around this time Diodorus has an odd story of Lysander sending Gylippus, the hero of Syracuse, back to Sparta with booty and money. Gylippus embezzled 300 of the 1,500 talents. However the money was marked and he was found out by the ephors and fled into exile being condemned to death in his absence. Diodorus Siculus, *Universal History V* 13.106 8–9. It is curious how little attention this tale has received. For instance the usually meticulous D Kagan, *The Fall of the Athenian Empire* fails to mentions it at all.
27. Details are from Lysias, *Against Agoratus*, translated by W R M Lamb and included in *Lysias*, (London and Cambridge, 1930).

Chapter 3: Liberation and Tyranny

1. It is unclear from the fragmentary and contradictory sources when all this took place in 404 and some argue for a later date in September. For a recent discussion of the evidence see, for instance, R Stem 'The Thirty at Athens in the summer of 404' in *Phoenix* 57 (2003) pp 18–34, though he postulates the existence of two different groups of Thirty, an idea first put forward by J A R Munro in 'The Constitution of Dracontides' in *CQ* 32 (1938) pp 152–166. In this he suggests that there was a group of Thirty elected early in the year to draft a constitution and then another group of Thirty established under the direction of Lysander to run the constitution. This admittedly obviates some of the chronological confusion but seems unnecessary, convoluted and unlikely.

2. For the makeup of the constitution see Lysias, *Against Eratosthenes*, translated by W R M Lamb and included in *Lysias*, (London and Cambridge, 1930) 12.76. Again the chronology of the institution of the Ten at Piraeus and its relationship with the Thirty is obscure. However in this we do agree with J A R Munro in his earlier article 'Theramenes against Lysander' in *CQ* 32 (1938) pp 18–26 when he argues that Lysander is likely to have imposed this when he sailed into the Piraeus early in 404 and thus almost certainly predates the Thirty.

   Interestingly both Munro's articles were written (or at least published) in 1938 and clearly show the influence of appeasement which was, of course, the dominant political trend in Britain at that time; a warning, perhaps, to consider treating academic articles with some scepticism.

3. Again the chronology of the garrison's arrival is completely obscure.

4. Xenophon, *Hellenica* 2.3.52–53. It has been argued that Xenophon was present at the debate and heard the speeches though he may have been too young to be a member of the assembly in circa 404 BC. However he probably had an informant who may have reported some of the actual words to him. For a summary of the arguments see S Usher 'Xenophon, Critias and Theramenes' in *JHS* 88 (1968) pp 128–135.

5. Quite what the Piraeus Ten had been doing while Thrasybulus' insurrection had occurred is unclear – presumably keeping their heads down.

6. The only source for this trial is his namesake Pausanias, the Greek traveller and writer of the second century AD. Pausanias, *Pausanias' Description of Greece* translated by W H S Jones and H A Ormerod in 4 Volumes (London and Cambridge, 1918) 3.5.2.

7. Xenophon, *Hellenica*, 3.3.5.

Chapter 4: The Hobbling Prince

1. Plutarch, *Agesilaus*, 2.2 translated by B Perrin and included in *Parallel Lives V* (London and Cambridge, Massachusetts, 1917).

2. Xenophon, *Hellenica* 3.2.26.

3. The accounts of the campaigns are Xenophon *Hellenica* 3.2.21–31 and Diodorus Siculus *Universal History VI* translated by C H Oldfather (London and Cambridge, Massachusetts, 1954) 14.17.4–12 and 14.34.1. For what it is worth *Pausanias' Description of Greece* 3.8.3–6 has Agis as the king in charge of the campaigns but adds little else. For a view of the context of the war and Sparta's aims see C Falkner, 'Sparta and the Elean War ca 401/400 BC; Revenge or Imperialism?' in *Phoenix* 50 (1996) pp 17–25.

4. Herodotus, *The Histories*, translated by A D Godley (London and Cambridge, 1920) 6.58–59 talks about the rites on the death of a king.

5. Plutarch, *Moralia* 348 F translated by F C Babbitt and included in Plutarch, *Moralia, Volume IV* (London and Cambridge, Massachusetts, 1936).

6. Implied in Plutarch, *Agesilaus*, 6.3.

7. Diodorus Siculus, *Universal History VI*, 14.37.3.

8. *Ibid*, 14.36.3.

9. See S M Rusch, *Sparta at War, Strategy, Tactics and Campaigns 550–362 BC* (Barnsley, 2011) p 156.

10. Diodorus Siculus, *Universal History VI*, 14.36.1.

11. Xenophon, *Hellenica* 3.1.14.

12. Scepsis' claim to fame is that Aristotle's library was there before being moved to Pergamum and Alexandria.
13. Xenophon, *Hellenica* 3.2.7.
14. Polyaenus, *Stratagems*, translated by R Shepherd (London 1793) 2.1.9 (*Agesilaus*).
15. The two versions of the Battle of Sardis are to be found in Xenophon *Hellenica* 3.4.20–24 *contra Hellenica Oxyrhynchia* 11 (6).4–6 and Diodorus Siculus, *Universal History VI* 14.80.1–6. They are completely irreconcilable. Up until the discovery of the Oxyrynchus manuscript in 1906 Xenophon's version had primacy but this view has gone out of favour. See for instance G L Cawkwell, *Xenophon, A History of my Times* (London, 1979) and in particular pp 405–6. But in more recent years Xenophon has regained some ground – see now J K Anderson, 'The Battle of Sardis in 395 B C' in *California Studies in Classical Antiquity* 7 (1974) pp 27–53; V J Gray, 'Two Different Approaches to the Battle of Sardis in 395 BC. Xenophon Hellenica 3.4.20–24 and Hellenica Oxyrhynchia 11 (6).4–6' in *California Studies in Classical Antiquity* 12 (1979) pp 183–200; and G. Wylie, 'Agesilaus and the Battle of Sardis' in *Klio* 74 (1992) pp 118–130. They all argue for Xenophon's probable first-hand military knowledge of the campaign and the fact that for all his alleged bias towards Agesilaus his version of the battle is much less laudatory of him than the alternative account inflating what was probably no more than a minor skirmish into a major battle.
16. Plutarch, *Agesilaus*, 10.5.
17. The information on this campaign is from the *Hellenica Oxyrhynchia* Fragment 24. Both Xenophon and Diodorus Siculus have *lacunae* on this period.
18. Xenophon, *Hellenica*, 4.1.37.

Chapter 5: A Year of Battles
1. *Hellenica Oxyrhynchia*, 21.2.
2. Plutarch, *Lysander*, 8.4.
3. Diodorus Siculus, *Universal History VI* 14.13.7.
4. For some interesting views on Lysander see A Andrewes, 'Two Notes on Lysander' in *Phoenix* 25 (1971) pp 206–226 and in particular W K Prentice, 'The Character of Lysander' in *AJA* 38 (1934) pp 37–42 who while providing a useful corrective perhaps goes too far in praising the general.
5. Plutarch, *Lysander* 30.2.
6. For detailed discussion of the sources for the whole of the Haliartus episode see H D Westlake, 'The Sources for the Spartan Debacle at Haliartus' in *Phoenix* 39 No 2 (1985) pp 119–133.
7. For two interesting views on the origins of the Corinthian War see S Perlman, 'The Causes and the Outbreak of the Corinthian War' in *CQ* 14 (1964) pp 64–81 and J E Lendon, 'The Oxyrynchus Historian and the Origins of the Corinthian War' in *Historia* 38 (1989) pp 300–313.
8. Xenophon, *Hellenica* 4.2.18.
9. *Ibid*, 4.2.19.
10. Thus J K Anderson, *Military Theory and Practice in the Age of Xenophon*, (Los Angeles, 1970) p 145.
11. V D Hanson, *Ripples of Battle* (New York, 2003) p 198.
12. Diodorus Siculus, *Universal History VI* 14.83.1.

Chapter 6: On Land and Sea

1. Plutarch, *Agesilaus* 16.3.
2. J K Lendon *Soldiers and Ghosts* (Connecticut, 2005) p 98.
3. As Heraclea had been taken by Medius shortly before it is somewhat puzzling it appears to be back in Spartan hands. For a solution to the problem see E Harrison 'A Problem in the Corinthian War' in *CQ* 7 (1913) p 132.
4. Plutarch, *Agesilaus* 17.3.
5. Xenophon, *Hellenica* 4.3.14.
6. Xenophon, *Agesilaus*, translated by E C Marchant and G W Bowersock, and included in *The works of Xenophon VII* (London and Cambridge, Massachusetts, 1925) 2.9.
7. Plutarch, *Agesilaus* 18.2.
8. *Ibid*, 18.2.
9. *Ibid*, 18.1. See also Xenophon, *Hellenica* 4.3.16 'how it proved to be like no other of the battles of our time.'
10. Though given the nature of his inadequate description of Leuctra and the fact that it was a Spartan defeat this assertion should be treated with some caution.
11. Plutarch, *Agesilaus* 18.3.
12. *Ibid*, 18.4.
13. See for instance Polyaenus, *Stratagems* 2.1.19. (*Agesilaus*) and Frontinus, *Stratagems*, translated by C E Bennett (London and Cambridge, 1925) 2.6.6.
14. Xenophon, *Hellenica* 4.3.19. and Xenophon, *Agesilaus* 2.12. 'In the end some of the Thebans broke through and reached Helicon, but many fell during the retreat.'
15. Plutarch, *Lycurgus*, translated by B Perrin and included in *Parallel Lives I* (London and Cambridge, Massachusetts, 1914) 22.5.
16. For a detailed study of the topography of the battle see W K Pritchett, *Studies in Ancient Greek Topography II* (Los Angeles, 1969) pp 77–89.
17. Plutarch, *Agesilaus* 19.1.
18. Justin, *Epitome of the Philippic History of Pompeius Trogus* 6.1.
19. Cornelius Nepos, *Lives of Eminent Commanders* (*Conon*) 9.2.
20. Justin, *Epitome of the Philippic History of Pompeius Trogus* 6.2.
21. Diodorus Siculus, *Universal History VI*, 14.81.4.
22. Cornelius Nepos, *Lives of Eminent Commanders* (Conon) 9.4.
23. Diodorus Siculus, *Universal History VI*, 14.83.6–7.
24. *Ibid*, 14.84.4.
25. Xenophon, *Hellenica*, 4.8.8.
26. Diodorus Siculus, *Universal History VI*, 14.84.6–7.

Chapter 7: A Corinthian Revolution and an Athenian General

1. Who exactly was involved in the massacre in terms of political factions is very difficult to ascertain given the thinness of our sources (Xenophon, Diodorus and some later extraneous sources). Similarly when the merger between Corinth and Argos takes place is also difficult to pin down. Some commentators have suggested it took part in two stages, see G Griffith, 'The Union of Corinth and Argos', (392–386 BC) in *Historia* vol. 1, no. 2 (1950) pp 236–256. This point of view was challenged by C Tuplin, 'The date of the Union of Corinth and Argos' in *CQ* 32(1982) pp 75–83 who argues that Xenophon is essentially right. However

Griffith has had more recent supporters, for this see M Whitby 'The Union of Corinth and Argos: A reconsideration' in *Historia* vol. 33 no. 3 (1984) pp 295–308. In reality the evidence is so thin that it will bear both interpretations. See also C D Hamilton, 'The Politics of the Revolution in Corinth 395–386 BC' in *Historia* vol. 21 no. 1 (1972) pp 21–37 and D Kagan, 'Corinthian Politics and the Revolution of 392 BC' in *Historia* vol. 11, no. 4 (1962) pp 447–457.

2. See S M Rusch, S M, *Sparta at War, Strategy, Tactics and Campaigns 550–362 BC.*

3. 'People who are ignorant of the danger also appear brave, and they are not far removed from those of a sanguine temper, but are inferior inasmuch as they have no self-reliance while these have. Hence also the sanguine hold their ground for a time; but those who have been deceived about the facts fly if they know or suspect that these are different from what they supposed, as happened to the Argives when they fell in with the Spartans and took them for Sicyonians.' Aristotle, *Nicomachean Ethics*, translated by H Rackham and included in *Aristotle in 23 Volumes, Vol. 19* (London and Cambridge, Massachusetts, 1934) 3.8.5.

4. Plutarch, *Apophthegms or Sayings of Kings and Commanders*, translated by E Hinton (Boston, 1878) *Iphicrates, 5.*

5. Polyaenus, *Stratagems*, 3.9.49. (Iphicrates).

6. S Yalichev, *Mercenaries of the ancient world* (London, 1997) p 119.

7. His first affray is described in Diodorus Siculus, *Universal History* VI, 14.86.1–6 and the second at 14.91.2–3.

Chapter 8: Attempts at War and Peace

1. Diodorus Siculus, *Universal History VI*, 14.85.4.

2. Xenophon omits all mention of these talks at Sparta which we learn from the extant speeches of Andocides (a delegate from Athens) an omission he has been heavily criticised for. Some scholars have argued for Sparta occurring before Sardis (see for instance J G DeVoto 'Agesilaus, Antalcidas and the failed peace of 392/391 BC' in *Classical Philology* 81 (1986) p 196 and R Seager 'Thrasybulus, Conon and Athenian Imperialism 396–386 BC' in *JHS* 87 (1967) p 105) though the evidence is tenuous either way.

3. Diodorus Siculus, *Universal History VI*, 14.99.1.

4. Xenophon, *Hellenica*, 4.8.20–22 contrasts Diphridas' behaviour strongly with that of Thibron; perhaps not surprisingly as Xenophon had history with Thibron who had apparently threatened him with execution during the *Anabasis* (Xenophon, *Anabasis*, translated by C L Brownson and included in *The works of Xenophon III* (London and Cambridge, Massachusetts, 1922) 7.6.43 ff.). As for Rhodes this is Xenophon's first mention of affairs there. Diodorus Siculus, *Universal History VI*, 14.79, 14.97 has further fragmentary information but it is slightly different from Xenophon. See also The Hobbling Prince.

5. For a summary of the chronological problems of this period see G Cawkwell 'The imperialism of Thrasybulus' in *CQ* 26 (1976) pp 270–277.

6. Xenophon *Hellenica* 4.8.31

Chapter 9: The King's Peace

1. Xenophon, *Hellenica*, 5.1.31.

2. Plutarch, *Artaxerxes*, translated by B Perrin and included in *Parallel Lives* XI (London and Cambridge, Massachusetts, 1926) 22.1.

3. J Adams, 'Antalcidas crushes liberty by deceit' in Adam's Defense No 42 Liberty Letters (1786)

4. See G L Cawkwell, 'Agesilaus and Sparta' in *CQ* 26 (1976) in particular pp 66–71. Teleutias is quoted by Xenophon, *Hellenica*, 5.1.14–18 criticising accepting Persian aid.

5. Plutarch, *Artaxerxes*, 22.2.

6. Xenophon, *Hellenica*, 4.5.18.

7. Diodorus Siculus, *Universal History VI*, 15.5.4.mentions five villages whilst Xenophon, *Hellenica* 5.2.7. claims there are four. Diodorus is the only source to mention the Mantineans' appeal to Athens. It also has the river not running through Mantinea but by it and Agesipolis diverts it into the polis. As G E A Underhill *A commentary on the Hellenica of Xenophon* (Oxford, 1900) p 180 notes, this can be possibly reconciled by the fact that the later reconstituted Mantinea had the river some distance from it so Diodorus and Plutarch made their accounts square with what they then knew of Mantinea.

8. Amyntas' appeal is only recorded in Diodorus Siculus, *Universal History VI*, 15.19.2–3 (who in turn does not mention the mission from Acanthus and Apollonia)! Xenophon chooses not to mention it as such though he is referred to in the ambassadors from the other city's speech. The reason for Xenophon's reticence is possibly because Amyntas was not party to the King's Peace and therefore the Spartans' subsequent support of him was not technically a legal requirement under the terms of the Peace which Apollonia and Acanthus were. See further G L Cawkwell, *Xenophon, A History of my Times* p 262 and P A Cartledge *Agesilaus and the Crisis of Sparta* (Baltimore, 1987) p 373.

9. Xenophon quotes liberally from the alleged speech of the Acanthian ambassador to the assembly leading one to wonder whether he was actually present.

10. Xenophon, *Hellenica*, 5.2.15.

11. *Ibid*, 5.2.18.

12. *Ibid*, 5.2.24.

13. Diodorus Siculus, *Universal History VII*, translated by C L Sherman (London and Cambridge, Massachusetts, 1952) 15.20 in an admittedly condensed version has Phoebidas in command of the whole expeditionary force.

14. Xenophon, *Hellenica*, 5.2.26.

15. *Ibid*, 5.2.28.

16. See for instance G L Cawkwell, *Xenophon, A History of my Times*, p 266.

17. Xenophon, *Hellenica*, 5.3.7.

18. See J F Lazenby, *The Spartan Army* (Barnsley, 2012) p 22.

19. Xenophon, *Hellenica* 5.2.8.

20. *Ibid*, 5.3.20.

21. Xenophon, *Hellenica*, 5.3.10 makes the case that Phlious acted as it did because they did not think Sparta would allow both their kings to be out of the city campaigning at the same time. Although this is mentioned by Herodotus, *Histories*, 5.75 there were several historical precedents for this happening; for instance in 395 king Pausanias had campaigned in Boeotia whilst Agesilaus was in Asia. And in any case Phlious was no great distance (60 to 70 miles) from Sparta.

22. Xenophon, *Hellenica*, 5.3.16.

23. *Ibid*, 5.3.26.

24. An event which some historians have regarded as disastrous. Their reasoning is that the League with its members comprising the most Hellenised cities of Macedonia with the

north Greek cities may well have stopped or at least curtailed the subsequent rise of Philip II of Macedon and all that his policy would eventually entail, namely the end of freedom for mainland Greece.

Chapter 10: Theban Campaigns

1. Xenophon, *Hellenica*, 5.4.3 claims there were only seven exiles involved.
2. Plutarch, *Pelopidas*, translated by B Perrin and included in *Parallel Lives V* (London and Cambridge, Massachusetts, 1917) 9.5.
3. *Ibid*, 9.7.
4. Plutarch has a lengthy version of the Theban affair in his *Discourse concerning the Daemon of Socrates*. Not significantly different (though Pelopidas plays a more minor part) in this account Charon hid the truth from no one.
5. The question of the Athenian response and the subsequent trial has been the subject of much academic dispute. See for instance discussion of this episode and Xenophon's inconsistency with Diodorus Siculus, *Universal History VII*, 15.25–27 and indeed Dinarchus, Minor Attic Orators in two volumes, 2, translated by J O Burtt, (London and Cambridge, Massachusetts 1962), Against Demosthenes, 1.39 confirms Diodorus' account. See further G L Cawkwell, *Xenophon, A History of my Times* p 282 and R B Strassler, *The Landmark Xenophon's Hellenica* (New York, 2009) p 205.
6. Diodorus Siculus, *Universal History* VII, 15.27.1.
7. *Ibid*, 15.27.1.
8. Xenophon, *Hellenica*, 5.4.13.
9. Diodorus Siculus, *Universal History* VII, 15.27.3.
10. For an explanation of why there appear to be three harmosts at Thebes see H W Parke, 'Herippidas, Harmost at Thebes' in *CQ* 21 (1927) pp 159–165.
11. Again this Athenian garrison has led to some scholarly dispute. Some see it as confirmation of the official help that Athens had sent so promptly whilst others see it as unofficial or posted there before an official request for help was received by Athens. However, as has been pointed out by G L Cawkwell, *Xenophon, A History of my Times* p 283, Chabrias cannot have been one of the two renegade generals as he is in command much later and therefore not punished as those two were. See further R B Strassler, *The Landmark Xenophon's Hellenica* p 378.
12. So P A Cartledge, *Agesilaus and the Crisis of Sparta* p 136.
13. Plutarch, *Agesilaus*, 24.3.
14. Xenophon, *Hellenica*, 5.4.32.
15. *Ibid*, 5.4 .32.
16. For very different interpretations of Sphodrias' actions see P A Cartledge, *Agesilaus and the Crisis of Sparta* pp 156–9, G E A Underhill, *A commentary on the Hellenica of Xenophon* pp 204–5, G L Cawkwell, *Xenophon, A History of my Times* pp 285–289 and R B Strassler, *The Landmark Xenophon's Hellenica* pp 208–11.
17. Diodorus Siculus, *Universal History* VII, 15.31.1.
18. *Ibid*, 15.31.2–3.
19. Xenophon, *Hellenica*, 5.4.39.
20. *Ibid*, 5.4.40.
21. Cornelius Nepos, *Lives of Eminent Commanders*, (Chabrias) 12.1.

22. Polyaenus, *Stratagems* 2.5.2. (Gorgidas)
23. *Ibid* 2.1.11. (Agesilaus)
24. *Ibid* 2.1.11. (Agesilaus)
25. *Ibid* 2.1.12. (Agesilaus)
26. *Ibid* 2.1.12. (Agesilaus)
27. Diodorus Siculus, *Universal History* VII, 15.34.2.
28. Plutarch, *Pelopidas*, 18.2.
29. *Ibid*, 17.2.
30. *Ibid*, 17.1.
31. *Ibid*, 17.3.
32. Plutarch, *Agesilaus*, 26.2.
33. Indeed not even the date of the treaty is absolutely assured. Some scholars think it belongs in 374 rather than 375. See for example N G L Hammond, *A History of Greece to 322 BC* (Oxford, 1959) pp 490–1.

Chapter 11: A Maritime Confederacy

1. Though in understanding the process, Xenophon is of no help as he conspicuously declines to mention the confederation at all, a failure for which he has persistently been taken to task.
2. Diodorus Siculus, *Universal History VII*, 15.34.3.
3. *Ibid*, 15.34.4.
4. *Ibid*, 15.34.6.
5. For Phocion see L A Tritle, *Phocion the Good* (London, 1988).
6. Polyaenus, *Stratagems*, 3.11.11. (Chabrias)
7. Xenophon, *Hellenica*, 5.4.61.
8. See Polyaenus, *Stratagems*, 3.11.6. (Chabrias)
9. Cornelius Nepos, *Lives of Eminent Commanders* 13.1. (Timotheus)
10. Polyaenus, *Stratagems* 3.10.4. (Timotheus)
11. An indication of the difficulty in relying on a historian like Polyaenus is that he has the crescent retreating story twice in near adjacent chapters, *Stratagems*, 3.10.13 and 3.10.17 which clearly seem to be referring to the same action.
12. Diodorus Siculus, *Universal History VII*, 15.45.3.
13. Xenophon is his most obtuse and unknowable whilst Diodorus, not the most reliable of copyists, is at his most garbled here. For a discussion of the problems of this period see for instance G L Cawkwell, 'Notes on the Peace of 375/4' in *Historia* 12 (1963) pp 84–95 or V J Gray 'The Years 375 to 371 BC: A Case Study in the Reliability of Diodorus Siculus and Xenophon' in *CQ* 30 (1980) pp 306–326.
14. Xenophon, *Hellenica*, 6.2.3 gives the number of ships as 60 while Diodorus Siculus, *Universal History VII*, 15.47.1 has 65. Both thankfully agree on 1,500 soldiers. Xenophon fails to mention the two earlier Spartan fleets under Aristocrates and Alcidas.
15. Xenophon, *Hellenica*, 6.2.6.
16. Iphicrates' successful voyage is derived from Xenophon *Hellenica* 6.2.13–17 whereas in contrast Diodorus Siculus, *Universal History VII*, 15.47.7 not only has Timotheus reappointed and in joint command with Iphicrates but say they achieved 'nothing worth mentioning'!!

Chapter 12: A Plain in Boeotia

1. Xenophon, *Hellenica*, 6.3.5.
2. Plutarch *Agesilaus* 28.1–3. Xenophon has it that the Thebans signed the treaty in the name of the city but then came back the following day and demanded to sign in the name of the Boeotian Confederacy which Agesilaus refused to let them do saying they could withdraw from the treaty completely; though it is not clear from Xenophon that Thebes actually did this. To muddy the waters even further Thebes was a member of the Second Athenian Confederacy as well!! But whatever the confusion in the sources the end result would prove to be the same.

   There also appears to have been a disagreement between Epaminondas and Callistratus about whether Thebes should sign as the Boeotian confederacy or not. This is reported in Diodorus Siculus *Universal History VII* 15.38.3. Though this appears to be referring to the peace of 375 most commentators agree that Diodorus is confused and it relates to 371.
3. Xenophon, *Hellenica*, 6.4.2.
4. See Diodorus Siculus, *Universal History VII*, 15.50–54. According to him the battle took place the year after the peace treaty not a mere twenty days as Xenophon has it.
5. This is the life by Plutarch where he is paralleled with the Roman Scipio Africanus, also sadly lost.
6. Polybius, *The Histories, Volume IV*, translated by W R Paton (London and Cambridge, Massachusetts, 1925) 9.23.7.
7. Thus Plutarch *Pelopidas*, 20.2–3
8. *Ibid*, 22.2.
9. Frontinus, *Stratagems*, 1.12.5.
10. Polyaenus, *Stratagems*, 2.3.12 (Epaminondas).
11. See for instance J K Anderson, *Military theory and practice in the age of Xenophon* p 197.
12. Thucydides, *History of the Peloponnesian War*, 5.71.1
13. Polyaenus, *Stratagems*, 2.3.15 (Epaminondas).
14. Xenophon, *Hellenica*, 6.4.10.
15. Diodorus Siculus, *Universal History VII*, 15.55.4.
16. *Ibid*, 15.55.5.
17. *Ibid*, 15.56.1.
18. Plutarch, *Pelopidas*, 23.1–2.
19. *Ibid*, 23.1.
20. Diodorus Siculus, *Universal History VII*, 15.55.2.
21. *Ibid*, 15.55.3.
22. Xenophon, *Hellenica*, 6.4.15.
23. Plutarch in his life of Agesilaus states that 1,000 Spartans died; Pausanias reports that over 1,000 died and Diodorus over 4,000, clearly a ludicrous figure. Xenophon reports that 400 out of the 700 Spartiates had fallen. As for the Thebans, Pausanias says that only 47 died in battle whilst Diodorus gives us the figure of 300. Xenophon with his pro-Spartan attitude disdains to give us any figures.

Conclusion

1. For this view and a general debunking of Epaminondas' military genius and innovation see V D Hanson, 'Epameinondas, the Battle of Leuktra (371 BC) and the "Revolution" in

Greek Battle Tactics' in *Classical Antiquity* 7 (1988) pp 190–207. For contrary and more conventionally held views see for example G L Cawkwell 'Epaminondas and Thebes' in *CQ* 22 (1972) pp 254–278 in particular pages pp 260–263 and J K Anderson, *Military theory and practice in the age of Xenophon* pp 192–220.

2. See on this T T B Ryder, 'Spartan Relations with Persia after the King's Peace: A Strange Story in Diodorus 15.9' in *CQ* 13 (1963) pp 105–9.

3. For instance Cartledge in his magisterial study of Agesilaus, P A Cartledge, *Agesilaus and the Crisis of Sparta* does not mention Glos at all.

Bibliography

Ancient Sources

Aristotle, *Nicomachean Ethics*, translated by H Rackham and included in *Aristotle in 23 Volumes*, *Vol 19* (London and Cambridge, Massachusetts, 1934)

Aristotle, *Athenian Constitution*, translated by H Rackham and included in *Aristotle in 23 Volumes, Vol 20* (London and Cambridge, Massachusetts, 1952)

Cornelius Nepos, *Lives of Eminent Commanders*, translated by J S Watson (London, 1886)

Dinarchus, Minor Attic Orators in two volumes, 2, translated by J O Burtt, (London and Cambridge, Massachusetts, 1962)

Diodorus Siculus, *Universal History V*, translated by C H Oldfather (London and Cambridge, Massachusetts, 1950)

Diodorus Siculus, *Universal History VI*, translated by C H Oldfather (London and Cambridge, Massachusetts, 1954)

Diodorus Siculus, *Universal History VII*, translated by C L Sherman (London and Cambridge, Massachusetts, 1952)

Frontinus, *Stratagems*, translated by C E Bennett (London and Cambridge, 1925)

Hellenica Oxyrhynchia, translated by J Marincola (Stuttgart, 1993)

Herodotus, *The Histories*, translated by A D Godley (London and Cambridge, 1920)

Justin, *Epitome of the Philippic History of Pompeius Trogus*, translated by J S Watson (London, 1853)

Lysias, *Against Agoratus*, translated by W R M Lamb and included in *Lysias*, (London and Cambridge, 1930)

Lysias, *Against Eratosthenes*, translated by W R M Lamb and included in *Lysias*, (London and Cambridge, 1930)

Pausanias, *Pausanias' Description of Greece* translated by W H S Jones and H A Ormerod in 4 Volumes (London and Cambridge, 1918)

Plutarch, *Agesilaus*, translated by B Perrin and included in *Parallel Lives V* (London and Cambridge, Massachusetts, 1917)

Plutarch, *Alcibiades*, translated by B Perrin and included in *Parallel Lives* IV (London and Cambridge, Massachusetts, 1916)

Plutarch, *Artaxerxes*, translated by B Perrin and included in *Parallel Lives* XI (London and Cambridge, Massachusetts, 1926)

Plutarch, *Apophthegms or Sayings of Kings and Commanders*, translated by E Hinton (Boston, 1878)

Plutarch, *Lycurgus*, translated by B Perrin and included in *Parallel Lives I* (London and Cambridge, Massachusetts, 1914)

Plutarch, *Lysander*, translated by B Perrin and included in *Parallel Lives IV* (London and Cambridge, Massachusetts, 1916)

Plutarch, *Pelopidas*, translated by B Perrin and included in *Parallel Lives V* (London and Cambridge, Massachusetts, 1917)

Plutarch, *Moralia, Volume III,* translated by F C Babbitt (London and Cambridge, Massachusetts, 1931)

Plutarch, *Moralia, Volume IV,* translated by F C Babbitt (London and Cambridge, Massachusetts, 1936)

Plutarch, *Moralia, Volume VII,* translated by P H De Lacey and B Einarson (London and Cambridge, Massachusetts, 1959)

Polyaenus, *Stratagems*, translated by R Shepherd (London, 1793)

Polybius, *The Histories, Volume IV*, translated by W R Paton (London and Cambridge, Massachusetts, 1925)

Thucydides, *History of the Peloponnesian War*, translated by B Jowett (London and Cambridge, Massachusetts, 1881)

Xenophon, *Agesilaus*, translated by E C Marchant and G W Bowersock, and included in *The works of Xenophon VII* (London and Cambridge, Massachusetts, 1925)

Xenophon, *Anabasis*, translated by C L Brownson and included in *The works of Xenophon III* (London and Cambridge, Massachusetts, 1922)

Xenophon, *Constitution of the Lacedaemonians*, translated by E C Marchant and G W Bowersock, and included in *The works of Xenophon VII* (London and Cambridge, Massachusetts, 1925)

Xenophon, *Hellenica*, translated by C L Brownson and included in *The works of Xenophon I* (London and Cambridge, Massachusetts, 1918)

Xenophon, *Hellenica*, translated by C L Brownson and included in *The works of Xenophon II* (London and Cambridge, Massachusetts, 1921)

Modern Authors

Adams, J 'Antalcidas crushes liberty by deceit' in Adam's Defense No 42 Liberty Letters (1786)

Anderson, J K, *Military theory and practice in the age of Xenophon* (Los Angeles, 1970)

Anderson, J K, 'The Battle of Sardis in 395 BC' in *California Studies in Classical Antiquity* 7 (1974) pp 27–53

Andrewes, A, 'Two Notes on Lysander' in *Phoenix* 25 (1971) pp 206–226

Andrewes, A, 'The Arginousai Trial' in *Phoenix* 28 (1974) pp 112–122

Cartledge, P A, *Agesilaus and the Crisis of Sparta* (Baltimore, 1987)

Cartledge, P A, *The Spartans, An Epic History* (London, 2002)

Cary, M, 'Heracleia Trachinia' in *CQ* 16 (1922) pp 98–99

Cawkwell, G L, 'Notes on the Peace of 375/4' in *Historia* 12 (1963) pp 84–95

Cawkwell, G L, 'Epaminondas and Thebes' in *CQ* 22 (1972) pp 254–278

Cawkwell, G L, 'Agesilaus and Sparta' in *CQ* 26 (1976) pp 62–84

Cawkwell, G L, 'The imperialism of Thrasybulus' in *CQ* 26 (1976) pp 270–277

Cawkwell G L, *Xenophon A History of my Times* (London, 1979)

DeVoto, J G, 'Agesilaus, Antalcidas and the failed peace of 392/391 BC' in *Classical Philology* 81 (1986) pp 191–202

Dusanic, S, 'The Attic-Chian alliance (IG II2 34) and the 'troubles in Greece' of the late 380s BC' in *ZPE* 133 (2000) pp 21–30

Ehrhardt, C, 'Xenophon and Diodorus on Aegospotami' in *Phoenix* 24 (1970) pp 225–228

Falkner, C, 'Sparta and the Elean War ca 401/400 B.C; Revenge or Imperialism?' in *Phoenix* 50 (1996) pp 17–25

Falkner, C, 'Astyochus, Sparta's Incompetent Navarch?' in *Phoenix* 53 (1999) pp 206–221

Forrest, W G A, *A History of Sparta 950–192 BC* (London, 1968)

Gray, V J, 'Two Different Approaches to the Battle of Sardis in 395 BC Xenophon Hellenica 3.4.20–24 and Hellenica Oxyrhynchia 11 (6).4–6' in *California Studies in Classical Antiquity* 12 (1979) pp 183–200

Gray, V J, 'The Years 375 to 371 BC: A Case Study in the Reliability of Diodorus Siculus and Xenophon' in *CQ* 30 (1980) pp 306–326

Griffith, G T, 'The Union of Corinth and Argos' (392–386 BC), in *Historia* vol. 1, no. 2 (1950) pp 236–256

Hamilton, C D, 'The Politics of the Revolution in Corinth 395–386 BC' in *Historia* vol. 21 no. 1 (1972) pp 21–37

Hammond, N G L, *A History of Greece to 322 BC* (Oxford, 1959)

Hanson, V D, 'Epameinondas, the Battle of Leuktra (371 BC) and the "Revolution" in Greek Battle Tactics' in *Classical Antiquity* 7 (1988) pp 190–207

Hanson, V D, *Ripples of Battle* (New York, 2003)

Harrison, E, 'A Problem in the Corinthian War' in *CQ* 7 (1913) p 132

Jones, A M H, *Sparta* (Oxford, 1967)

Kagan, D, 'Corinthian Politics and the Revolution of 392 BC' in *Historia* vol. 11, no. 4 (1962) pp 447–457

Kagan, D, *The Fall of the Athenian Empire*, (New York, 1987)

Lazenby J F, *The Spartan Army* (Barnsley, 2012)

Lendon, J E, 'The Oxyrynchus Historian and the Origins of the Corinthian War' in *Historia* 38 (1989) pp 300–313

Lendon J E, *Soldiers and Ghosts* (Connecticut, 2005)

Littman R J, 'The Strategy of the Battle of Cyzicus' in *TAPA* 99 (1968) pp 265–72

March, D A, 'Konon and the Great King's Fleet, 396–394' in *Historia* vol. 46, no. 3 (1997) pp 257–269

Munn, M H, *The Defense of Attica*, (Los Angeles, 1993)

Munro, J A R, 'Theramenes against Lysander' in *CQ* 32 (1938) pp 18–26

Munro, J A R, 'The Constitution of Dracontides' in *CQ* 32 (1938) pp 152–166

Parke, H W, 'Herippidas, Harmost at Thebes' in *CQ* 21 (1927) pp 159–165

Perlman, S, 'The Causes and the Outbreak of the Corinthian War' in *CQ* 14 (1964) pp 64–81

Prentice, W K, 'The Character of Lysander' in *AJA* 38 (1934) pp 37–42

Pritchett, W K, *Studies in Ancient Greek Topography II* (Los Angeles, 1969)

Rhodes, P J, *Alcibiades* (Barnsley, 2011)

Roy, J, 'Agis II of Sparta at Heraea' in *CQ* 59 (2009) pp 437–443

Ryder, T T B, 'Spartan Relations with Persia after the King's Peace: A Strange Story in Diodorus 15.9' in *CQ* 13 (1963) pp 105–9

Rusch, S M, *Sparta at War, Strategy, Tactics and Campaigns 550–362 BC* (Barnsley, 2011)

Seager, R, 'Thrasybulus, Conon and Athenian Imperialism 396–386 BC' in *JHS* 87 (1967) pp 95–115

Stem, R, 'The Thirty at Athens in the summer of 404' in *Phoenix* 57 (2003) pp 18–34

Strassler, R B, *The Landmark Xenophon's Hellenica* (New York, 2009)

Strauss, B S, 'Aegospotami Reexamined' in *AJP* 104 (1983) pp 24–35

Strauss, B S, 'Thrasybulus and Conon: A rivalry in Athens in the 390s BC' in *AJP* 105 (1984) pp 37–48

Strauss, B S, 'A Note on the Topography and Tactics of the Battle of Aegospotami' in *AJP* 108 (1987) pp 741–745

Tritle, L A, *Phocion the Good* (London, 1988)

Tuplin, C, 'The date of the Union of Corinth and Argos' in *CQ* 32 (1982) pp 75–83

Underhill, G E, A *commentary on the Hellenica of Xenophon* (Oxford, 1900)

Usher, S, 'Xenophon, Critias and Theramenes' in *JHS* 88 (1968) pp 128–135

Welsh, F, *Building the Trireme* (London, 1988)

Westlake, H D, 'The Sources for the Spartan Debacle at Haliartus' in *Phoenix* 39 No 2 (1985) pp 119–133

Whitby, M, 'The Union of Corinth and Argos: A reconsideration' in *Historia* vol. 33 no. 3 (1984) pp 295–308

Wylie, G, 'Agesilaus and the Battle of Sardis' in *Klio* 74 (1992) pp 118–130

Yalichev, S, *Mercenaries of the Ancient World* (London, 1997)

Index